SHIVER
SHIVER
SHIVER

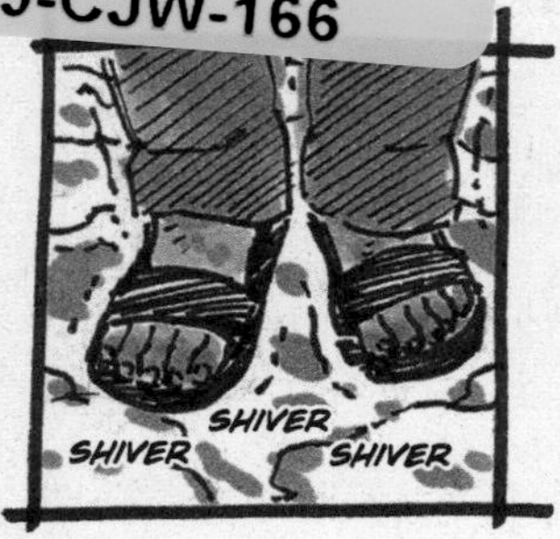

岸本斉史

I visited my family home for the first time in a while and planned to take a really short stroll in the winter snow with my feet exposed. But everything was so nostalgic that I kept going and going. Though I was shivering from the cold, I'd walked over three miles before I realized it. I ended up having someone come give me a ride back.

—Masashi Kishimoto, 2014

Author/artist Masashi Kishimoto was born in 1974 in rural Okayama Prefecture, Japan. After spending time in art college, he won the Hop Step Award for new manga artists with his manga **Karakuri** (Mechanism). Kishimoto decided to base his next story on traditional Japanese culture. His first version of **Naruto**, drawn in 1997, was a one-shot story about fox spirits; his final version, which debuted in **Weekly Shonen Jump** in 1999, quickly became the most popular ninja manga in Japan.

一楽
ラーメン一楽

NARUTO VOL. 68
SHONEN JUMP Manga Edition

STORY AND ART BY MASASHI KISHIMOTO

Translation/Mari Morimoto
Touch-up Art & Lettering/John Hunt
Design/Sam Elzway
Editor/Alexis Kirsch

Printed in the U.S.A.

Published by VIZ Media, LLC
P.O. Box 77010
San Francisco, CA 94107

10 9 8 7 6 5 4 3 2 1
First printing, December 2014

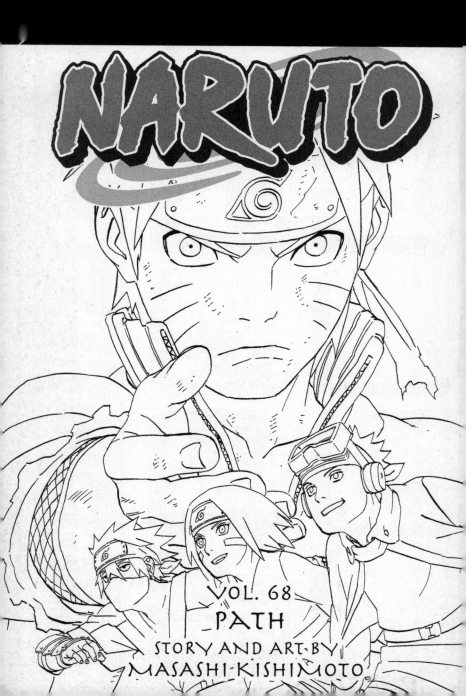

NARUTO

VOL. 68
PATH
STORY AND ART BY
MASASHI KISHIMOTO

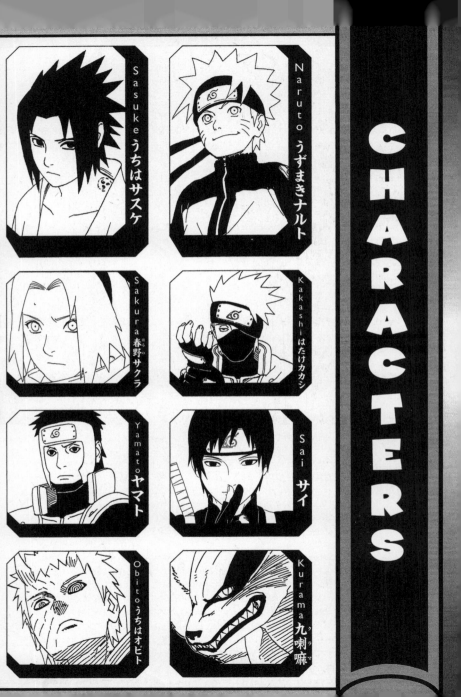

CHARACTERS

Naruto うずまきナルト

Sasuke うちはサスケ

Kakashi はたけカカシ

Sakura 春野サクラ

Sai サイ

Yamato ヤマト

Kurama 九喇嘛

Obito うちはオビト

Tsuchikage 土影
Raikage 雷影
Gaara 我愛羅
Orochimaru 大蛇丸
Eight Tails 八尾
Killer Bee キラービー
Jugo 重吾
Karin 香燐
Suigetsu 水月
Minato 波風ミナト
Hiruzen 猿飛ヒルゼン
Tobirama 千手扉間

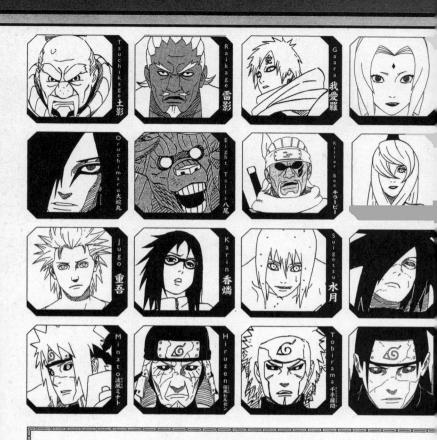

THE STORY SO FAR...

Naruto, the biggest troublemaker at the Ninja Academy in the Village of Konohagakure, finally becomes a ninja along with his classmates Sasuke and Sakura. They grow and mature through countless trials and battles. However, Sasuke, unable to give up his quest for vengeance, leaves Konohagakure to seek Orochimaru and his power…

Two years pass. Naruto grows up and engages in fierce battles against the Tailed Beast-targeting Akatsuki. And the Fourth Great Ninja War against the Akatsuki finally begins. Naruto and his companions face off against the reunited Obito and Madara in order to stop the resurrected Ten Tails! But soon, Obito absorbs the Ten Tails and becomes a Jinchuriki. Then, in order to complete the Infinite Tsukuyomi, he summons forth the Divine Tree. The alliance appears powerless against these forces but Naruto and Sasuke stand tall. Can they stop Obito?!

NARUTO

VOL. 68
PATH

CONTENTS

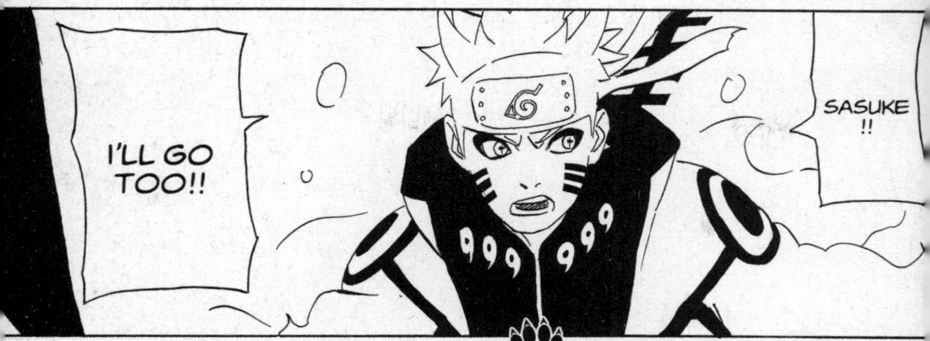
SASUKE !!
I'LL GO TOO!!

Number 648: A Shinobi's Dream

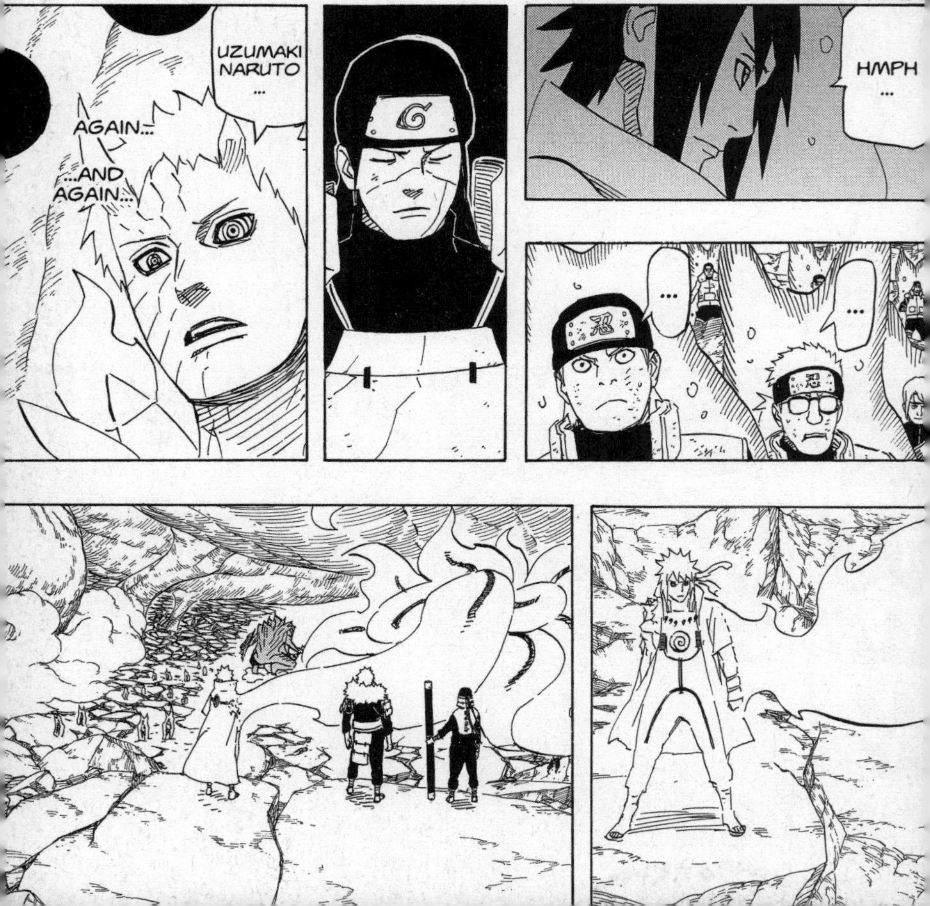
HMPH ...
UZUMAKI NARUTO ...
AGAIN...
...AND AGAIN...
...
...

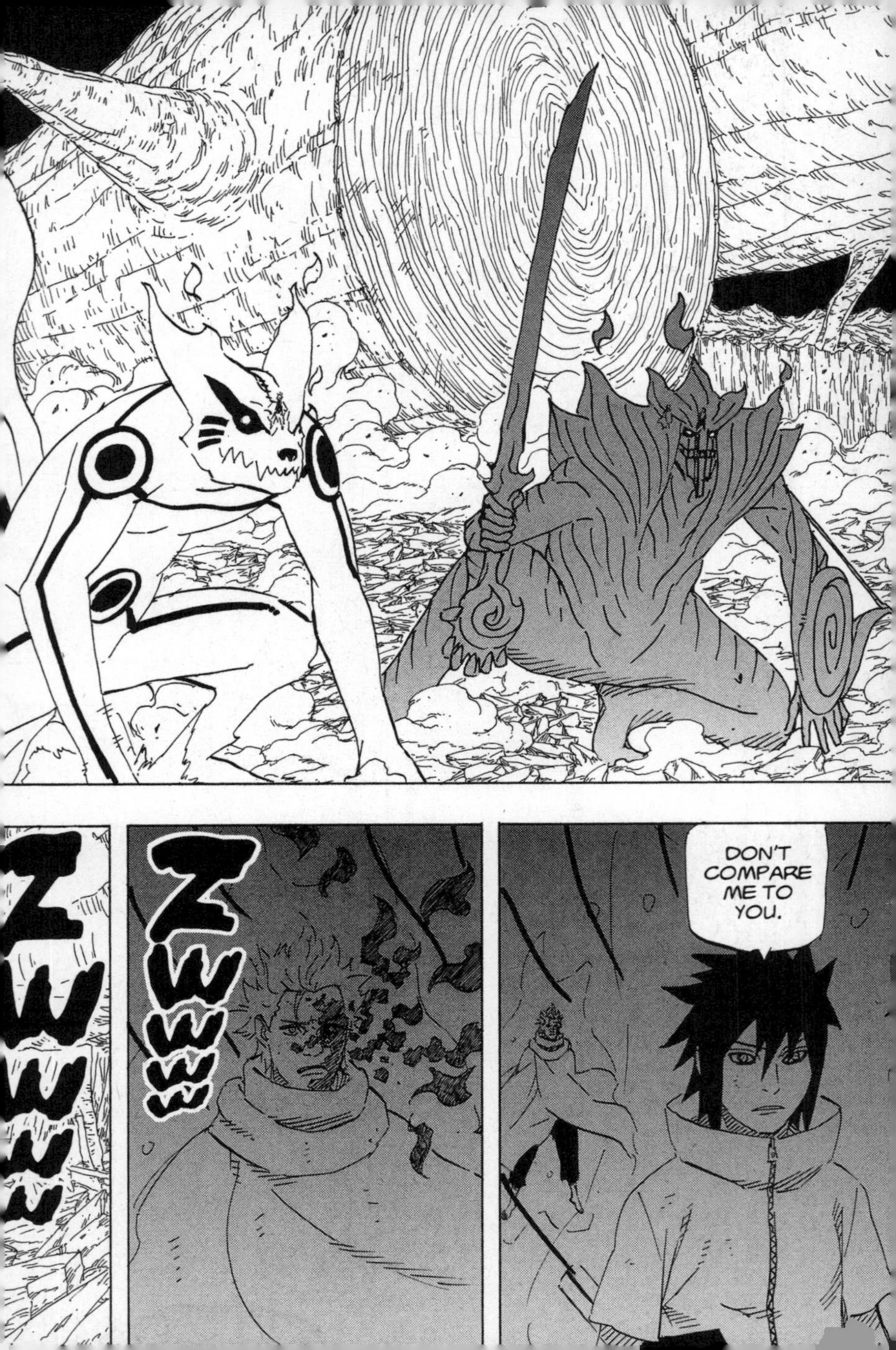
DON'T COMPARE ME TO YOU.
ZWWWW
ZWWWW

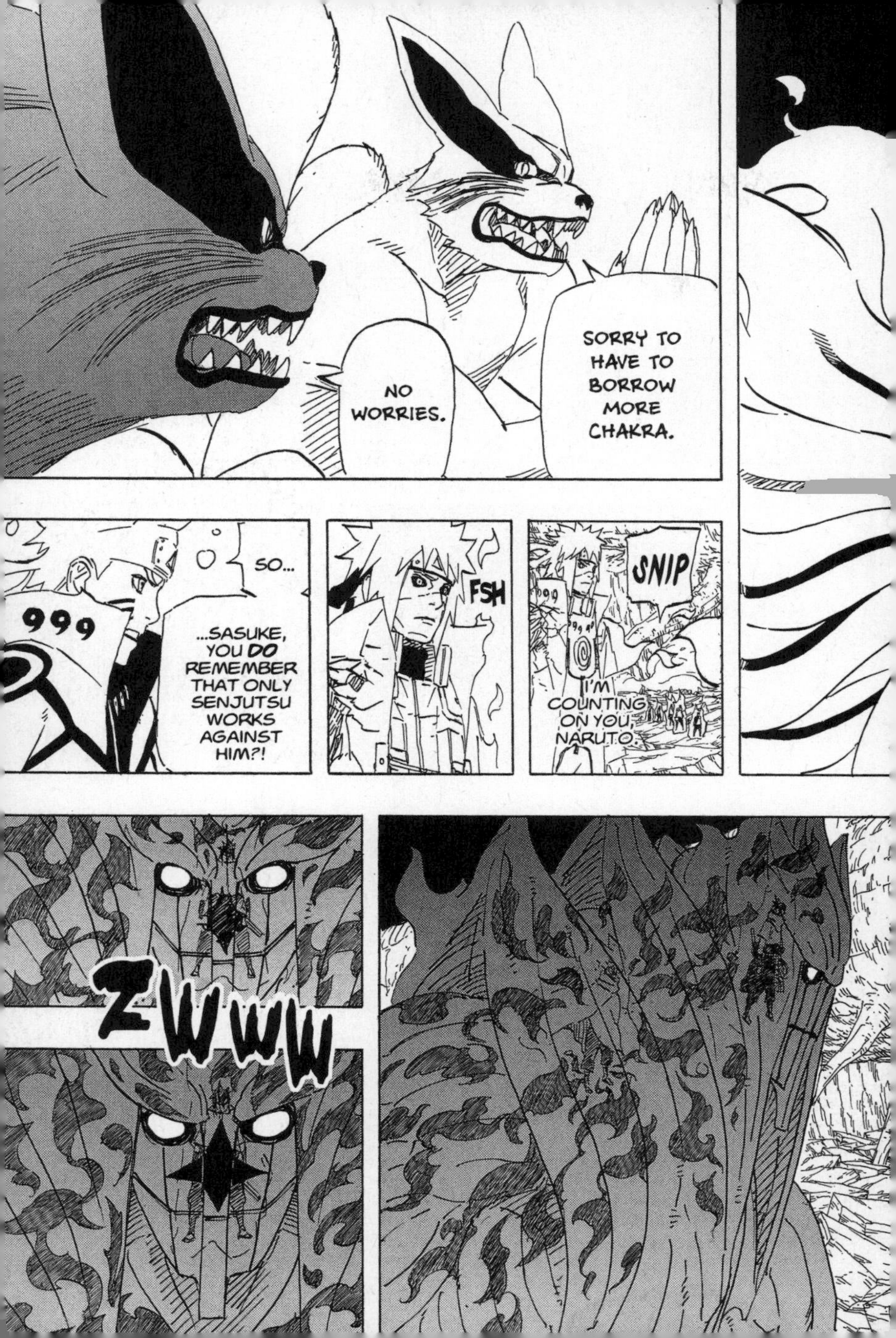

SORRY TO HAVE TO BORROW MORE CHAKRA.
NO WORRIES.
SNIP
I'M COUNTING ON YOU, NARUTO.
FSH
SO...
...SASUKE, YOU DO REMEMBER THAT ONLY SENJUTSU WORKS AGAINST HIM?!
ZWWW

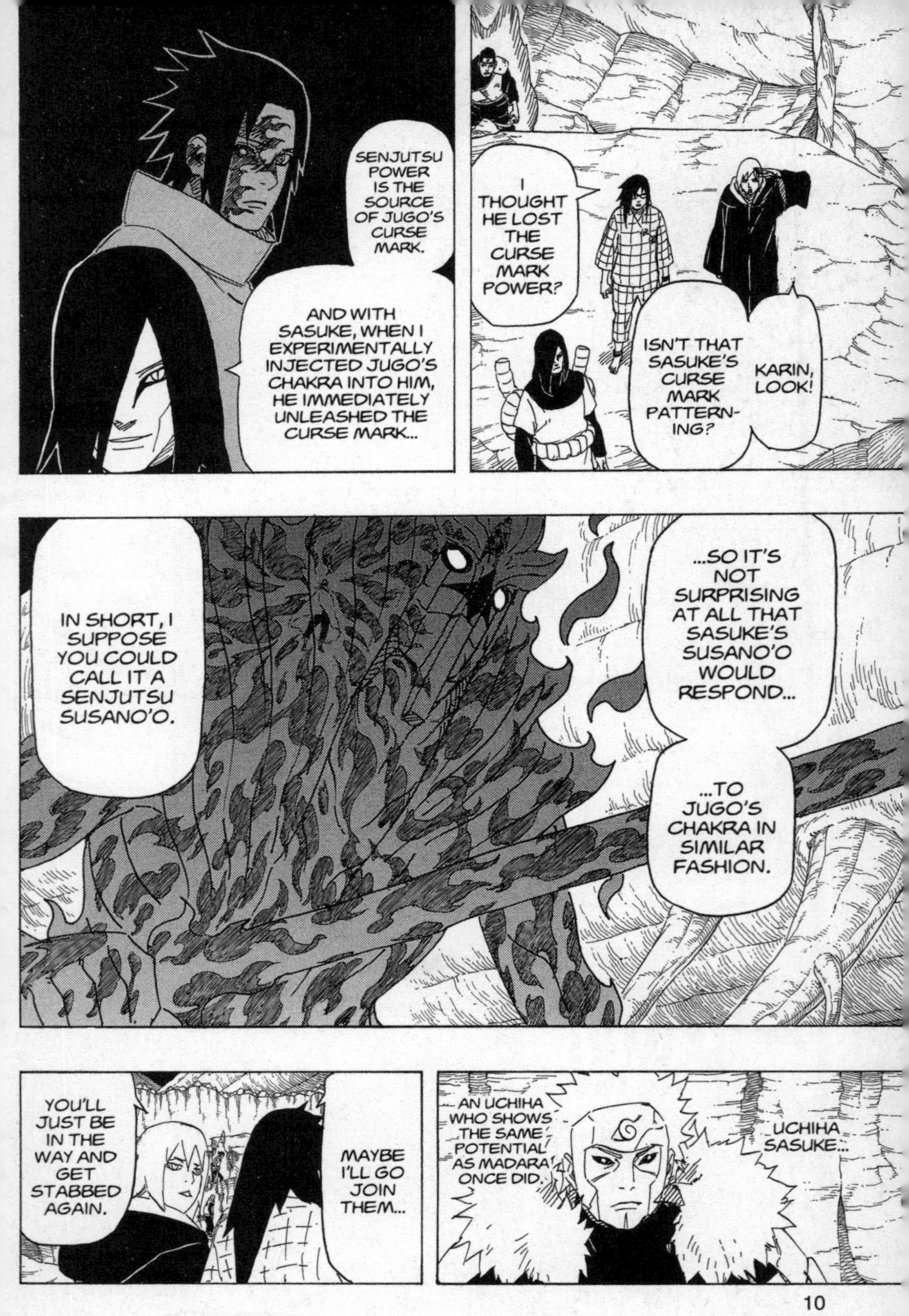
KARIN, LOOK!
ISN'T THAT SASUKE'S CURSE MARK PATTERN-ING?
I THOUGHT HE LOST THE CURSE MARK POWER?
SENJUTSU POWER IS THE SOURCE OF JUGO'S CURSE MARK.
AND WITH SASUKE, WHEN I EXPERIMENTALLY INJECTED JUGO'S CHAKRA INTO HIM, HE IMMEDIATELY UNLEASHED THE CURSE MARK...
...SO IT'S NOT SURPRISING AT ALL THAT SASUKE'S SUSANO'O WOULD RESPOND...
...TO JUGO'S CHAKRA IN SIMILAR FASHION.
IN SHORT, I SUPPOSE YOU COULD CALL IT A SENJUTSU SUSANO'O.
UCHIHA SASUKE...
AN UCHIHA WHO SHOWS THE SAME POTENTIAL AS MADARA ONCE DID.
MAYBE I'LL GO JOIN THEM...
YOU'LL JUST BE IN THE WAY AND GET STABBED AGAIN.

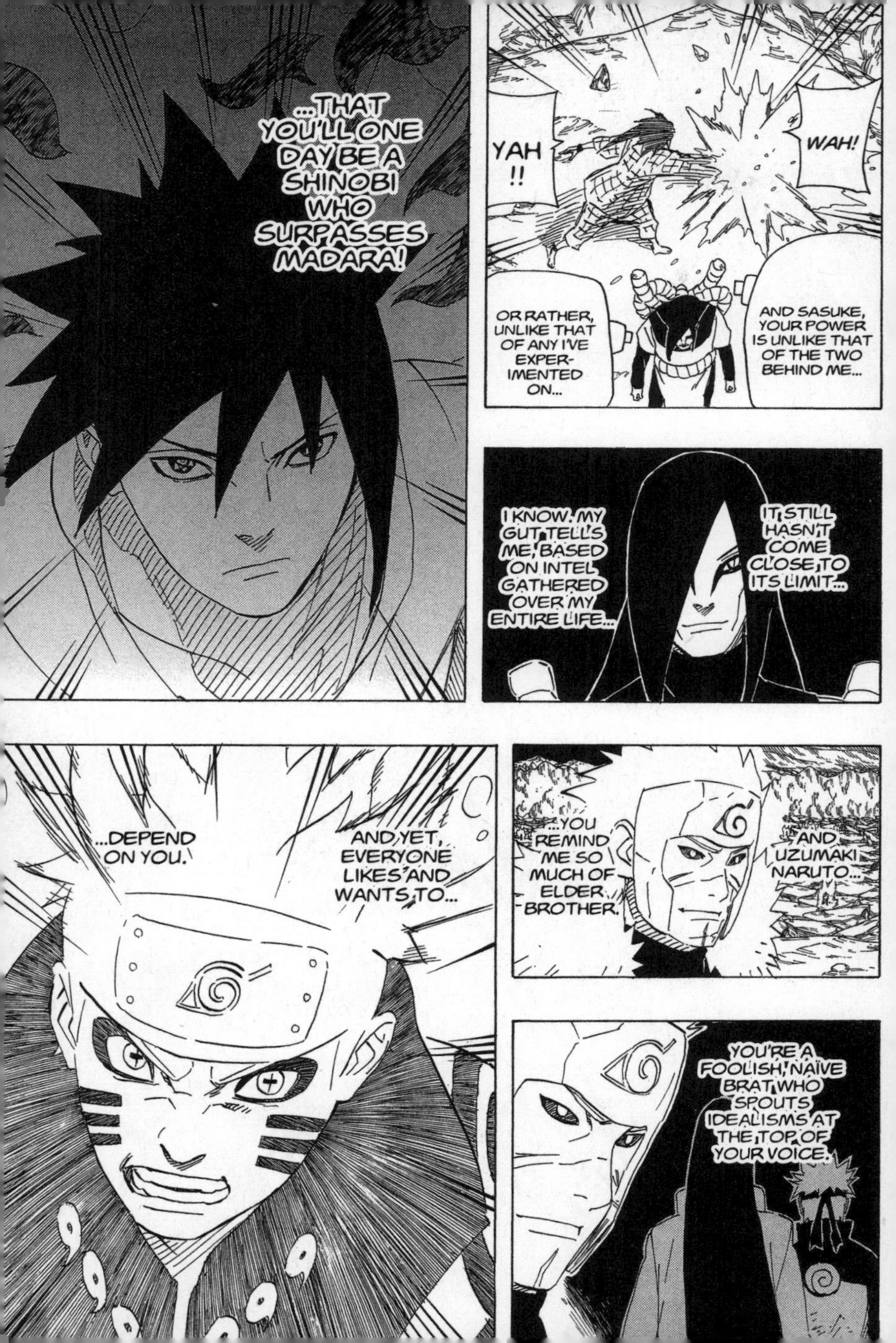
WAH!
YAH !!
AND SASUKE, YOUR POWER IS UNLIKE THAT OF THE TWO BEHIND ME...
OR RATHER, UNLIKE THAT OF ANY I'VE EXPER-IMENTED ON...
IT STILL HASN'T COME CLOSE TO ITS LIMIT...
I KNOW. MY GUT TELLS ME, BASED ON INTEL GATHERED OVER MY ENTIRE LIFE...
...THAT YOU'LL ONE DAY BE A SHINOBI WHO SURPASSES MADARA!
AND UZUMAKI NARUTO...
...YOU REMIND ME SO MUCH OF ELDER BROTHER.
YOU'RE A FOOLISH, NAÏVE BRAT WHO SPOUTS IDEALISMS AT THE TOP OF YOUR VOICE.
AND YET, EVERYONE LIKES AND WANTS TO...
...DEPEND ON YOU.

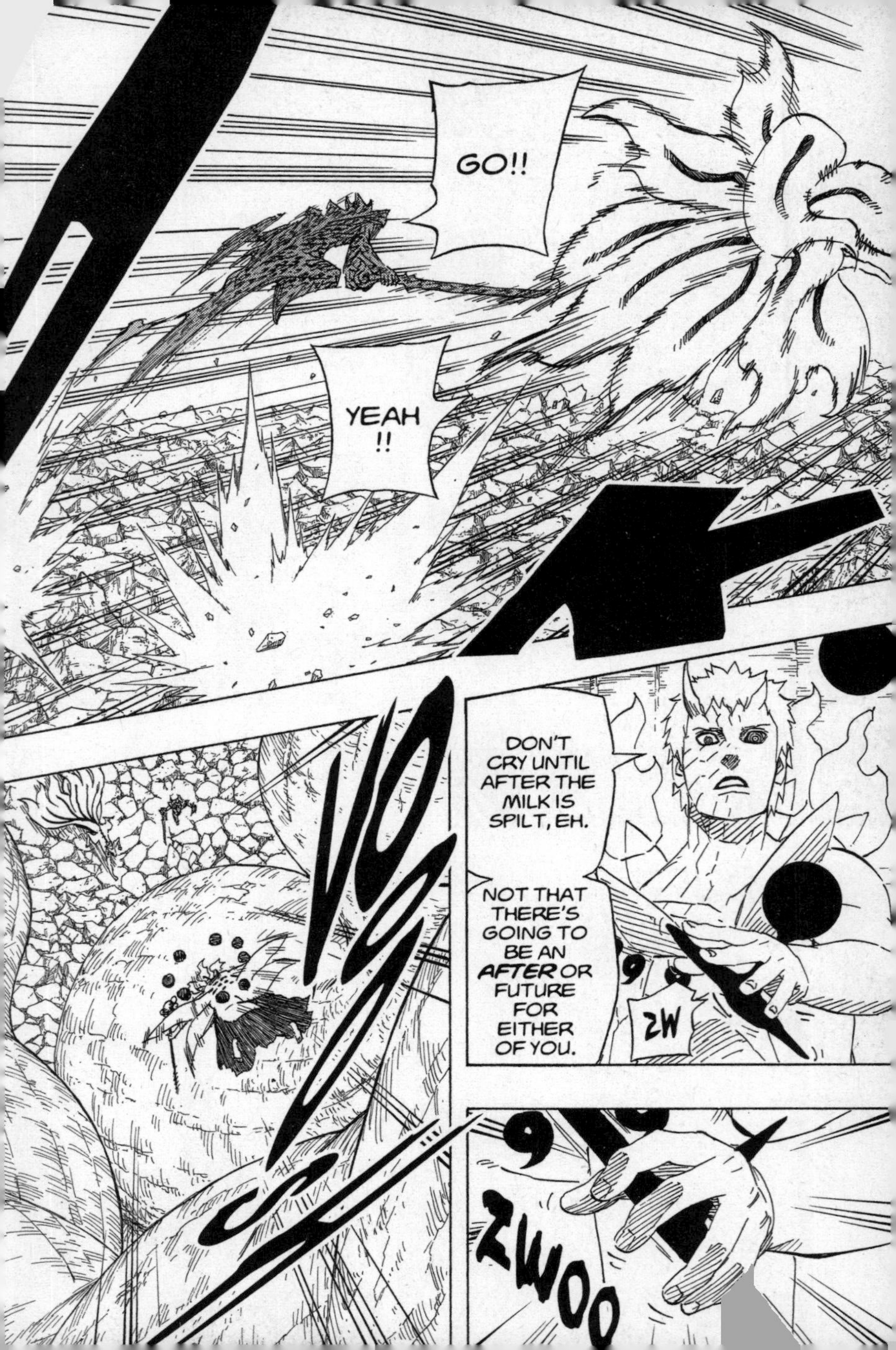
GO!!
YEAH !!
DON'T CRY UNTIL AFTER THE MILK IS SPILT, EH.
NOT THAT THERE'S GOING TO BE AN *AFTER* OR FUTURE FOR EITHER OF YOU.
ZW
ZWOO

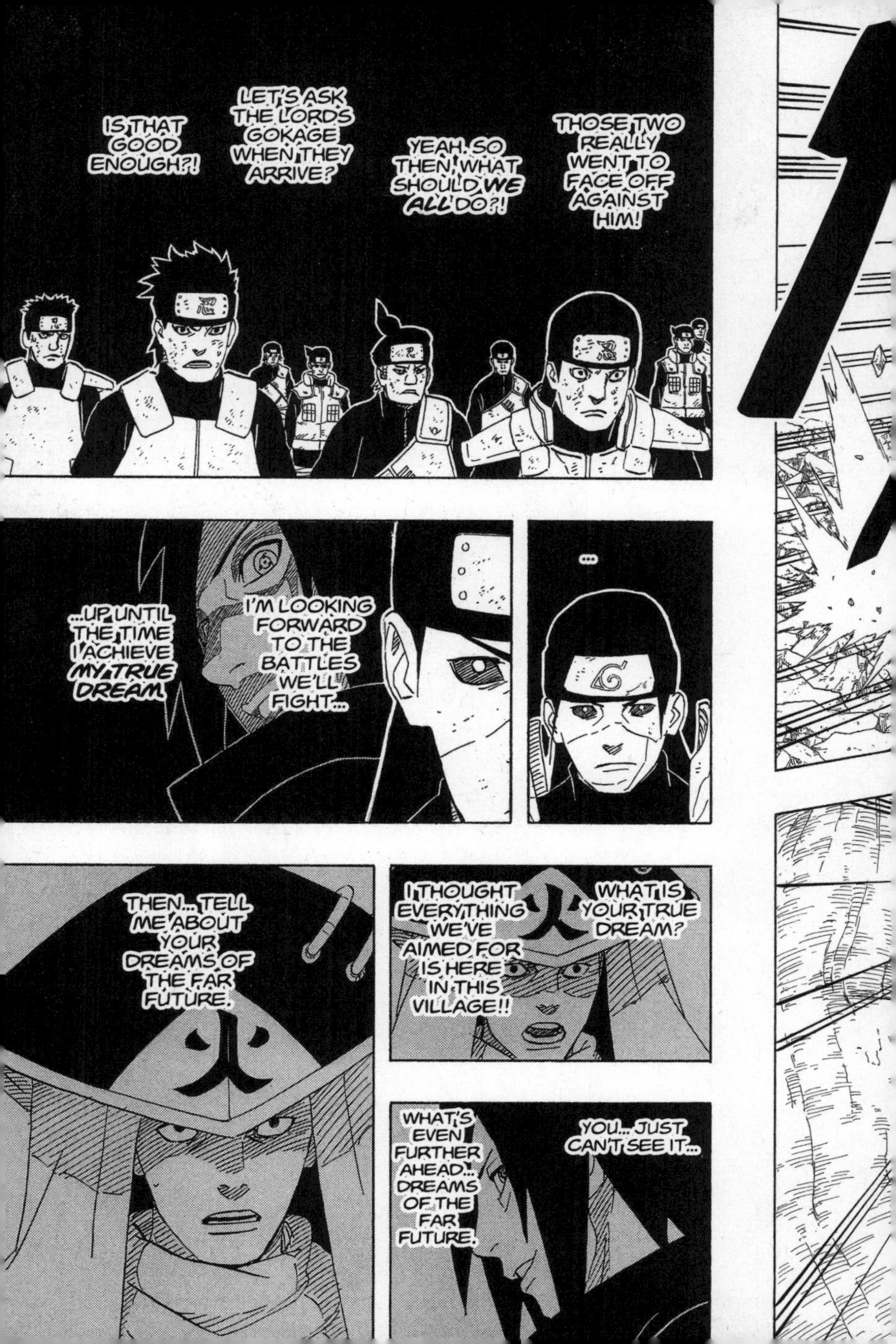
THOSE TWO REALLY WENT TO FACE OFF AGAINST HIM!
YEAH, SO THEN, WHAT SHOULD WE ALL DO?!
LET'S ASK THE LORDS GOKAGE WHEN THEY ARRIVE?
IS THAT GOOD ENOUGH?!
...
I'M LOOKING FORWARD TO THE BATTLES WE'LL FIGHT...
...UP UNTIL THE TIME I ACHIEVE MY TRUE DREAM.
WHAT IS YOUR TRUE DREAM?
I THOUGHT EVERYTHING WE'VE AIMED FOR IS HERE IN THIS VILLAGE!!
YOU... JUST CAN'T SEE IT...
WHAT'S EVEN FURTHER AHEAD... DREAMS OF THE FAR FUTURE.
THEN... TELL ME ABOUT YOUR DREAMS OF THE FAR FUTURE.

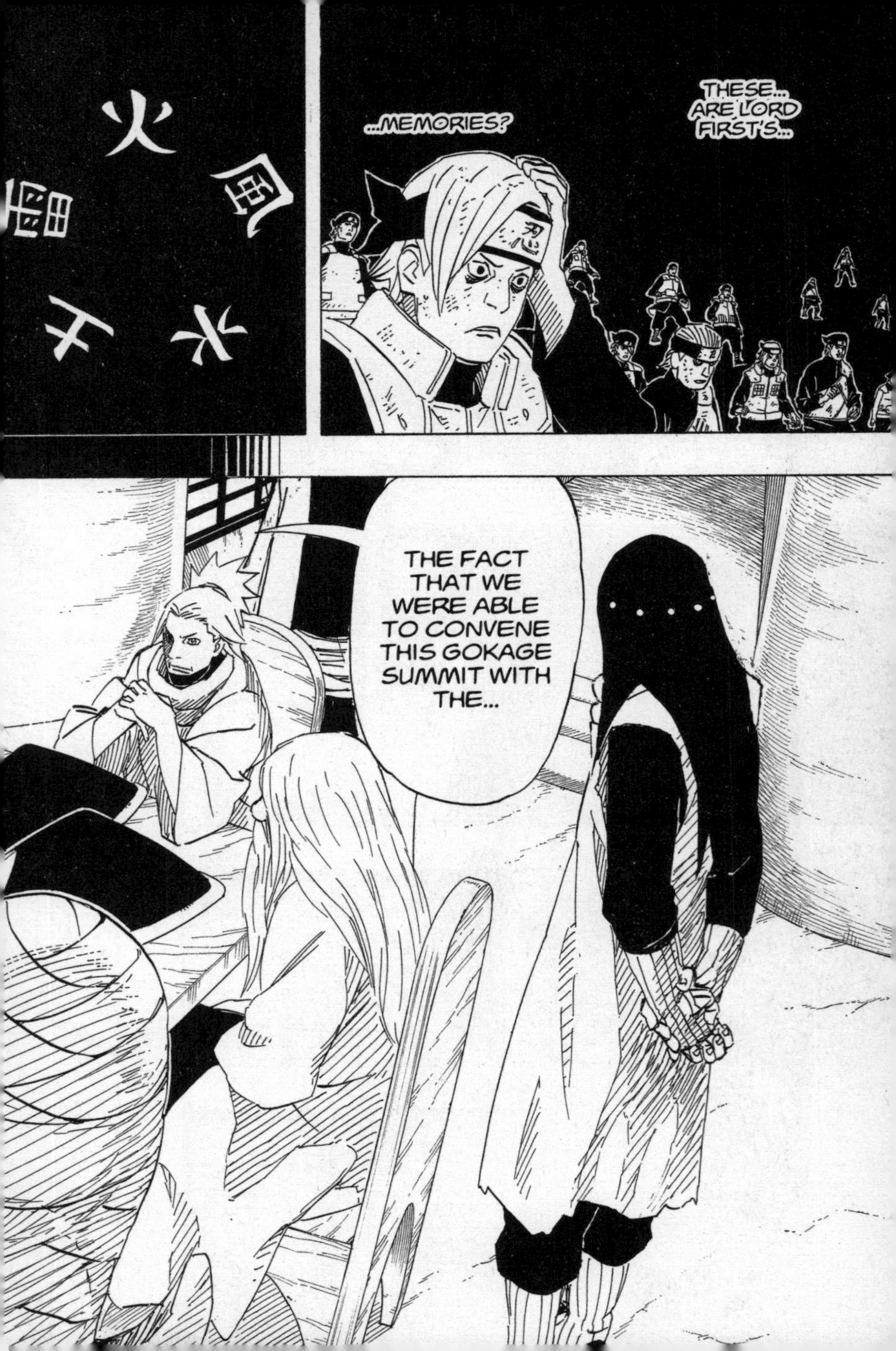
THESE... ARE LORD FIRST'S...
...MEMORIES?
火 風 水 土 雷
THE FACT THAT WE WERE ABLE TO CONVENE THIS GOKAGE SUMMIT WITH THE...

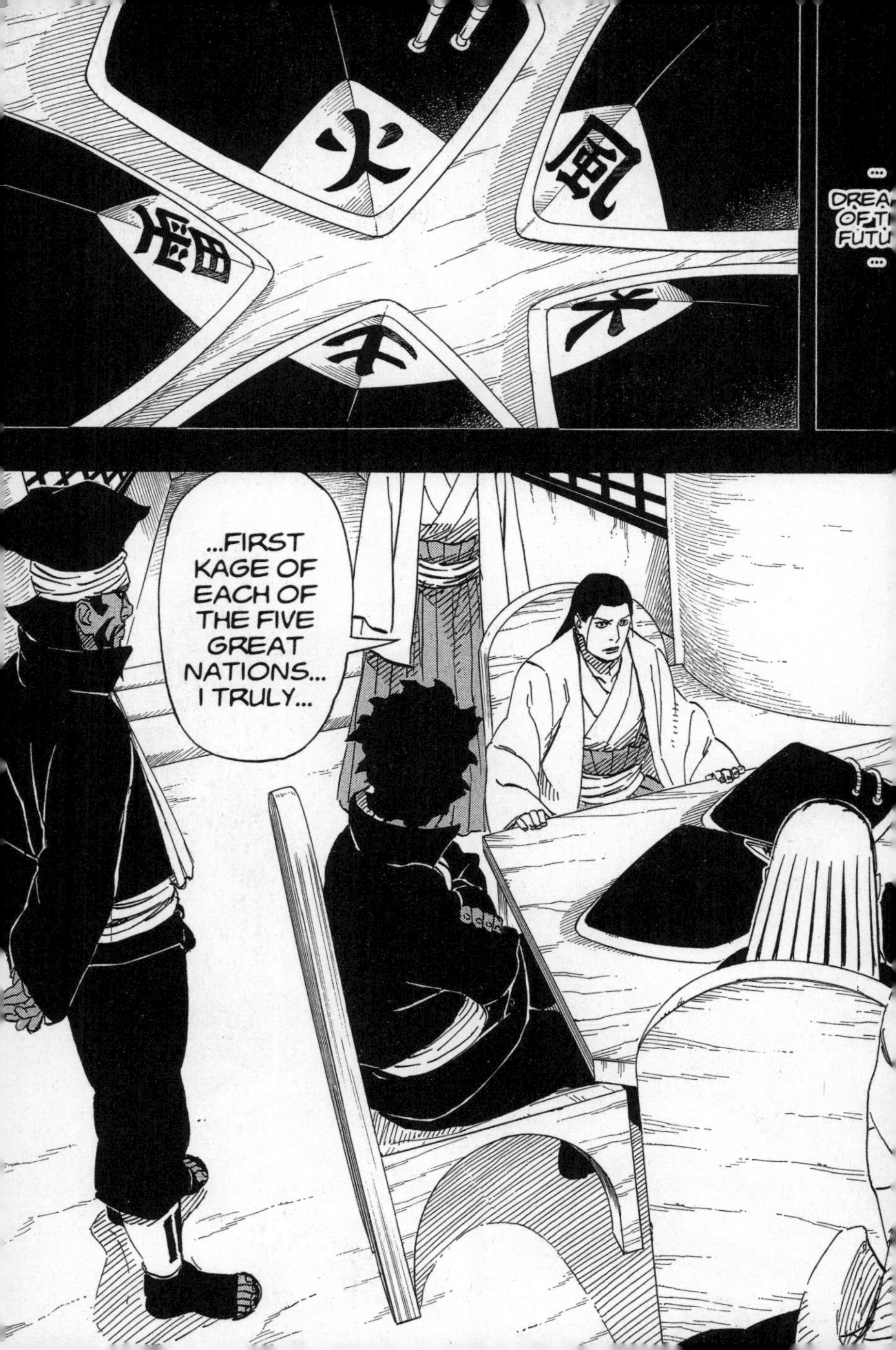
...DREA OF T FUTU...
...FIRST KAGE OF EACH OF THE FIVE GREAT NATIONS... I TRULY...

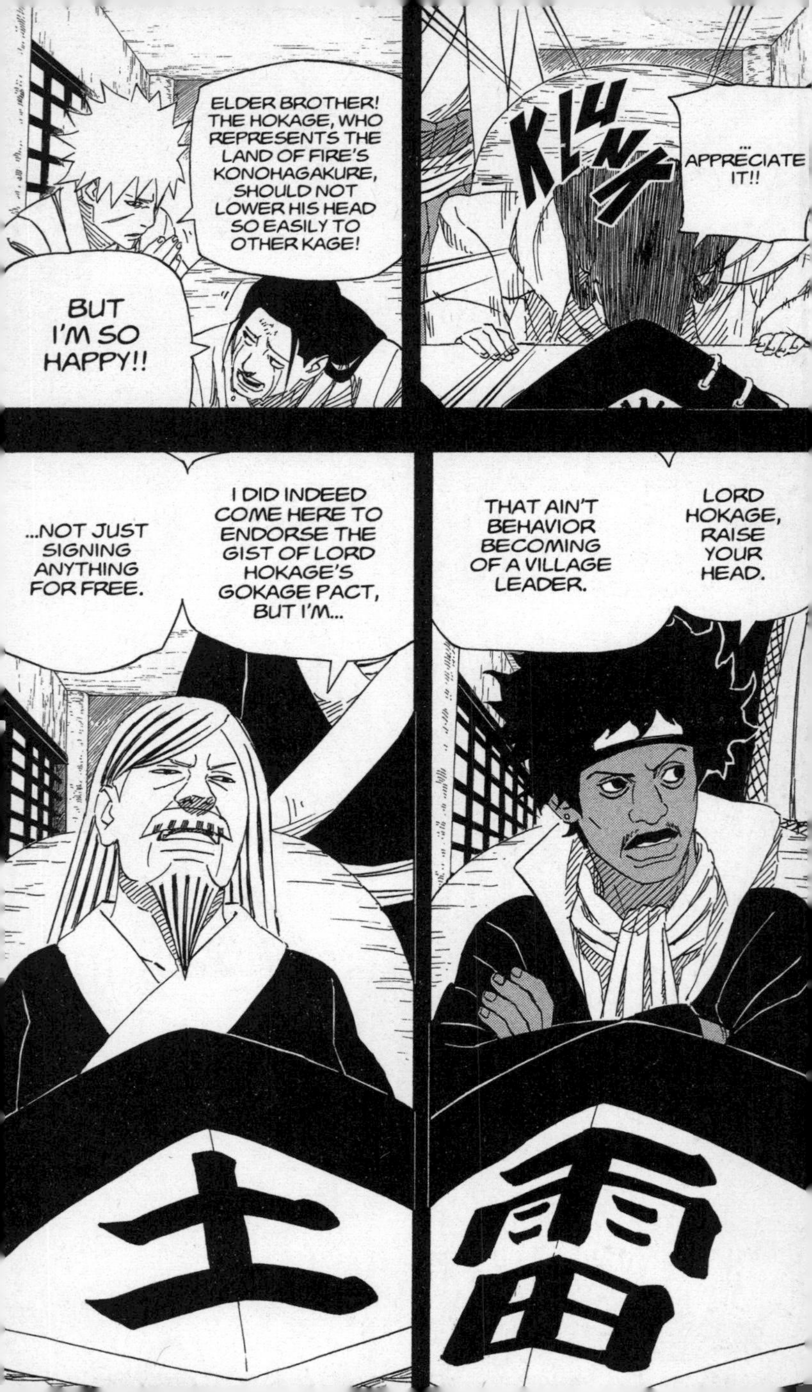
KLUNK
...APPRECIATE IT!!
ELDER BROTHER! THE HOKAGE, WHO REPRESENTS THE LAND OF FIRE'S KONOHAGAKURE, SHOULD NOT LOWER HIS HEAD SO EASILY TO OTHER KAGE!
BUT I'M SO HAPPY!!
LORD HOKAGE, RAISE YOUR HEAD.
THAT AIN'T BEHAVIOR BECOMING OF A VILLAGE LEADER.
雷
I DID INDEED COME HERE TO ENDORSE THE GIST OF LORD HOKAGE'S GOKAGE PACT, BUT I'M...
...NOT JUST SIGNING ANYTHING FOR FREE.
土

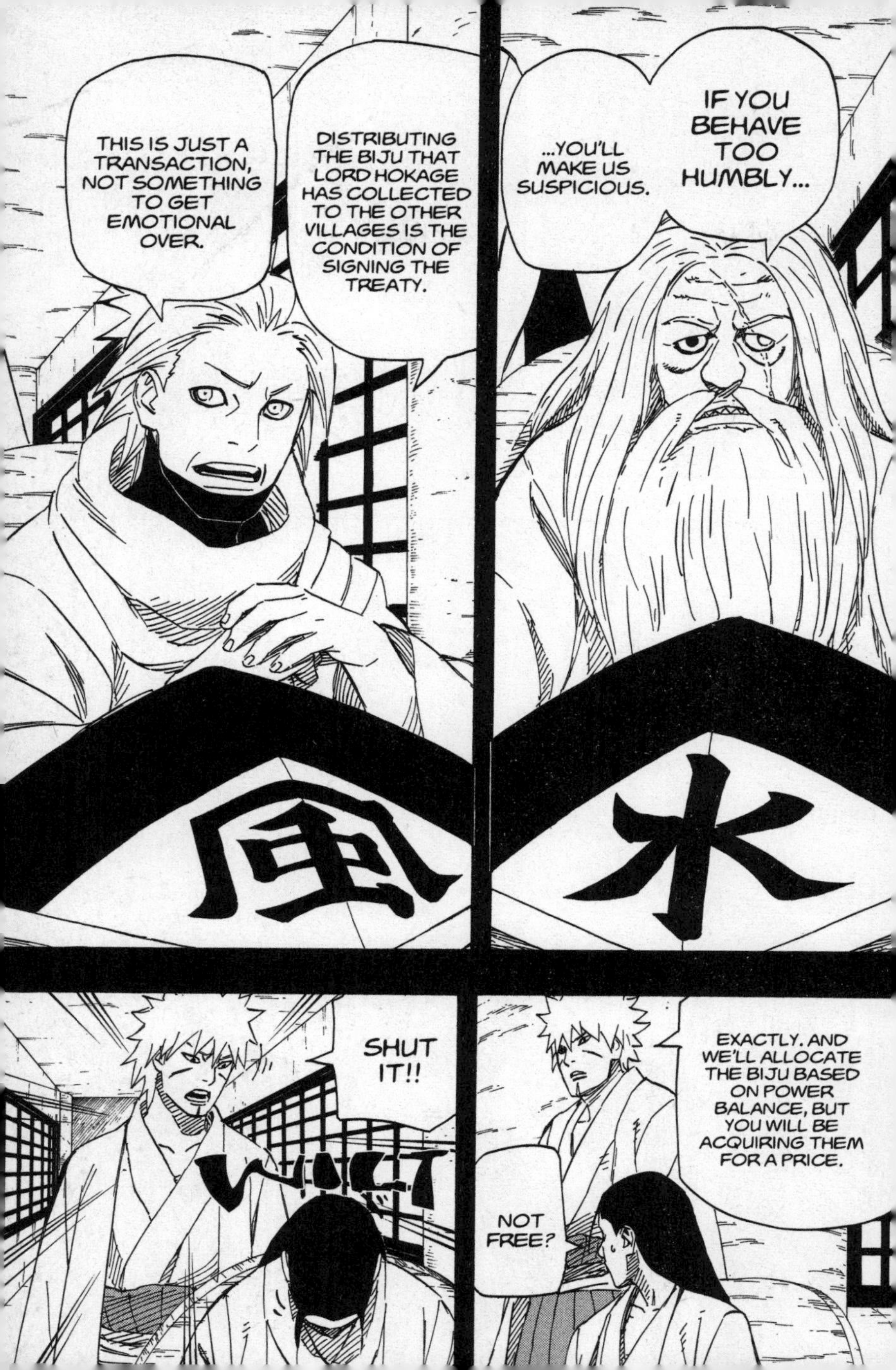
IF YOU BEHAVE TOO HUMBLY...
...YOU'LL MAKE US SUSPICIOUS.
水
DISTRIBUTING THE BIJU THAT LORD HOKAGE HAS COLLECTED TO THE OTHER VILLAGES IS THE CONDITION OF SIGNING THE TREATY.
THIS IS JUST A TRANSACTION, NOT SOMETHING TO GET EMOTIONAL OVER.
風
EXACTLY. AND WE'LL ALLOCATE THE BIJU BASED ON POWER BALANCE, BUT YOU WILL BE ACQUIRING THEM FOR A PRICE.
NOT FREE?
SHUT IT!!

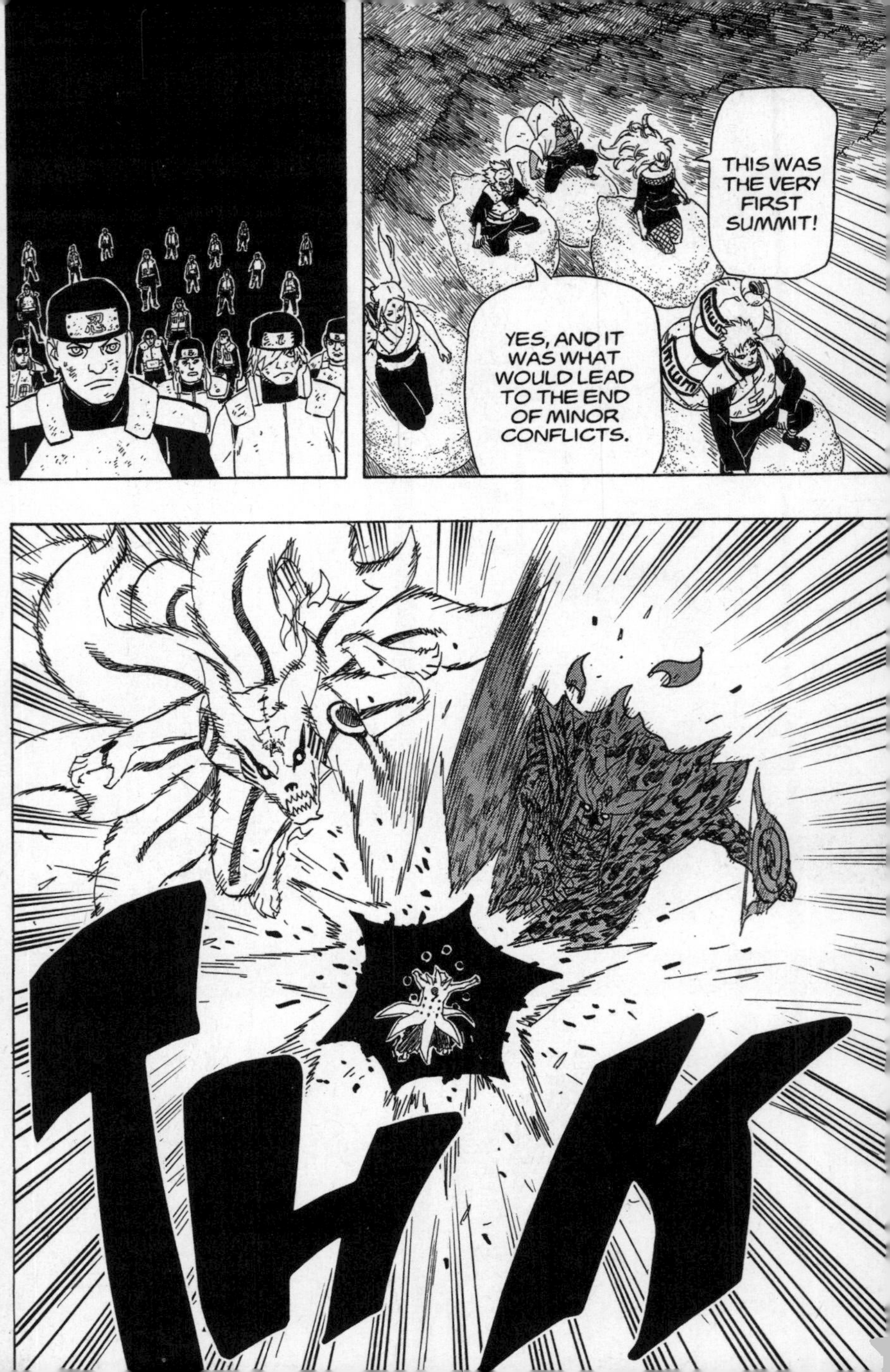
THIS WAS THE VERY FIRST SUMMIT!
YES, AND IT WAS WHAT WOULD LEAD TO THE END OF MINOR CONFLICTS.

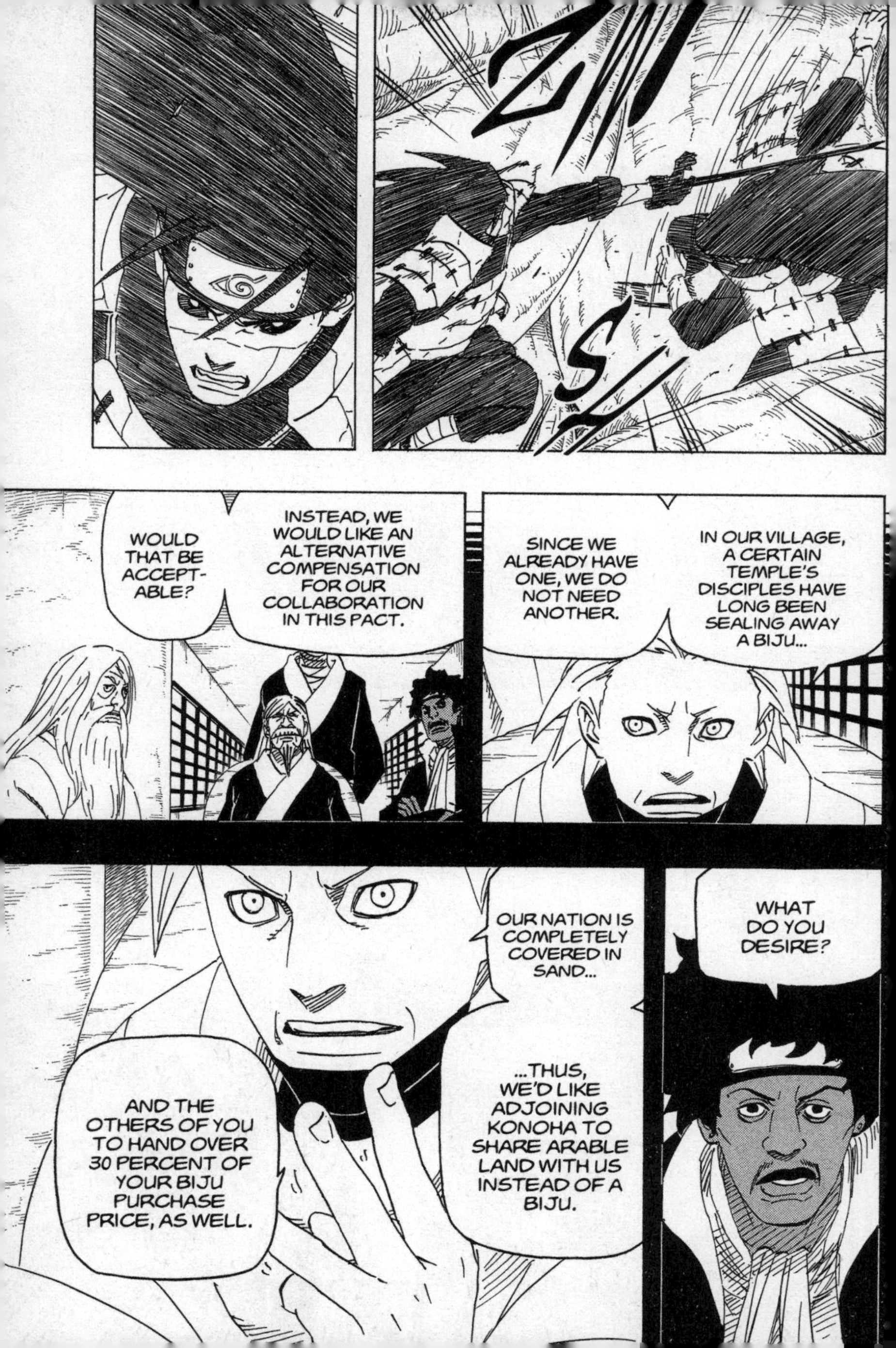
IN OUR VILLAGE, A CERTAIN TEMPLE'S DISCIPLES HAVE LONG BEEN SEALING AWAY A BIJU...
SINCE WE ALREADY HAVE ONE, WE DO NOT NEED ANOTHER.
INSTEAD, WE WOULD LIKE AN ALTERNATIVE COMPENSATION FOR OUR COLLABORATION IN THIS PACT.
WOULD THAT BE ACCEPT-ABLE?
WHAT DO YOU DESIRE?
OUR NATION IS COMPLETELY COVERED IN SAND...
...THUS, WE'D LIKE ADJOINING KONOHA TO SHARE ARABLE LAND WITH US INSTEAD OF A BIJU.
AND THE OTHERS OF YOU TO HAND OVER 30 PERCENT OF YOUR BIJU PURCHASE PRICE, AS WELL.

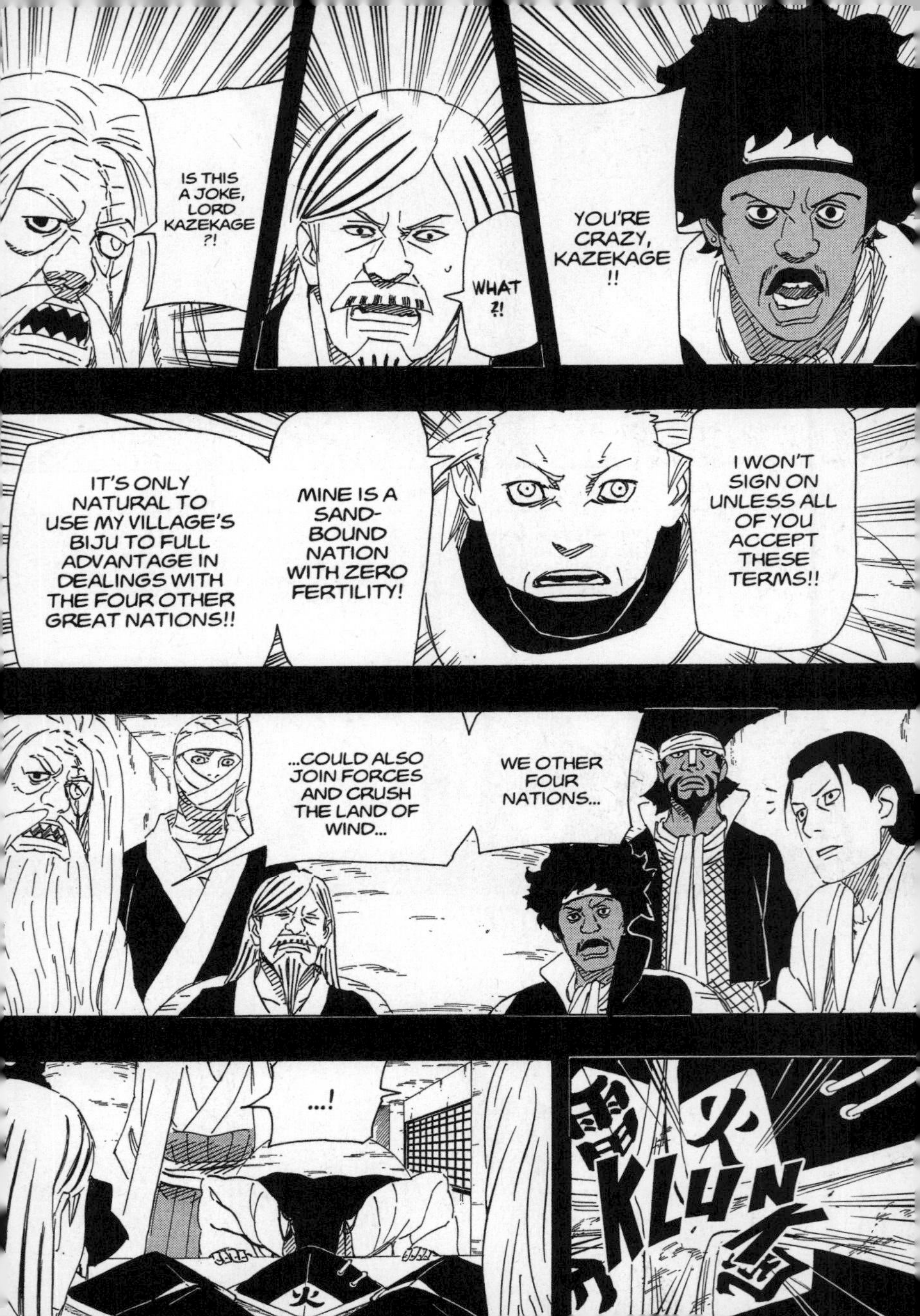
YOU'RE CRAZY, KAZEKAGE!!
WHAT?!
IS THIS A JOKE, LORD KAZEKAGE?!
I WON'T SIGN ON UNLESS ALL OF YOU ACCEPT THESE TERMS!!
MINE IS A SAND-BOUND NATION WITH ZERO FERTILITY!
IT'S ONLY NATURAL TO USE MY VILLAGE'S BIJU TO FULL ADVANTAGE IN DEALINGS WITH THE FOUR OTHER GREAT NATIONS!!
WE OTHER FOUR NATIONS...
...COULD ALSO JOIN FORCES AND CRUSH THE LAND OF WIND...
KLUN
...!

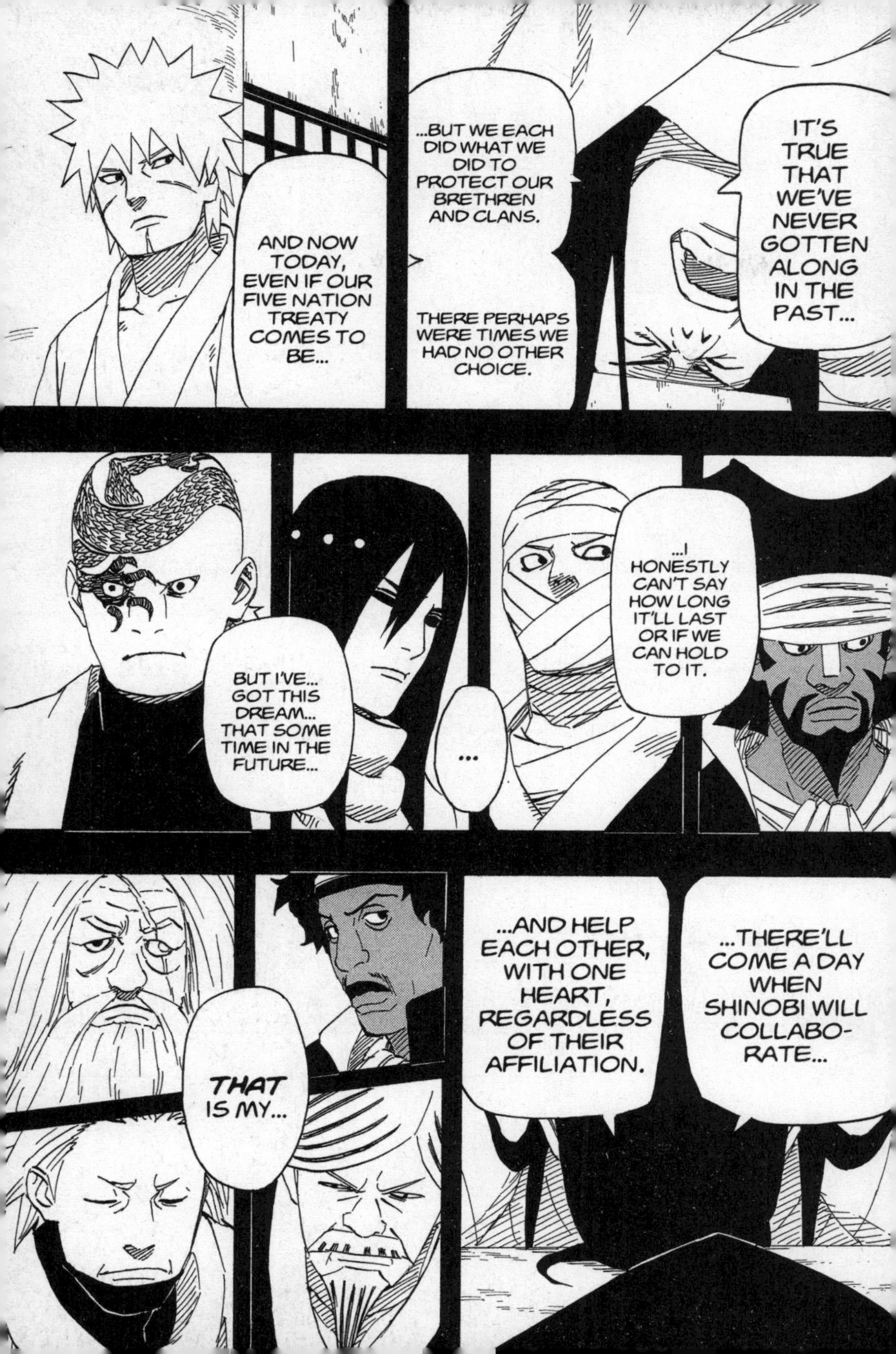
IT'S TRUE THAT WE'VE NEVER GOTTEN ALONG IN THE PAST...
...BUT WE EACH DID WHAT WE DID TO PROTECT OUR BRETHREN AND CLANS.
THERE PERHAPS WERE TIMES WE HAD NO OTHER CHOICE.
AND NOW TODAY, EVEN IF OUR FIVE NATION TREATY COMES TO BE...
...I HONESTLY CAN'T SAY HOW LONG IT'LL LAST OR IF WE CAN HOLD TO IT.
...
BUT I'VE... GOT THIS DREAM... THAT SOME TIME IN THE FUTURE...
...THERE'LL COME A DAY WHEN SHINOBI WILL COLLABO-RATE...
...AND HELP EACH OTHER, WITH ONE HEART, REGARDLESS OF THEIR AFFILIATION.
THAT IS MY...

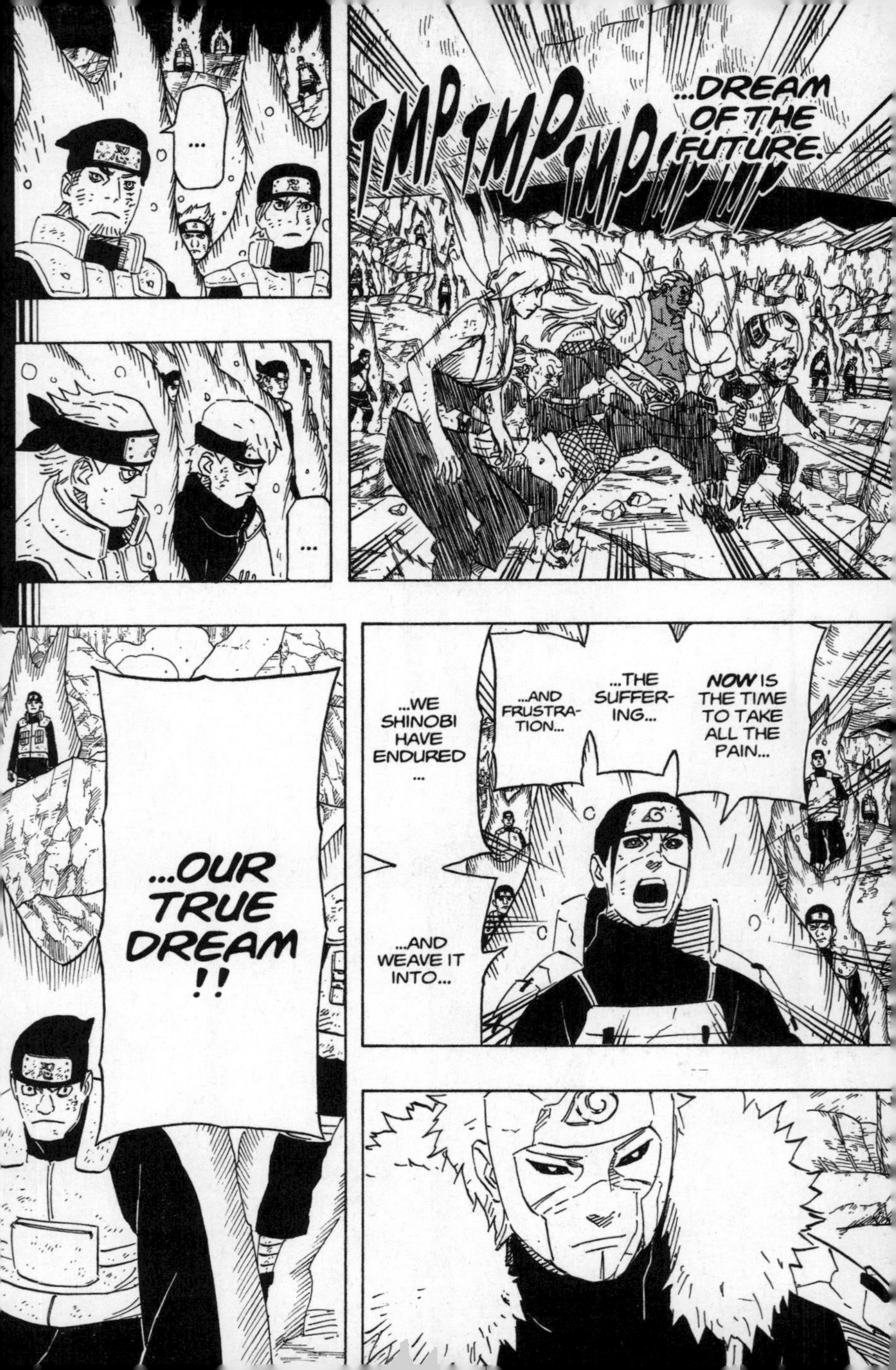
...DREAM OF THE FUTURE.
TMP TMP TMP
...
...
NOW IS THE TIME TO TAKE ALL THE PAIN...
...THE SUFFERING...
...AND FRUSTRATION...
...WE SHINOBI HAVE ENDURED...
...AND WEAVE IT INTO...
...OUR TRUE DREAM!!

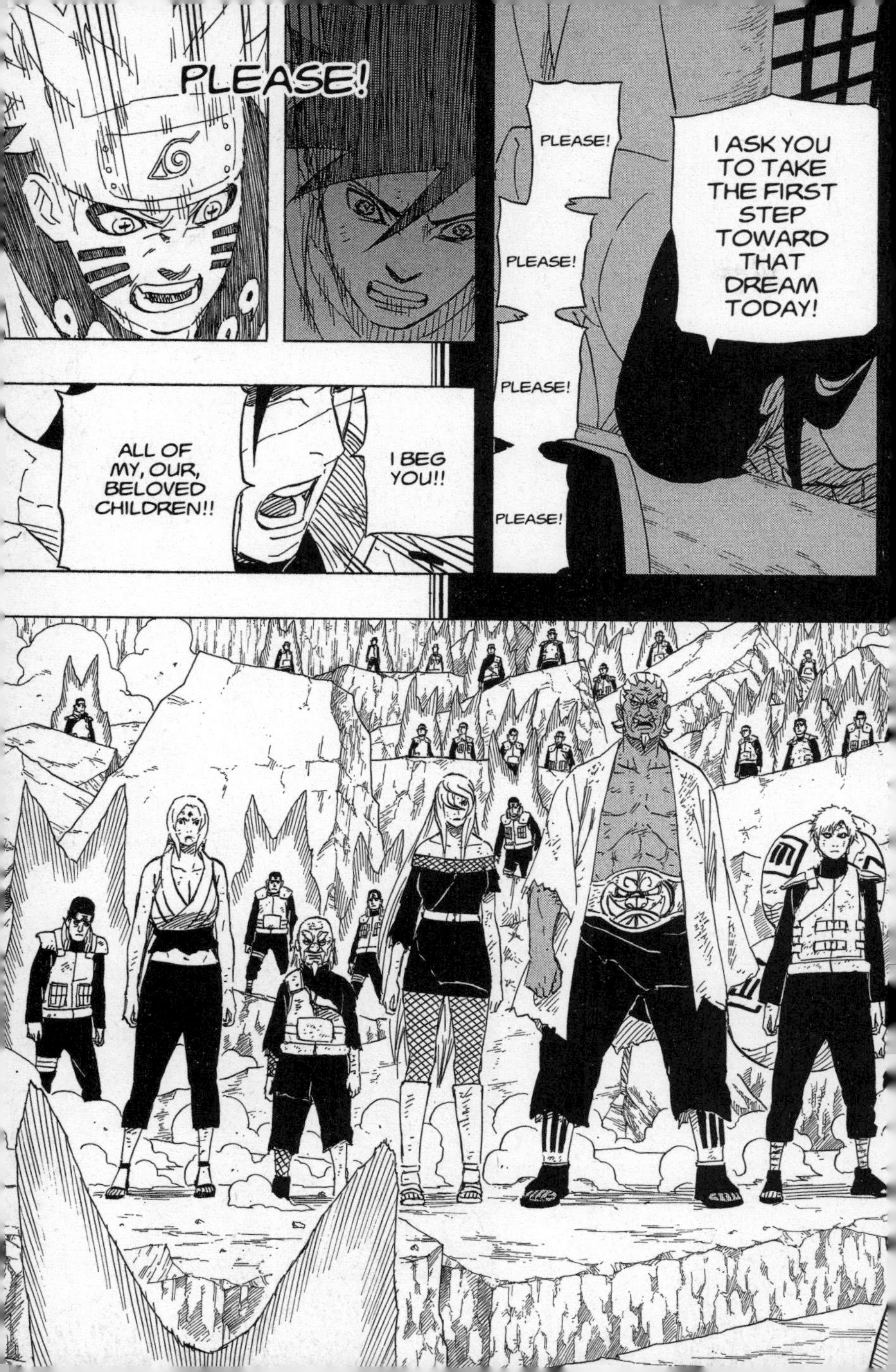
I ASK YOU TO TAKE THE FIRST STEP TOWARD THAT DREAM TODAY!
PLEASE!
PLEASE!
PLEASE!
PLEASE!
PLEASE!
I BEG YOU!!
ALL OF MY, OUR, BELOVED CHILDREN!!

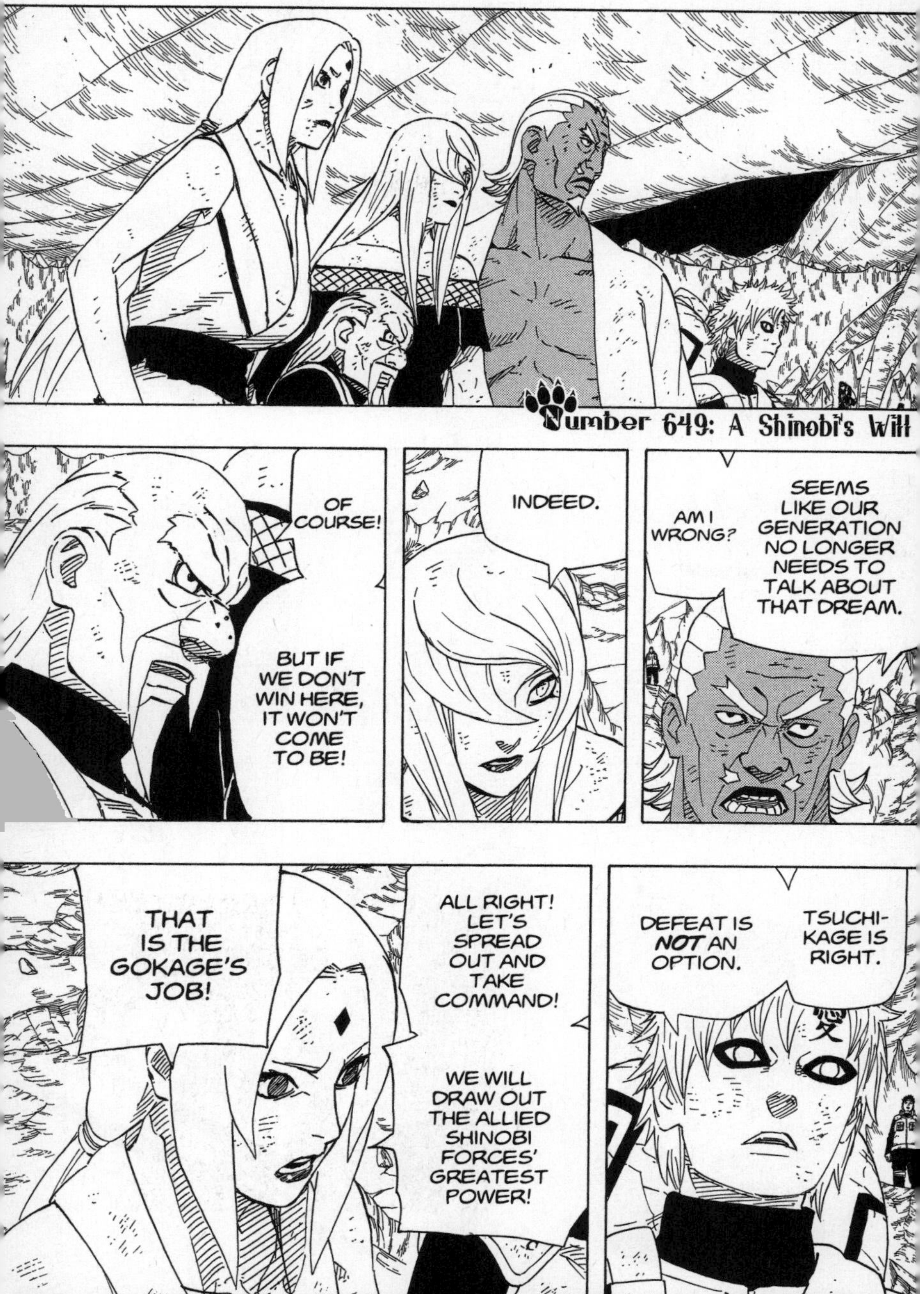
Number 649: A Shinobi's Will
SEEMS LIKE OUR GENERATION NO LONGER NEEDS TO TALK ABOUT THAT DREAM.
AM I WRONG?
INDEED.
OF COURSE!
BUT IF WE DON'T WIN HERE, IT WON'T COME TO BE!
TSUCHIKAGE IS RIGHT.
DEFEAT IS *NOT* AN OPTION.
ALL RIGHT! LET'S SPREAD OUT AND TAKE COMMAND!
WE WILL DRAW OUT THE ALLIED SHINOBI FORCES' GREATEST POWER!
THAT IS THE GOKAGE'S JOB!

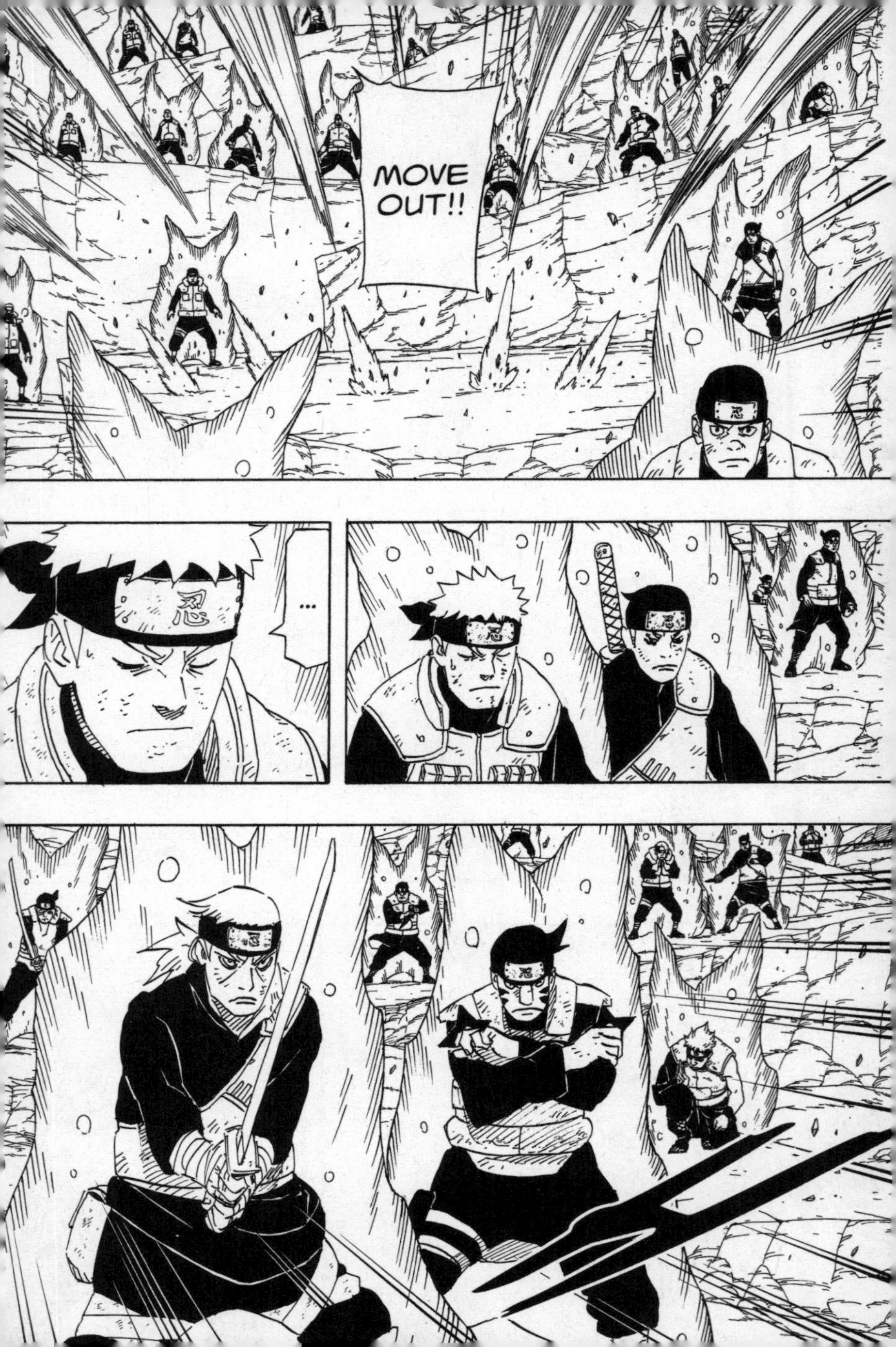
MOVE OUT!!
...

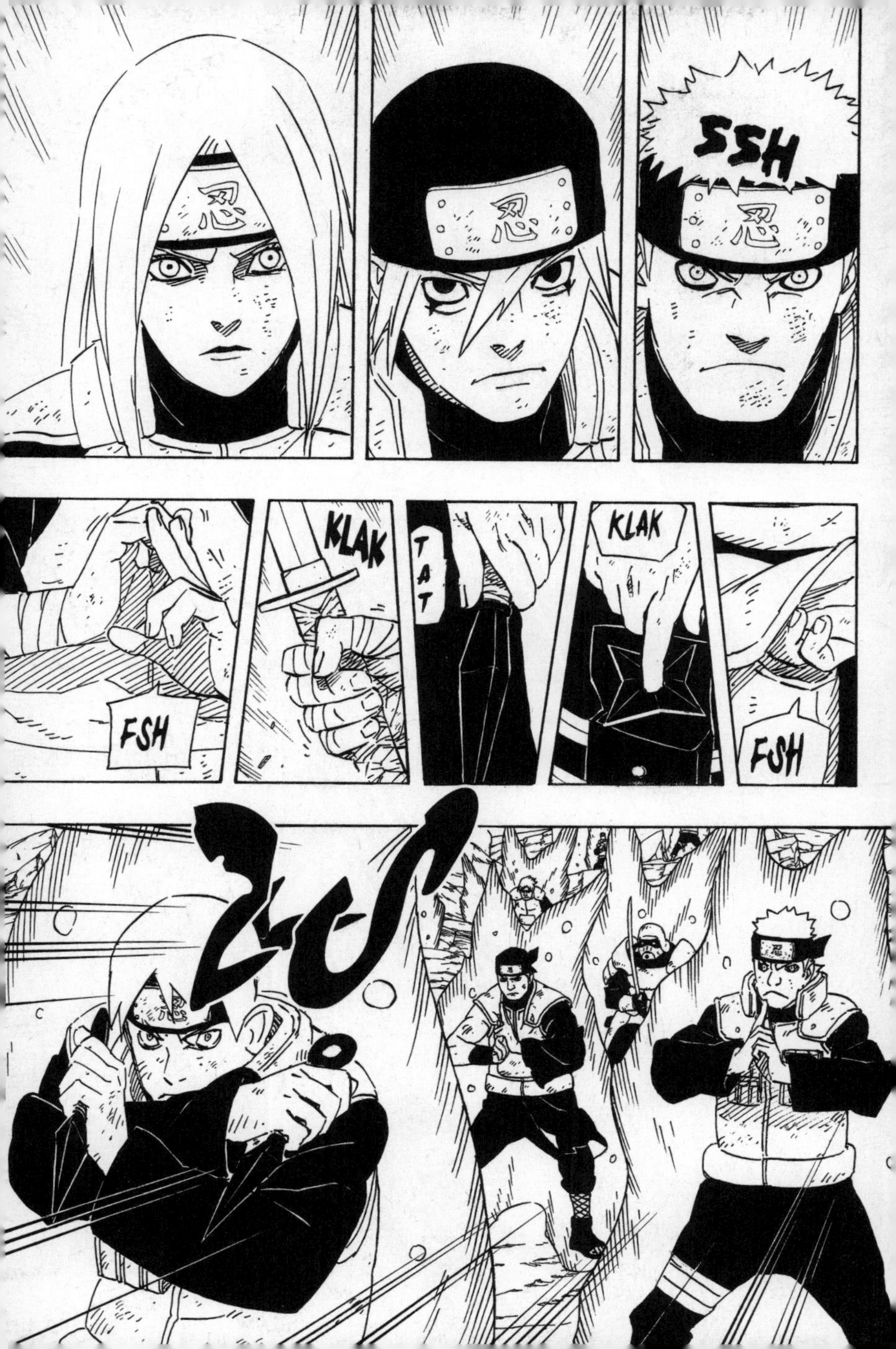
SSH
FSH
KLAK
TAT
KLAK
FSH

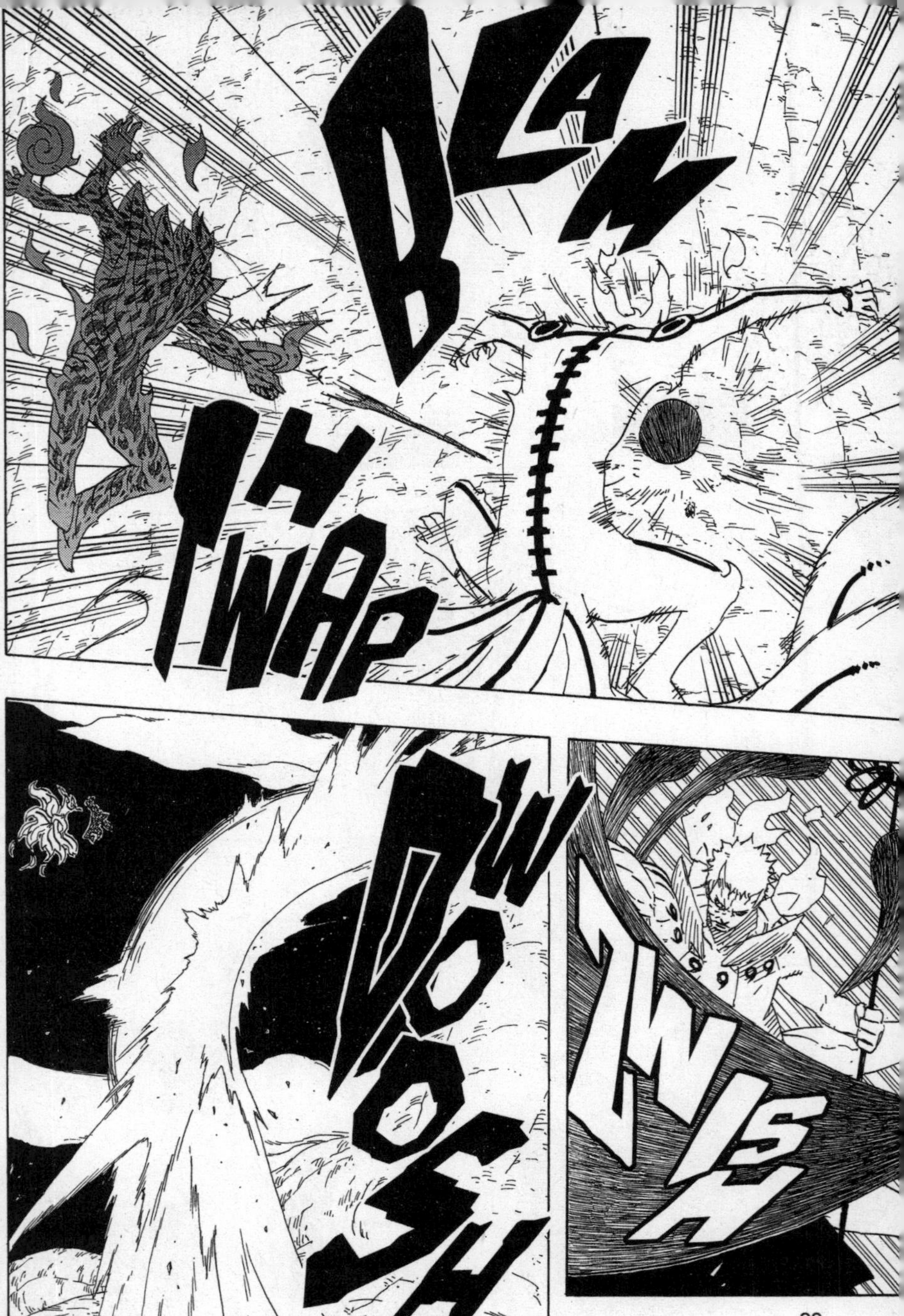
BLAM
THWAP
ZWISH
VWOOSH

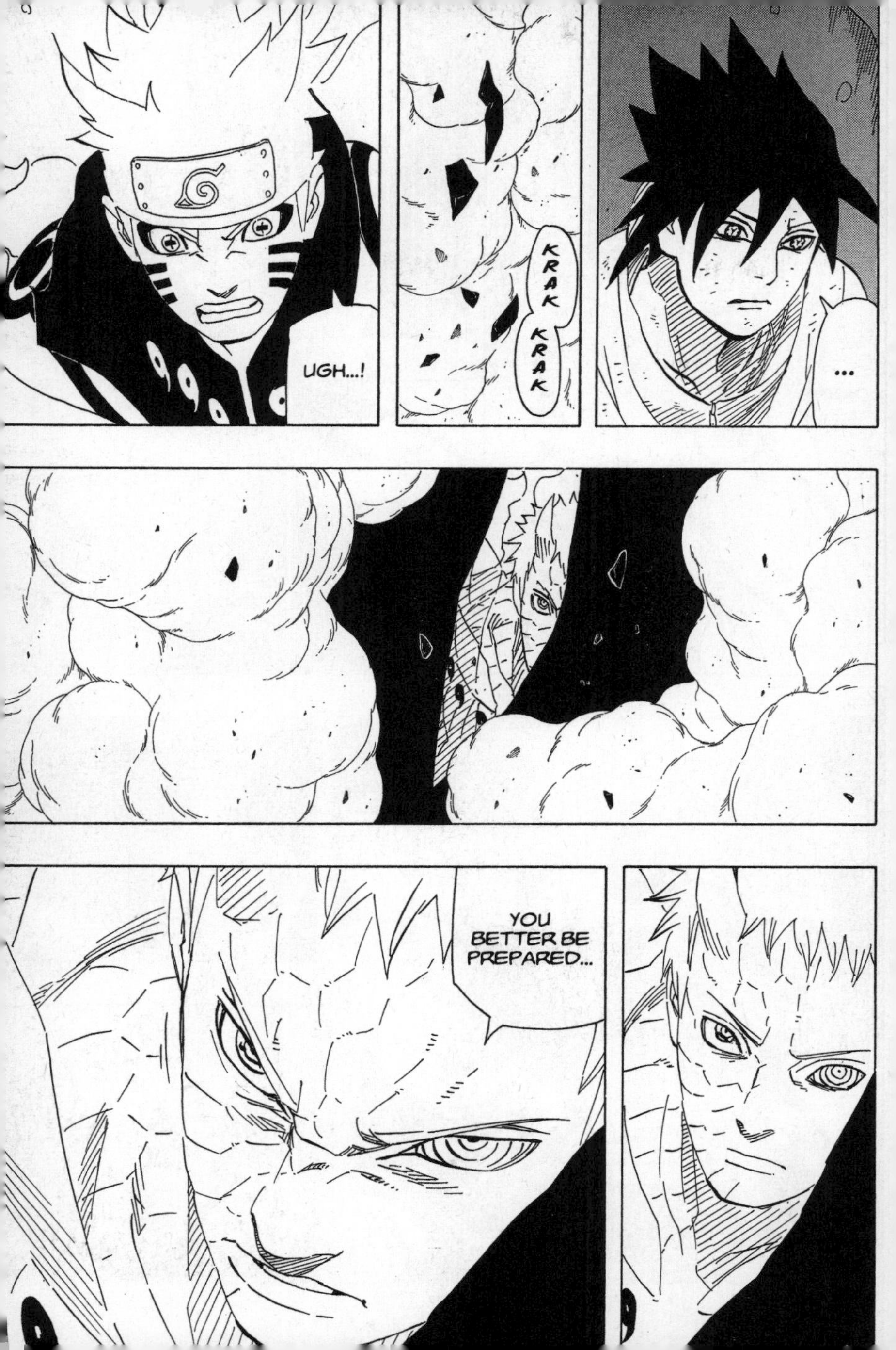
...
KRAK KRAK
UGH...!
YOU BETTER BE PREPARED...

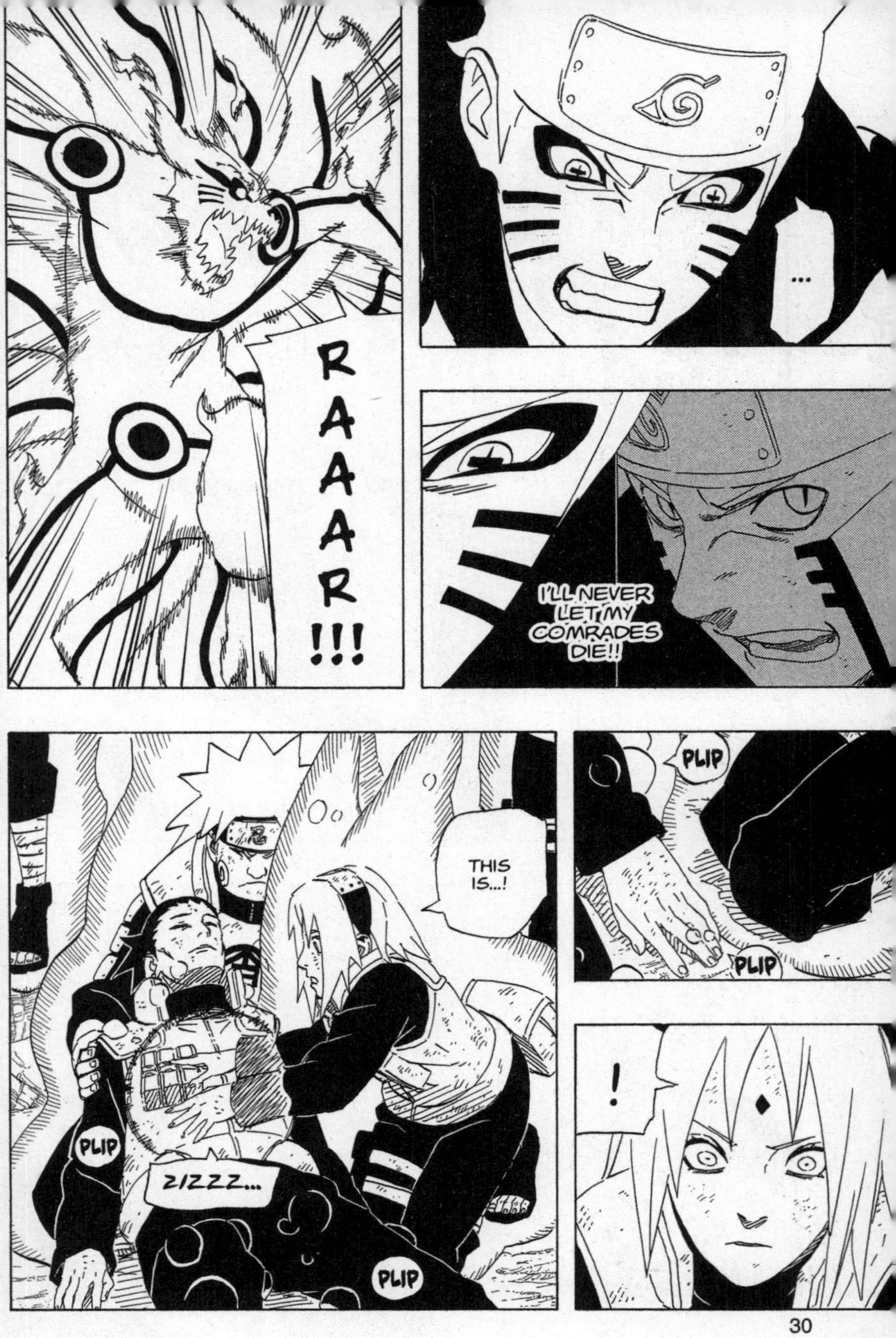
...
I'LL NEVER LET MY COMRADES DIE!!
RAAAAR!!!
PLIP
PLIP
!
THIS IS...!
PLIP
ZIZZZ...
PLIP

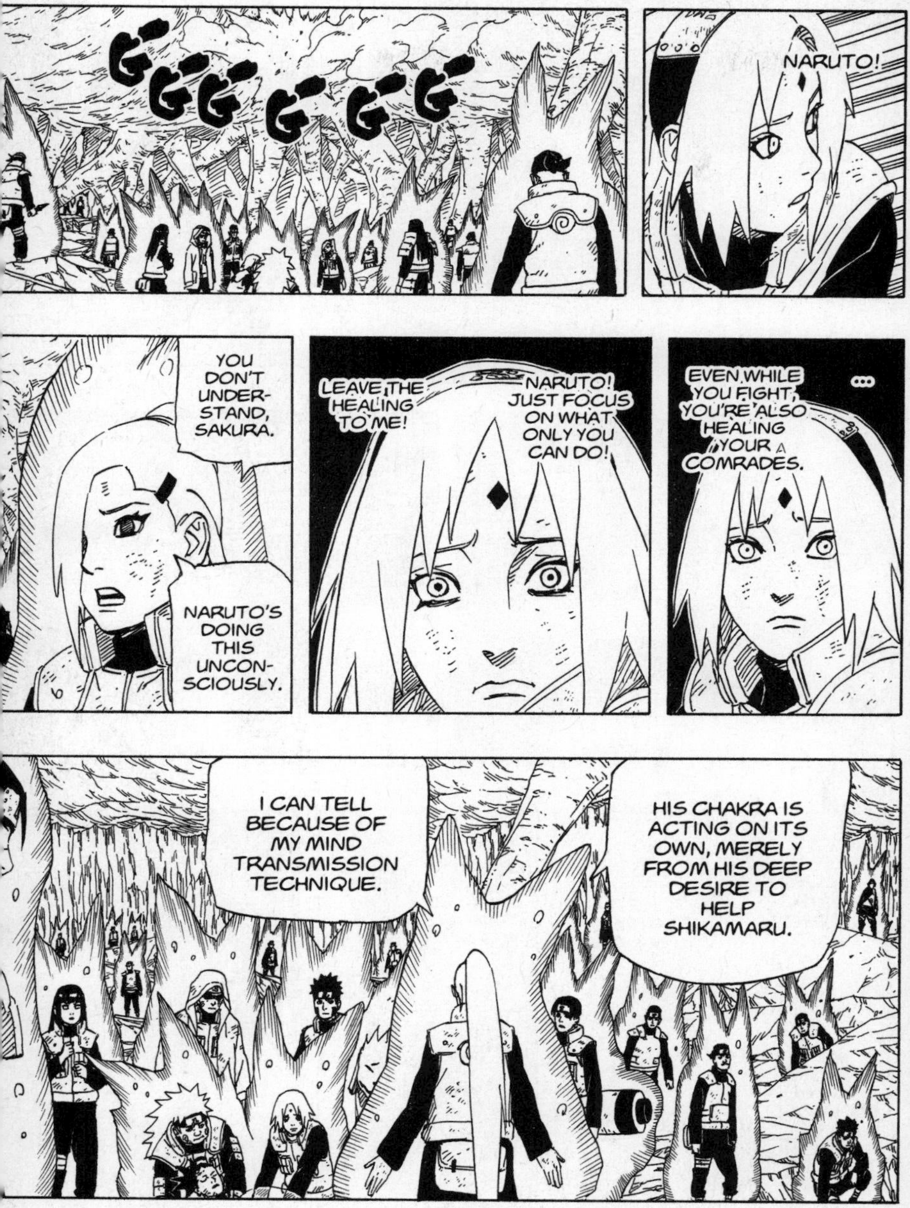
NARUTO!
GGGGGG
...
EVEN WHILE YOU FIGHT, YOU'RE ALSO HEALING YOUR COMRADES.
NARUTO! JUST FOCUS ON WHAT ONLY YOU CAN DO!
LEAVE THE HEALING TO ME!
YOU DON'T UNDER-STAND, SAKURA.
NARUTO'S DOING THIS UNCON-SCIOUSLY.
HIS CHAKRA IS ACTING ON ITS OWN, MERELY FROM HIS DEEP DESIRE TO HELP SHIKAMARU.
I CAN TELL BECAUSE OF MY MIND TRANSMISSION TECHNIQUE.

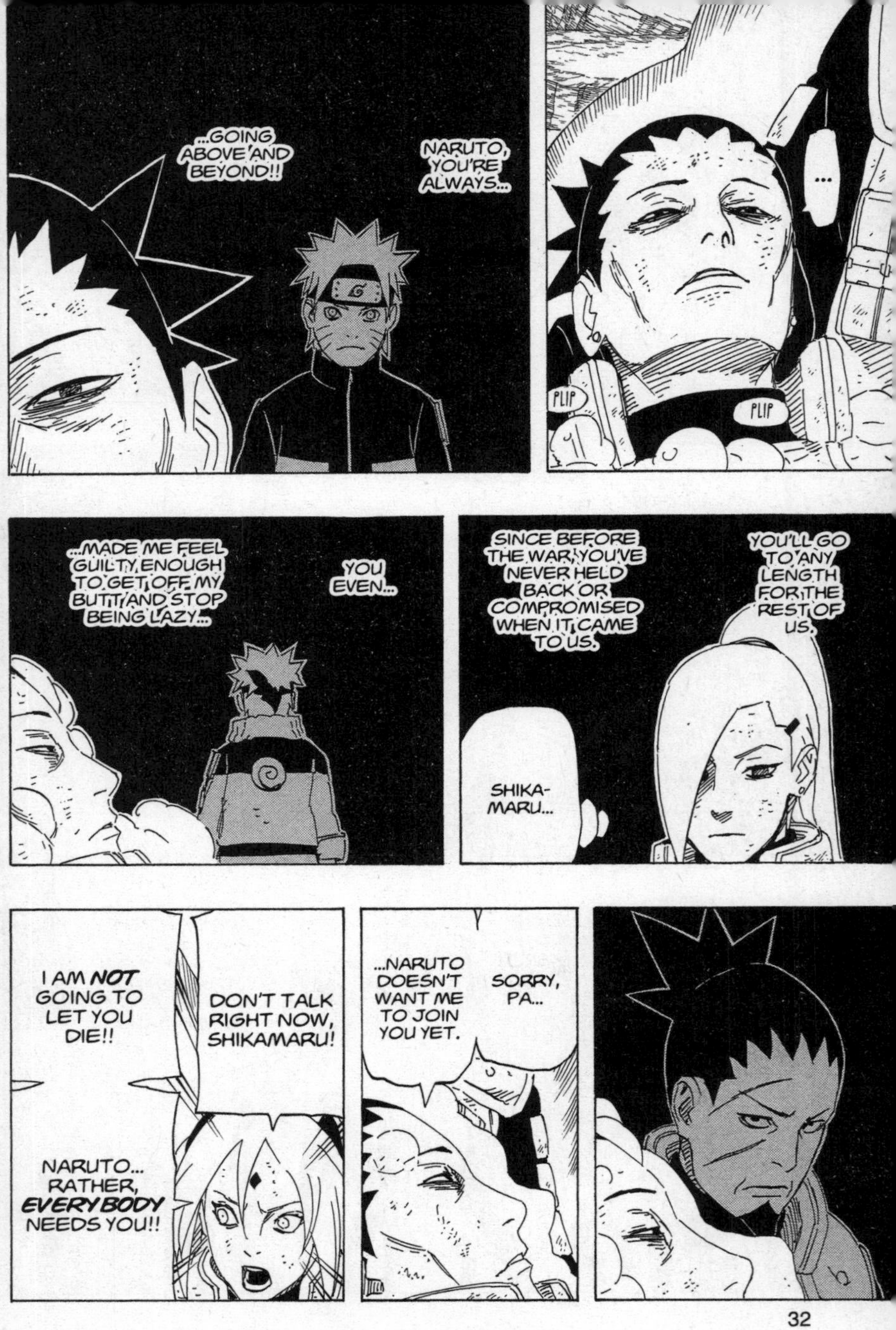
...
PLIP
PLIP
NARUTO, YOU'RE ALWAYS...
...GOING ABOVE AND BEYOND!!
YOU'LL GO TO ANY LENGTH FOR THE REST OF US.
SINCE BEFORE THE WAR, YOU'VE NEVER HELD BACK OR COMPROMISED WHEN IT CAME TO US.
SHIKAMARU...
YOU EVEN...
...MADE ME FEEL GUILTY ENOUGH TO GET OFF MY BUTT AND STOP BEING LAZY...
SORRY, PA...
...NARUTO DOESN'T WANT ME TO JOIN YOU YET.
DON'T TALK RIGHT NOW, SHIKAMARU!
I AM **NOT** GOING TO LET YOU DIE!!
NARUTO... RATHER, ***EVERYBODY*** NEEDS YOU!!

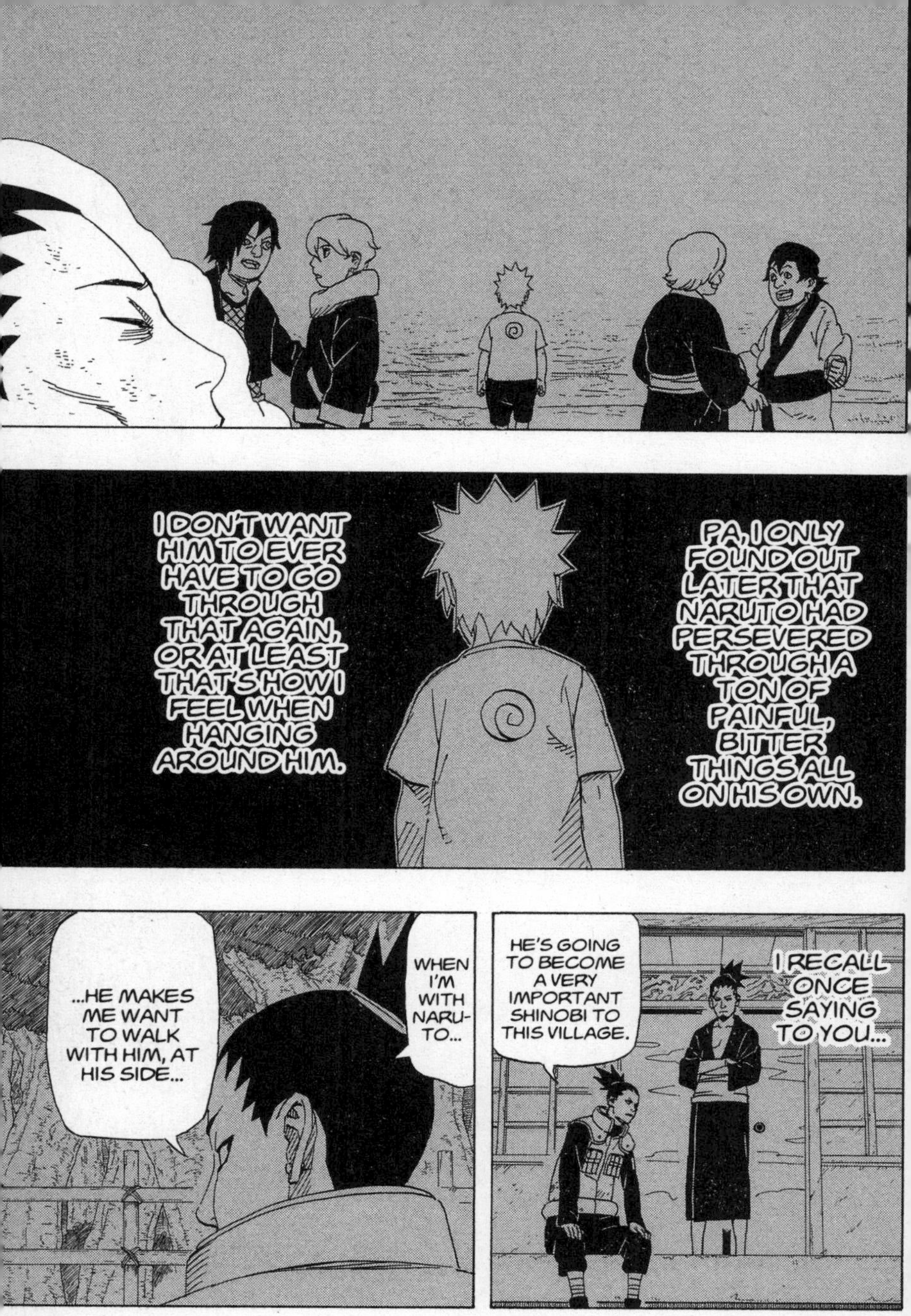
PA, I ONLY FOUND OUT LATER THAT NARUTO HAD PERSEVERED THROUGH A TON OF PAINFUL, BITTER THINGS ALL ON HIS OWN.
I DON'T WANT HIM TO EVER HAVE TO GO THROUGH THAT AGAIN, OR AT LEAST THAT'S HOW I FEEL WHEN HANGING AROUND HIM.
I RECALL ONCE SAYING TO YOU...
HE'S GOING TO BECOME A VERY IMPORTANT SHINOBI TO THIS VILLAGE.
WHEN I'M WITH NARUTO...
...HE MAKES ME WANT TO WALK WITH HIM, AT HIS SIDE...

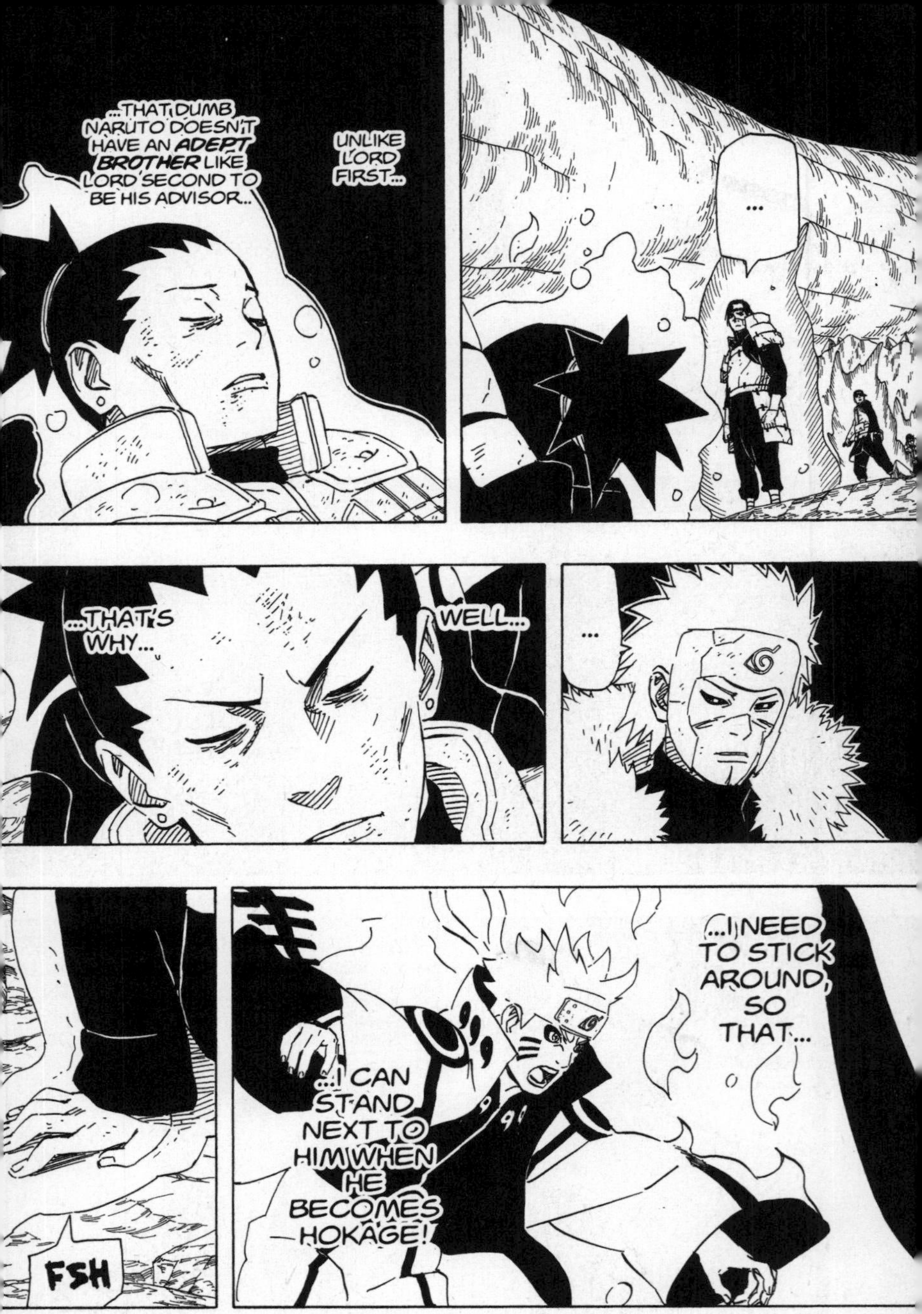
...
...
UNLIKE LORD FIRST...
...THAT DUMB NARUTO DOESN'T HAVE AN *ADEPT BROTHER* LIKE LORD SECOND TO BE HIS ADVISOR...
...
WELL...
...THAT'S WHY...
...I NEED TO STICK AROUND, SO THAT...
...I CAN STAND NEXT TO HIM WHEN HE BECOMES HOKAGE!
FSH

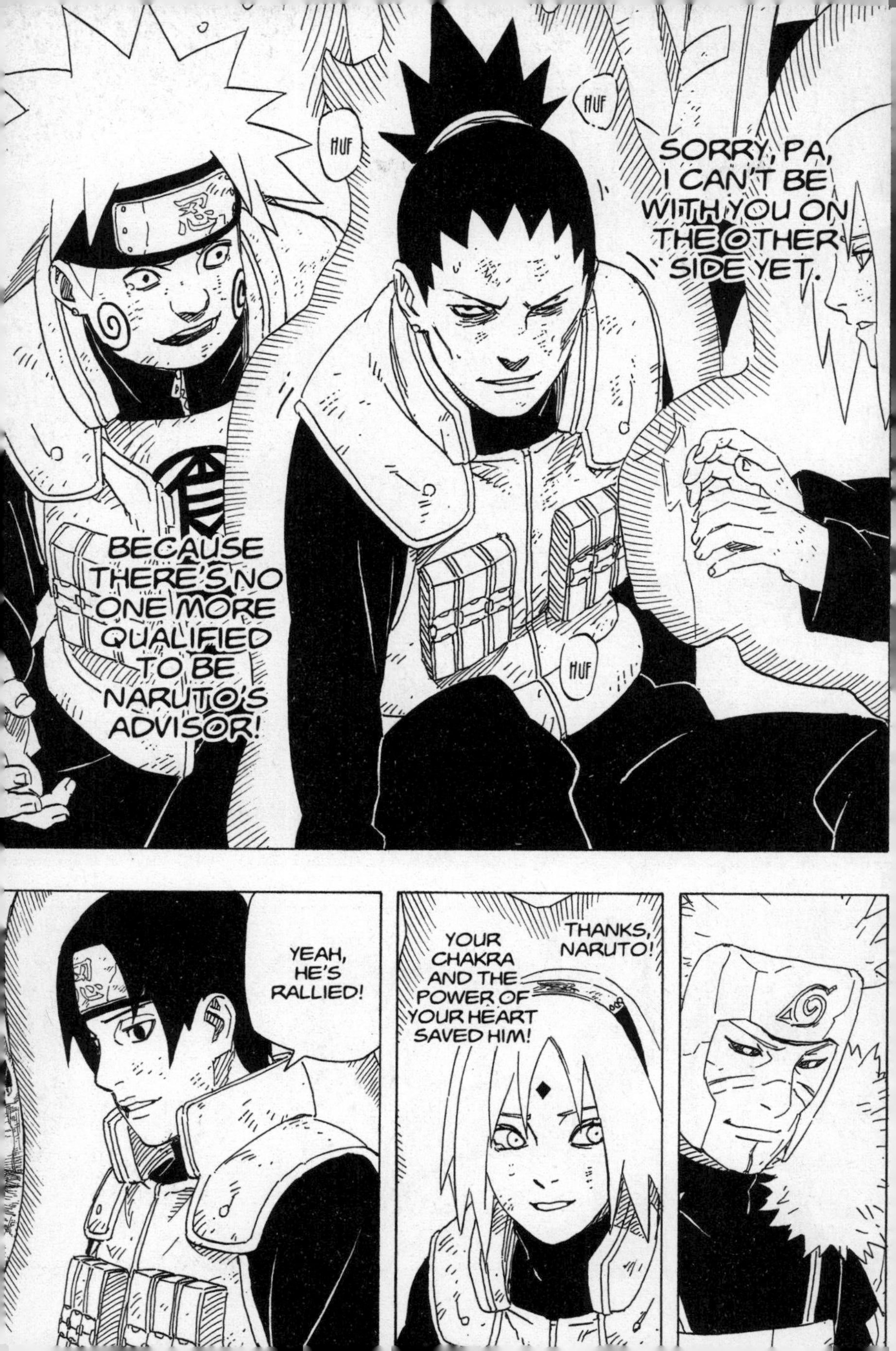
HUF
SORRY, PA, I CAN'T BE WITH YOU ON THE OTHER SIDE YET.
HUF
HUF
BECAUSE THERE'S NO ONE MORE QUALIFIED TO BE NARUTO'S ADVISOR!
THANKS, NARUTO!
YOUR CHAKRA AND THE POWER OF YOUR HEART SAVED HIM!
YEAH, HE'S RALLIED!

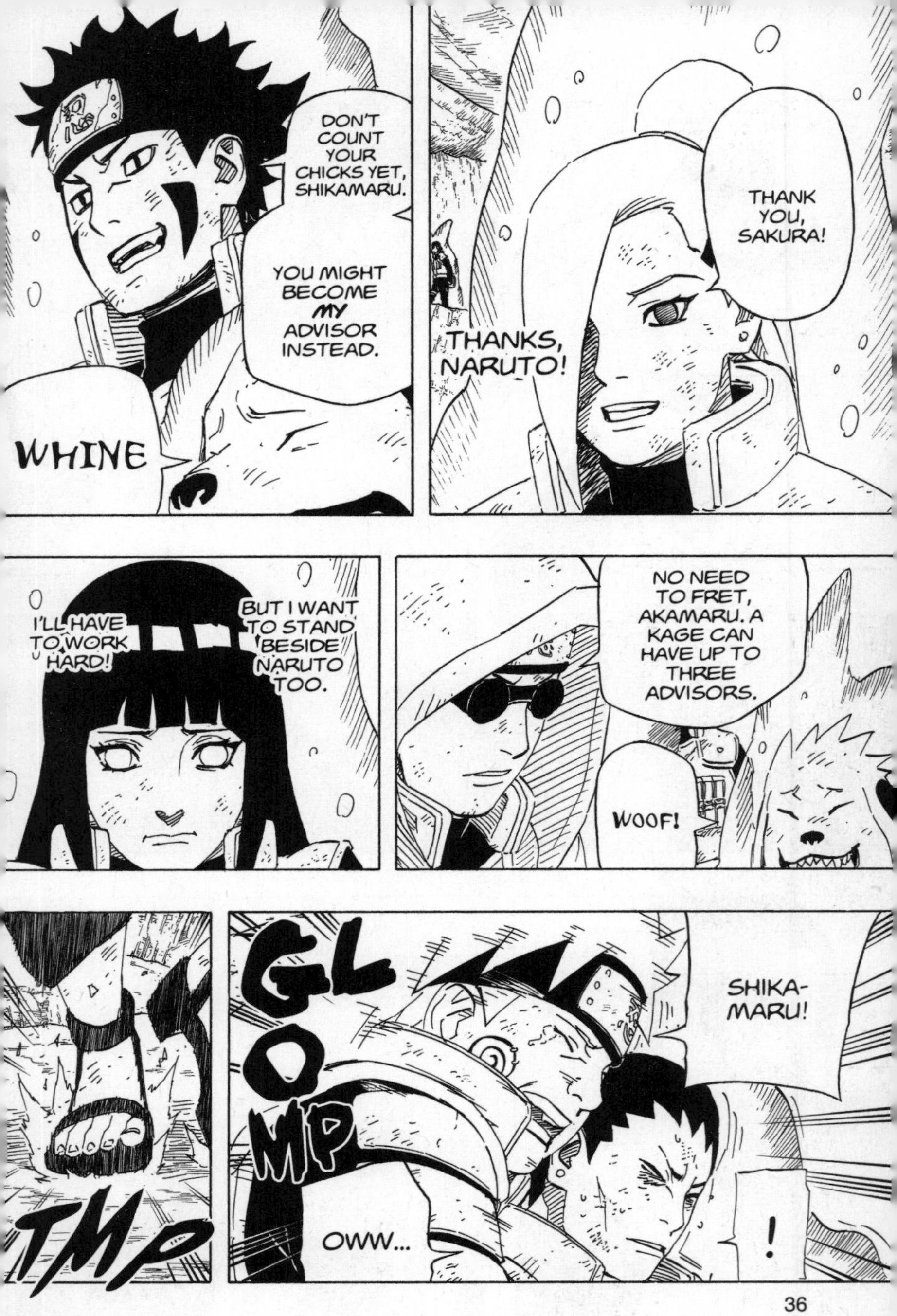
THANK YOU, SAKURA!
THANKS, NARUTO!
DON'T COUNT YOUR CHICKS YET, SHIKAMARU.
YOU MIGHT BECOME MY ADVISOR INSTEAD.
WHINE
NO NEED TO FRET, AKAMARU. A KAGE CAN HAVE UP TO THREE ADVISORS.
WOOF!
BUT I WANT TO STAND BESIDE NARUTO TOO.
I'LL HAVE TO WORK HARD!
SHIKA-MARU!
!
GLOMP
OWW...
TMP

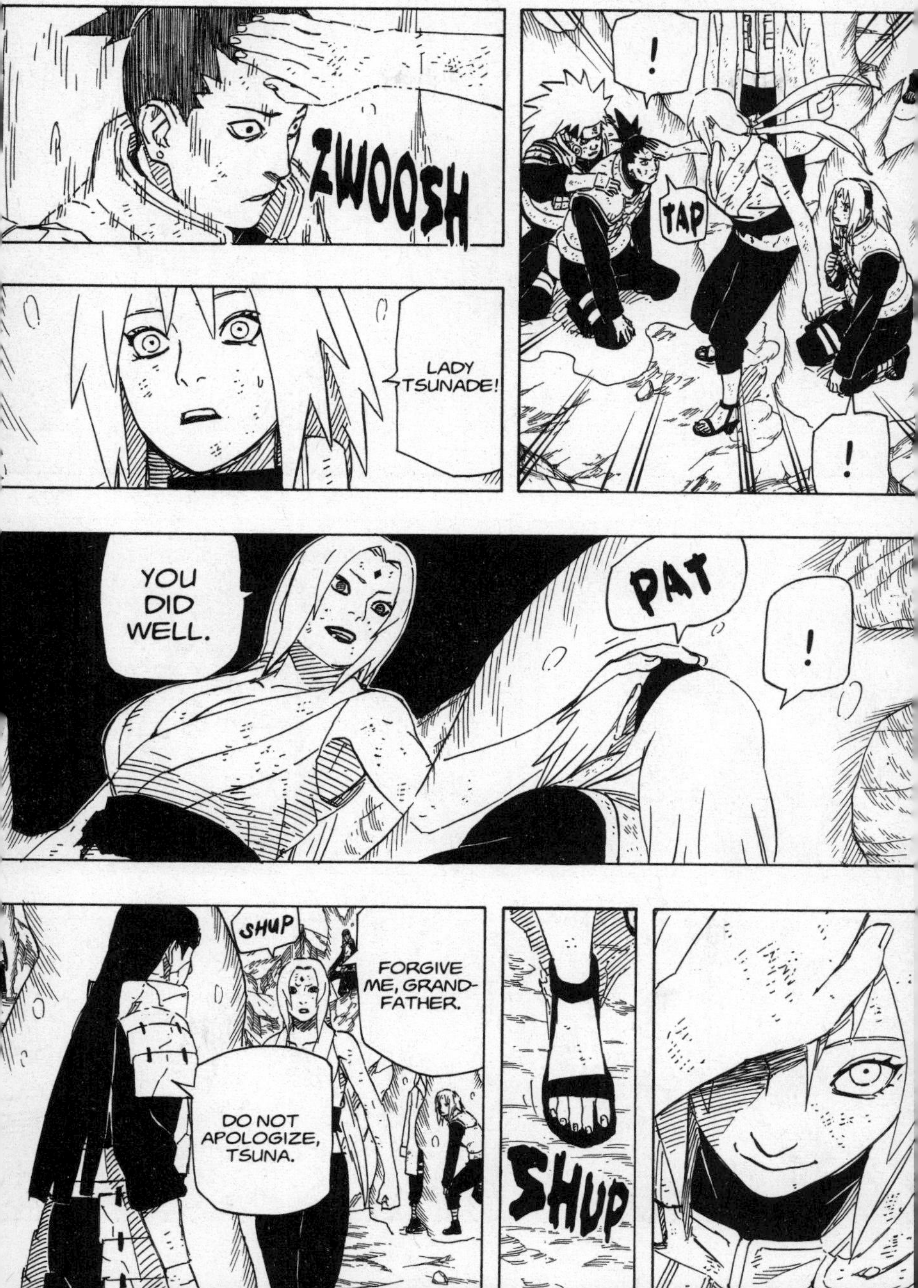
!
TAP
!
ZWOOSH
LADY TSUNADE!
!
PAT
YOU DID WELL.
SHUP
SHUP
FORGIVE ME, GRAND-FATHER.
DO NOT APOLOGIZE, TSUNA.

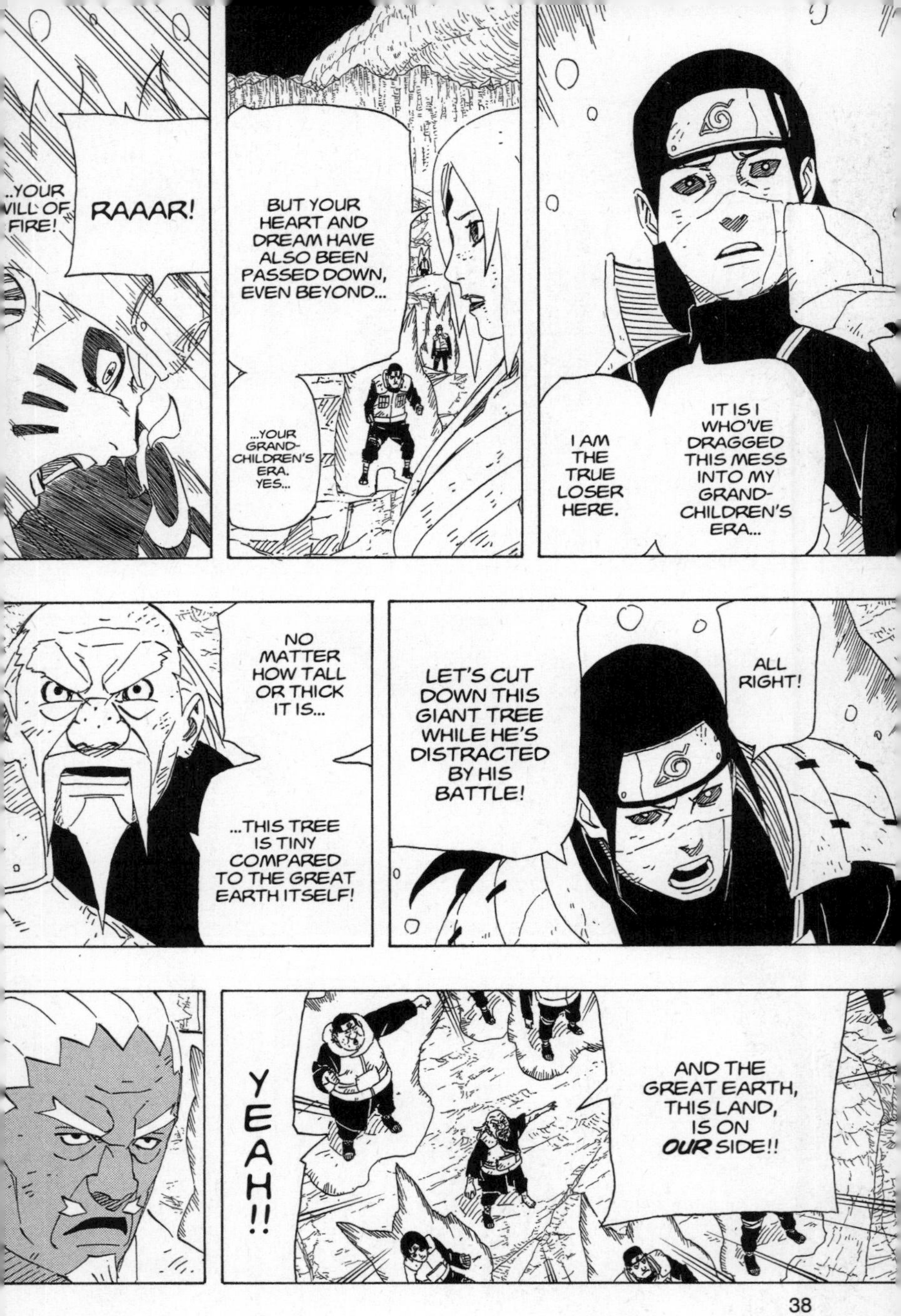
IT IS I WHO'VE DRAGGED THIS MESS INTO MY GRAND-CHILDREN'S ERA...
I AM THE TRUE LOSER HERE.
BUT YOUR HEART AND DREAM HAVE ALSO BEEN PASSED DOWN, EVEN BEYOND...
...YOUR GRAND-CHILDREN'S ERA. YES...
RAAAR!
..YOUR WILL OF FIRE!
ALL RIGHT!
LET'S CUT DOWN THIS GIANT TREE WHILE HE'S DISTRACTED BY HIS BATTLE!
NO MATTER HOW TALL OR THICK IT IS...
...THIS TREE IS TINY COMPARED TO THE GREAT EARTH ITSELF!
AND THE GREAT EARTH, THIS LAND, IS ON ***OUR*** SIDE!!
YEAH!!

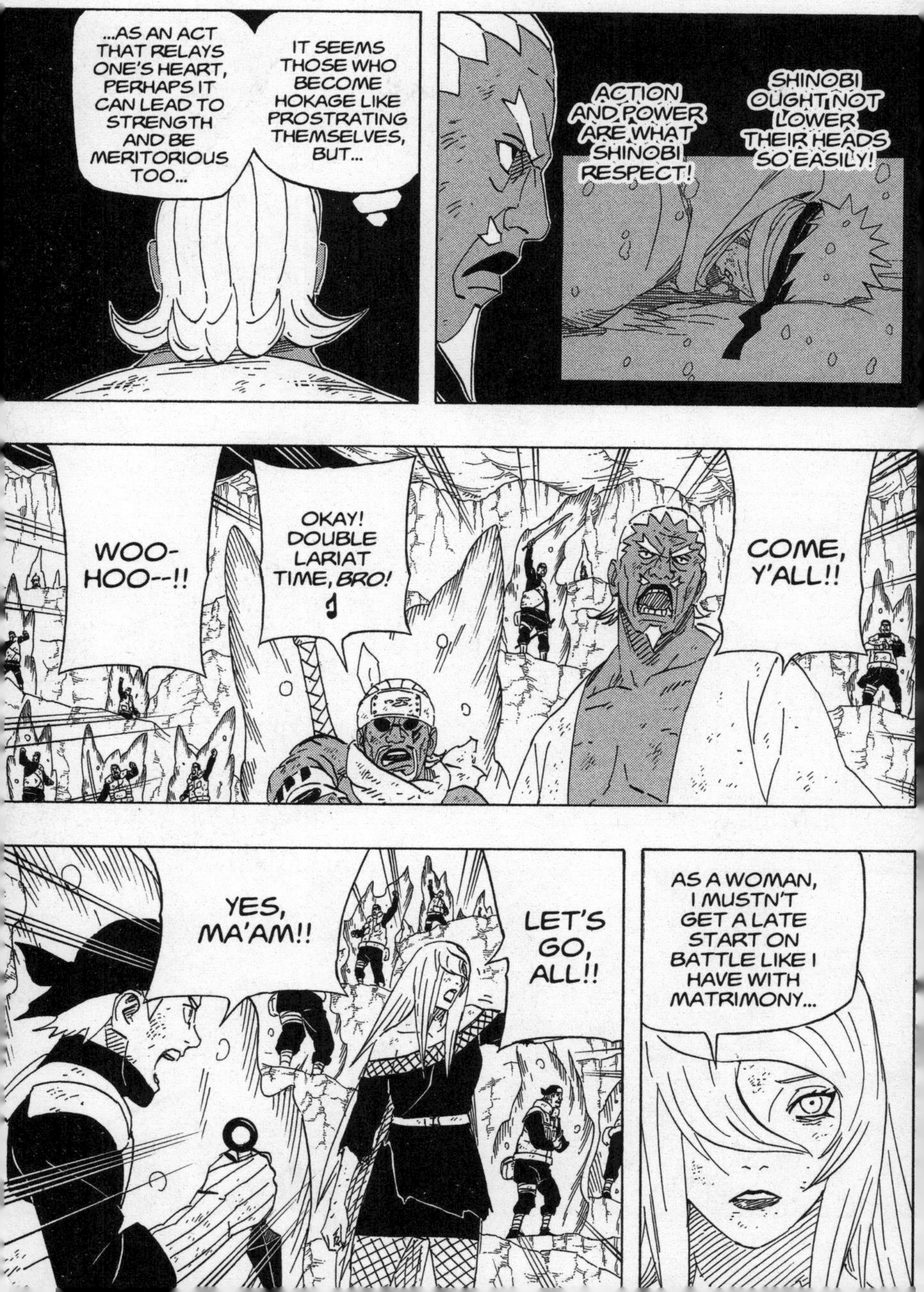
SHINOBI OUGHT NOT LOWER THEIR HEADS SO EASILY!
ACTION AND POWER ARE WHAT SHINOBI RESPECT!
IT SEEMS THOSE WHO BECOME HOKAGE LIKE PROSTRATING THEMSELVES, BUT...
...AS AN ACT THAT RELAYS ONE'S HEART, PERHAPS IT CAN LEAD TO STRENGTH AND BE MERITORIOUS TOO...
COME, Y'ALL!!
OKAY! DOUBLE LARIAT TIME, *BRO!* ♪
WOO-HOO--!!
AS A WOMAN, I MUSTN'T GET A LATE START ON BATTLE LIKE I HAVE WITH MATRIMONY...
LET'S GO, ALL!!
YES, MA'AM!!

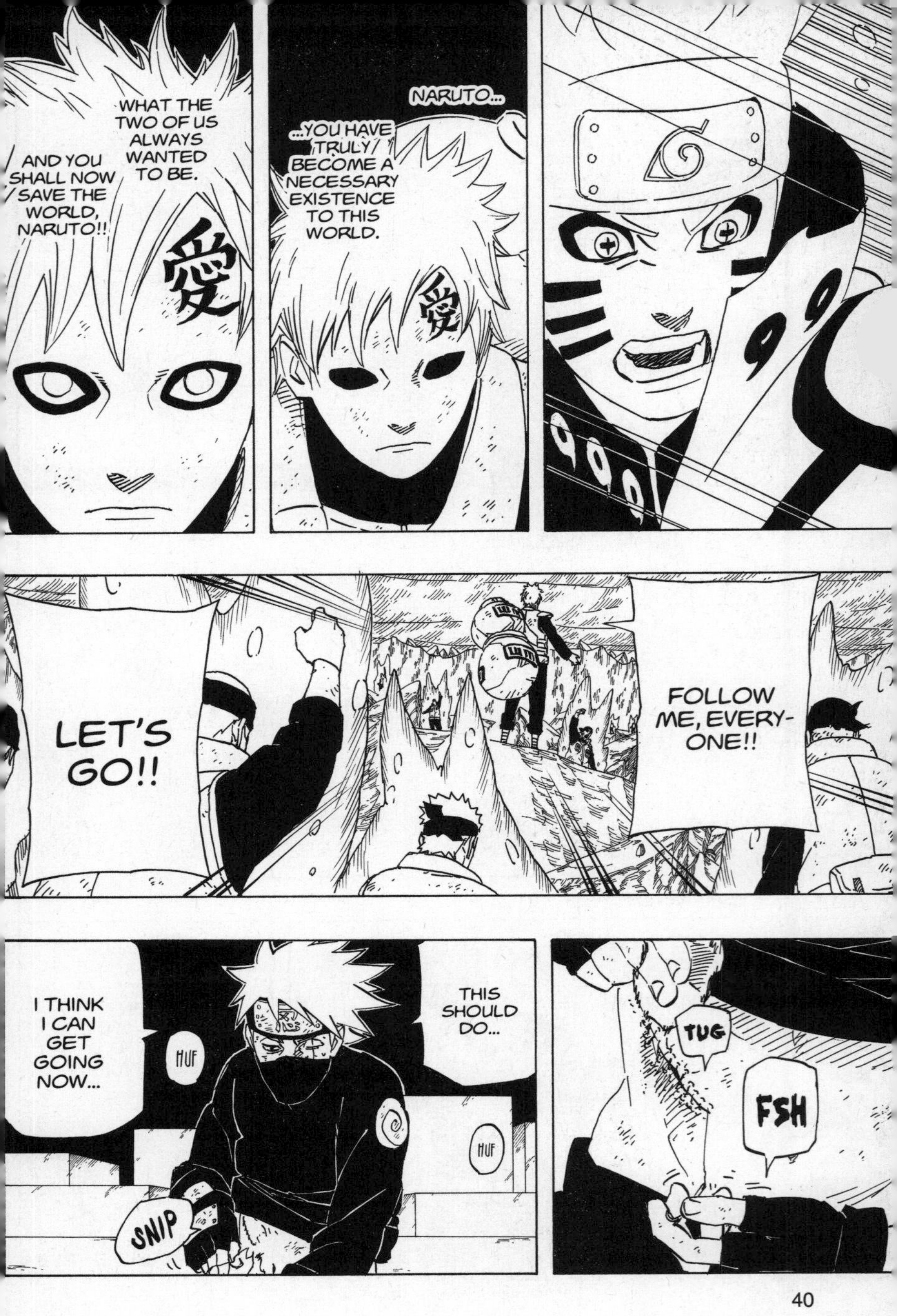
NARUTO...
...YOU HAVE TRULY BECOME A NECESSARY EXISTENCE TO THIS WORLD.
WHAT THE TWO OF US ALWAYS WANTED TO BE.
AND YOU SHALL NOW SAVE THE WORLD, NARUTO!!
FOLLOW ME, EVERY-ONE!!
LET'S GO!!
TUG
FSH
THIS SHOULD DO...
HUF
I THINK I CAN GET GOING NOW...
HUF
SNIP

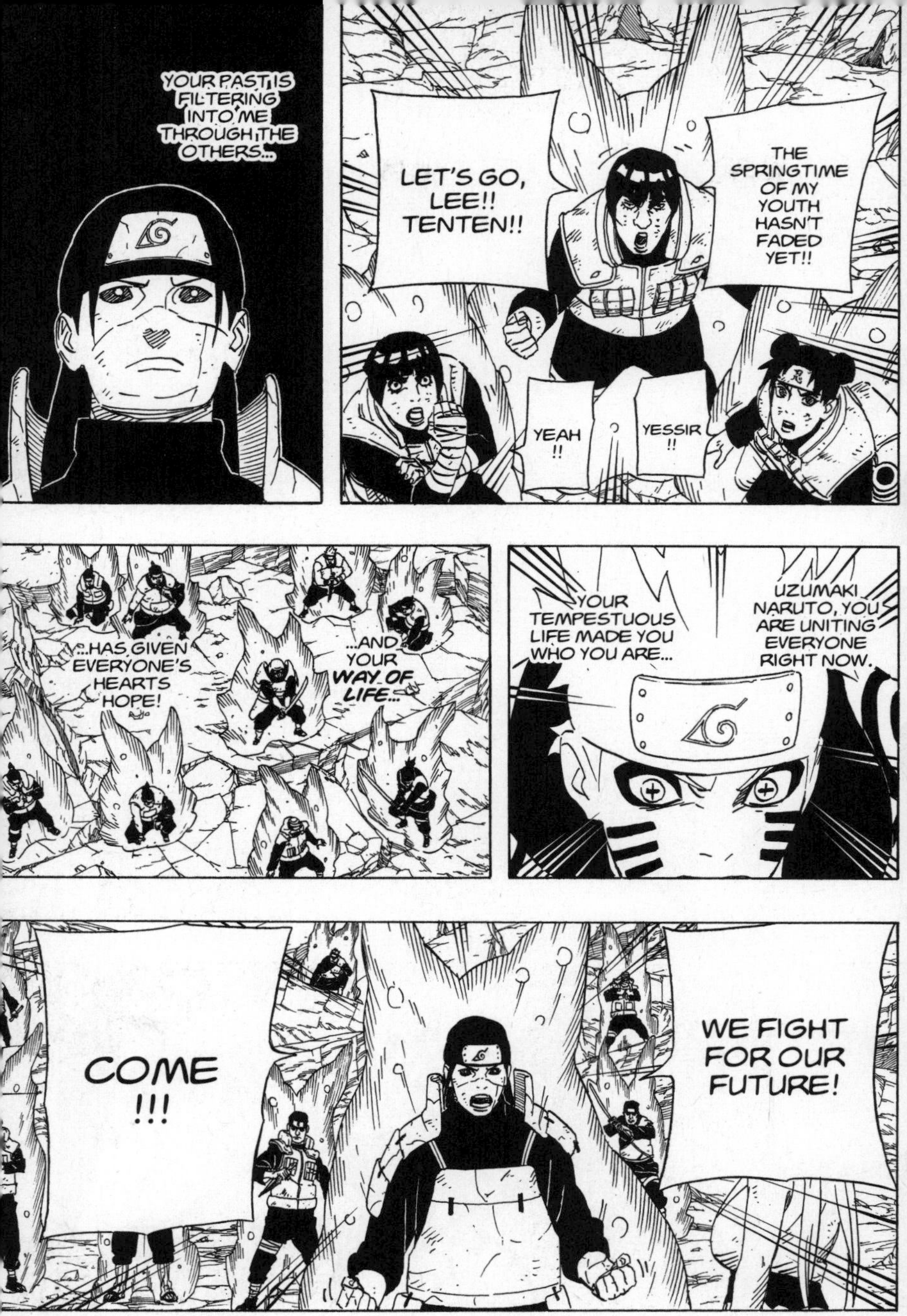
THE SPRINGTIME OF MY YOUTH HASN'T FADED YET!!
LET'S GO, LEE!! TENTEN!!
YESSIR!!
YEAH!!
YOUR PAST IS FILTERING INTO ME THROUGH THE OTHERS...
UZUMAKI NARUTO, YOU ARE UNITING EVERYONE RIGHT NOW.
YOUR TEMPESTUOUS LIFE MADE YOU WHO YOU ARE...
...AND YOUR WAY OF LIFE...
...HAS GIVEN EVERYONE'S HEARTS HOPE!
WE FIGHT FOR OUR FUTURE!
COME!!!

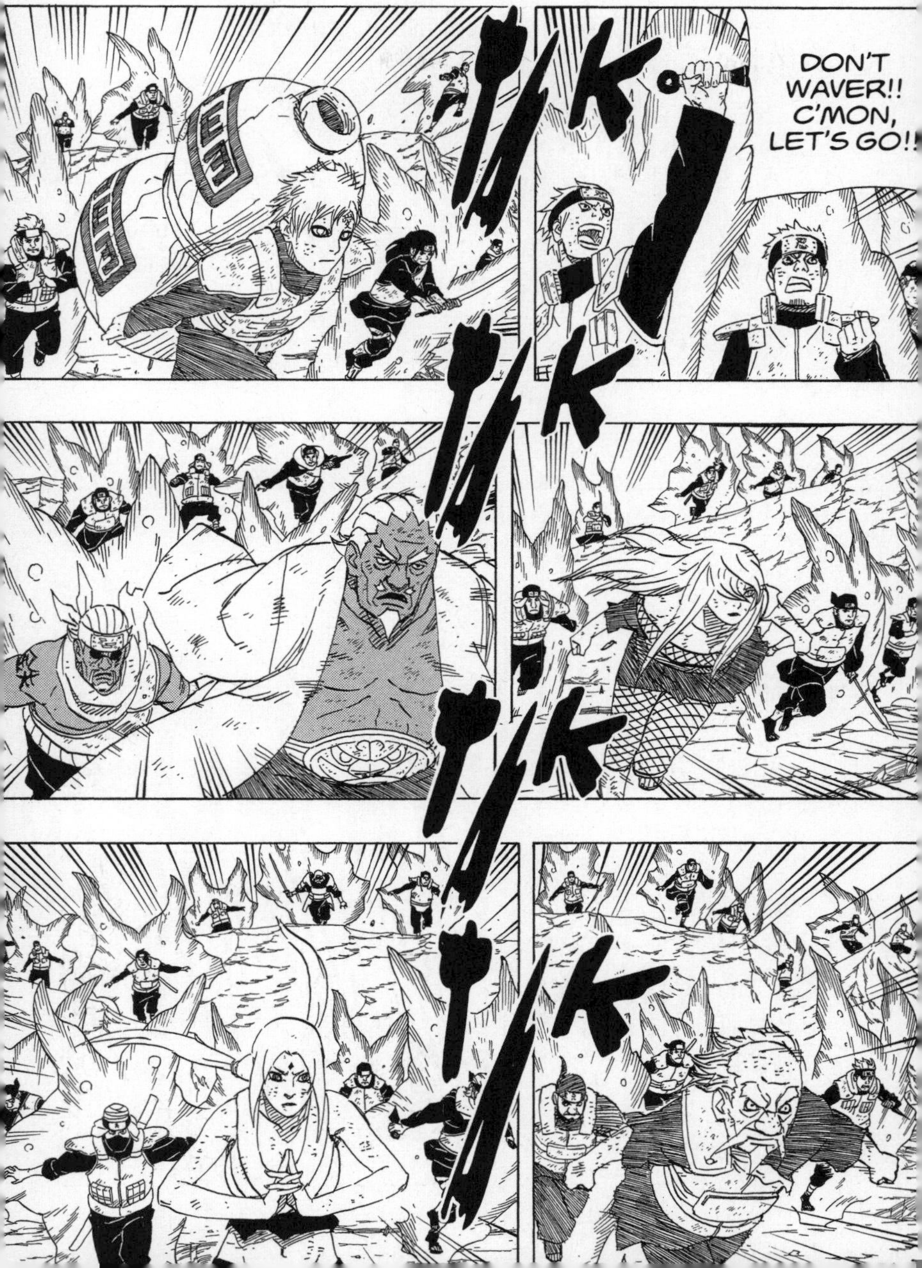
DON'T WAVER!! C'MON, LET'S GO!!

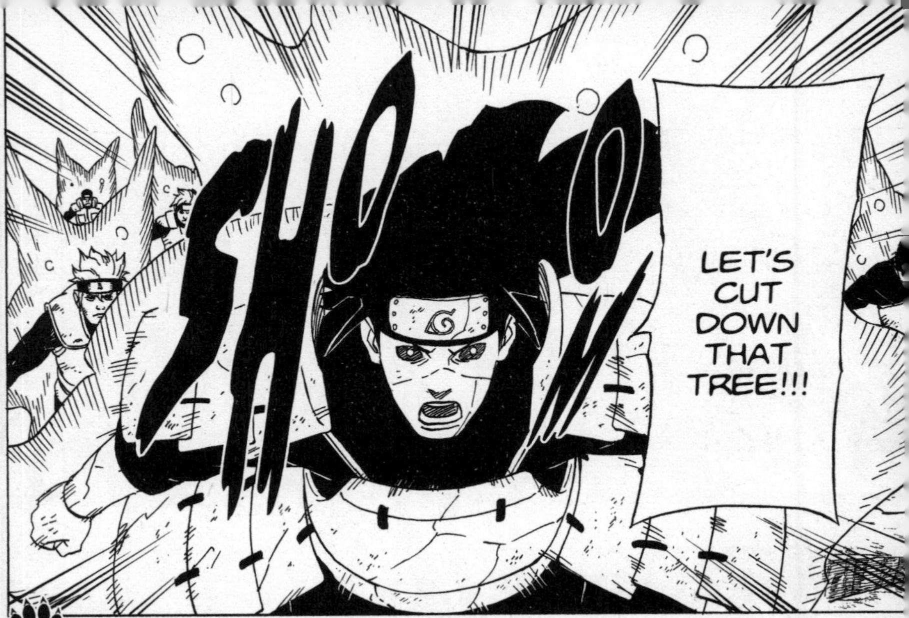
SHOOOM
LET'S CUT DOWN THAT TREE!!!

Number650: Those Who Shall Sleep

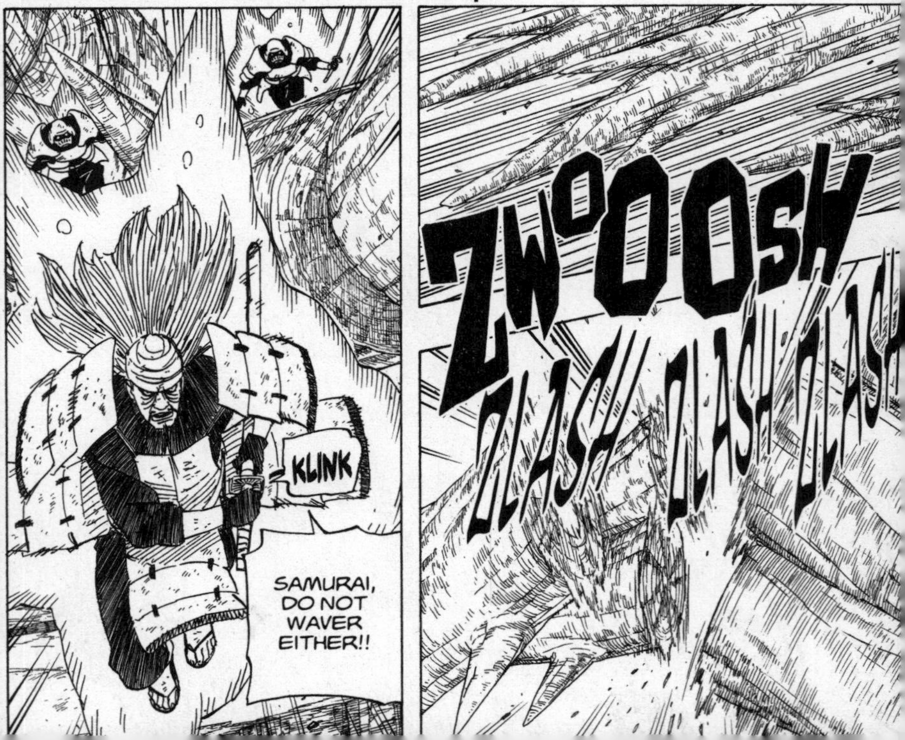
ZWOOOSH
SLASH SLASH SLASH
KLINK
SAMURAI, DO NOT WAVER EITHER!!

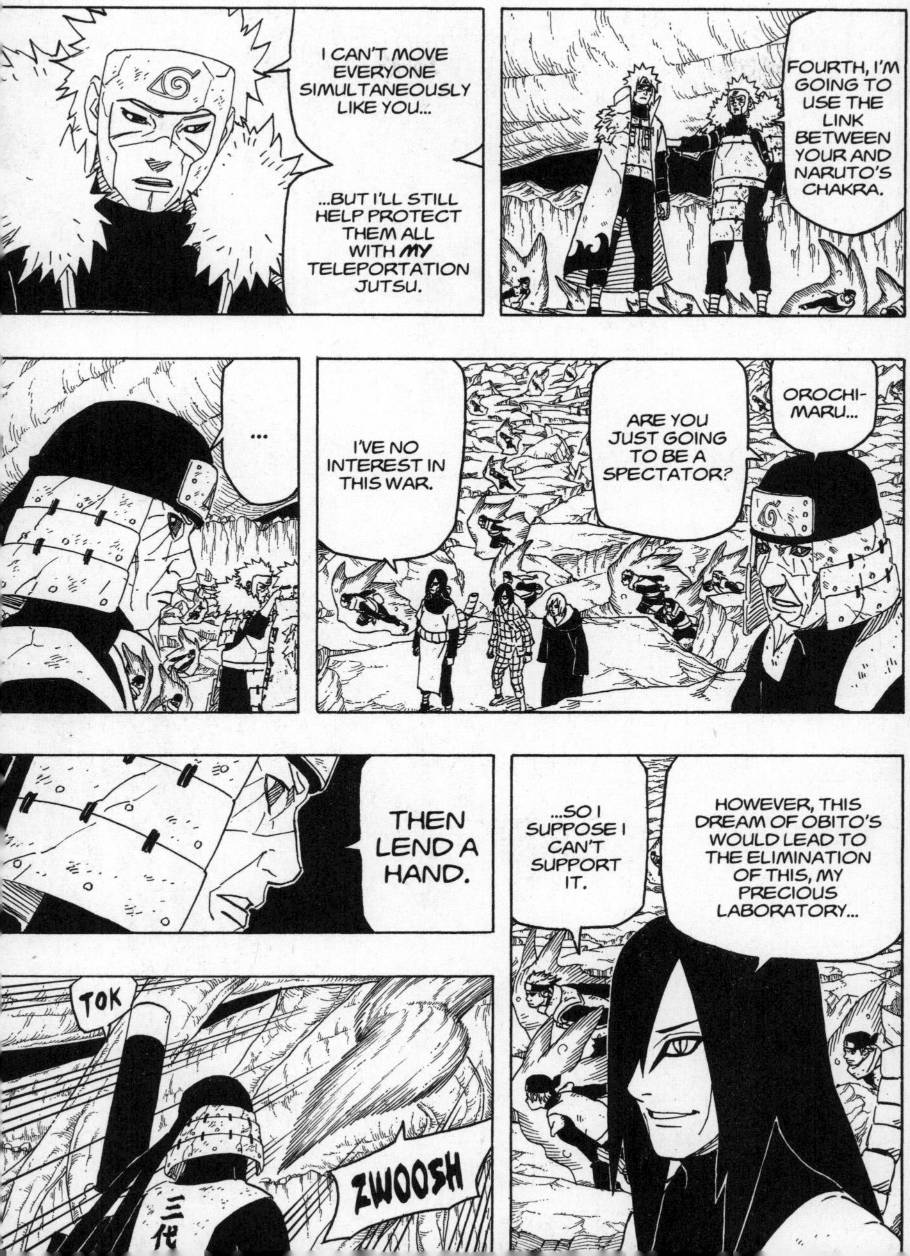
FOURTH, I'M GOING TO USE THE LINK BETWEEN YOUR AND NARUTO'S CHAKRA.
I CAN'T MOVE EVERYONE SIMULTANEOUSLY LIKE YOU...
...BUT I'LL STILL HELP PROTECT THEM ALL WITH *MY* TELEPORTATION JUTSU.
OROCHI-MARU...
ARE YOU JUST GOING TO BE A SPECTATOR?
I'VE NO INTEREST IN THIS WAR.
...
HOWEVER, THIS DREAM OF OBITO'S WOULD LEAD TO THE ELIMINATION OF THIS, MY PRECIOUS LABORATORY...
...SO I SUPPOSE I CAN'T SUPPORT IT.
THEN LEND A HAND.
TOK
ZWOOSH
三代

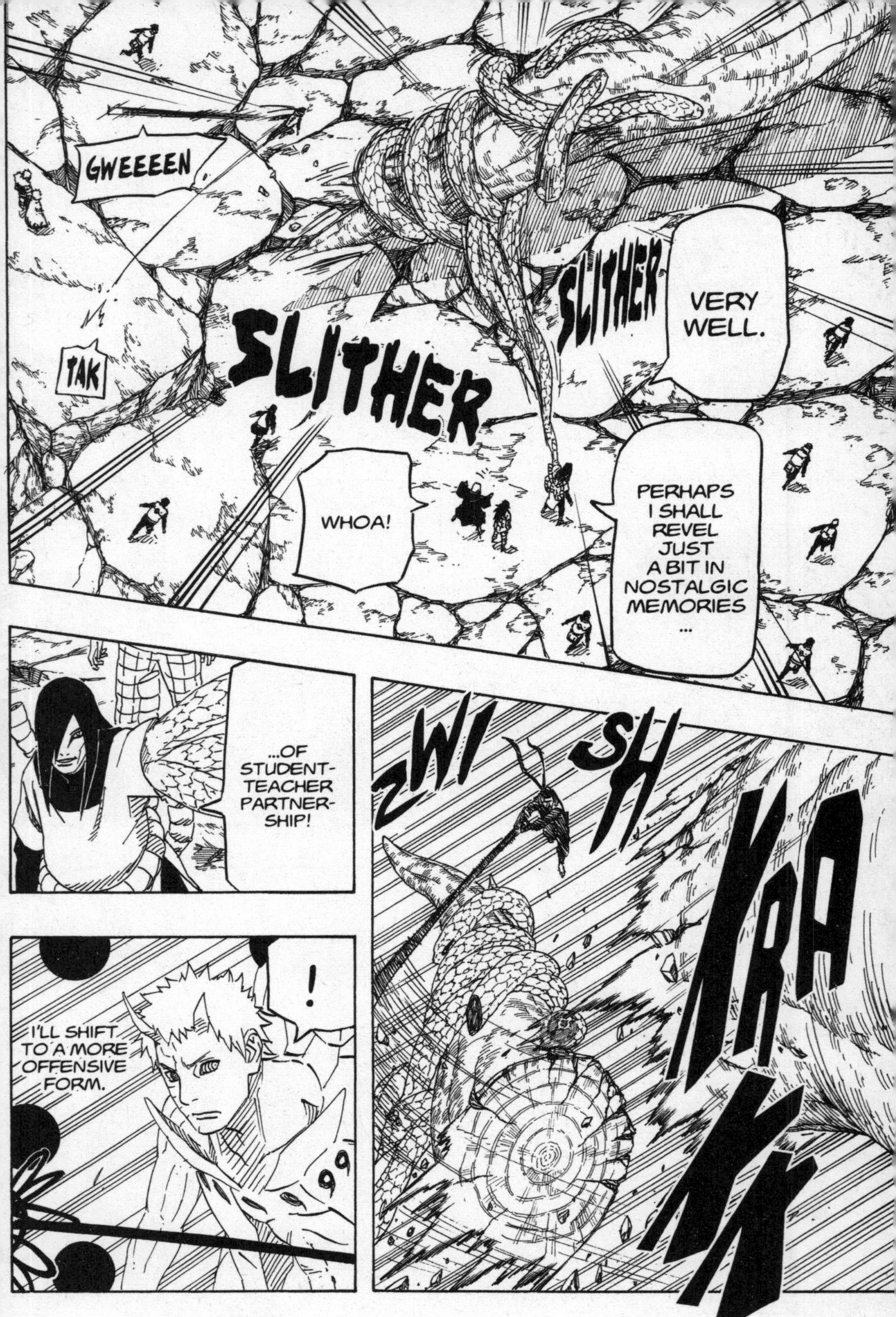
VERY WELL.
SLITHER
GWEEEEN
SLITHER
PERHAPS I SHALL REVEL JUST A BIT IN NOSTALGIC MEMORIES ...
WHOA!
TAK
ZWISH
KRAKK
...OF STUDENT-TEACHER PARTNERSHIP!
!
I'LL SHIFT TO A MORE OFFENSIVE FORM.

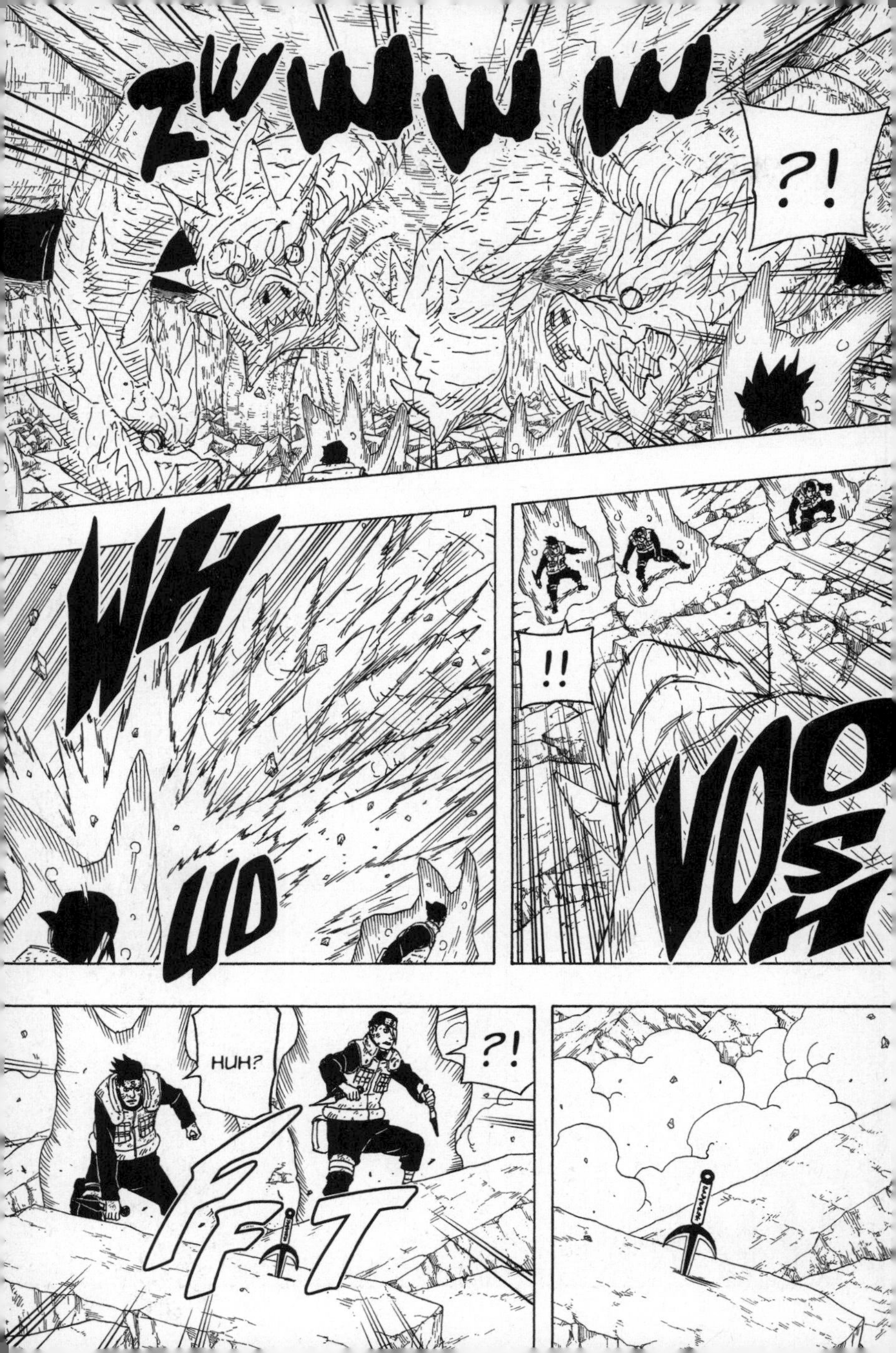
ZWWWW
?!
VOOSH
!!
WHUD
?!
HUH?
FFT

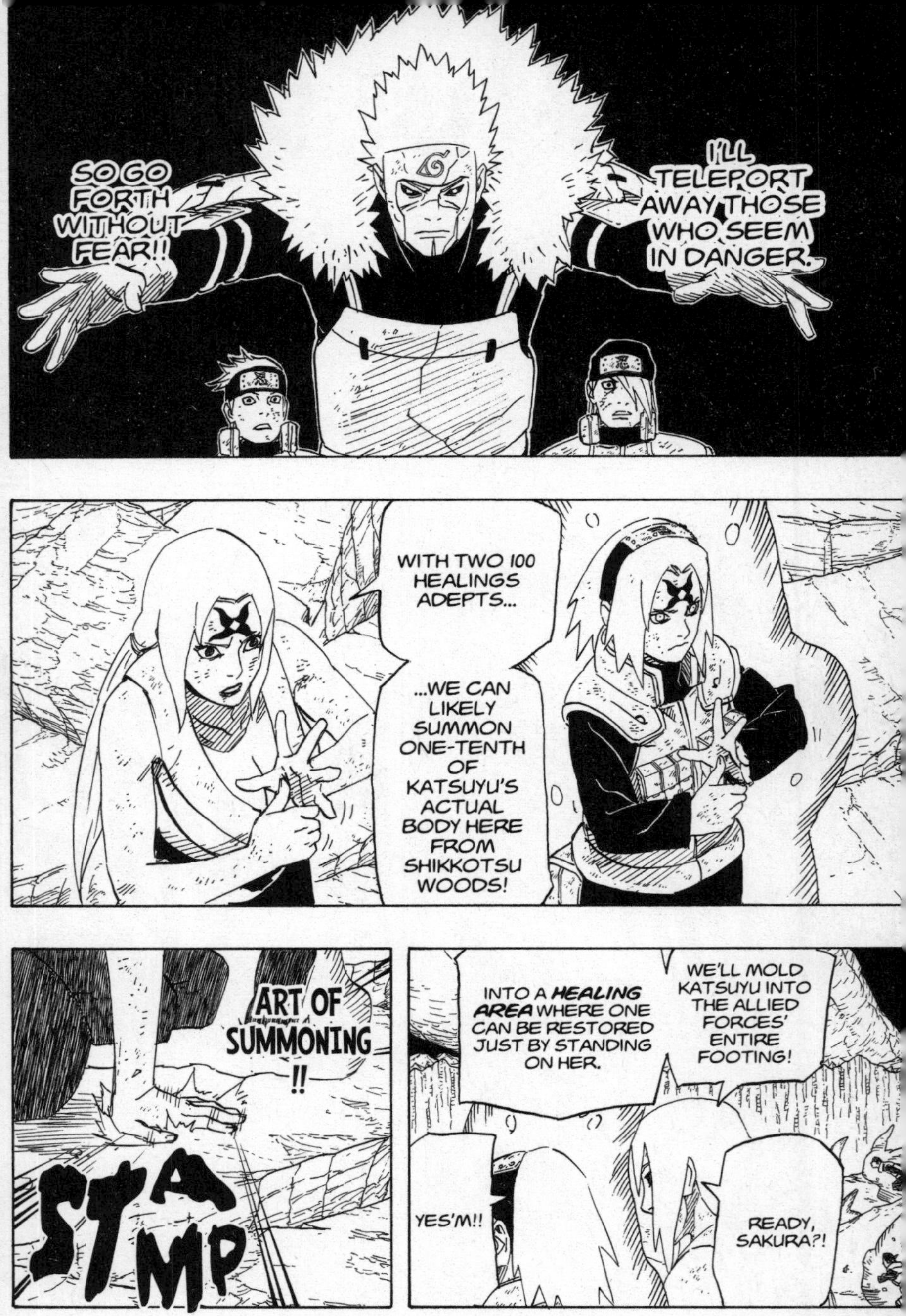
I'LL TELEPORT AWAY THOSE WHO SEEM IN DANGER.
SO GO FORTH WITHOUT FEAR!!
WITH TWO 100 HEALINGS ADEPTS...
...WE CAN LIKELY SUMMON ONE-TENTH OF KATSUYU'S ACTUAL BODY HERE FROM SHIKKOTSU WOODS!
WE'LL MOLD KATSUYU INTO THE ALLIED FORCES' ENTIRE FOOTING!
INTO A ***HEALING AREA*** WHERE ONE CAN BE RESTORED JUST BY STANDING ON HER.
READY, SAKURA?!
YES'M!!
ART OF SUMMONING!!
STAMP

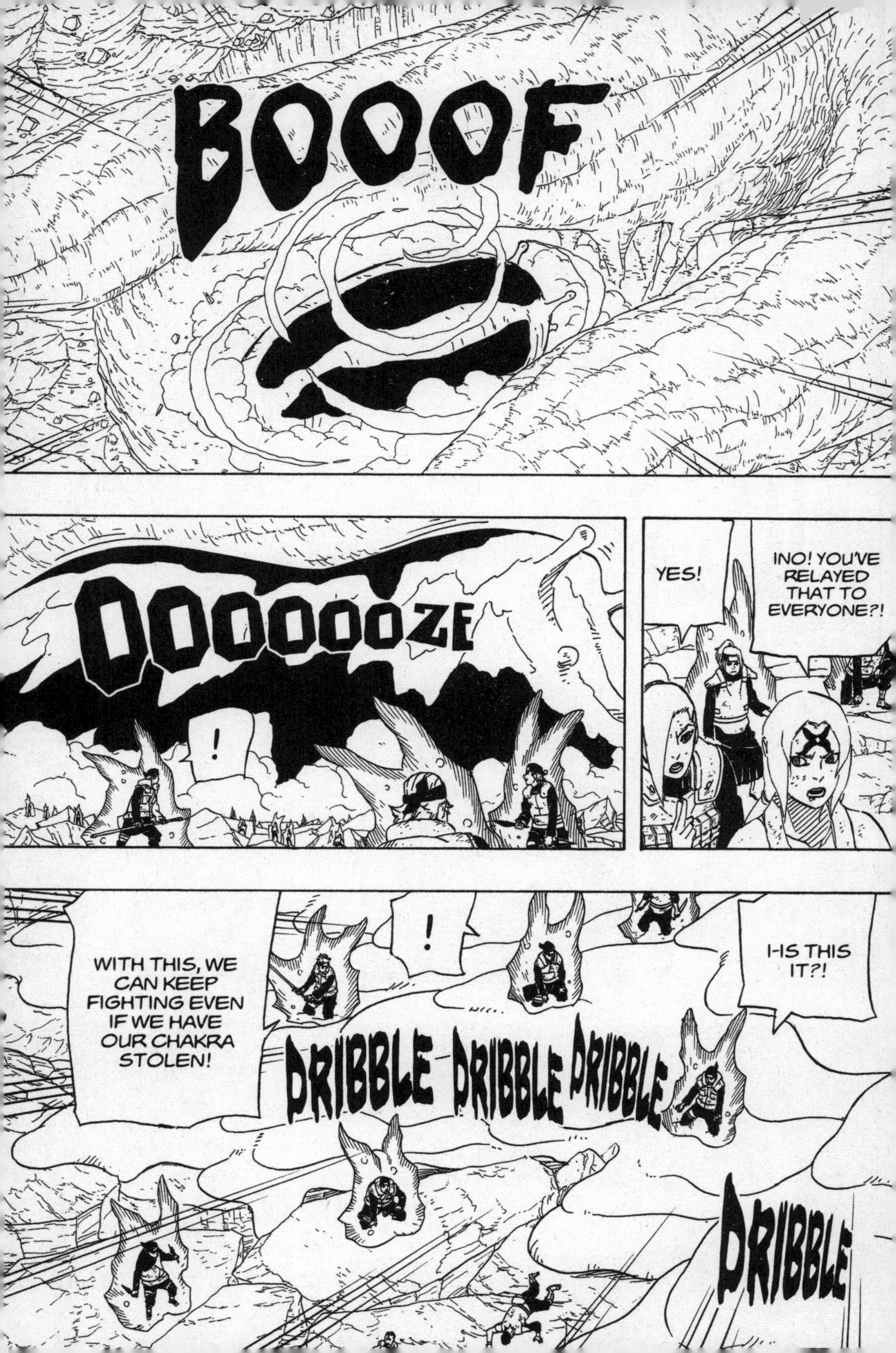
BOOOF
INO! YOU'VE RELAYED THAT TO EVERYONE?!
YES!
OOOOOOOZE
!
I-IS THIS IT?!
!
DRIBBLE DRIBBLE DRIBBLE
DRIBBLE
WITH THIS, WE CAN KEEP FIGHTING EVEN IF WE HAVE OUR CHAKRA STOLEN!

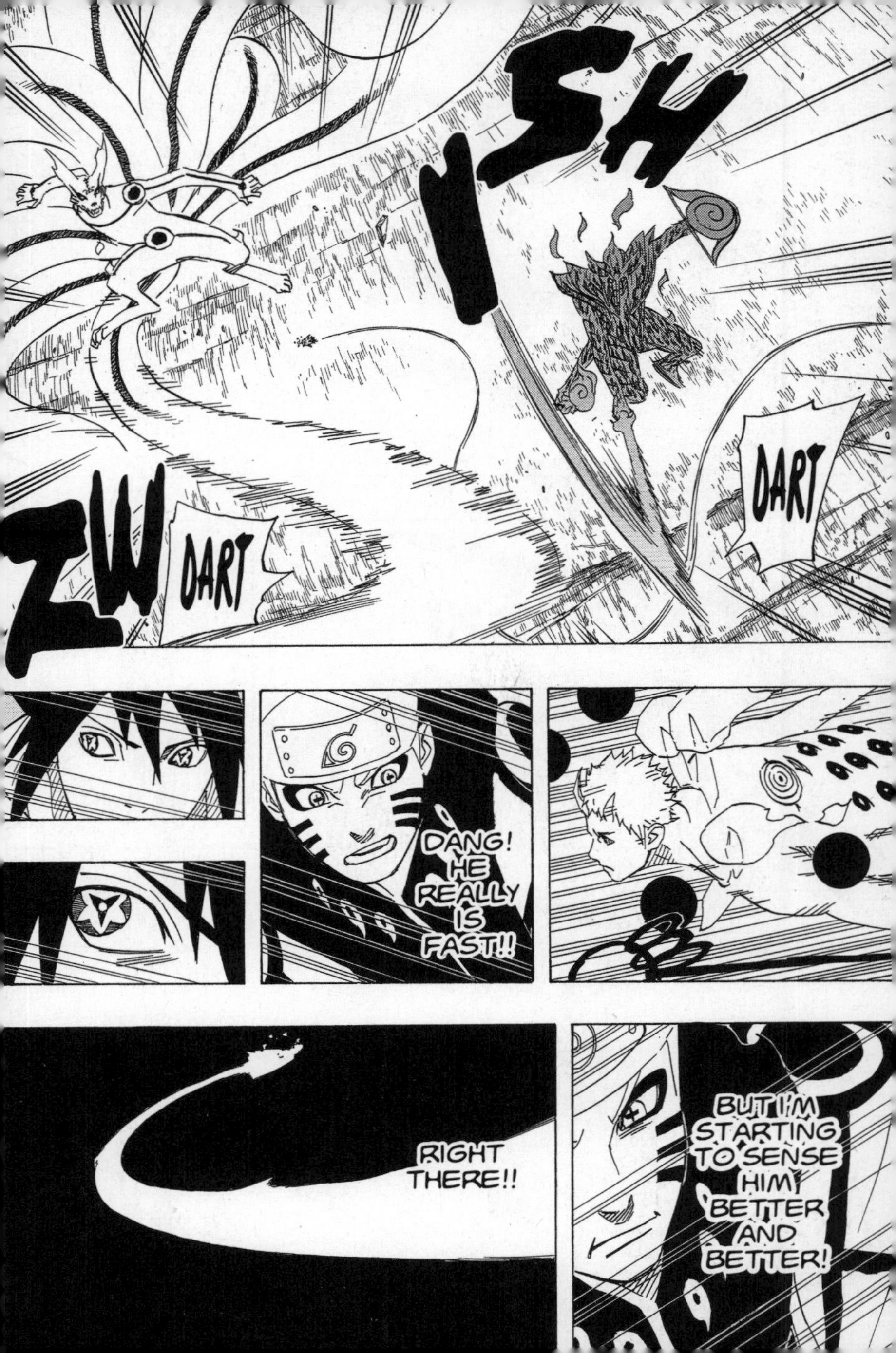
SH
DART
ZW
DART
DANG! HE REALLY IS FAST!!
BUT I'M STARTING TO SENSE HIM BETTER AND BETTER!
RIGHT THERE!!

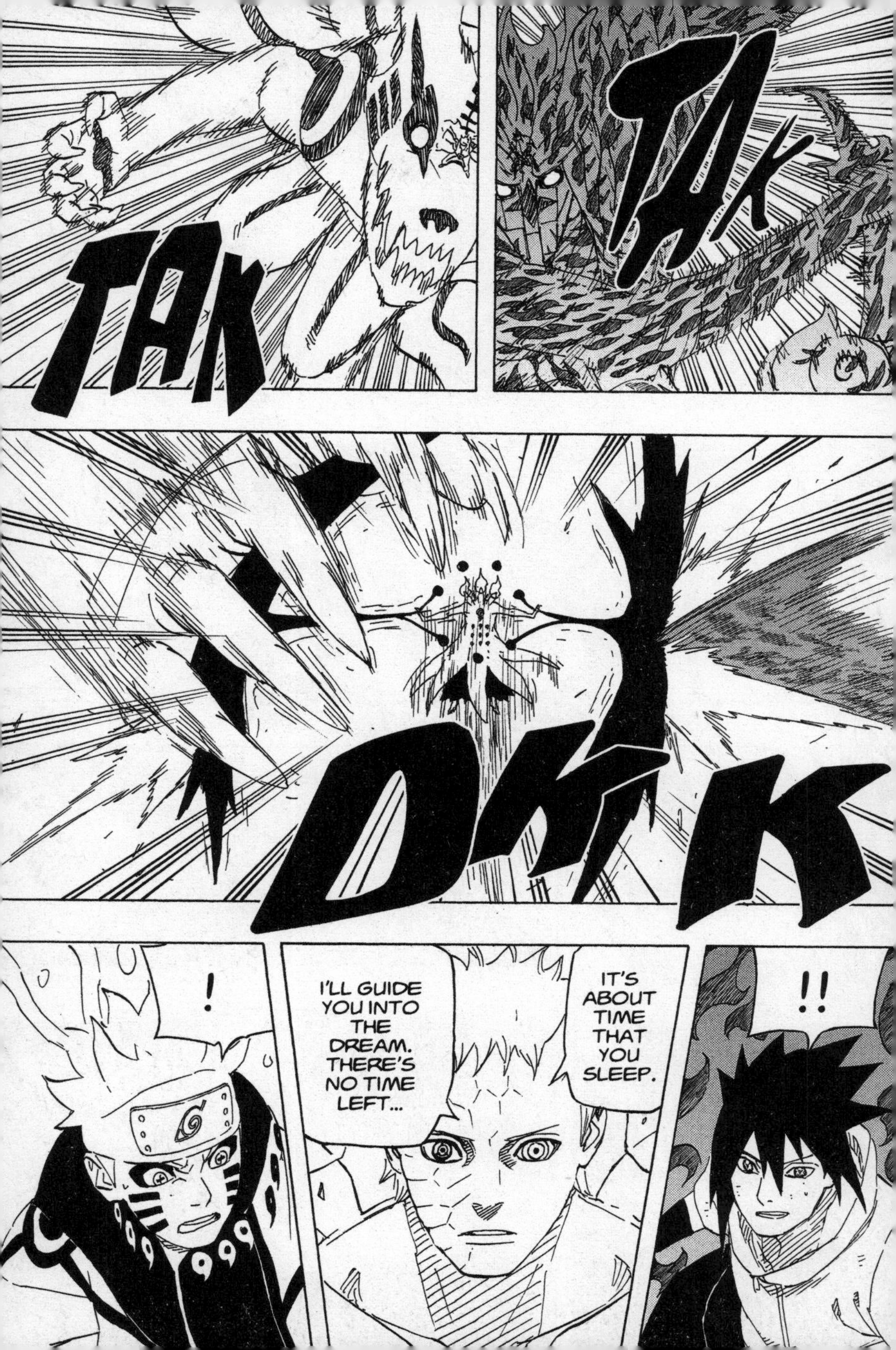
TAK
TAK
DKK
!!
IT'S ABOUT TIME THAT YOU SLEEP.
I'LL GUIDE YOU INTO THE DREAM. THERE'S NO TIME LEFT...
!

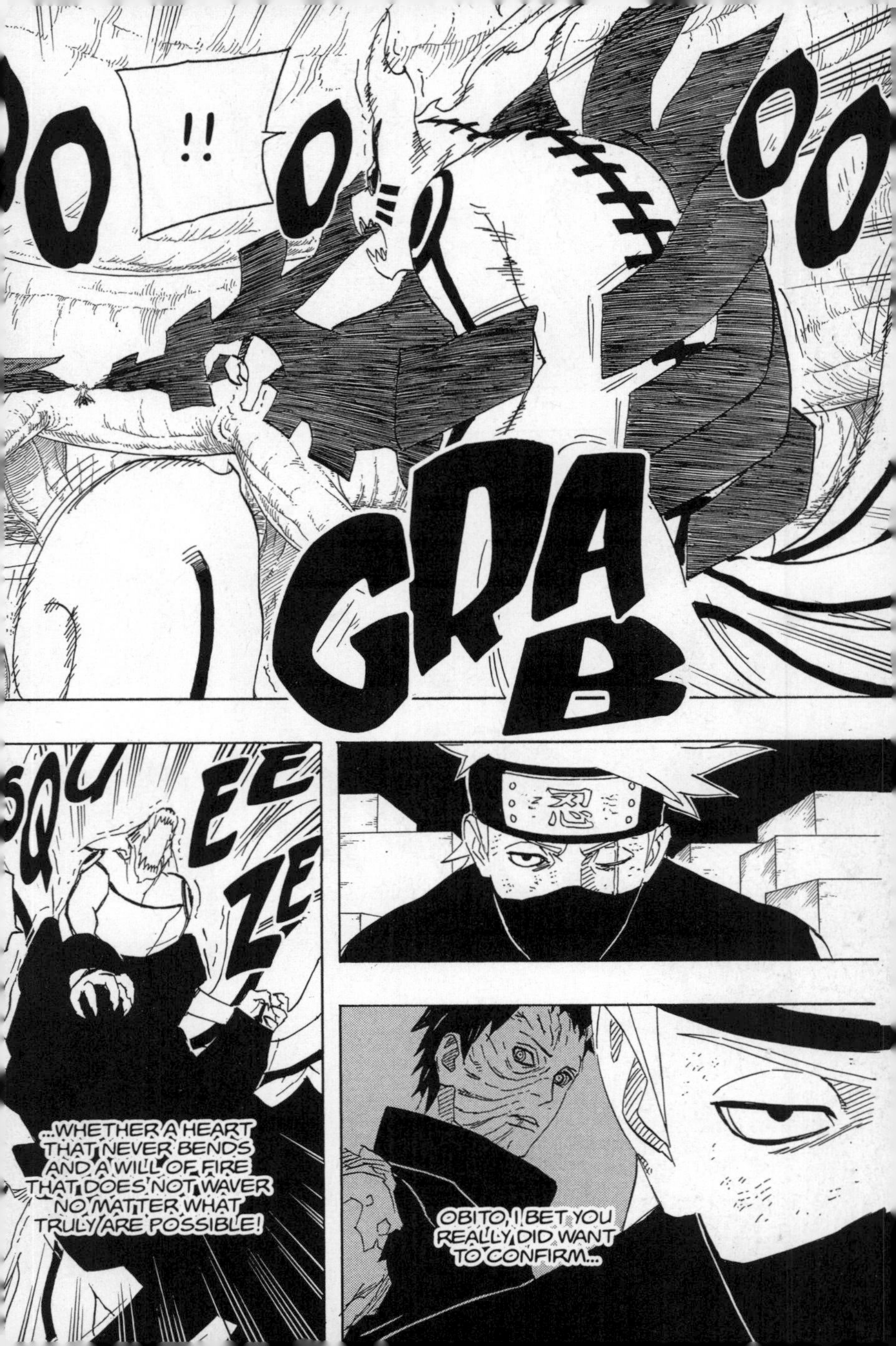
POOOO
!!
GRAB
OBITO, I BET YOU REALLY DID WANT TO CONFIRM...
SQUEEZE
...WHETHER A HEART THAT NEVER BENDS AND A WILL OF FIRE THAT DOES NOT WAVER NO MATTER WHAT TRULY ARE POSSIBLE!

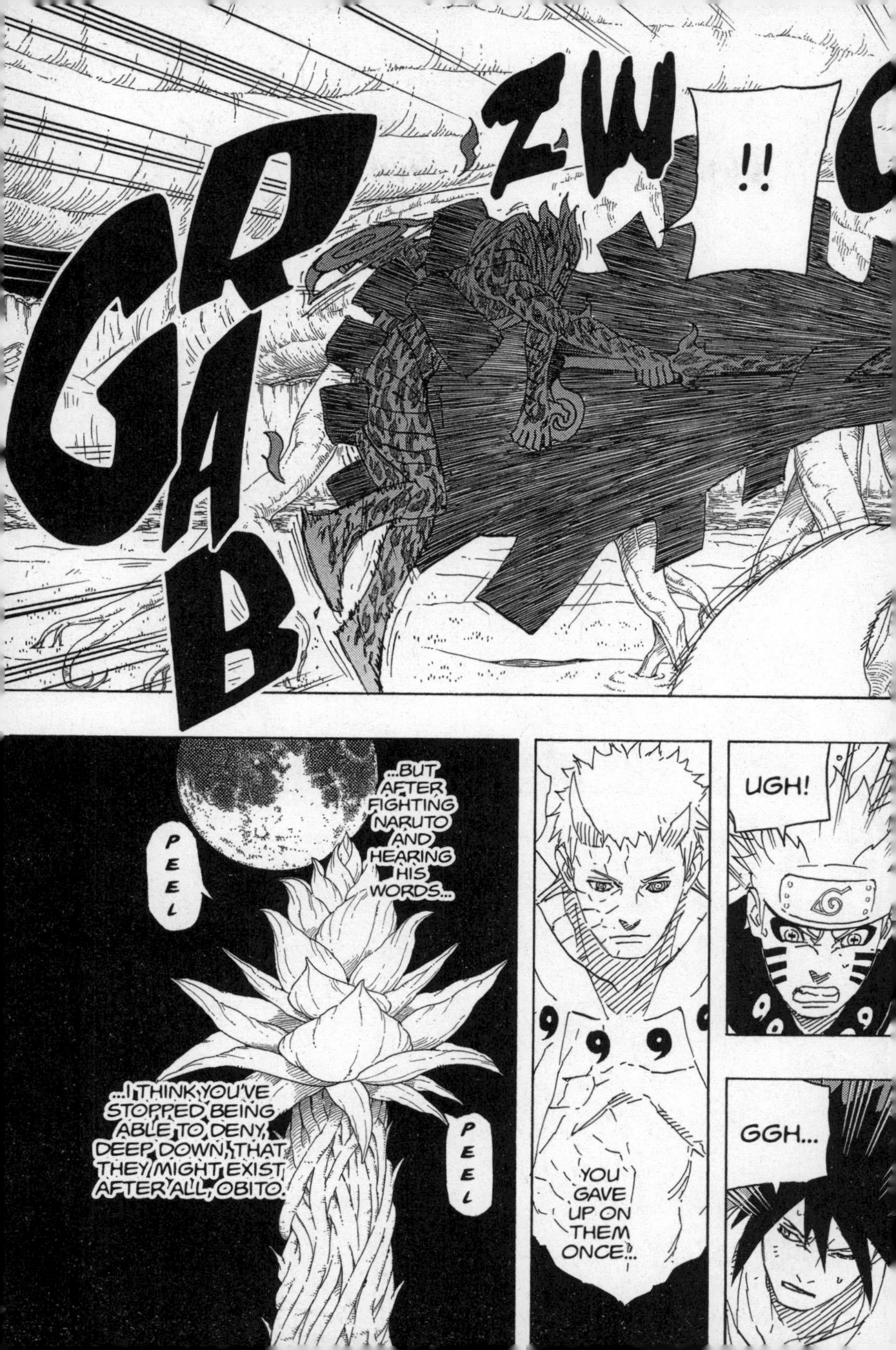
!!
ZW
GRAB
UGH!
GGH...
YOU GAVE UP ON THEM ONCE...
...BUT AFTER FIGHTING NARUTO AND HEARING HIS WORDS...
PEEL
...I THINK YOU'VE STOPPED BEING ABLE TO DENY, DEEP DOWN, THAT THEY MIGHT EXIST AFTER ALL, OBITO.
PEEL

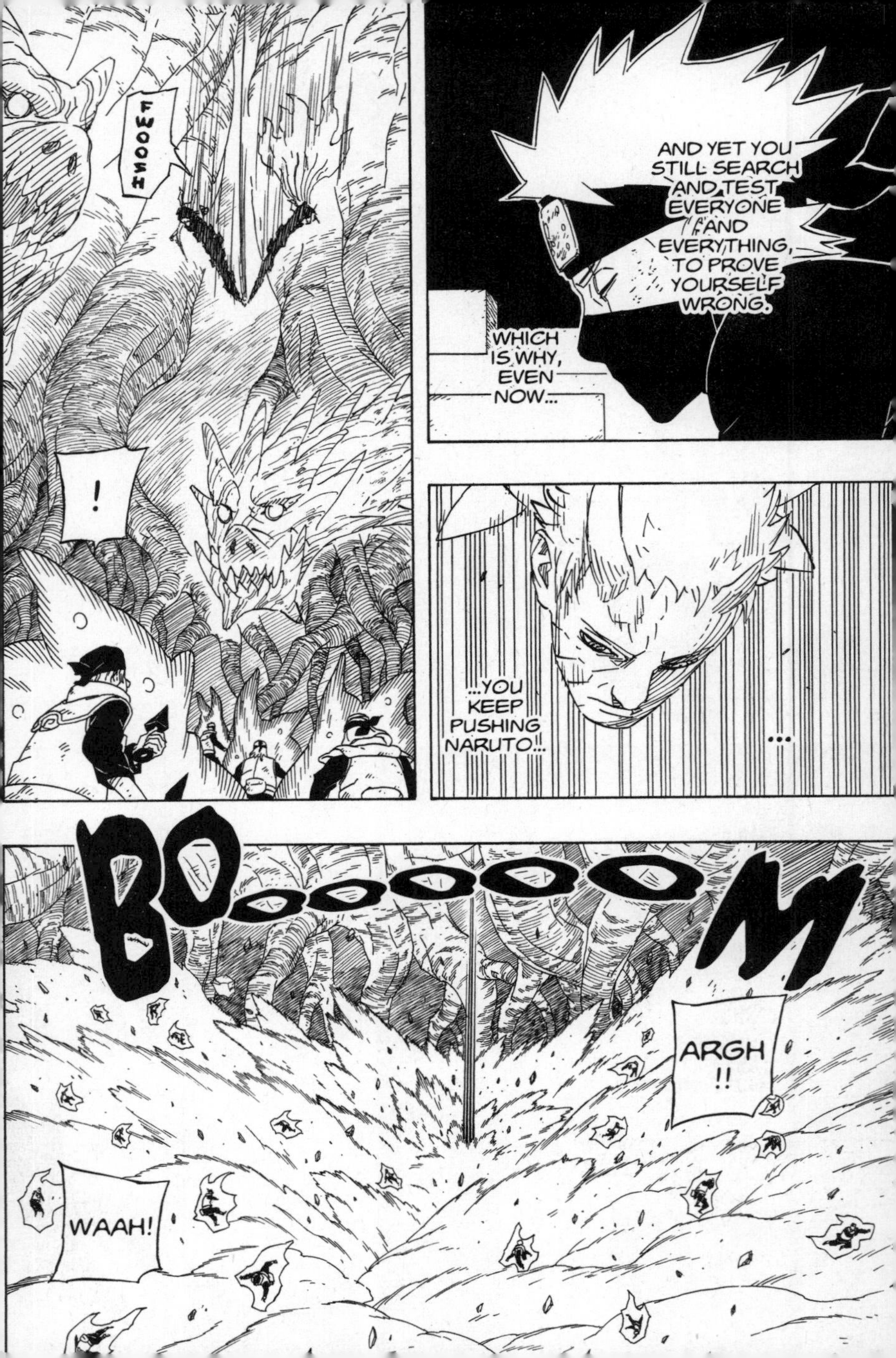
AND YET YOU STILL SEARCH AND TEST EVERYONE AND EVERYTHING, TO PROVE YOURSELF WRONG.
WHICH IS WHY, EVEN NOW...
...YOU KEEP PUSHING NARUTO...
...
FWOOSH
!
BOOOOOOM
ARGH!!
WAAH!

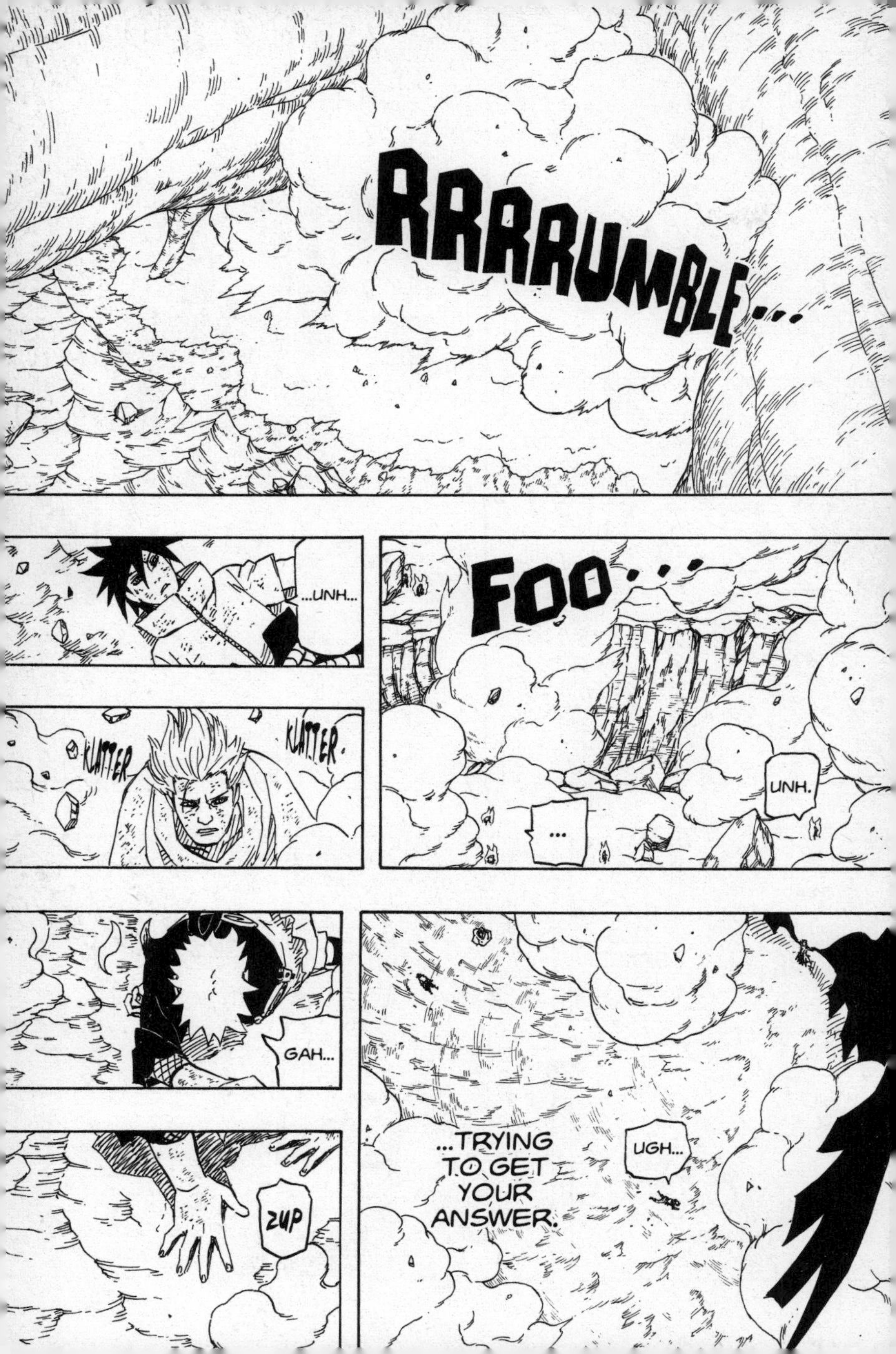
RRRRUMBLE...
FOO...
UNH.
...
...UNH...
KLATTER
KLATTER
UGH...
...TRYING TO GET YOUR ANSWER.
GAH...
ZUP

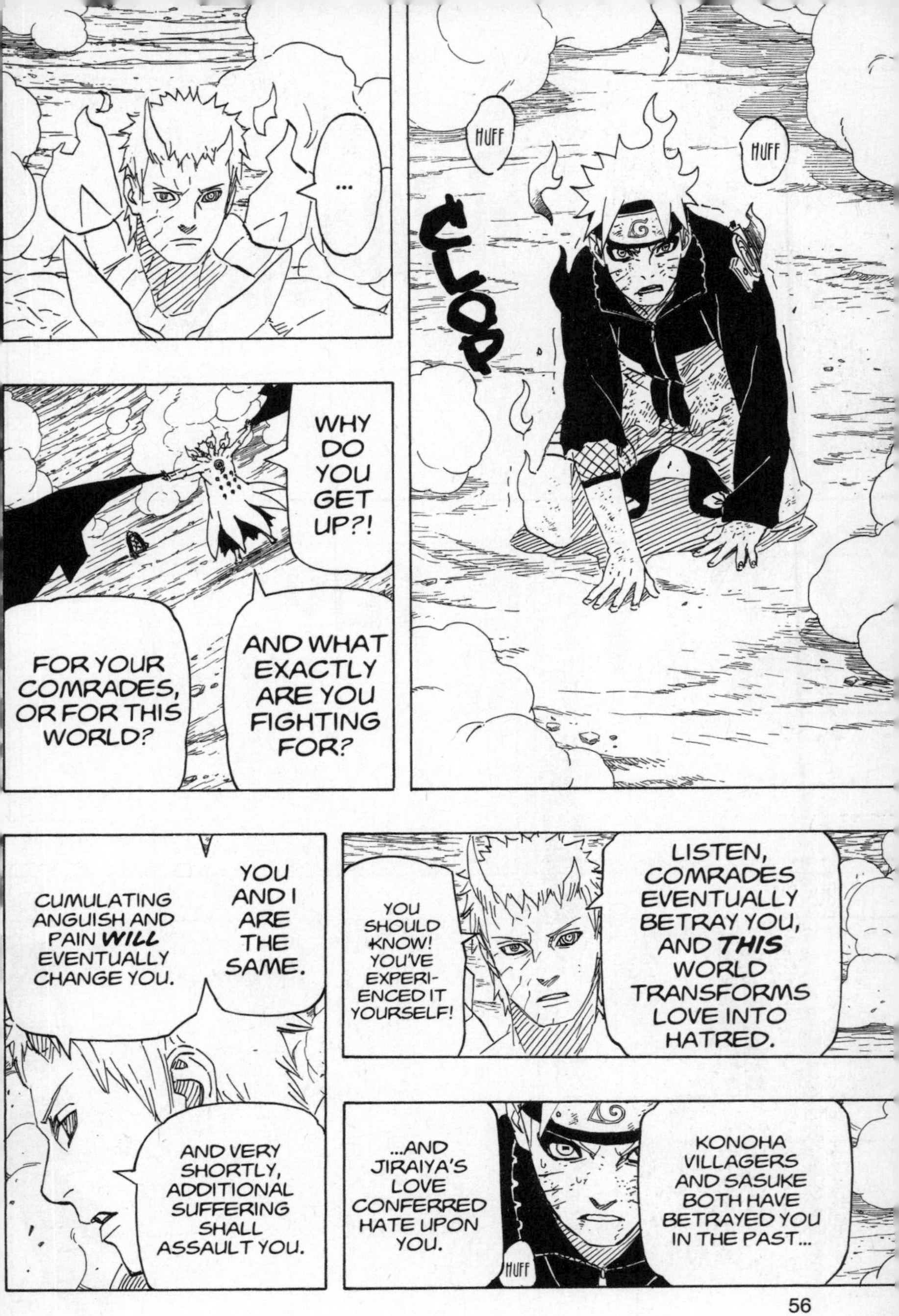
HUFF
HUFF
CLOP
...
WHY DO YOU GET UP?!
AND WHAT EXACTLY ARE YOU FIGHTING FOR?
FOR YOUR COMRADES, OR FOR THIS WORLD?
LISTEN, COMRADES EVENTUALLY BETRAY YOU, AND *THIS* WORLD TRANSFORMS LOVE INTO HATRED.
YOU SHOULD KNOW! YOU'VE EXPERI-ENCED IT YOURSELF!
KONOHA VILLAGERS AND SASUKE BOTH HAVE BETRAYED YOU IN THE PAST...
...AND JIRAIYA'S LOVE CONFERRED HATE UPON YOU.
HUFF
YOU AND I ARE THE SAME.
CUMULATING ANGUISH AND PAIN *WILL* EVENTUALLY CHANGE YOU.
AND VERY SHORTLY, ADDITIONAL SUFFERING SHALL ASSAULT YOU.

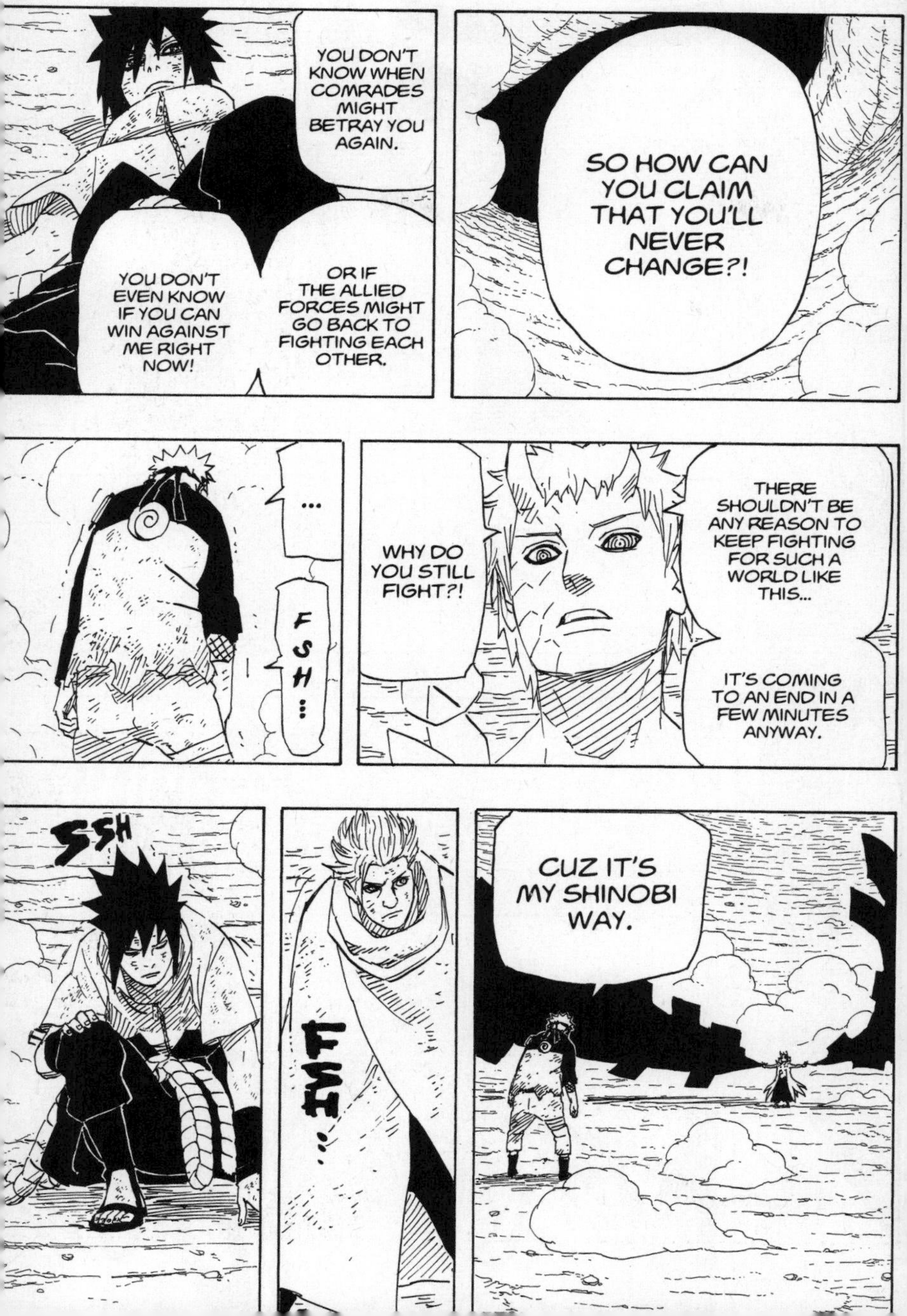

SO HOW CAN YOU CLAIM THAT YOU'LL NEVER CHANGE?!
YOU DON'T KNOW WHEN COMRADES MIGHT BETRAY YOU AGAIN.
OR IF THE ALLIED FORCES MIGHT GO BACK TO FIGHTING EACH OTHER.
YOU DON'T EVEN KNOW IF YOU CAN WIN AGAINST ME RIGHT NOW!
THERE SHOULDN'T BE ANY REASON TO KEEP FIGHTING FOR SUCH A WORLD LIKE THIS...
IT'S COMING TO AN END IN A FEW MINUTES ANYWAY.
WHY DO YOU STILL FIGHT?!
...
FSH...
CUZ IT'S MY SHINOBI WAY.
FSH...
SSH

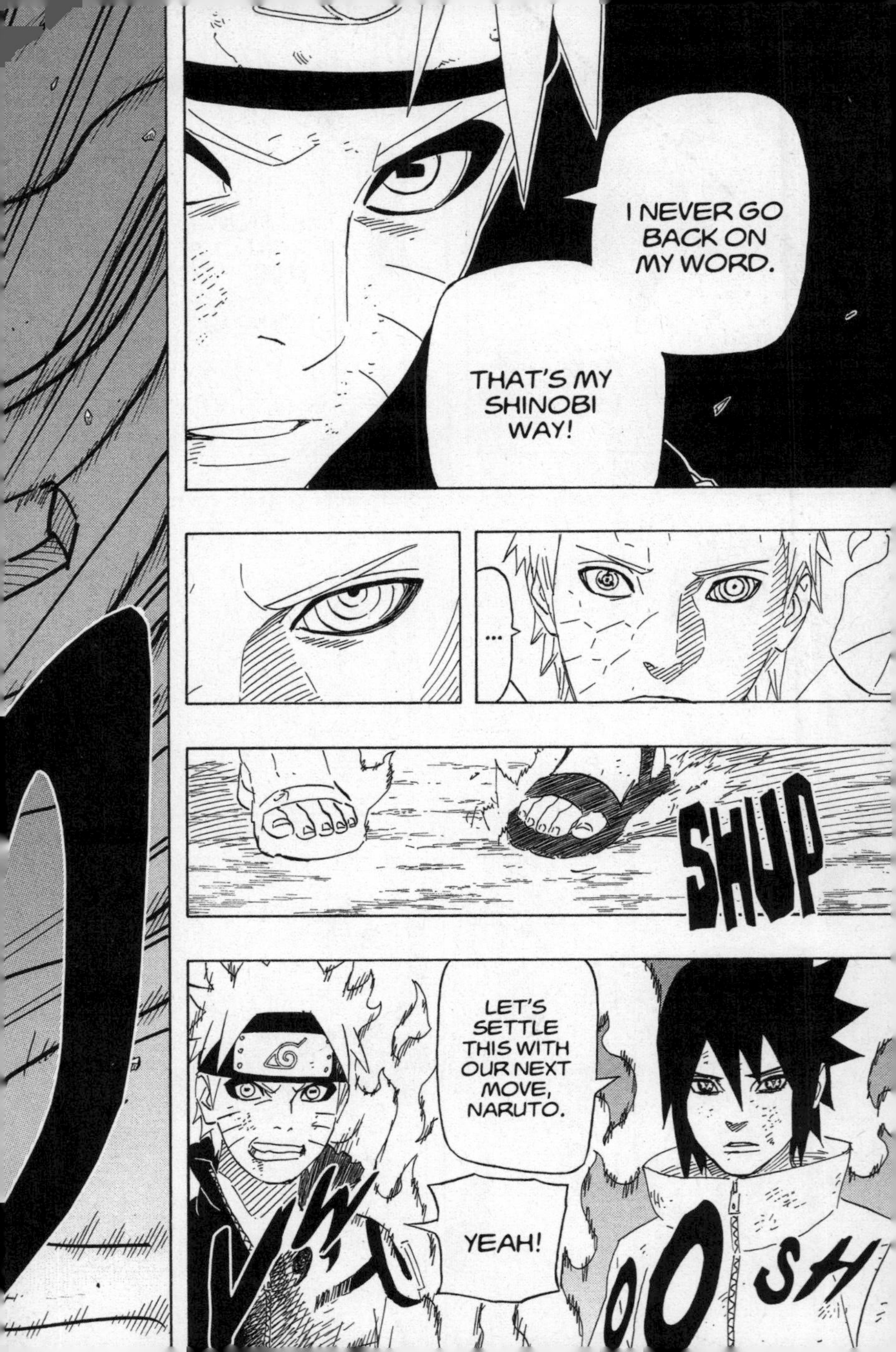
I NEVER GO BACK ON MY WORD.
THAT'S MY SHINOBI WAY!
...
SHUP
LET'S SETTLE THIS WITH OUR NEXT MOVE, NARUTO.
YEAH!
WOOSH

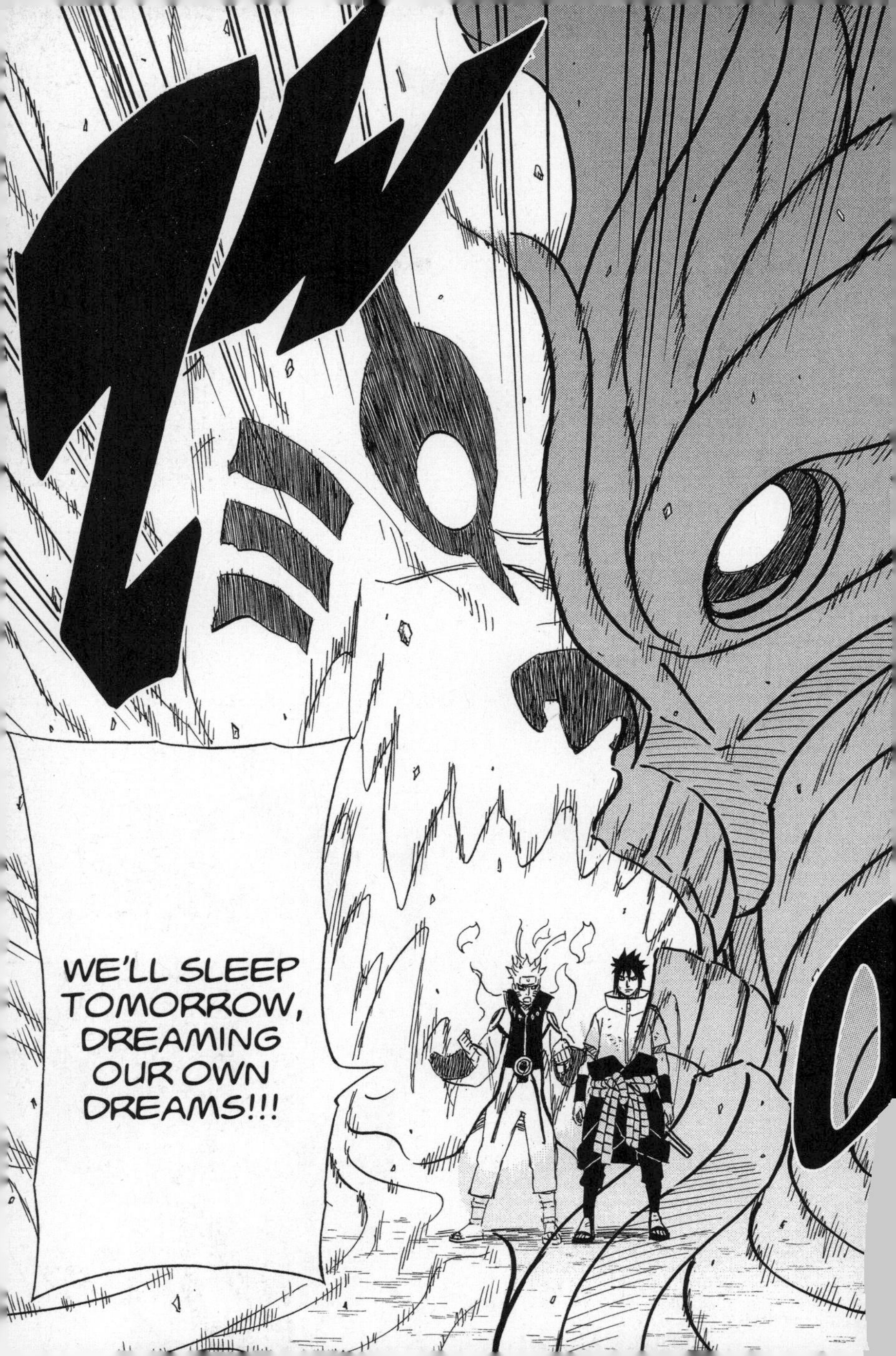
WE'LL SLEEP TOMORROW, DREAMING OUR OWN DREAMS!!!

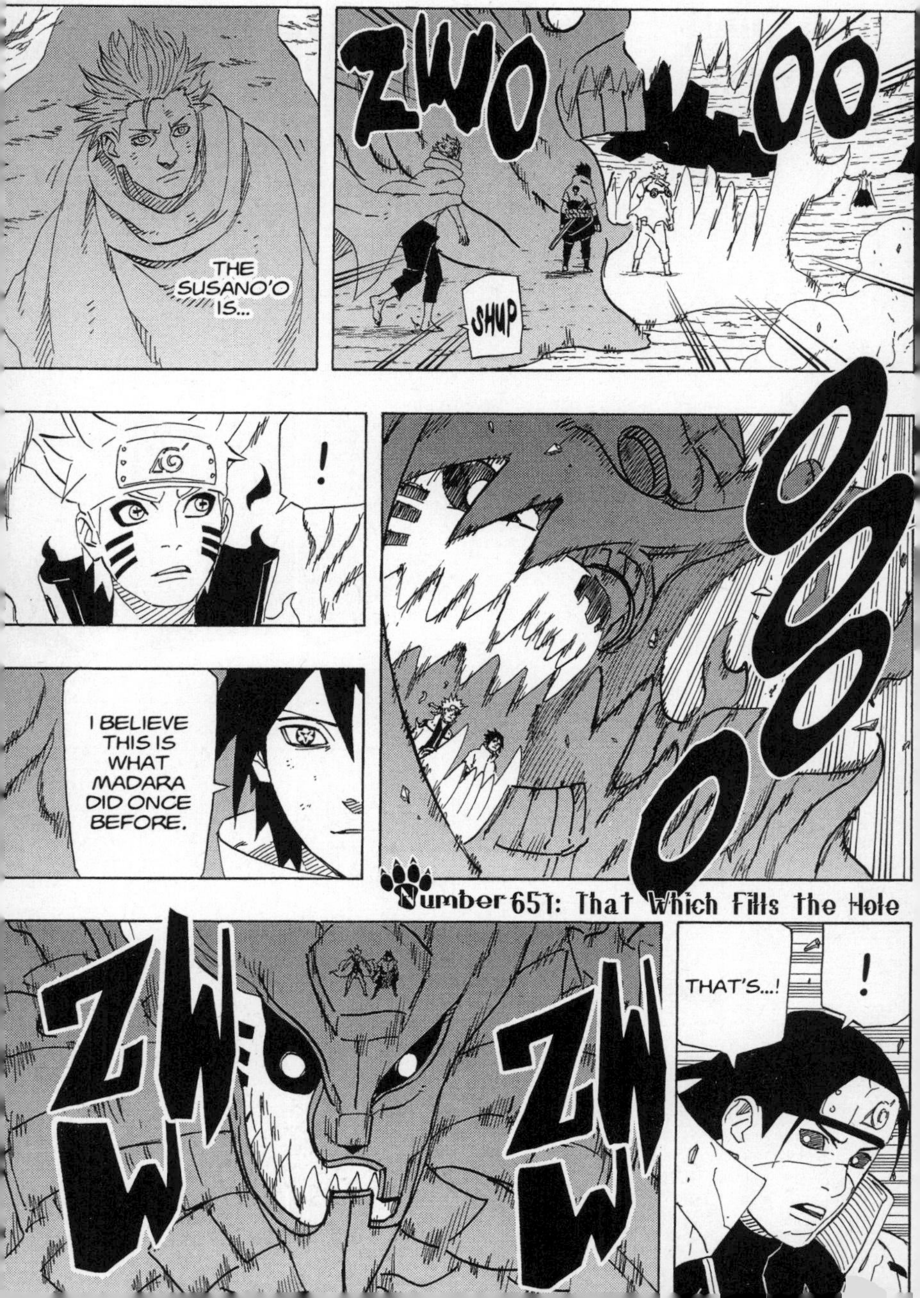
ZWO
OO
SHUP
THE SUSANO'O IS...
OOOOOO
!
I BELIEVE THIS IS WHAT MADARA DID ONCE BEFORE.
Number 651: That Which Fills the Hole
!
THAT'S...!
ZW
W
ZW
W

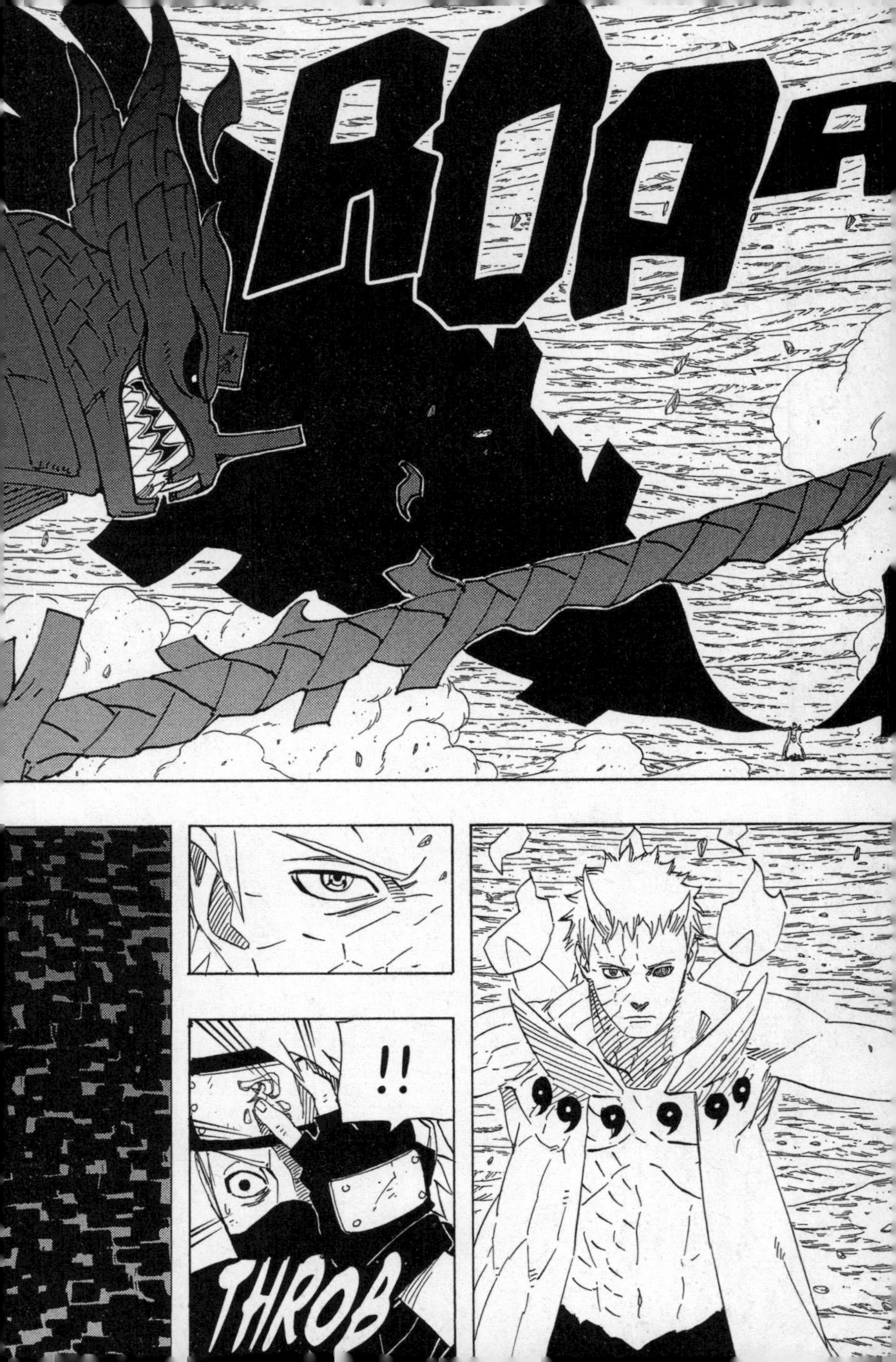
ROAA
!!
THROB

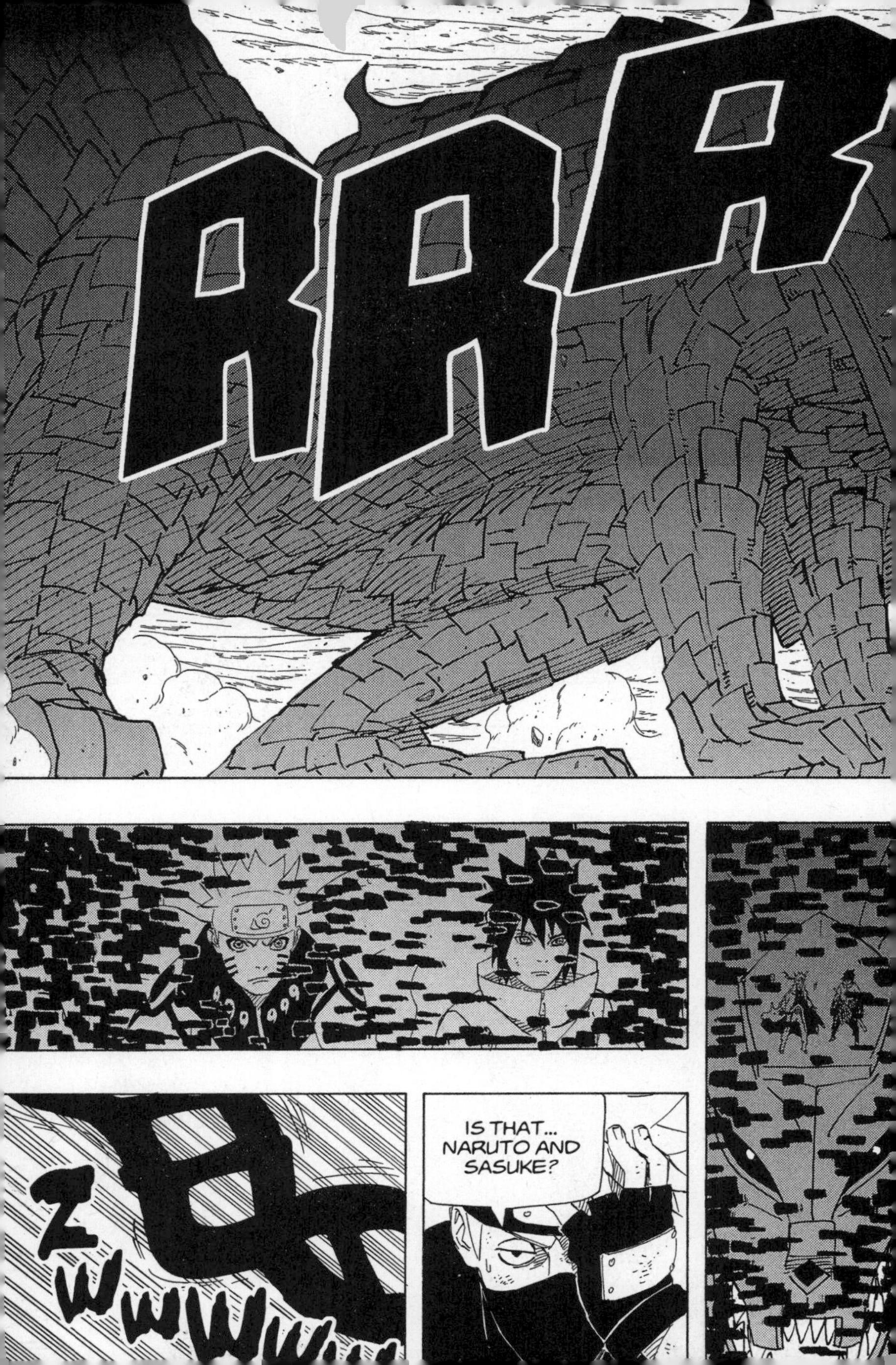
RRR
IS THAT... NARUTO AND SASUKE?

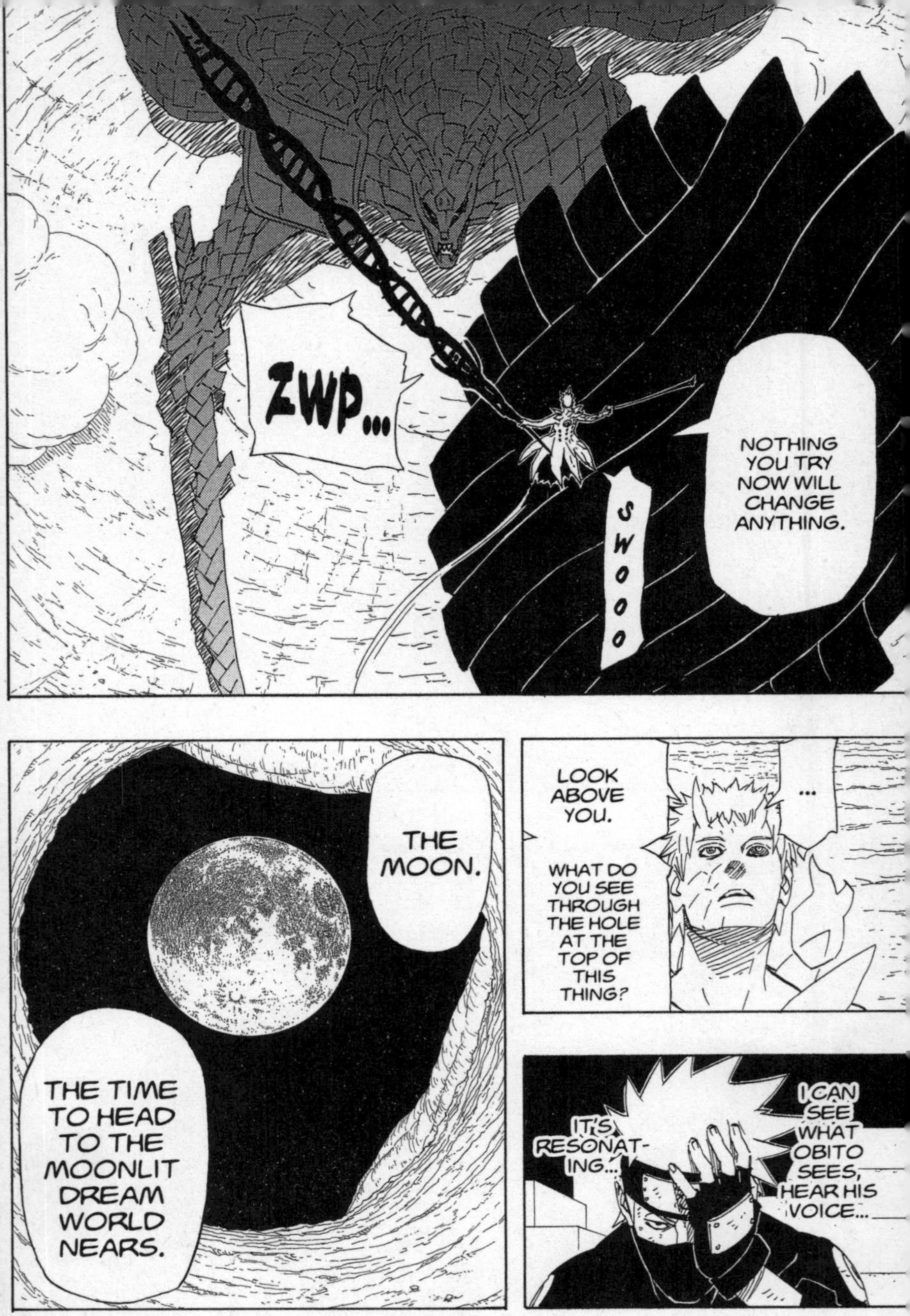
NOTHING YOU TRY NOW WILL CHANGE ANYTHING.
SWOOO
ZWP...
...
LOOK ABOVE YOU.
WHAT DO YOU SEE THROUGH THE HOLE AT THE TOP OF THIS THING?
I CAN SEE WHAT OBITO SEES, HEAR HIS VOICE...
IT'S RESONATING...
THE MOON.
THE TIME TO HEAD TO THE MOONLIT DREAM WORLD NEARS.

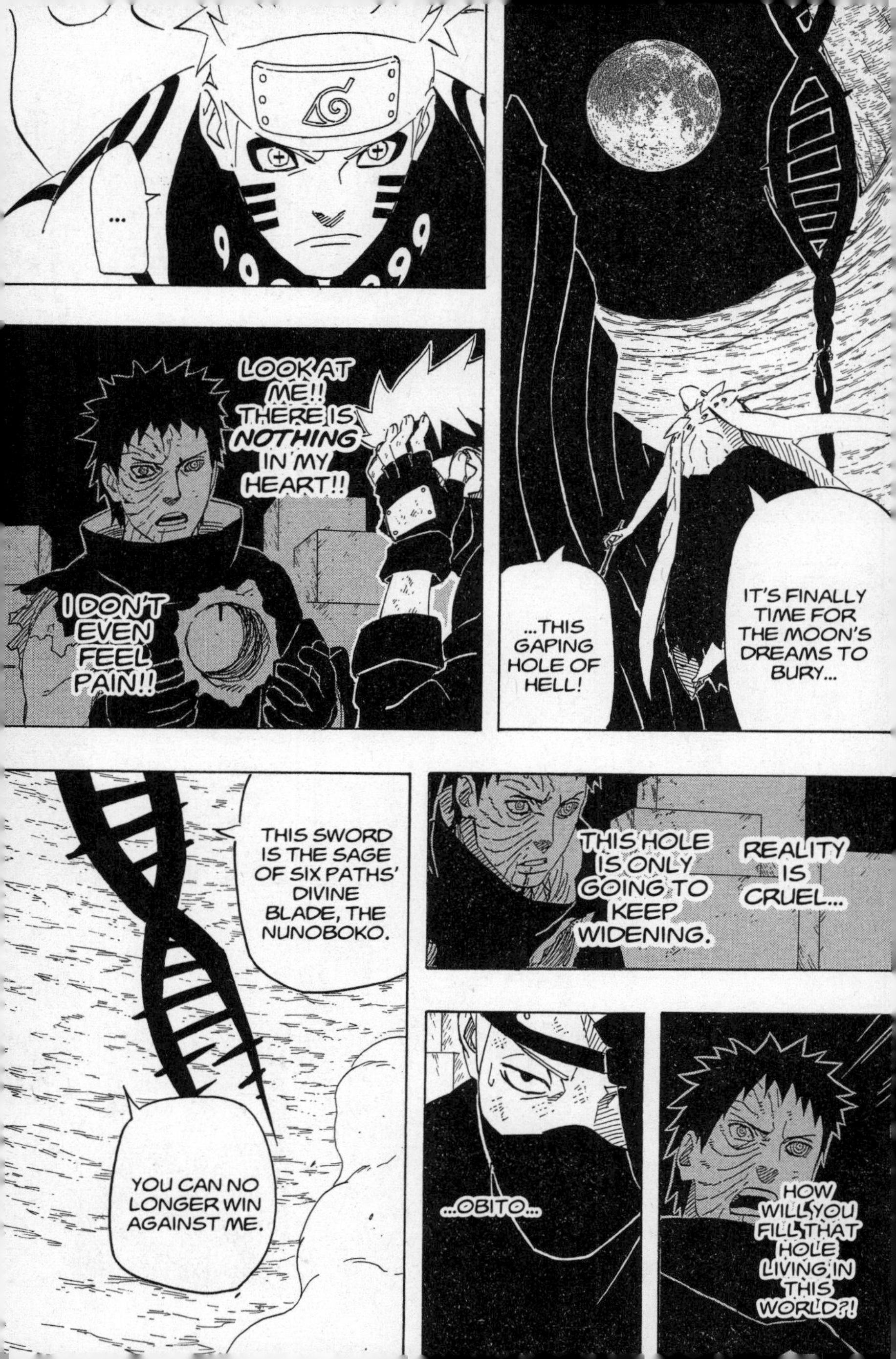
IT'S FINALLY TIME FOR THE MOON'S DREAMS TO BURY...
...THIS GAPING HOLE OF HELL!
...
LOOK AT ME!! THERE IS *NOTHING* IN MY HEART!!
I DON'T EVEN FEEL PAIN!!
REALITY IS CRUEL...
THIS HOLE IS ONLY GOING TO KEEP WIDENING.
HOW WILL YOU FILL THAT HOLE LIVING IN THIS WORLD?!
...OBITO...
THIS SWORD IS THE SAGE OF SIX PATHS' DIVINE BLADE, THE NUNOBOKO.
YOU CAN NO LONGER WIN AGAINST ME.

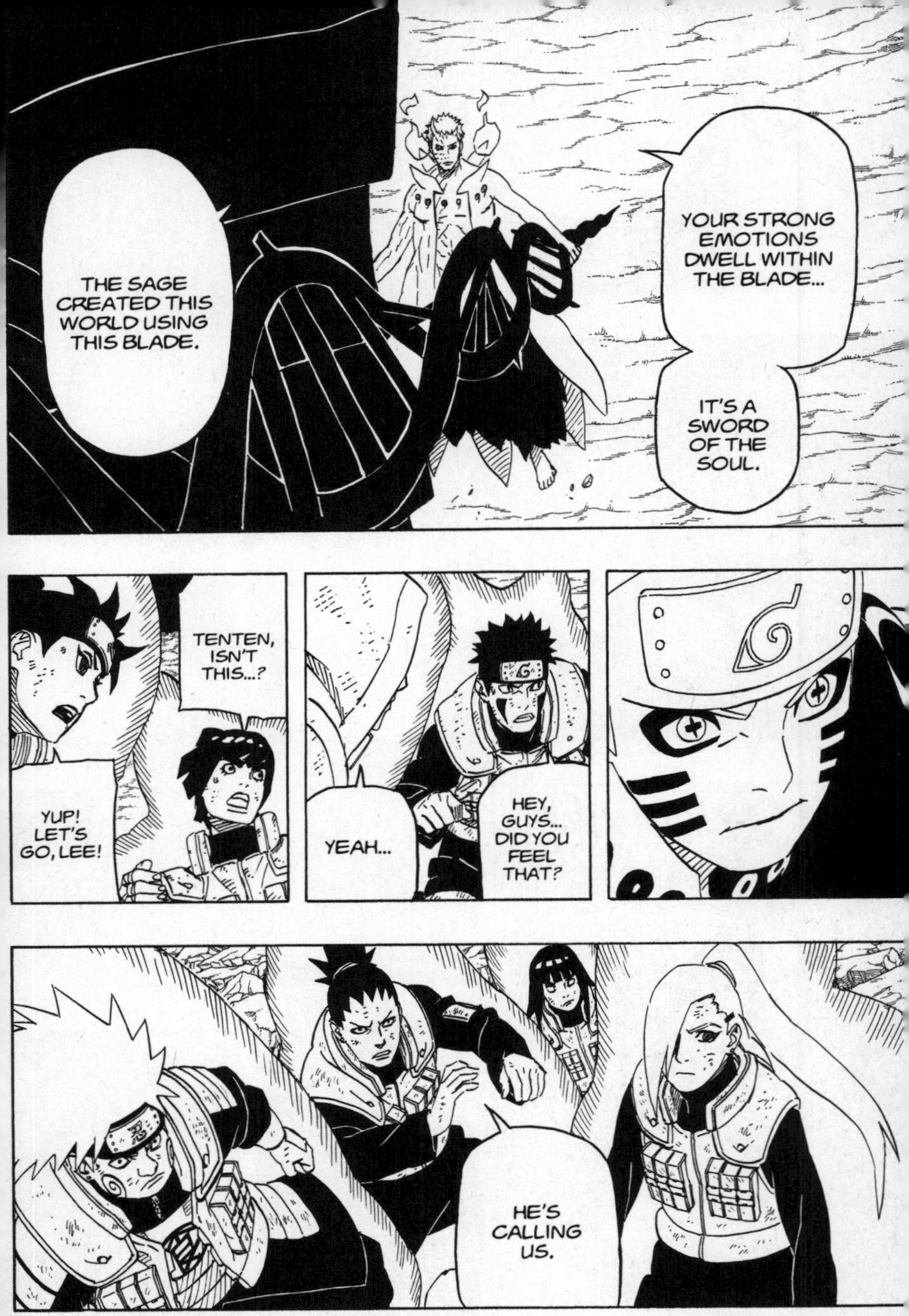
YOUR STRONG EMOTIONS DWELL WITHIN THE BLADE...
IT'S A SWORD OF THE SOUL.
THE SAGE CREATED THIS WORLD USING THIS BLADE.
HEY, GUYS... DID YOU FEEL THAT?
YEAH...
TENTEN, ISN'T THIS...?
YUP! LET'S GO, LEE!
HE'S CALLING US.

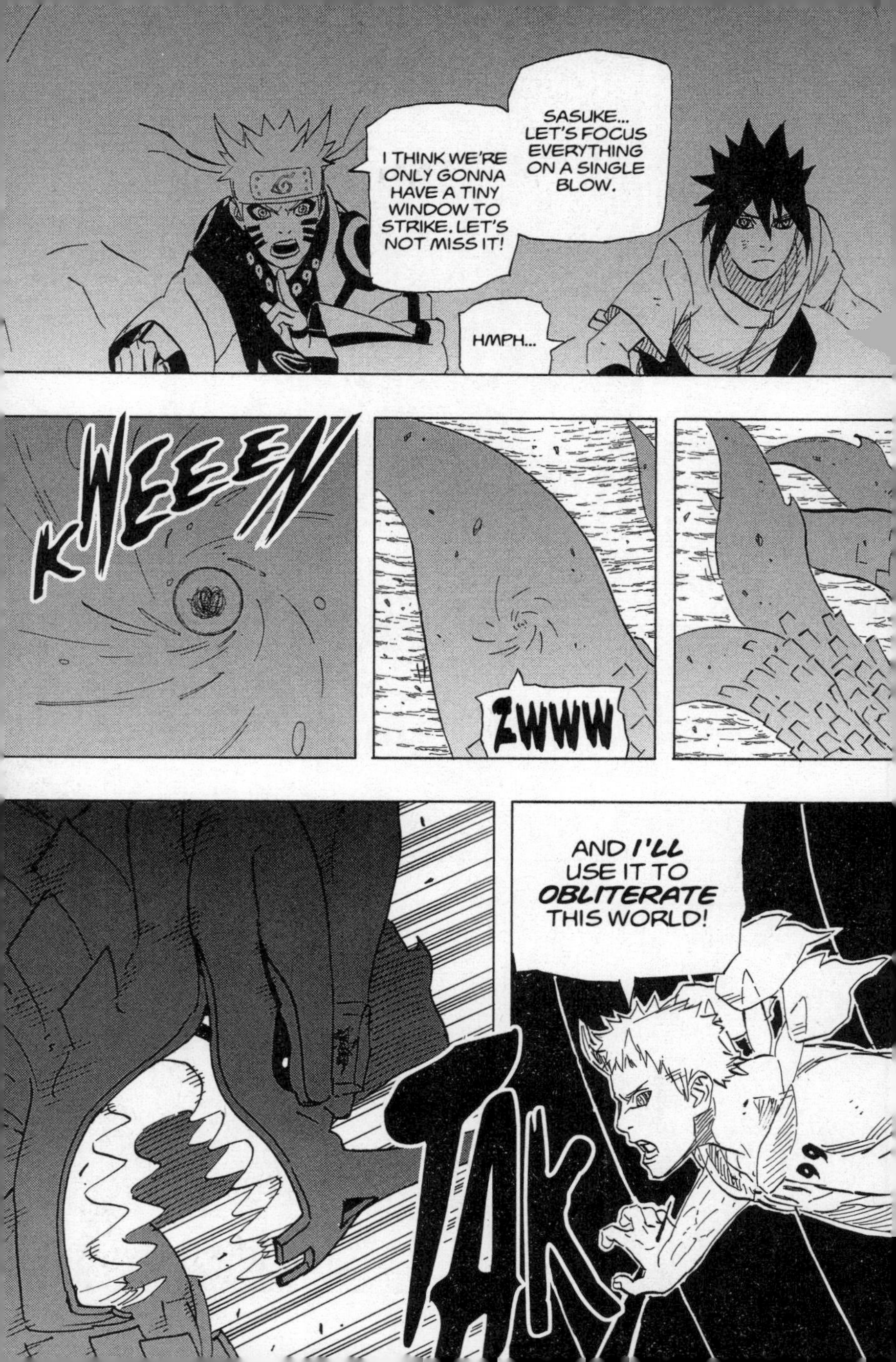
SASUKE... LET'S FOCUS EVERYTHING ON A SINGLE BLOW.
I THINK WE'RE ONLY GONNA HAVE A TINY WINDOW TO STRIKE. LET'S NOT MISS IT!
HMPH...
ZWWW
KWEEEN
AND I'LL USE IT TO OBLITERATE THIS WORLD!
TAK

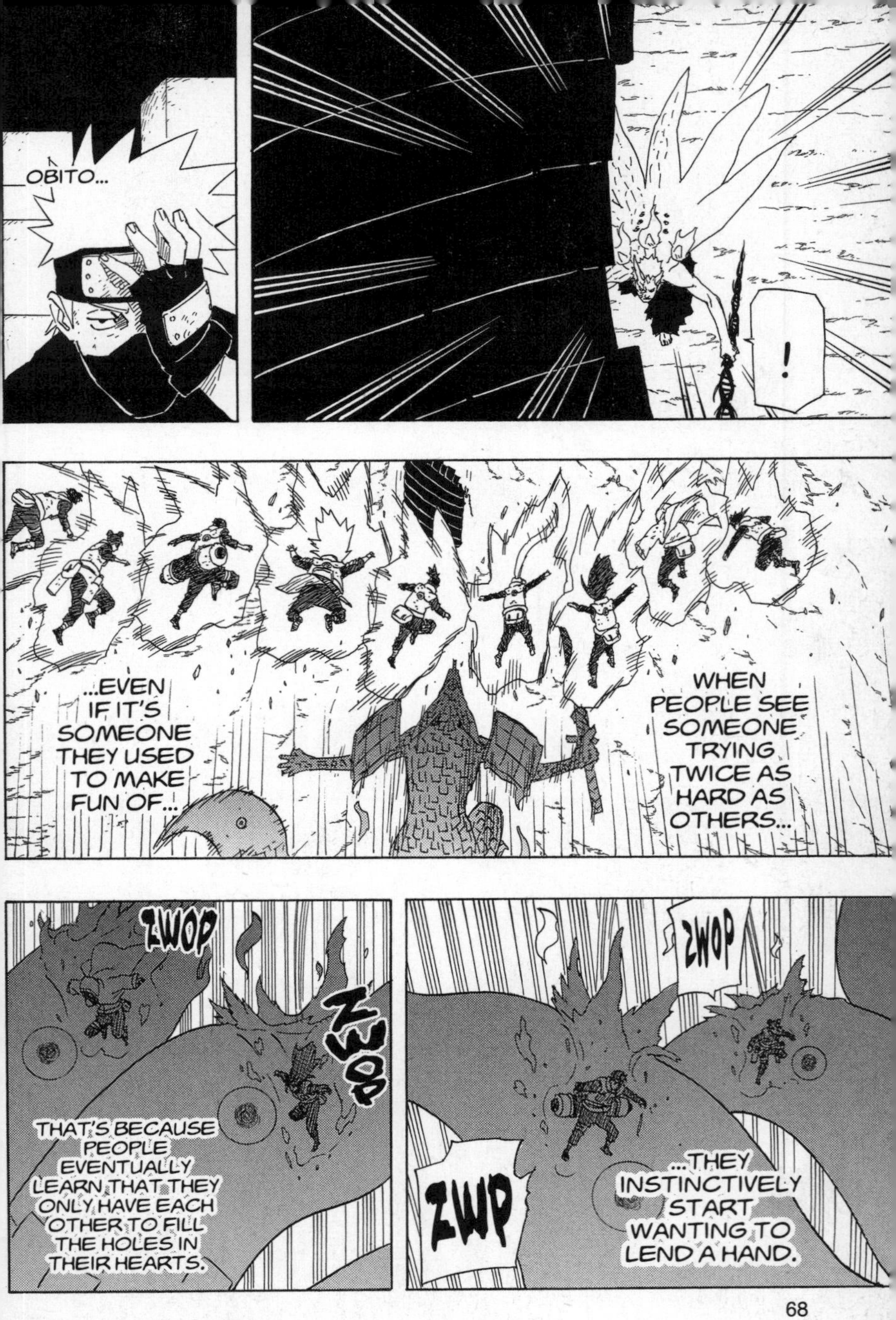
!
OBITO...
WHEN PEOPLE SEE SOMEONE TRYING TWICE AS HARD AS OTHERS...
...EVEN IF IT'S SOMEONE THEY USED TO MAKE FUN OF...
ZWOP
ZWP
...THEY INSTINCTIVELY START WANTING TO LEND A HAND.
ZWOP
ZWOP
THAT'S BECAUSE PEOPLE EVENTUALLY LEARN THAT THEY ONLY HAVE EACH OTHER TO FILL THE HOLES IN THEIR HEARTS.

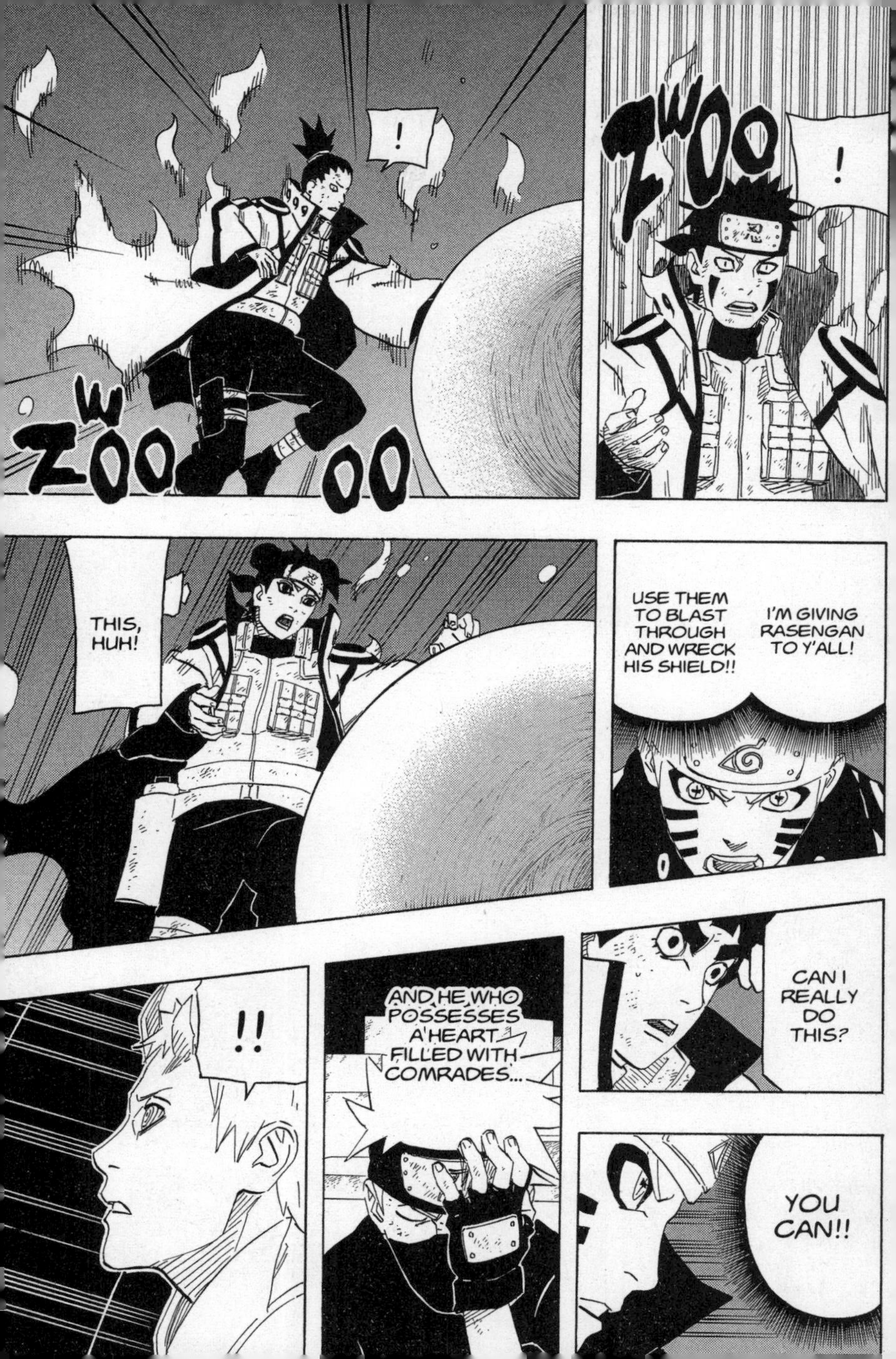

ZWOO
!
!
ZWOO OO
I'M GIVING RASENGAN TO Y'ALL!
USE THEM TO BLAST THROUGH AND WRECK HIS SHIELD!!
THIS, HUH!
CAN I REALLY DO THIS?
YOU CAN!!
AND HE WHO POSSESSES A HEART FILLED WITH COMRADES...
!!

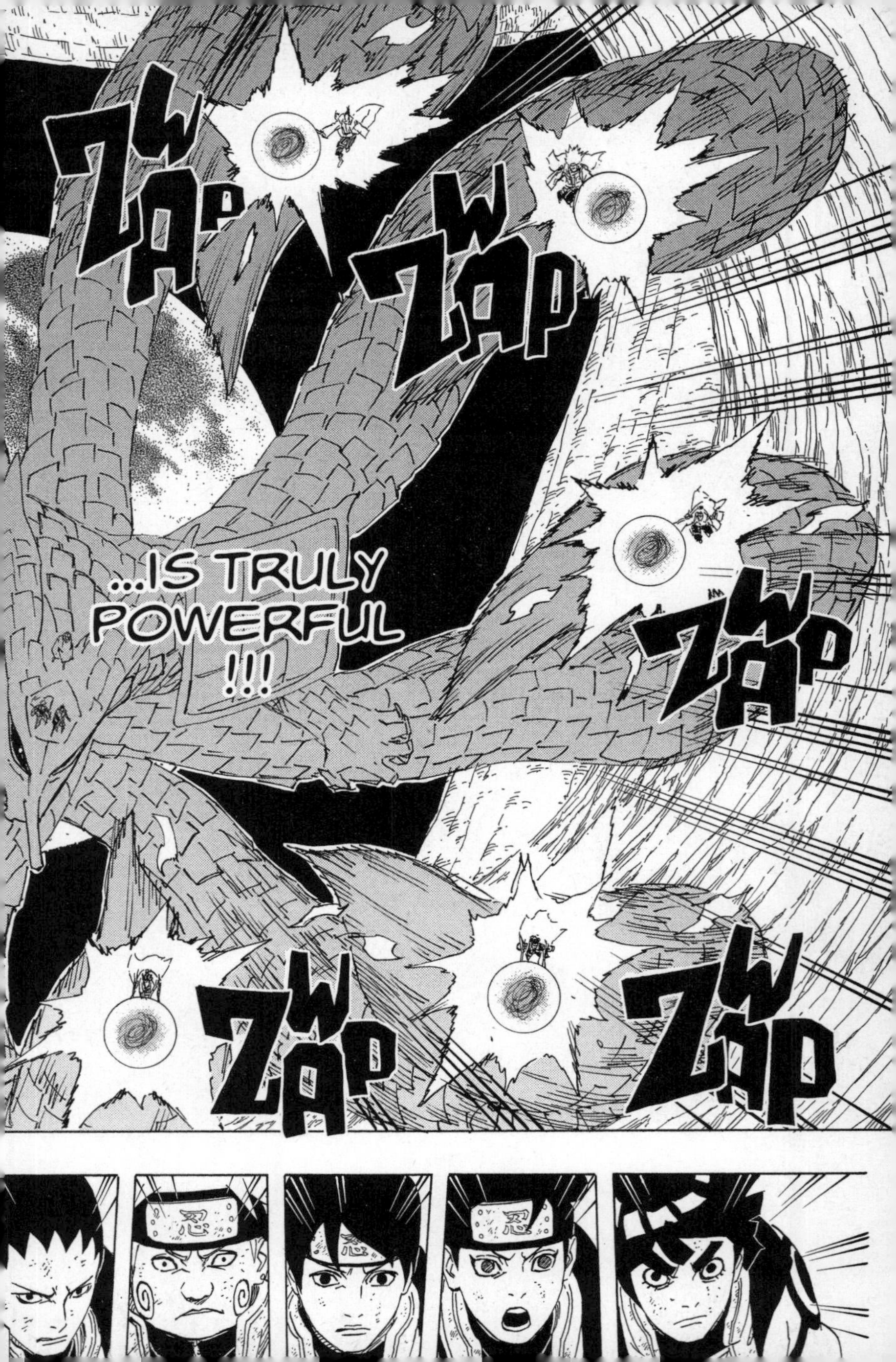
ZAP
ZAP
ZAP
...IS TRULY POWERFUL !!!
ZAP
ZAP
ZAP

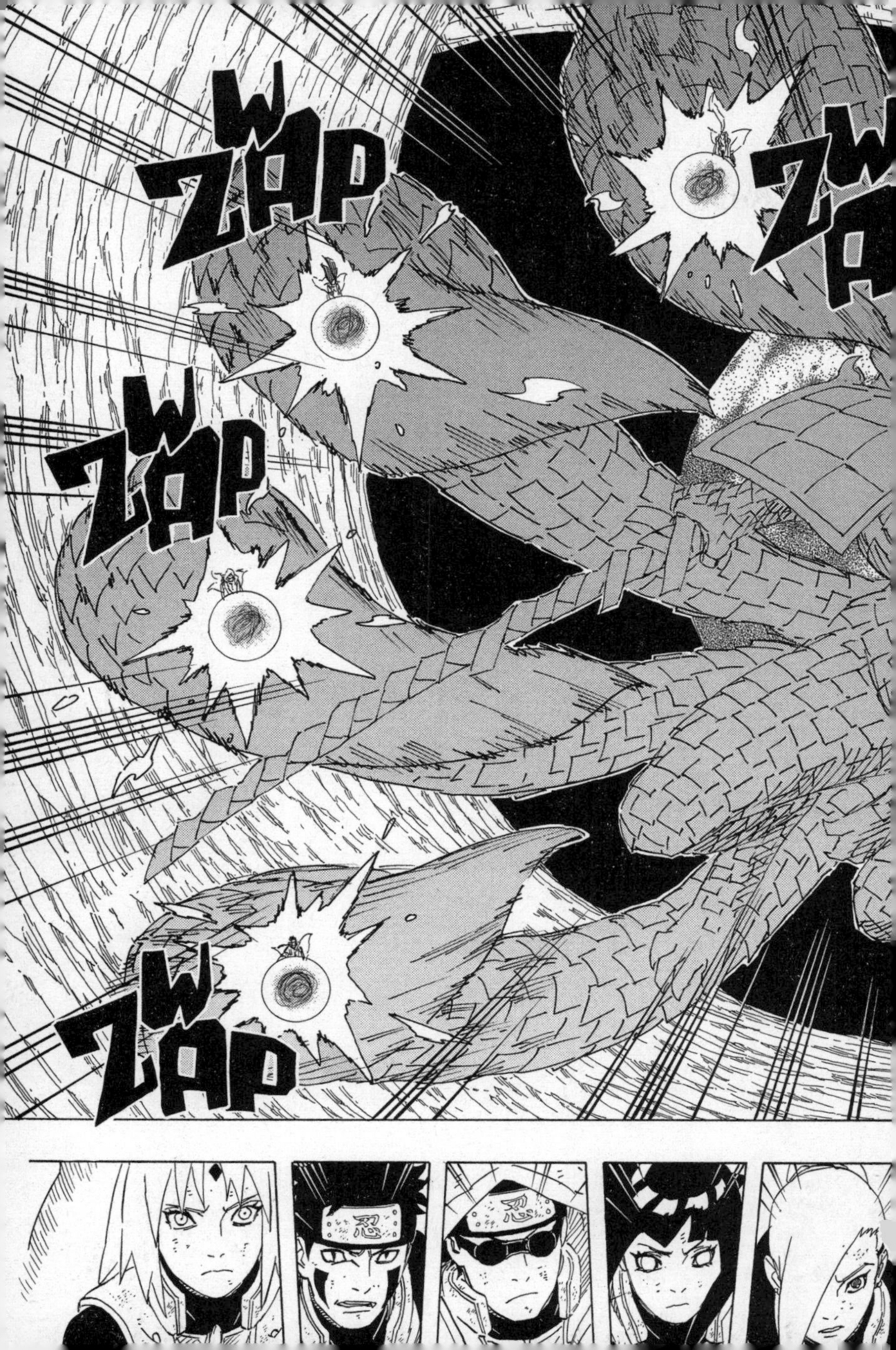
ZWA
ZWAP
ZWAP
ZWAP

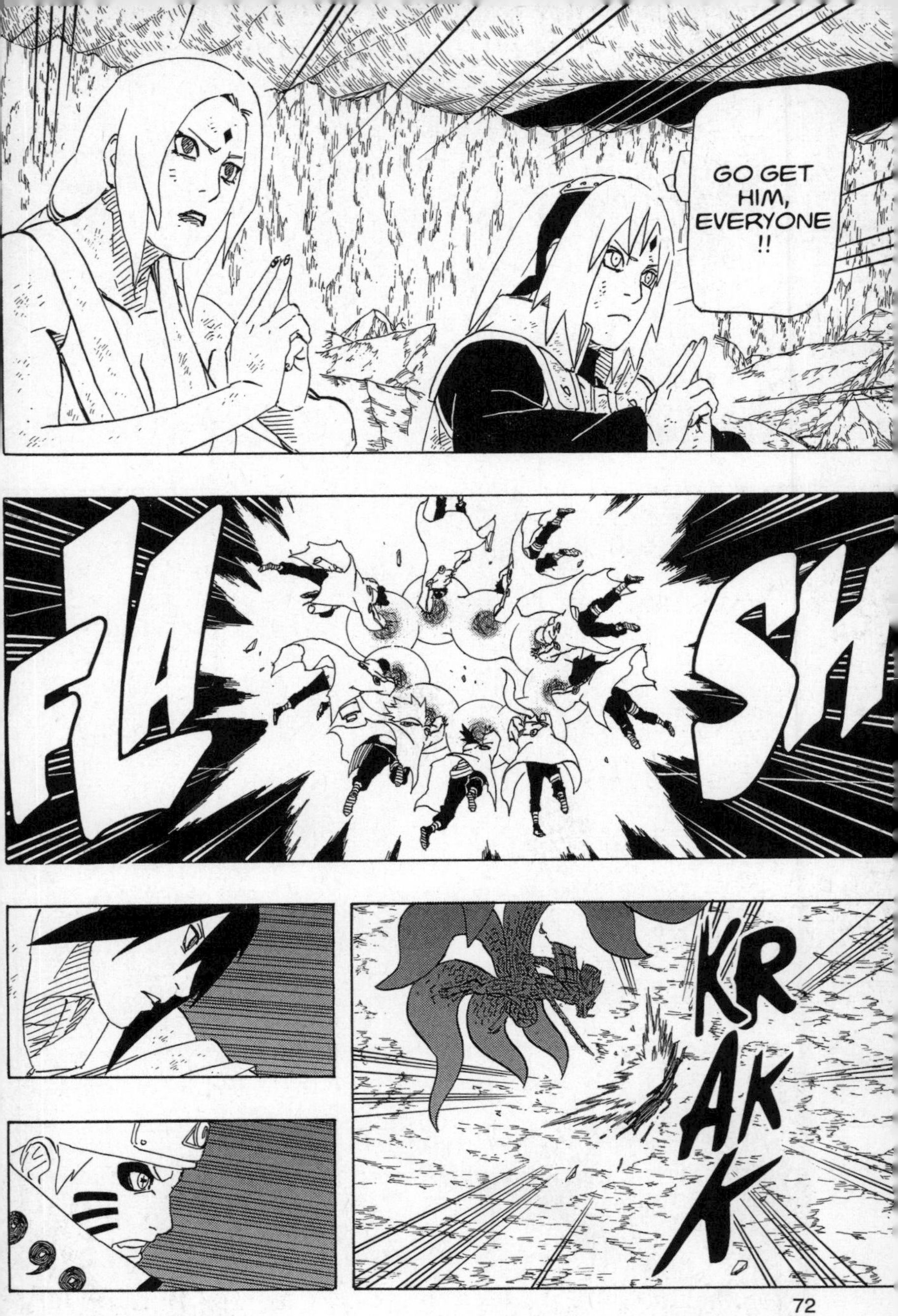
GO GET HIM, EVERYONE !!
FLASH
KRAKK

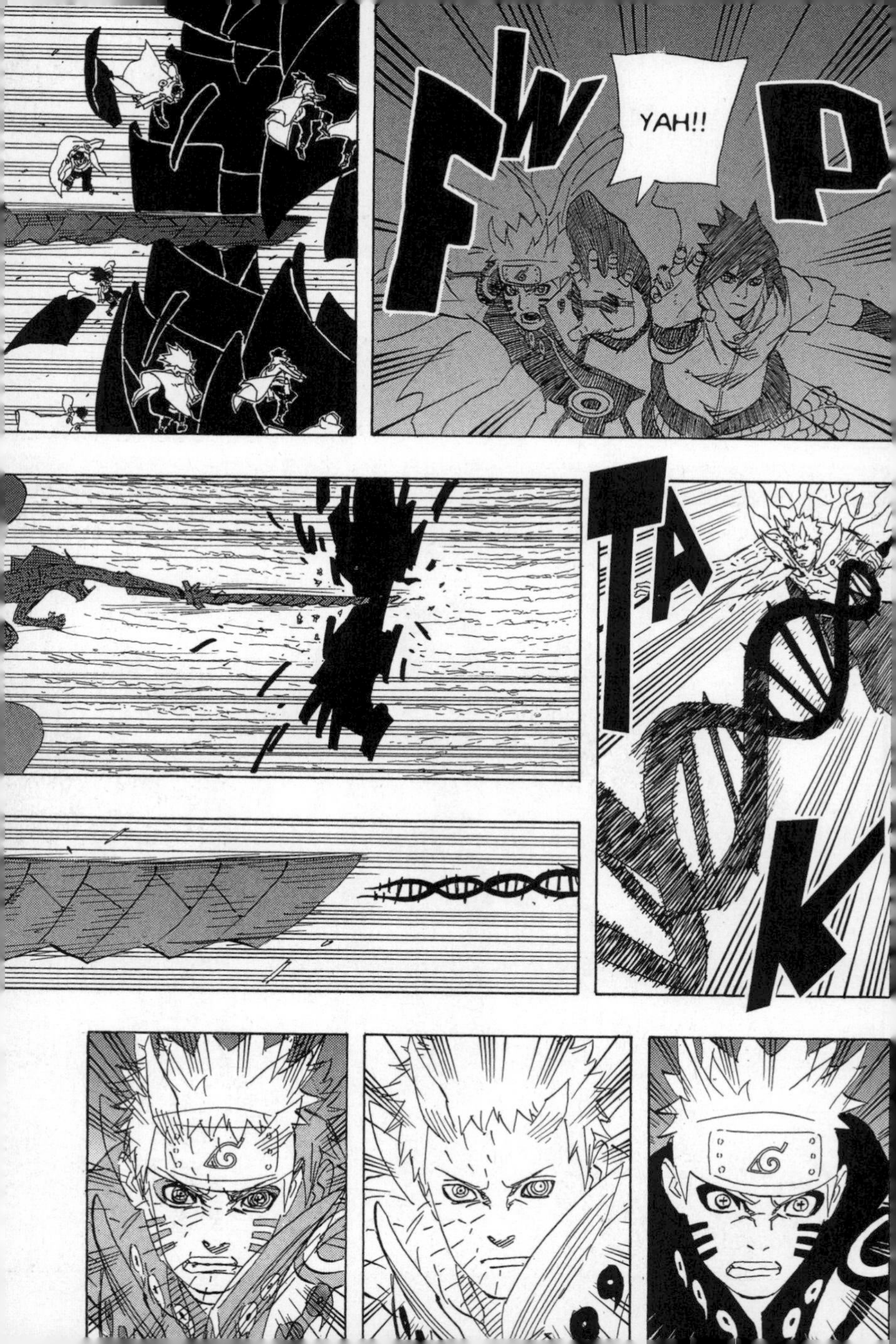
FWP
YAH!!
TAK

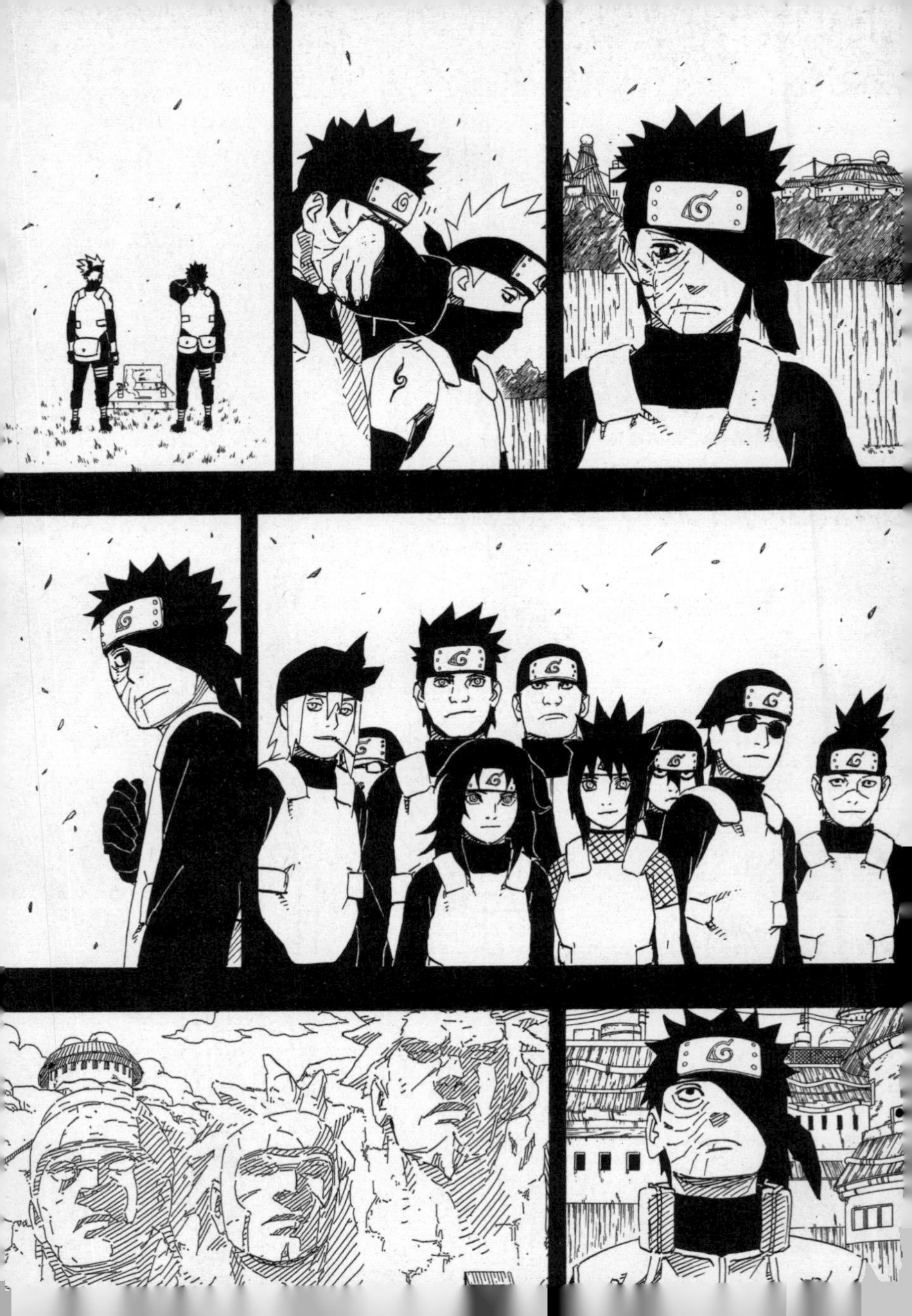

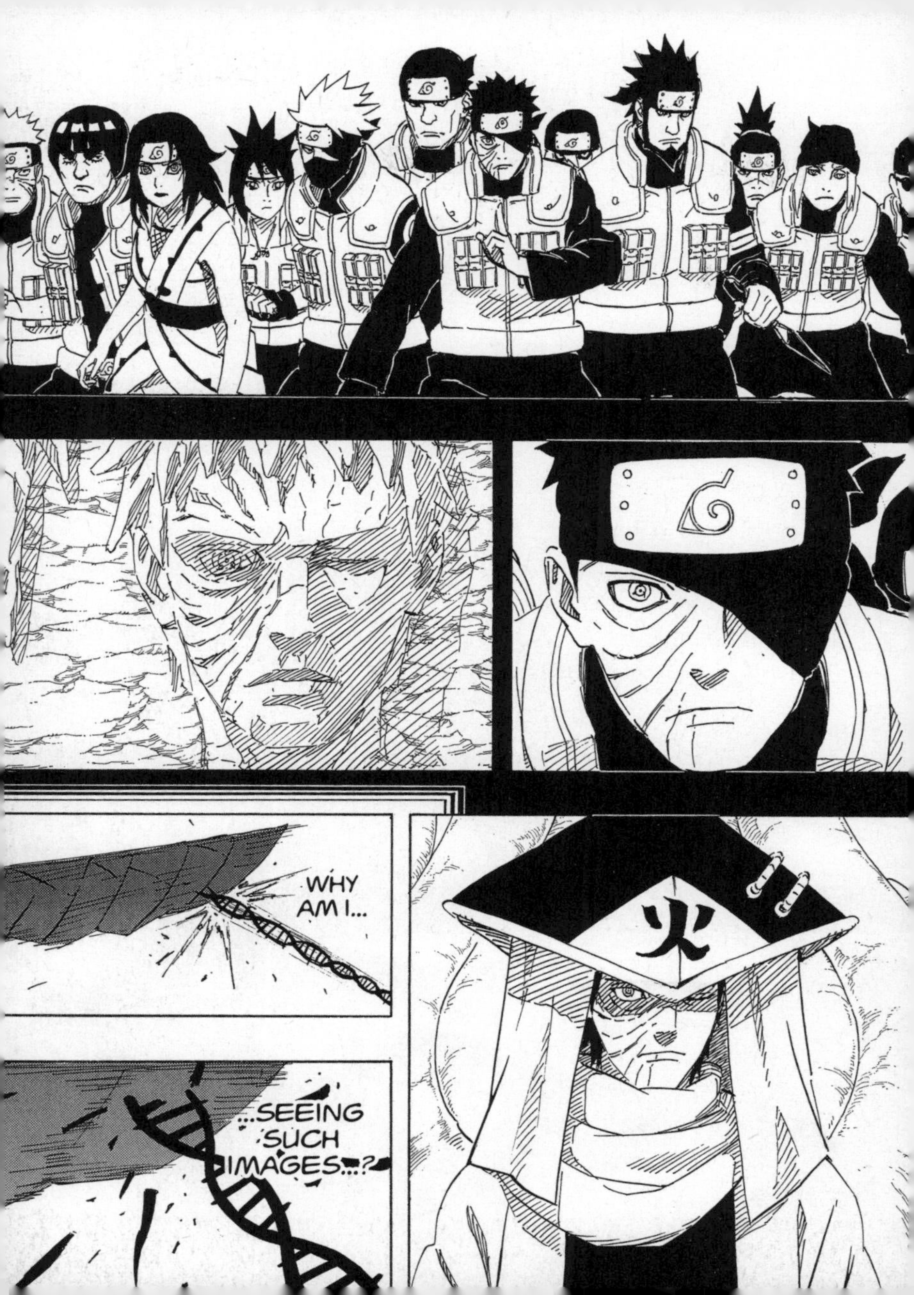
WHY AM I...
...SEEING SUCH IMAGES...?

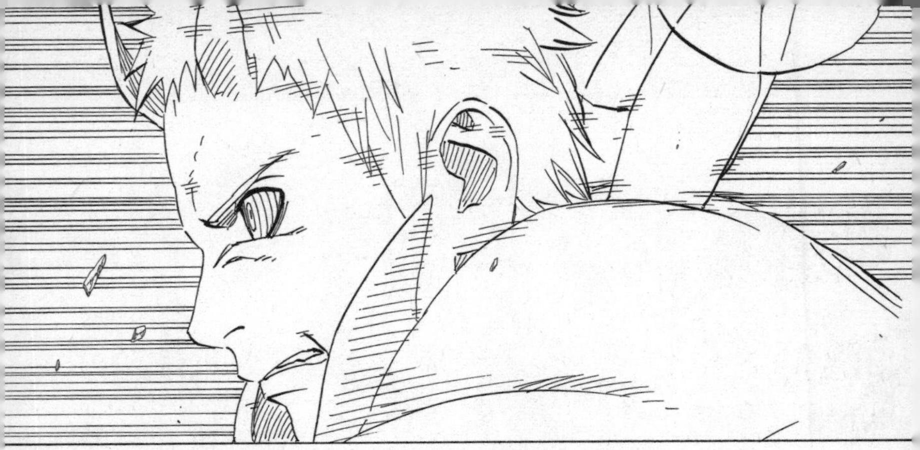
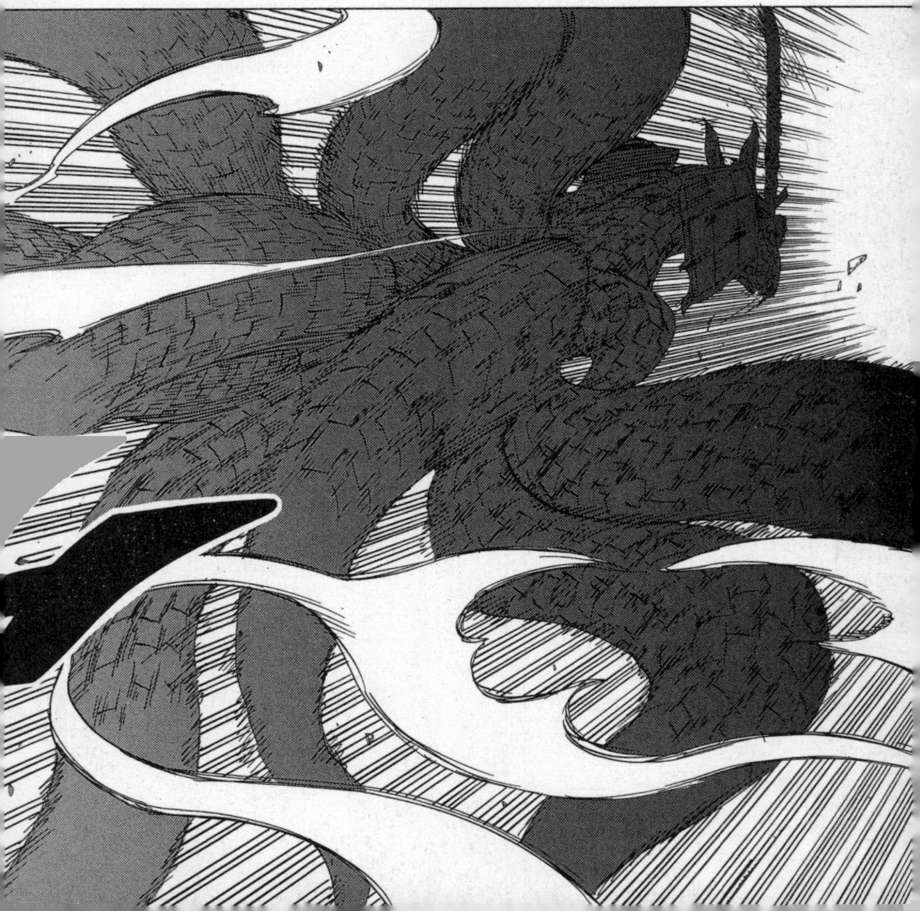

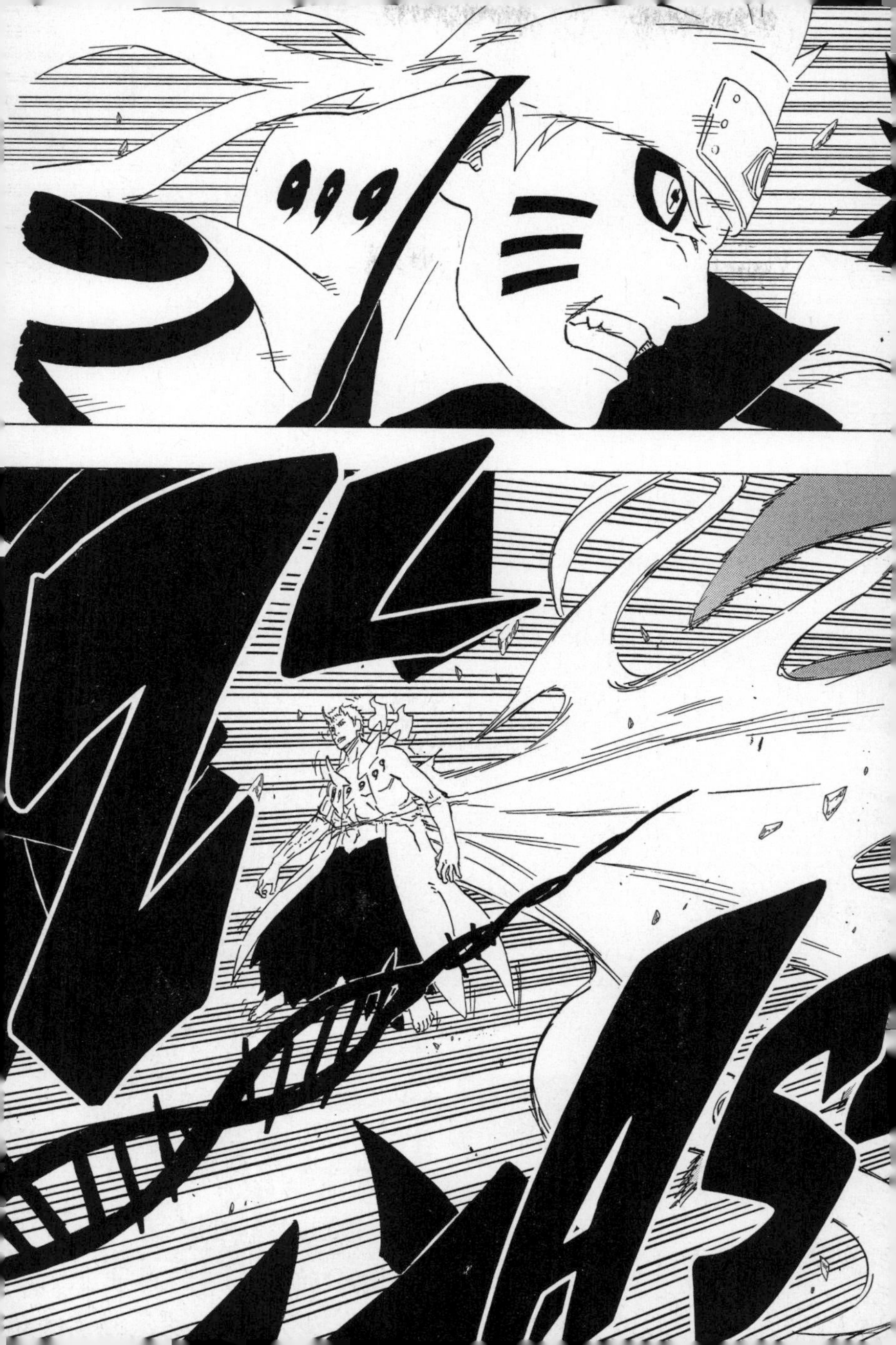

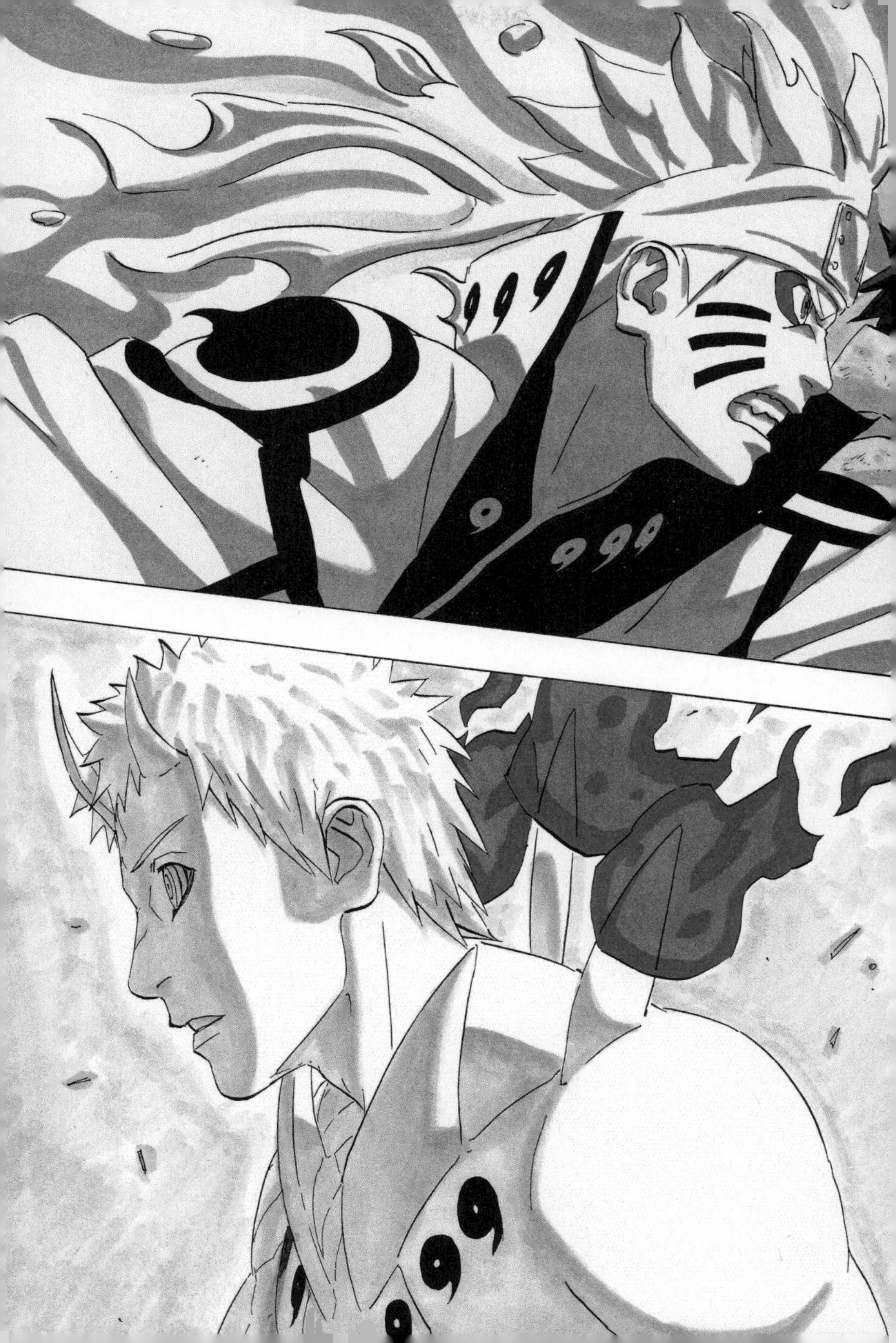

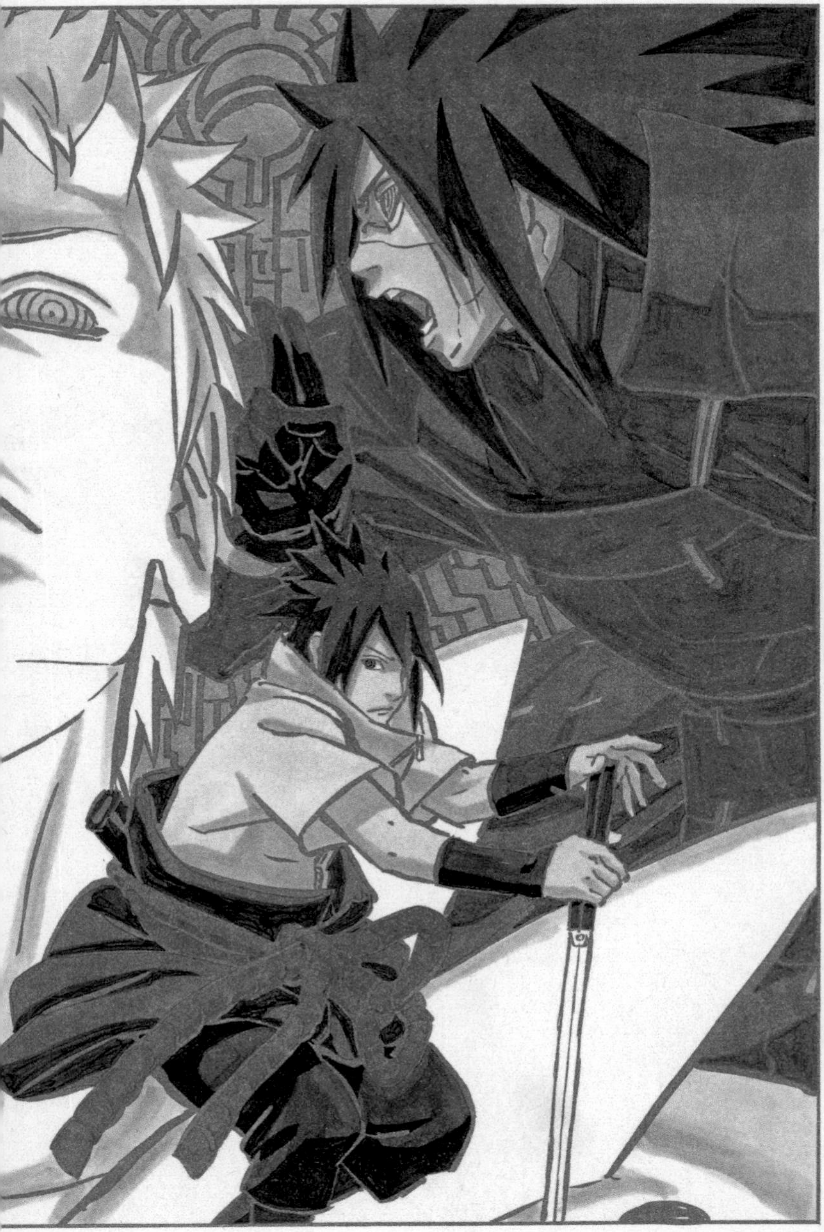

Number 652: Naruto's Path

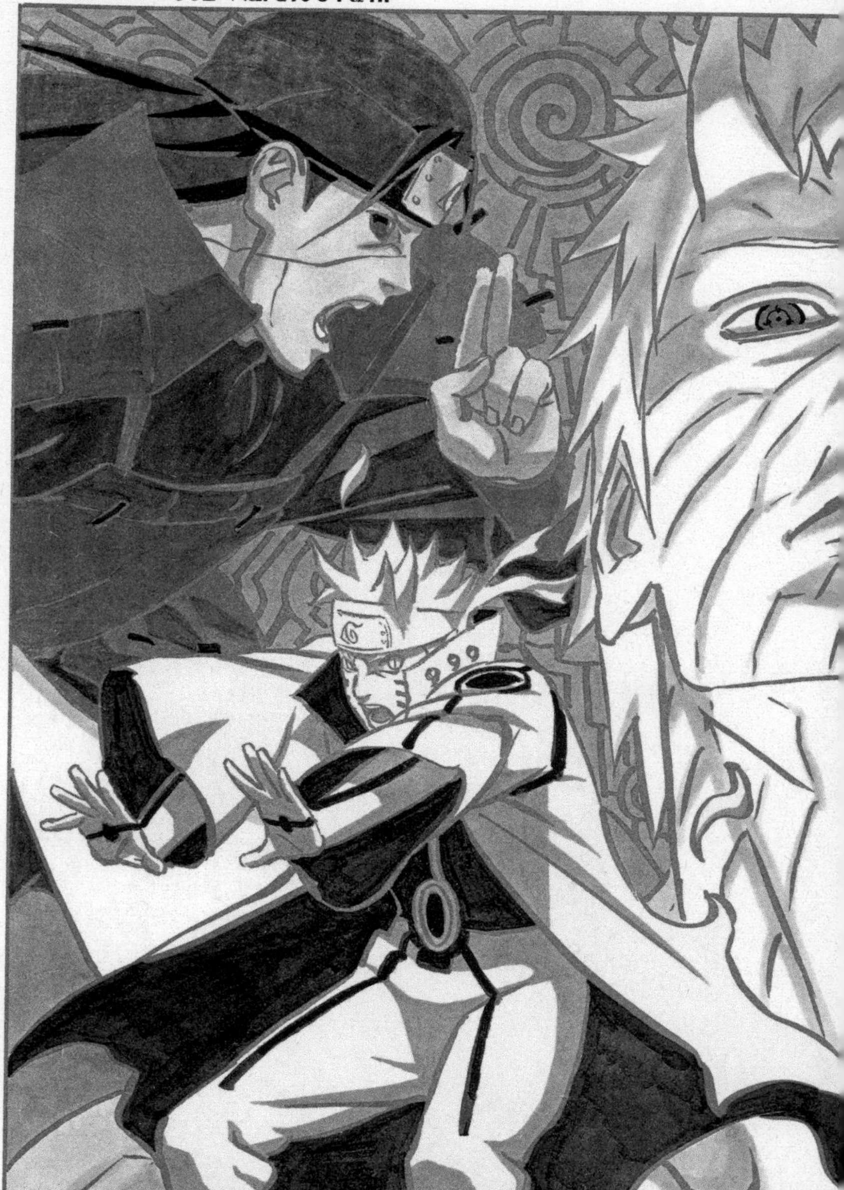

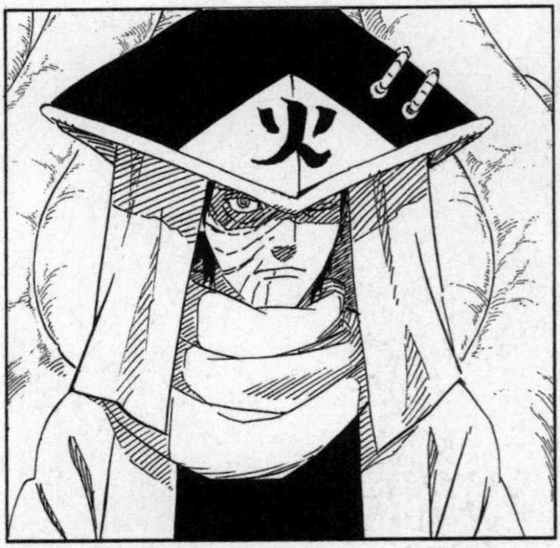
火

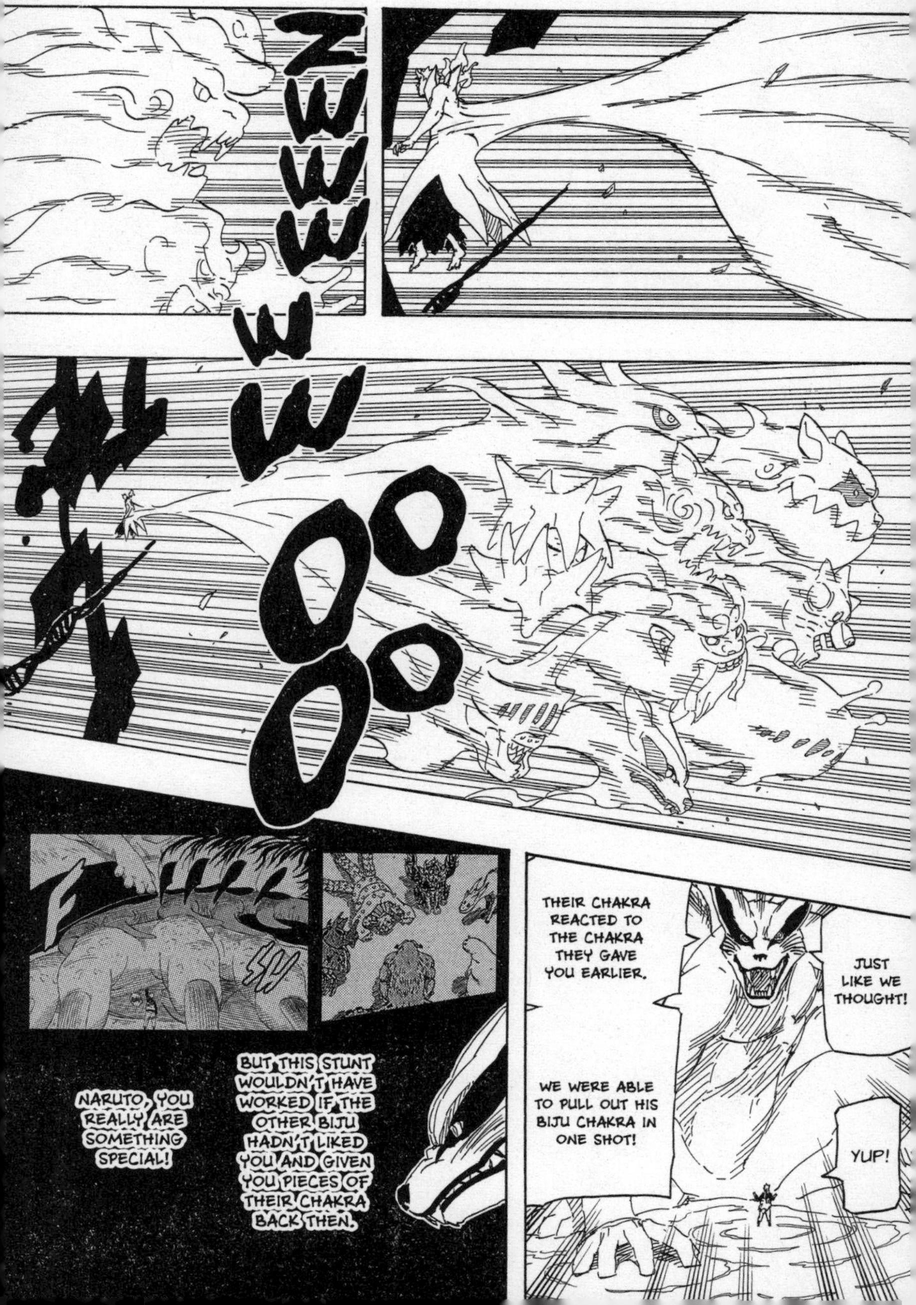
ZWWWWWWOOOO
THEIR CHAKRA REACTED TO THE CHAKRA THEY GAVE YOU EARLIER.
JUST LIKE WE THOUGHT!
WE WERE ABLE TO PULL OUT HIS BIJU CHAKRA IN ONE SHOT!
YUP!
BUT THIS STUNT WOULDN'T HAVE WORKED IF THE OTHER BIJU HADN'T LIKED YOU AND GIVEN YOU PIECES OF THEIR CHAKRA BACK THEN.
NARUTO, YOU REALLY ARE SOMETHING SPECIAL!

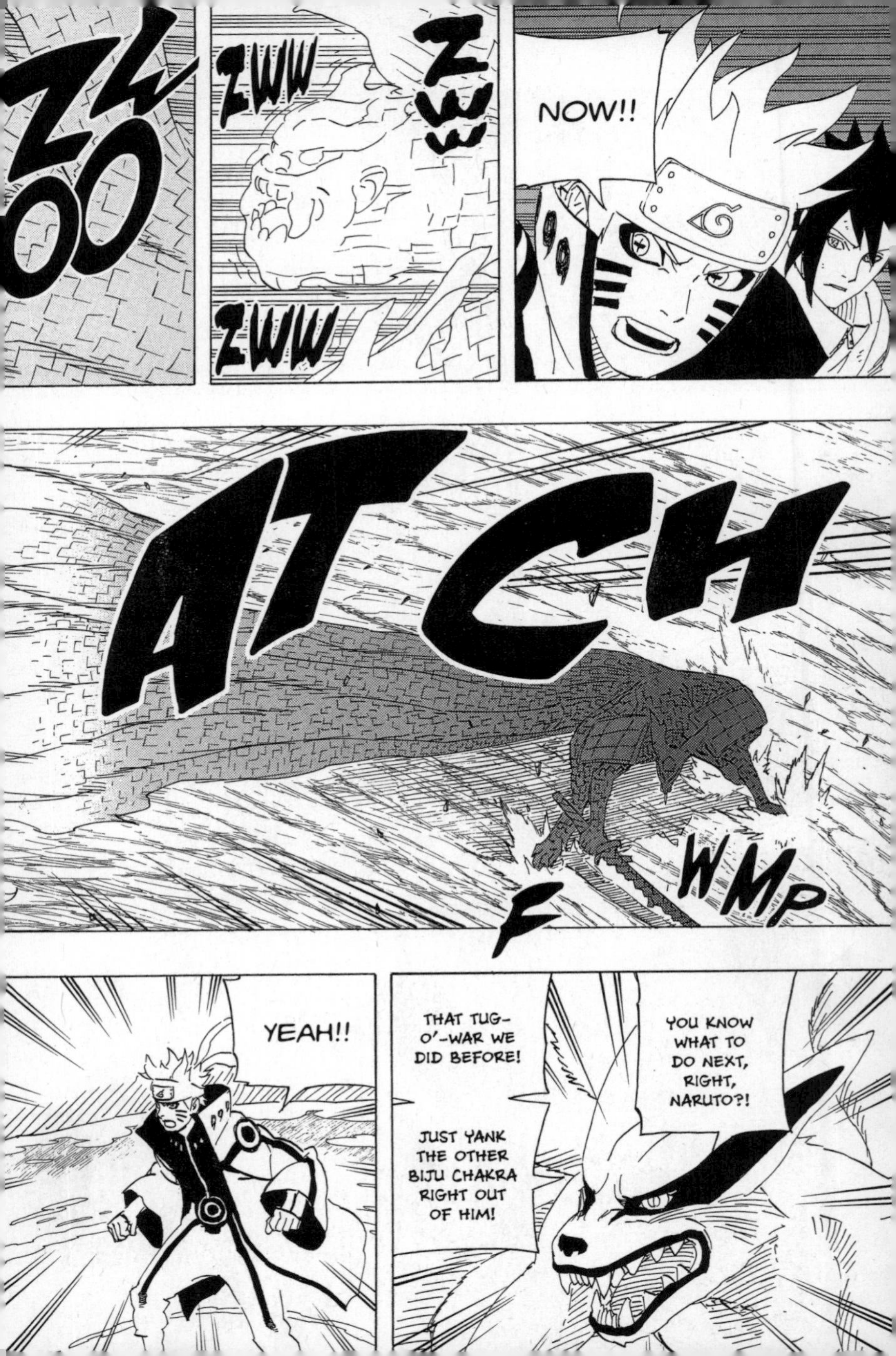
NOW!!
ZWW
ZWW
ZWW
ZWOO
ATCH
FWMP
YOU KNOW WHAT TO DO NEXT, RIGHT, NARUTO?!
THAT TUG-O'-WAR WE DID BEFORE!
JUST YANK THE OTHER BIJU CHAKRA RIGHT OUT OF HIM!
YEAH!!

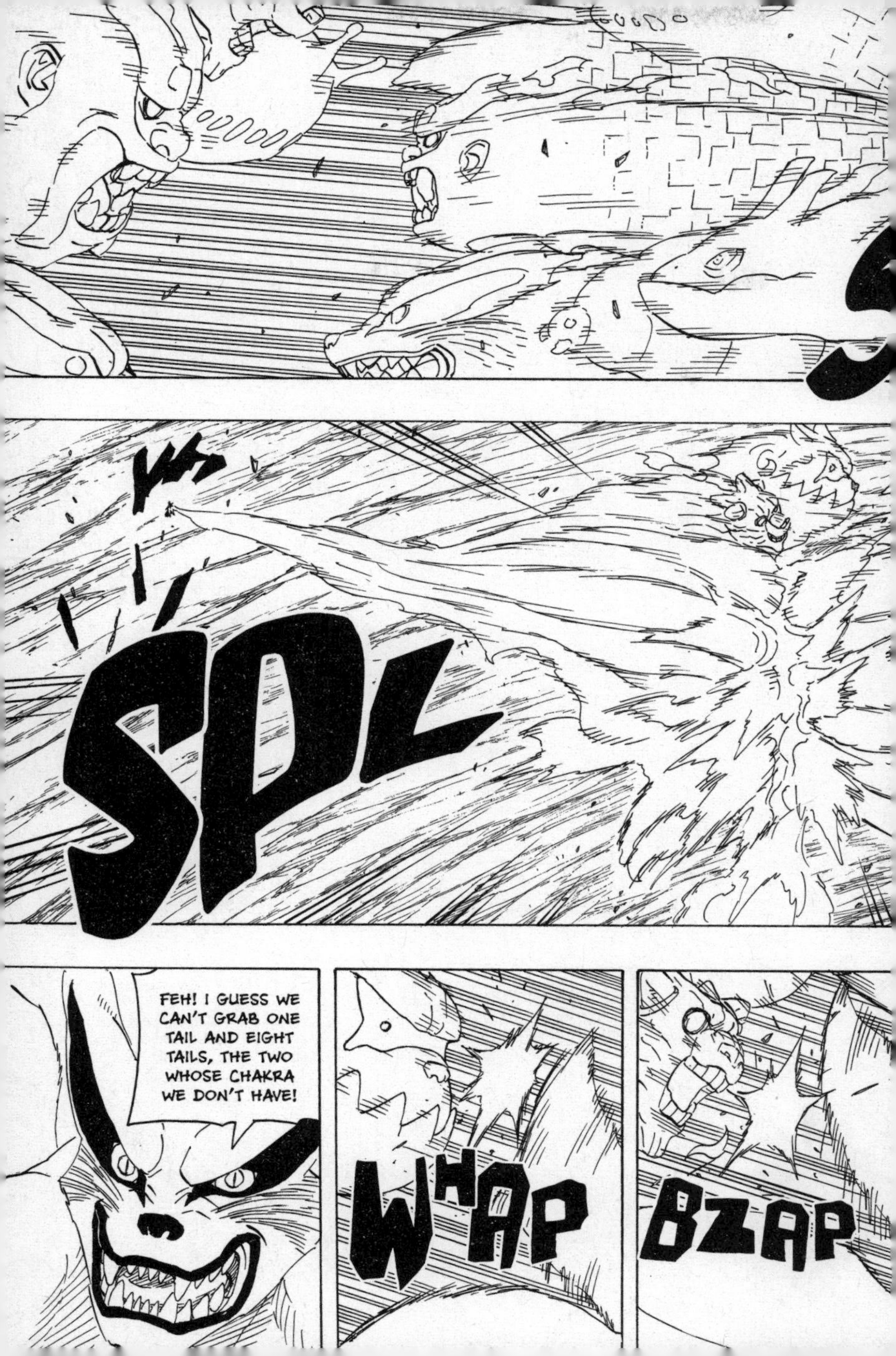
SPL
BZAP
WHAP
FEH! I GUESS WE CAN'T GRAB ONE TAIL AND EIGHT TAILS, THE TWO WHOSE CHAKRA WE DON'T HAVE!

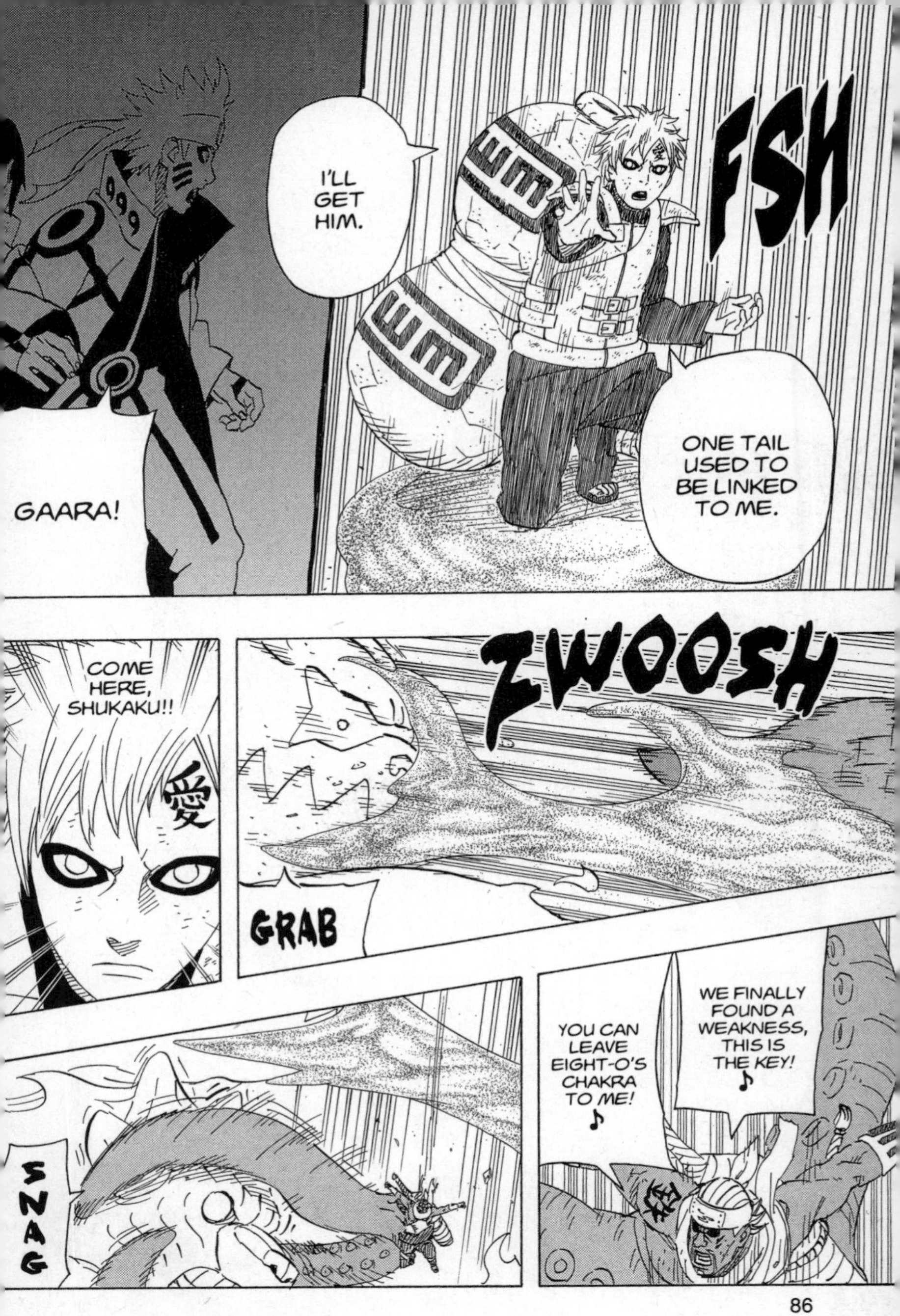
FSH
I'LL GET HIM.
ONE TAIL USED TO BE LINKED TO ME.
GAARA!
ZWOOSH
GRAB
COME HERE, SHUKAKU!!
WE FINALLY FOUND A WEAKNESS, THIS IS THE KEY! ♪
YOU CAN LEAVE EIGHT-O'S CHAKRA TO ME! ♪
SNAG

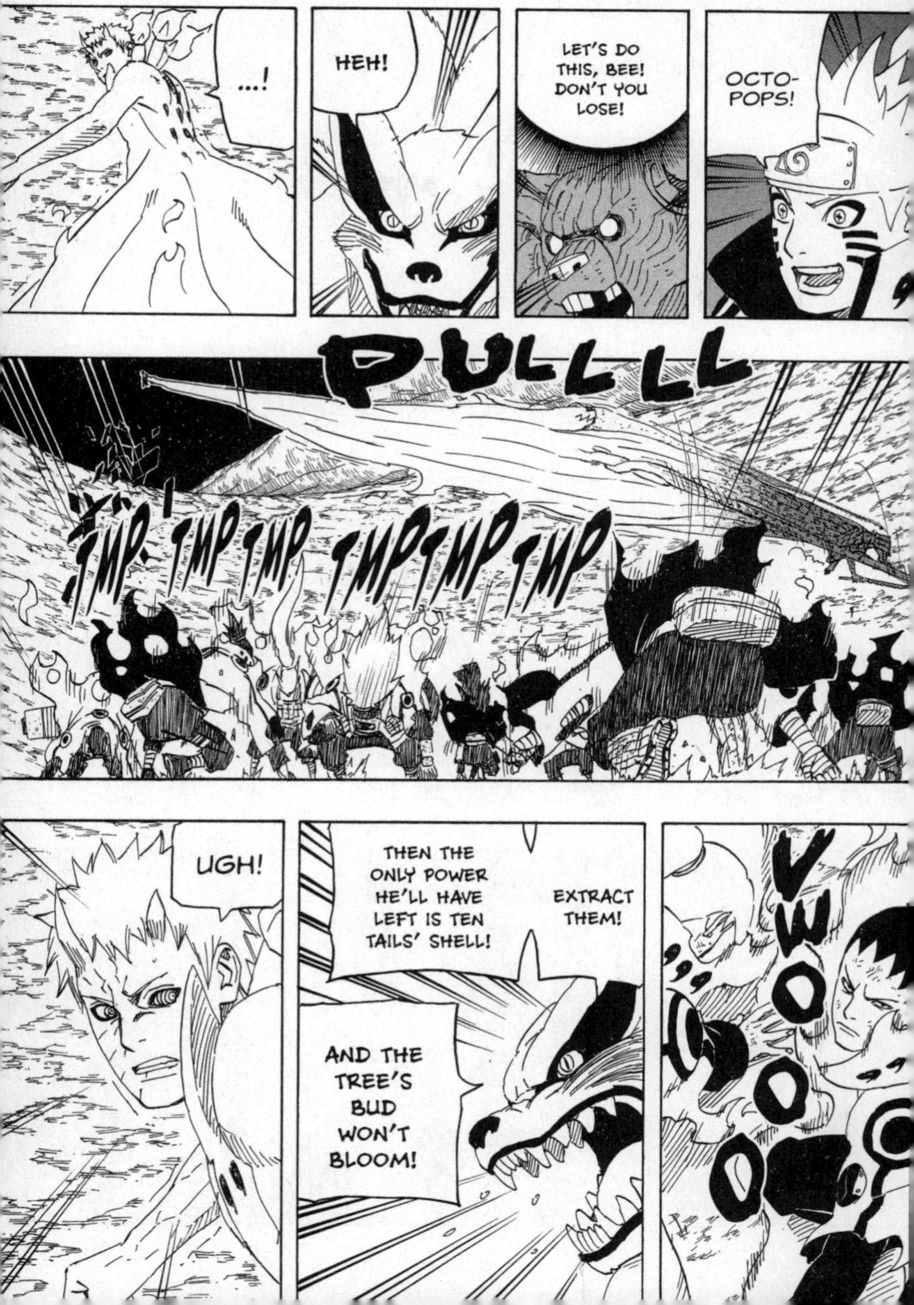
OCTO-POPS!
LET'S DO THIS, BEE! DON'T YOU LOSE!
HEH!
...!
PULLLL
TMP TMP TMP TMP TMP TMP TMP
VWOOOO
EXTRACT THEM!
THEN THE ONLY POWER HE'LL HAVE LEFT IS TEN TAILS' SHELL!
AND THE TREE'S BUD WON'T BLOOM!
UGH!

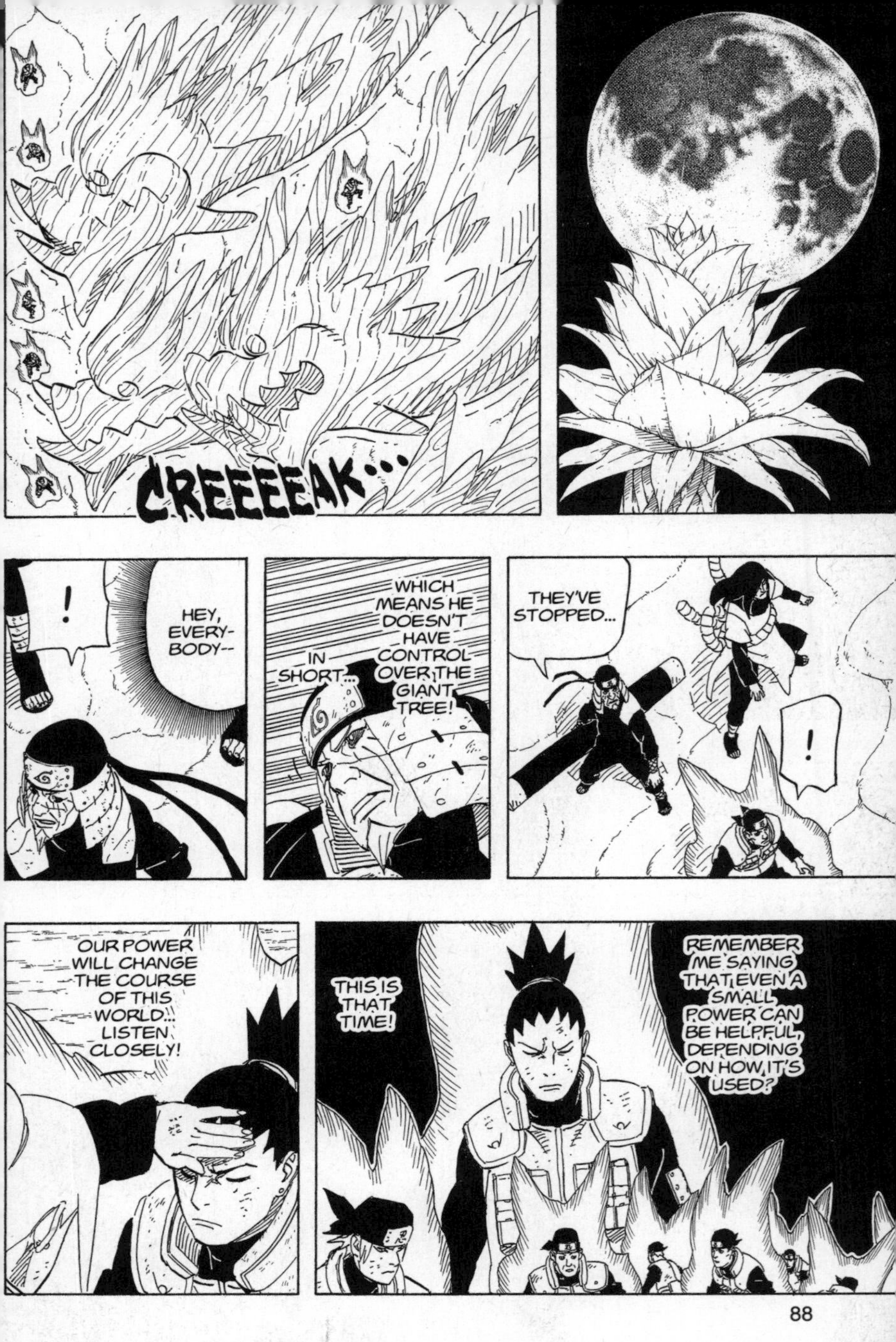
CREEEEAK...
THEY'VE STOPPED...
!
WHICH MEANS HE DOESN'T HAVE CONTROL OVER THE GIANT TREE!
IN SHORT...
HEY, EVERY-BODY--
!
REMEMBER ME SAYING THAT EVEN A SMALL POWER CAN BE HELPFUL, DEPENDING ON HOW IT'S USED?
THIS IS THAT TIME!
OUR POWER WILL CHANGE THE COURSE OF THIS WORLD... LISTEN CLOSELY!

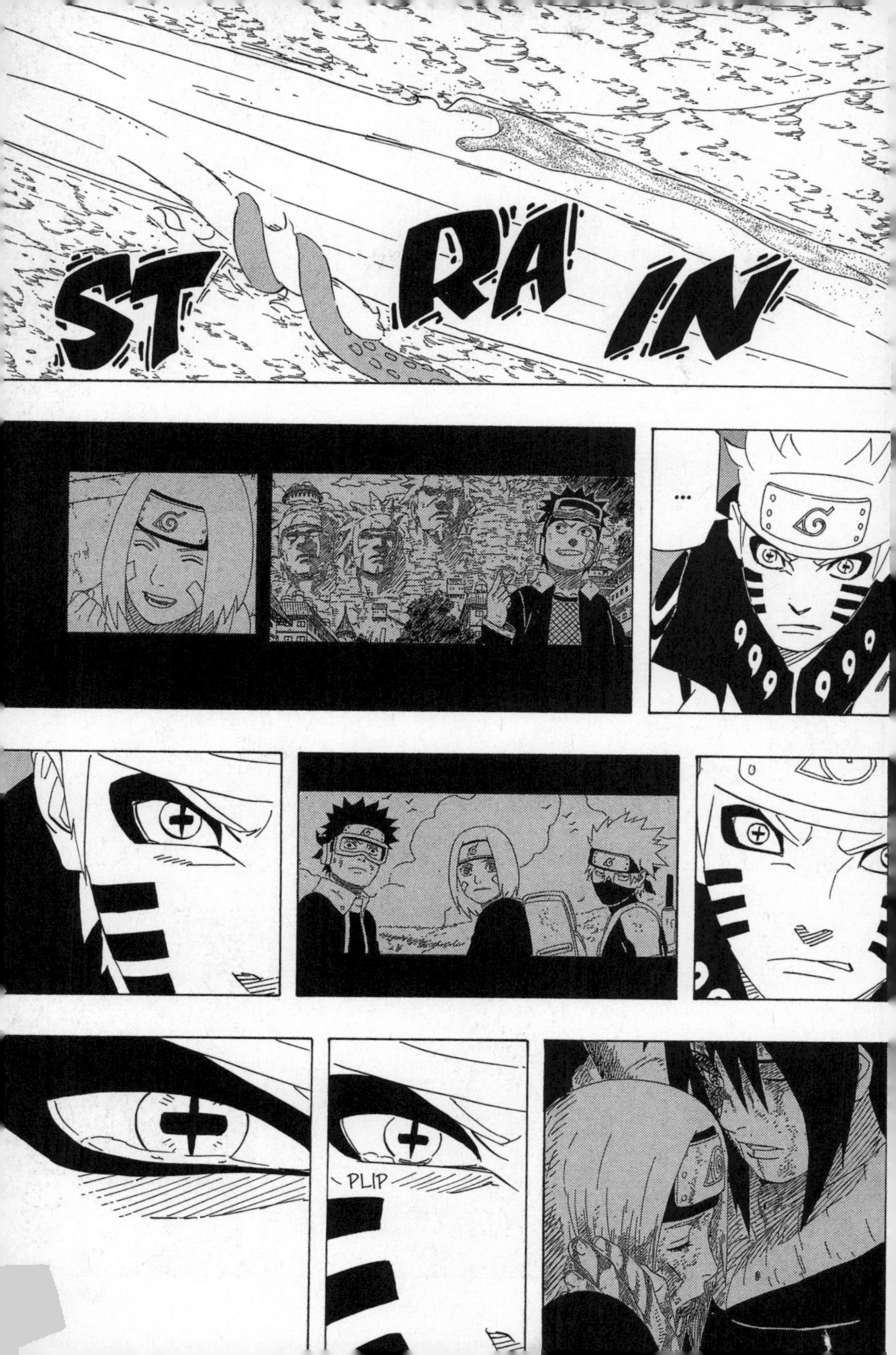
STRAIN
...
PLIP

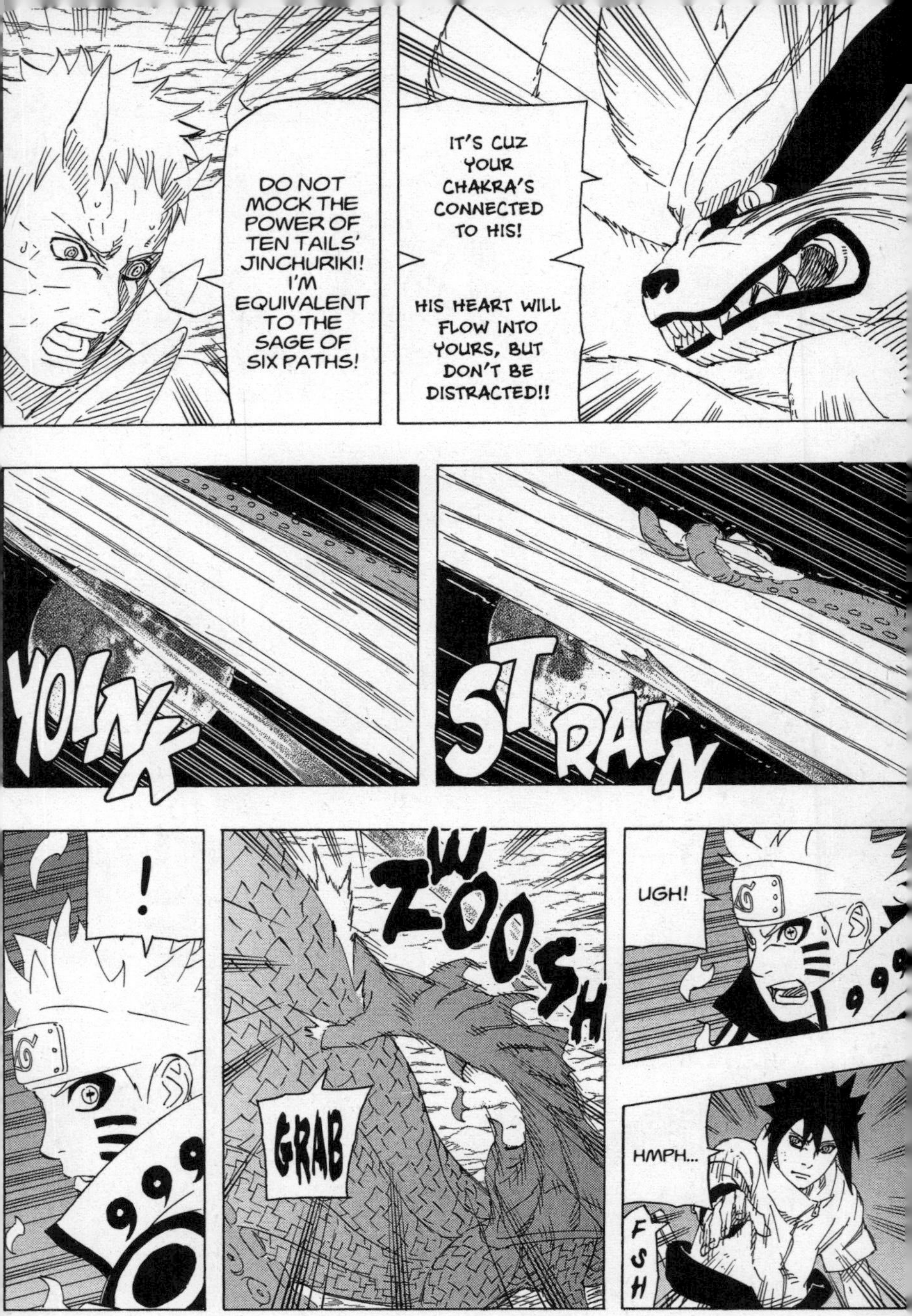

IT'S CUZ YOUR CHAKRA'S CONNECTED TO HIS!
HIS HEART WILL FLOW INTO YOURS, BUT DON'T BE DISTRACTED!!
DO NOT MOCK THE POWER OF TEN TAILS' JINCHURIKI! I'M EQUIVALENT TO THE SAGE OF SIX PATHS!
STRAIN
YOINK
UGH!
HMPH...
FSH
ZWOOSH
GRAB
!

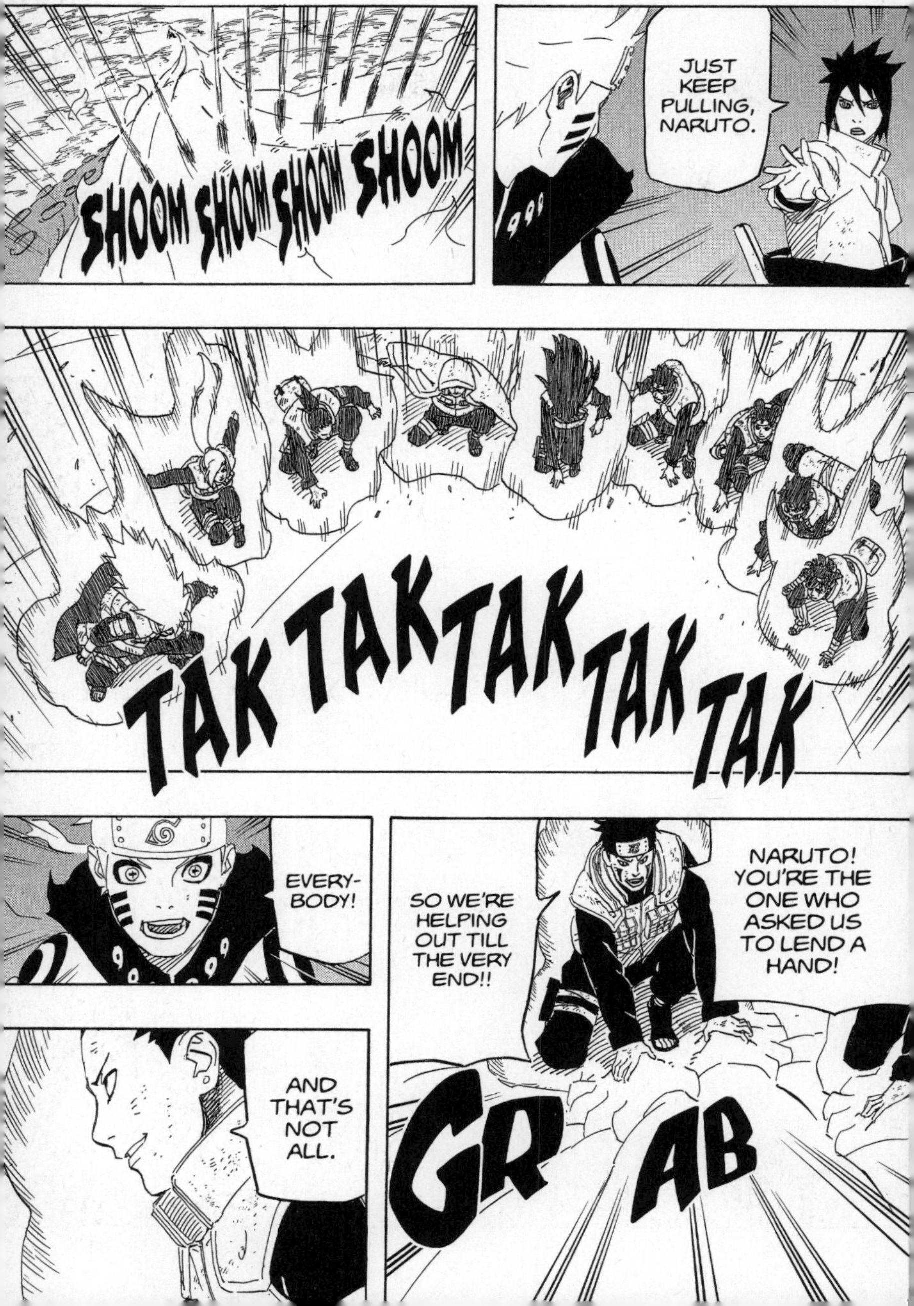

JUST KEEP PULLING, NARUTO.
SHOOM SHOOM SHOOM SHOOM
TAK TAK TAK TAK TAK TAK
NARUTO! YOU'RE THE ONE WHO ASKED US TO LEND A HAND!
SO WE'RE HELPING OUT TILL THE VERY END!!
GRAB
EVERY-BODY!
AND THAT'S NOT ALL.

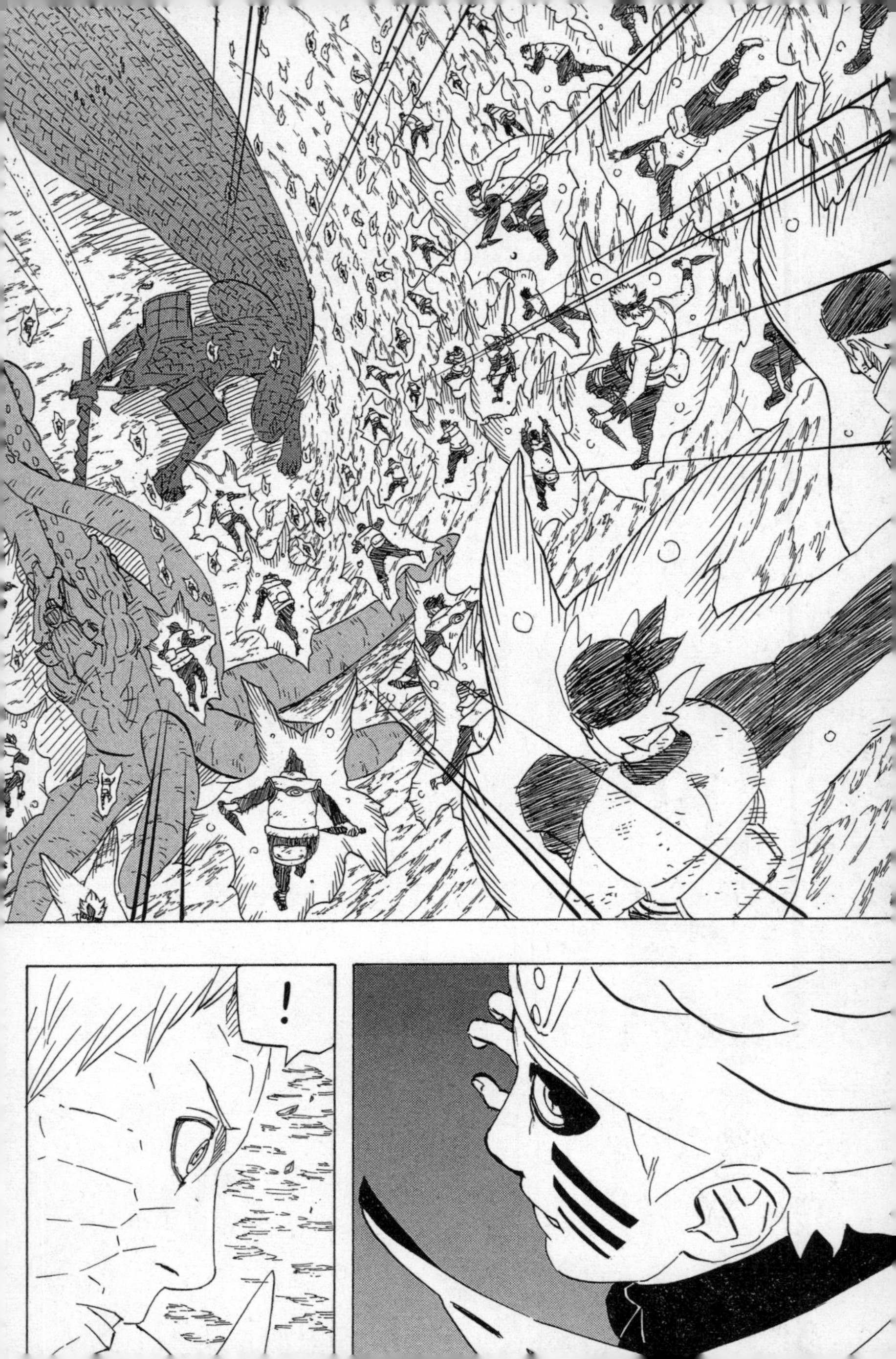
!

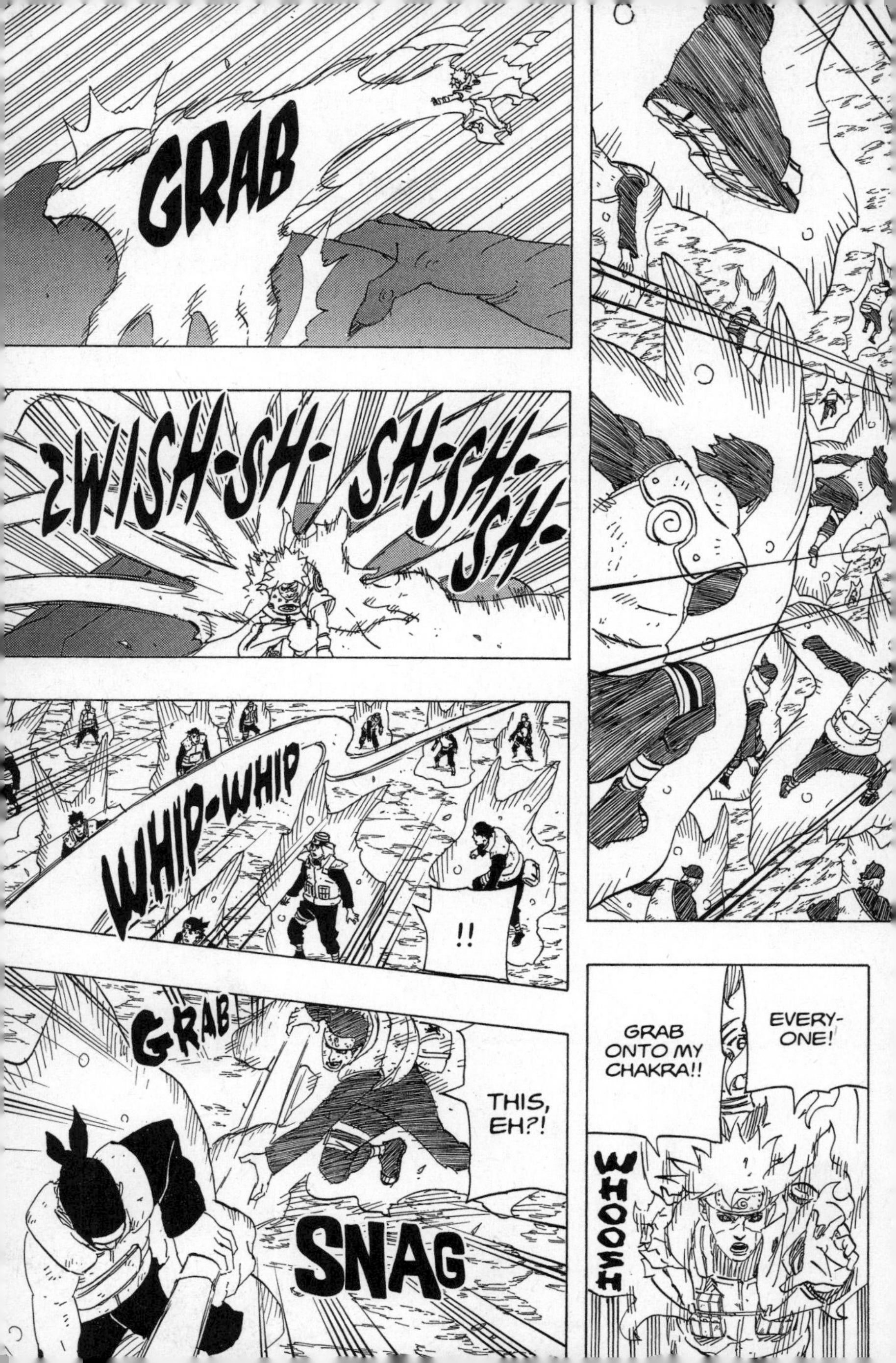
GRAB
ZWISH-SH-SH-SH-SH-SH-
WHIP-WHIP
!!
EVERY-ONE!
GRAB ONTO MY CHAKRA!!
WHOOSH
GRAB
THIS, EH?!
SNAG

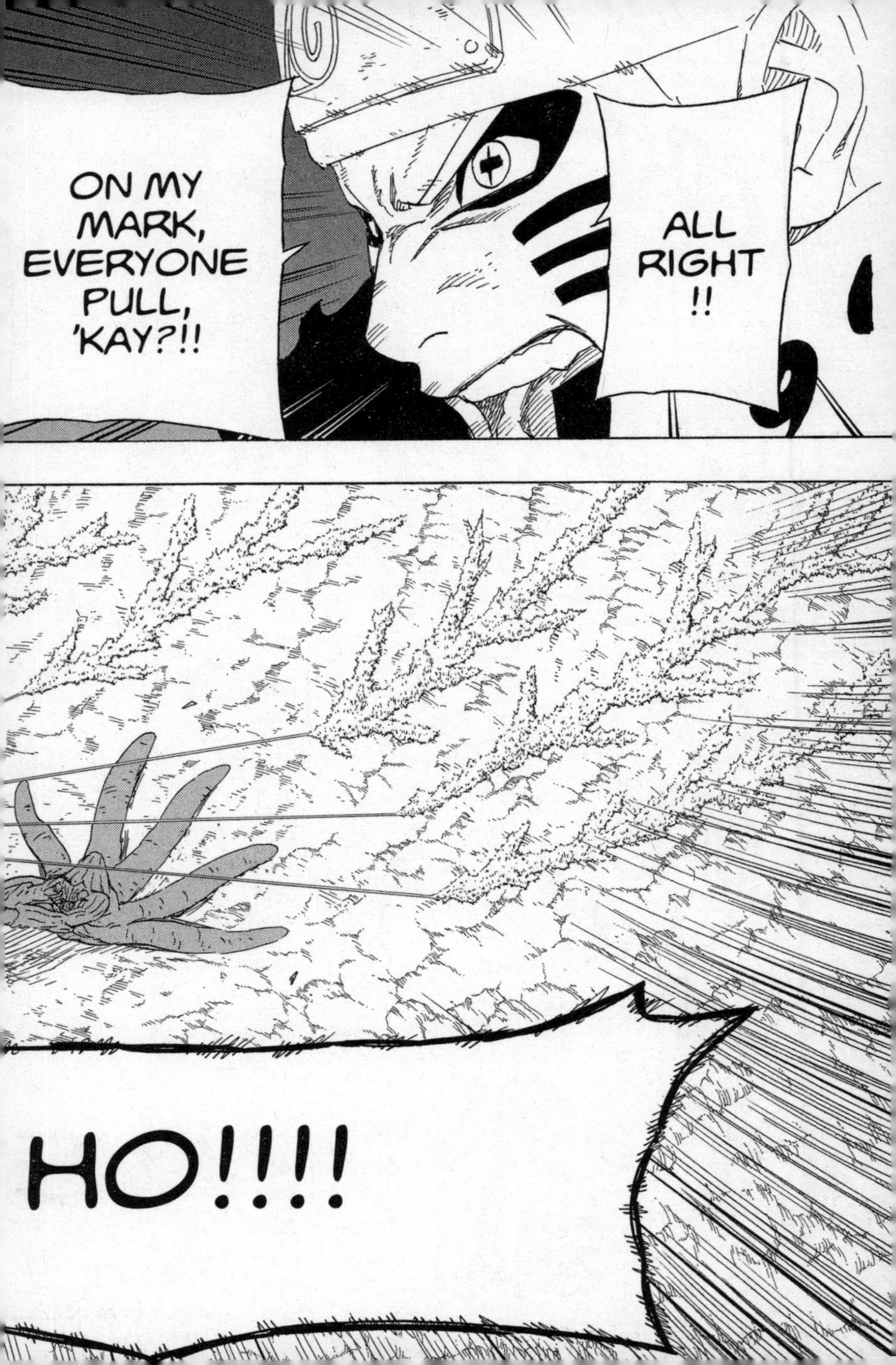
ON MY MARK, EVERYONE PULL, 'KAY?!!
ALL RIGHT!!
HO!!!!

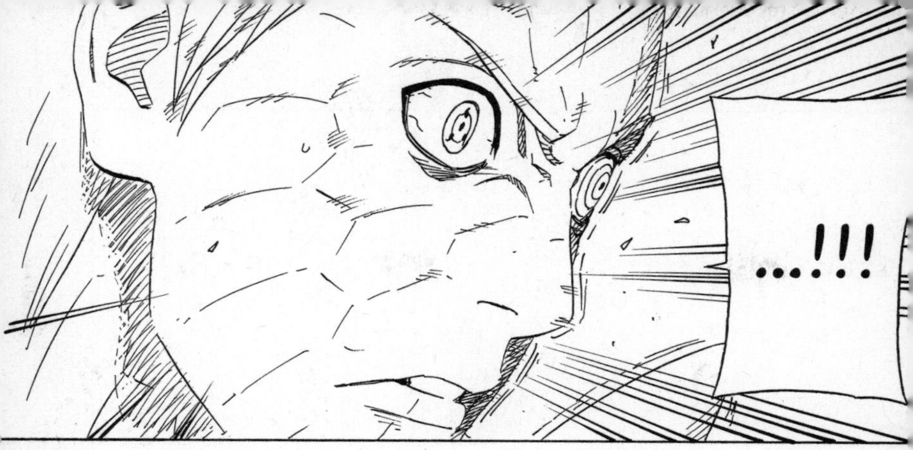
...!!!
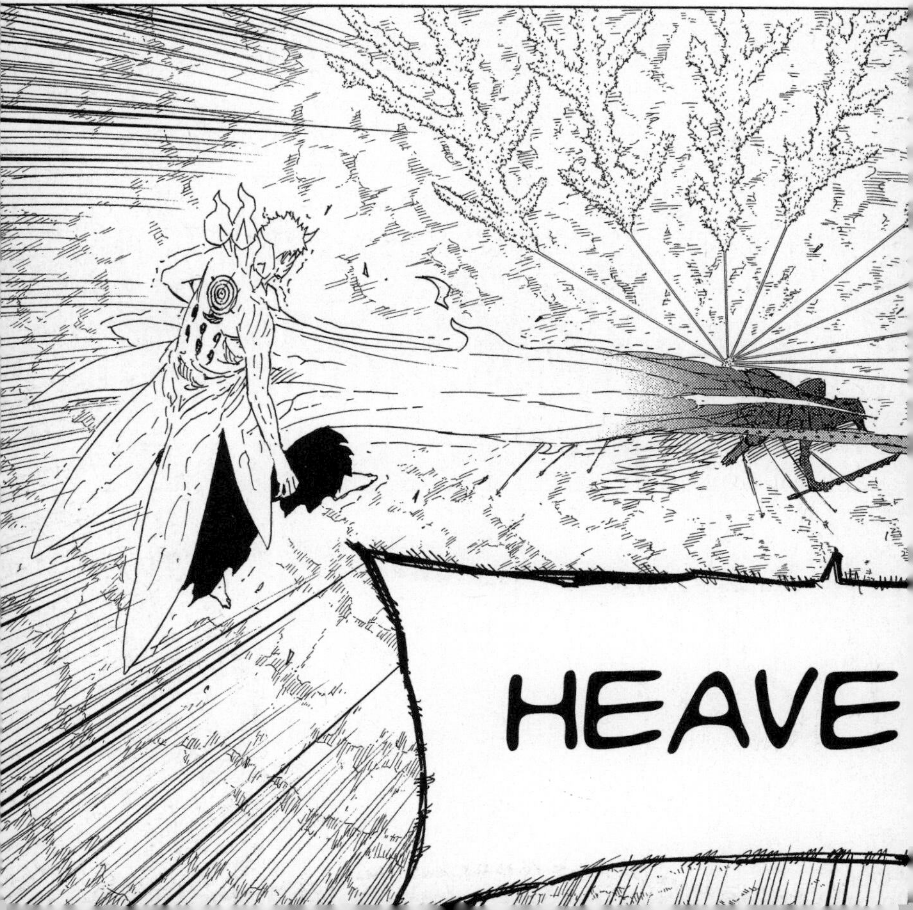
HEAVE

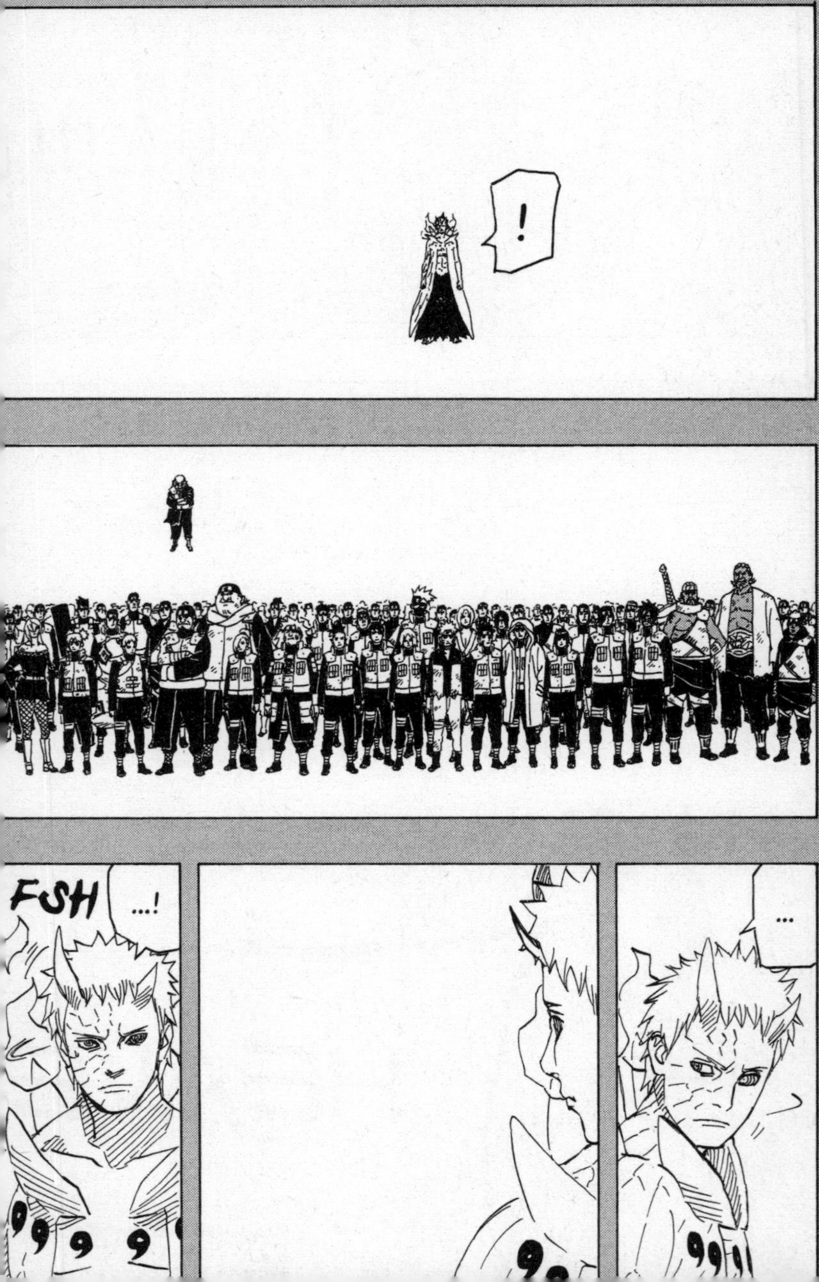
!
...
FSH
...!

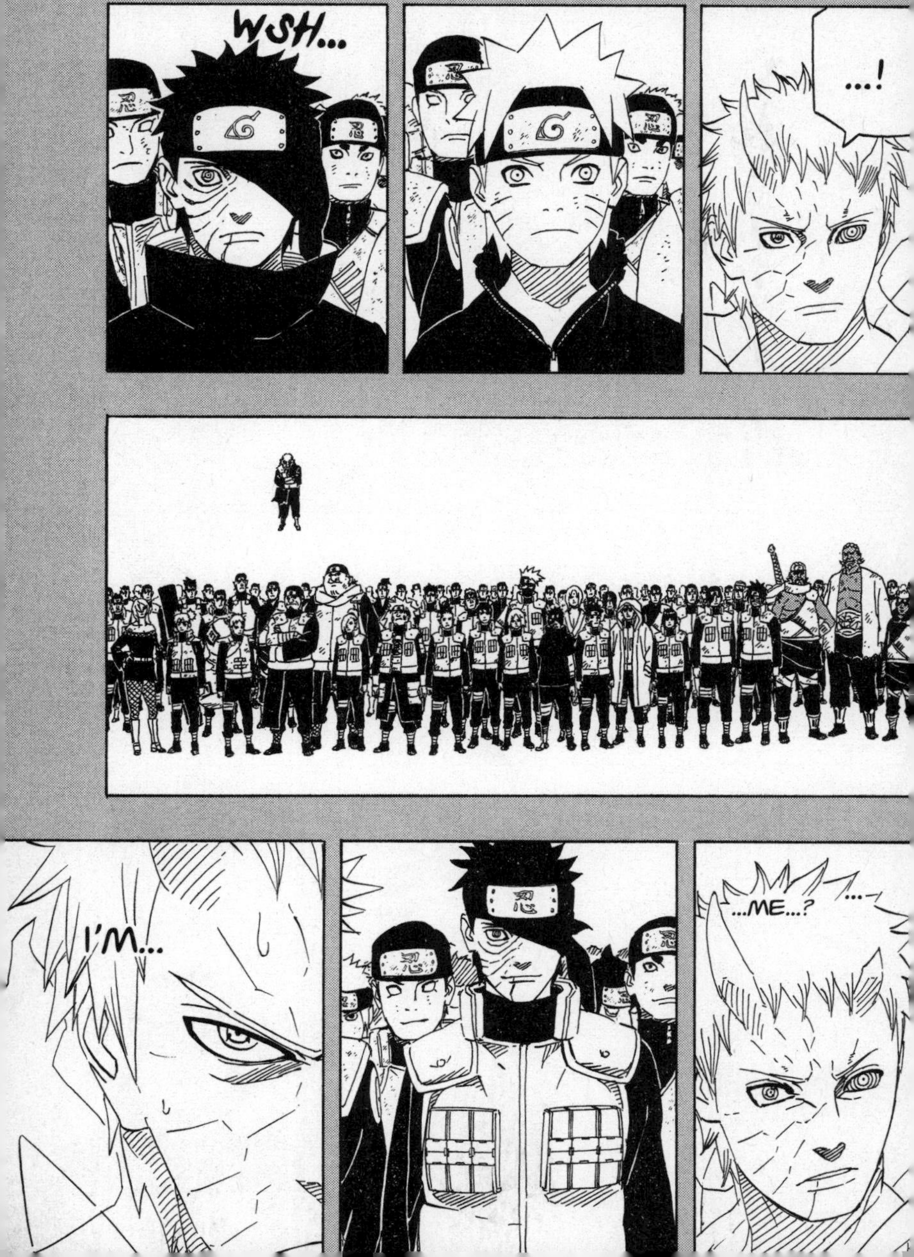
...!
WSH...
...
...ME...?
I'M...

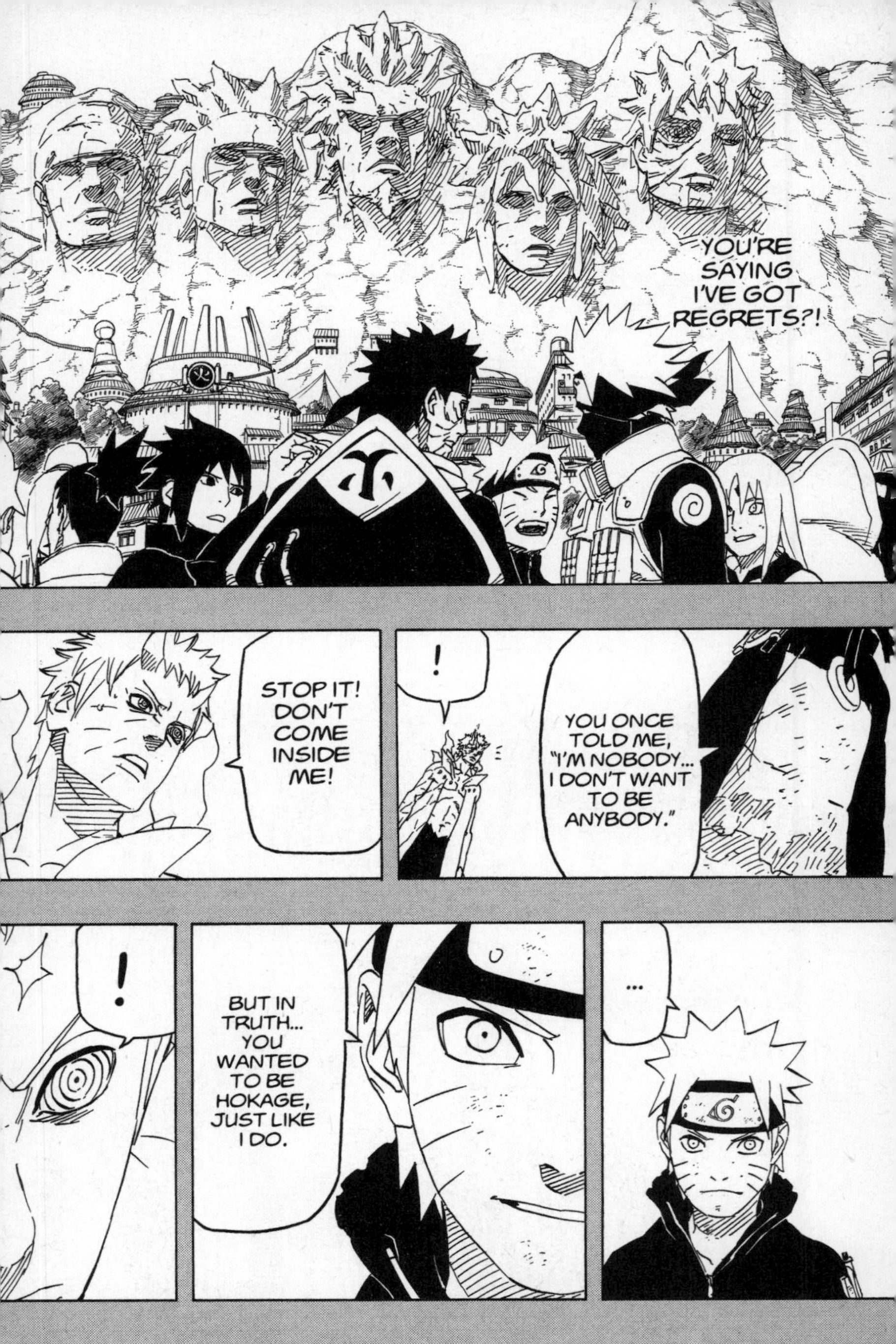
YOU'RE SAYING I'VE GOT REGRETS?!
YOU ONCE TOLD ME, "I'M NOBODY... I DON'T WANT TO BE ANYBODY."
!
STOP IT! DON'T COME INSIDE ME!
...
BUT IN TRUTH... YOU WANTED TO BE HOKAGE, JUST LIKE I DO.
!

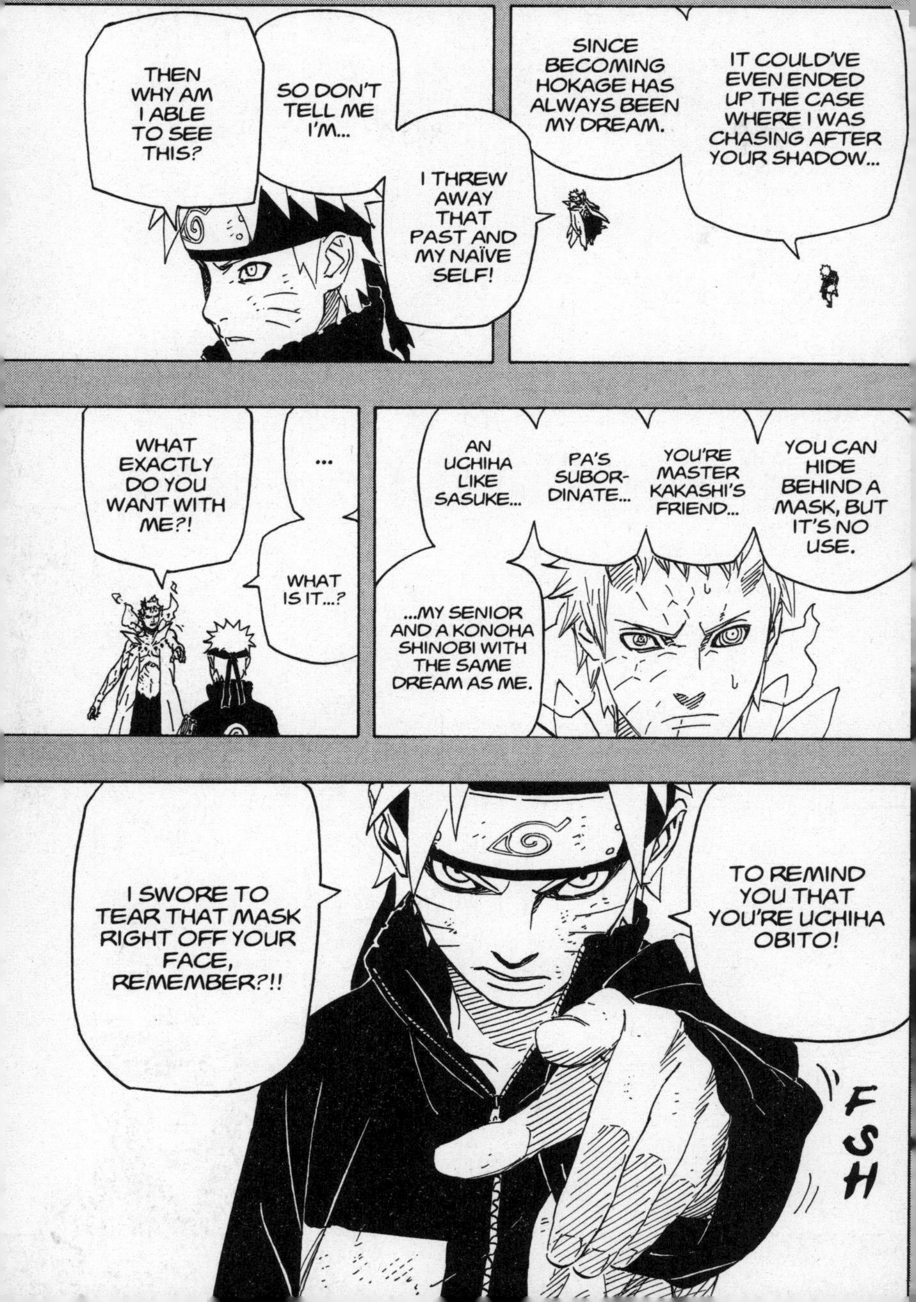
IT COULD'VE EVEN ENDED UP THE CASE WHERE I WAS CHASING AFTER YOUR SHADOW...
SINCE BECOMING HOKAGE HAS ALWAYS BEEN MY DREAM.
I THREW AWAY THAT PAST AND MY NAÏVE SELF!
SO DON'T TELL ME I'M...
THEN WHY AM I ABLE TO SEE THIS?
YOU CAN HIDE BEHIND A MASK, BUT IT'S NO USE.
YOU'RE MASTER KAKASHI'S FRIEND...
PA'S SUBORDINATE...
AN UCHIHA LIKE SASUKE...
...MY SENIOR AND A KONOHA SHINOBI WITH THE SAME DREAM AS ME.
...
WHAT IS IT...?
WHAT EXACTLY DO YOU WANT WITH ME?!
TO REMIND YOU THAT YOU'RE UCHIHA OBITO!
I SWORE TO TEAR THAT MASK RIGHT OFF YOUR FACE, REMEMBER?!!
FSH

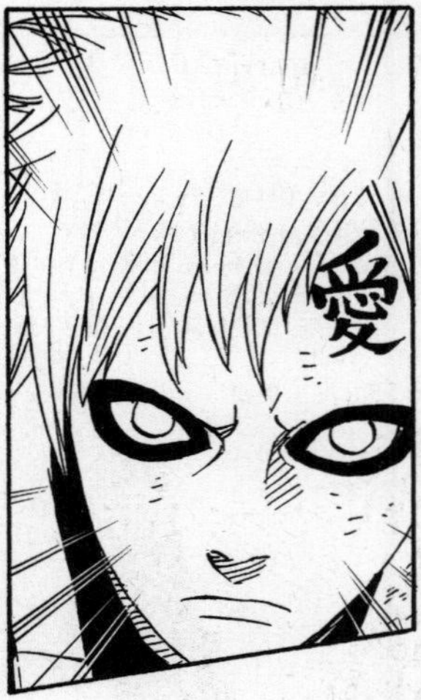
愛

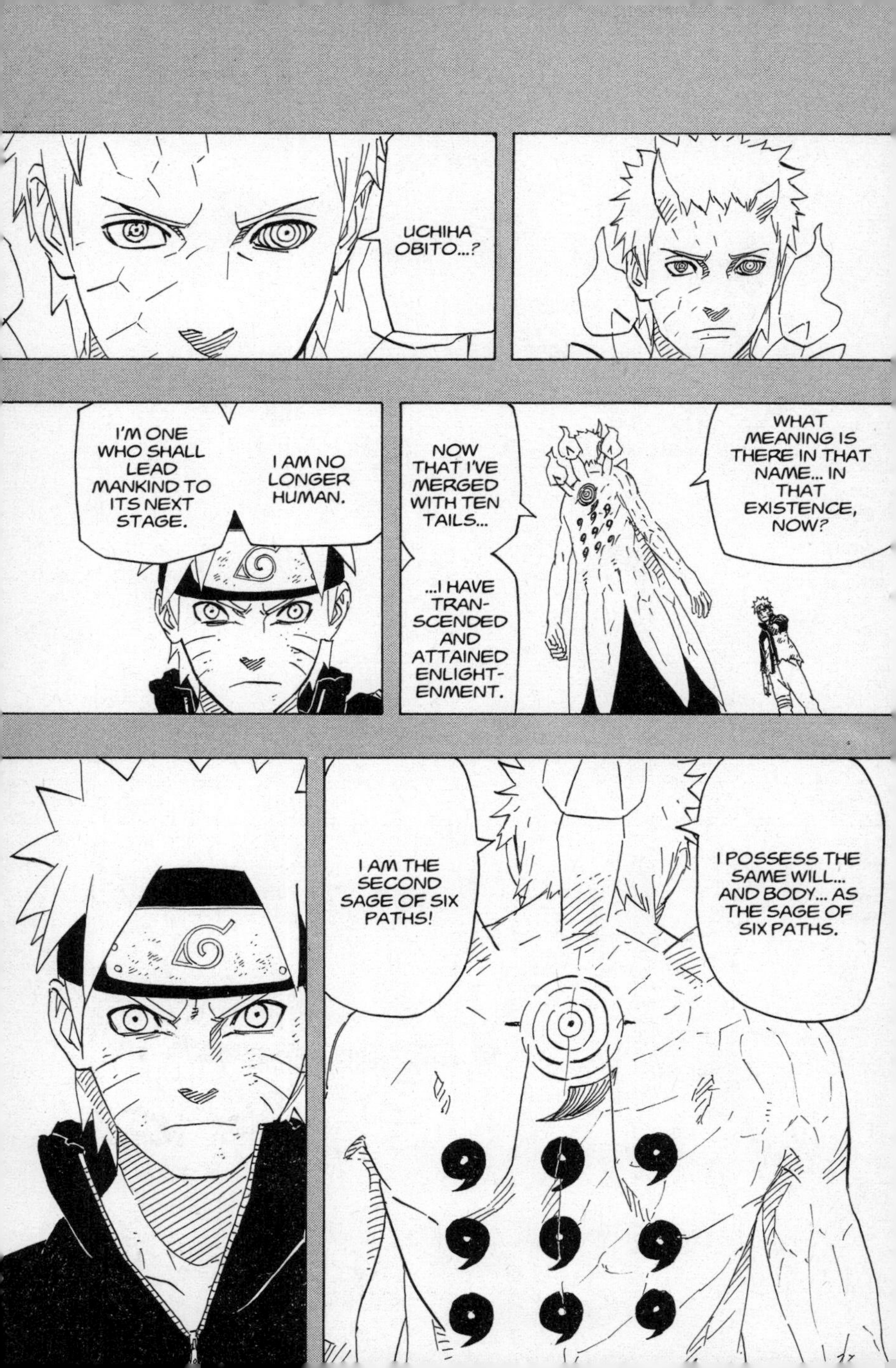
UCHIHA OBITO...?
WHAT MEANING IS THERE IN THAT NAME... IN THAT EXISTENCE, NOW?
NOW THAT I'VE MERGED WITH TEN TAILS...
...I HAVE TRANSCENDED AND ATTAINED ENLIGHTENMENT.
I AM NO LONGER HUMAN.
I'M ONE WHO SHALL LEAD MANKIND TO ITS NEXT STAGE.
I POSSESS THE SAME WILL... AND BODY... AS THE SAGE OF SIX PATHS.
I AM THE SECOND SAGE OF SIX PATHS!

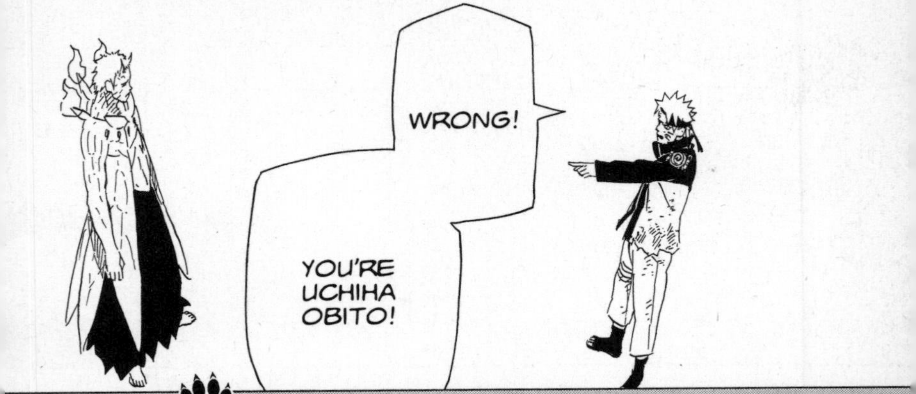
WRONG!
YOU'RE UCHIHA OBITO!

Number 653: I'm Always Watching

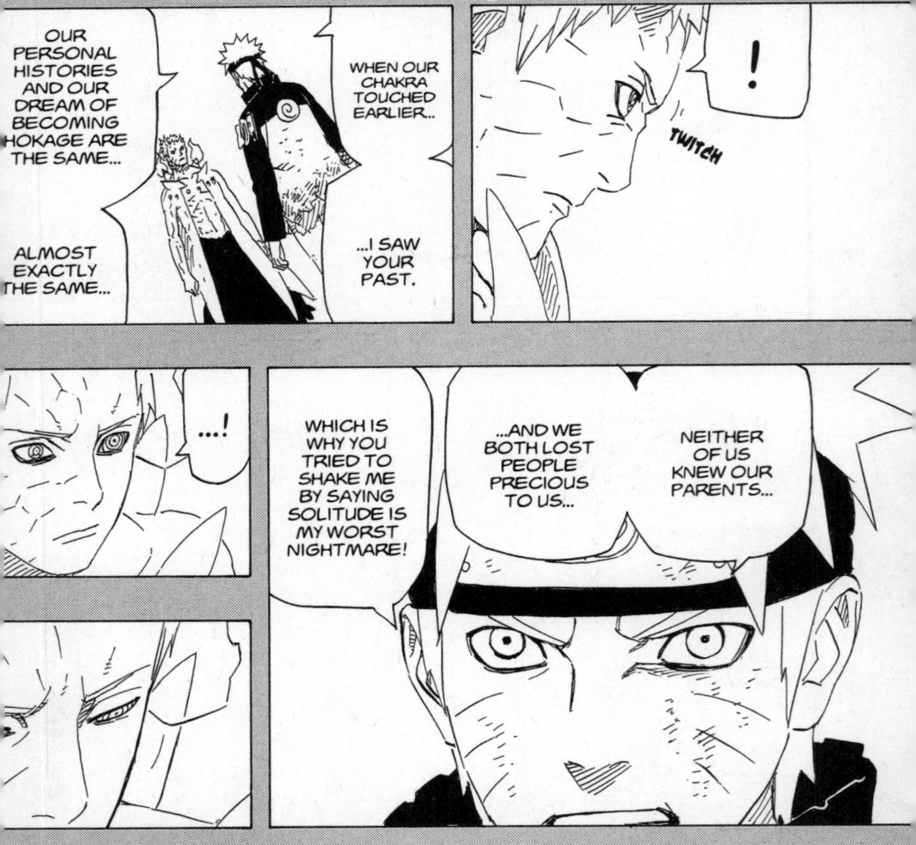
!
TWITCH
WHEN OUR CHAKRA TOUCHED EARLIER...
...I SAW YOUR PAST.
OUR PERSONAL HISTORIES AND OUR DREAM OF BECOMING HOKAGE ARE THE SAME...
ALMOST EXACTLY THE SAME...
NEITHER OF US KNEW OUR PARENTS...
...AND WE BOTH LOST PEOPLE PRECIOUS TO US...
WHICH IS WHY YOU TRIED TO SHAKE ME BY SAYING SOLITUDE IS MY WORST NIGHTMARE!
...!

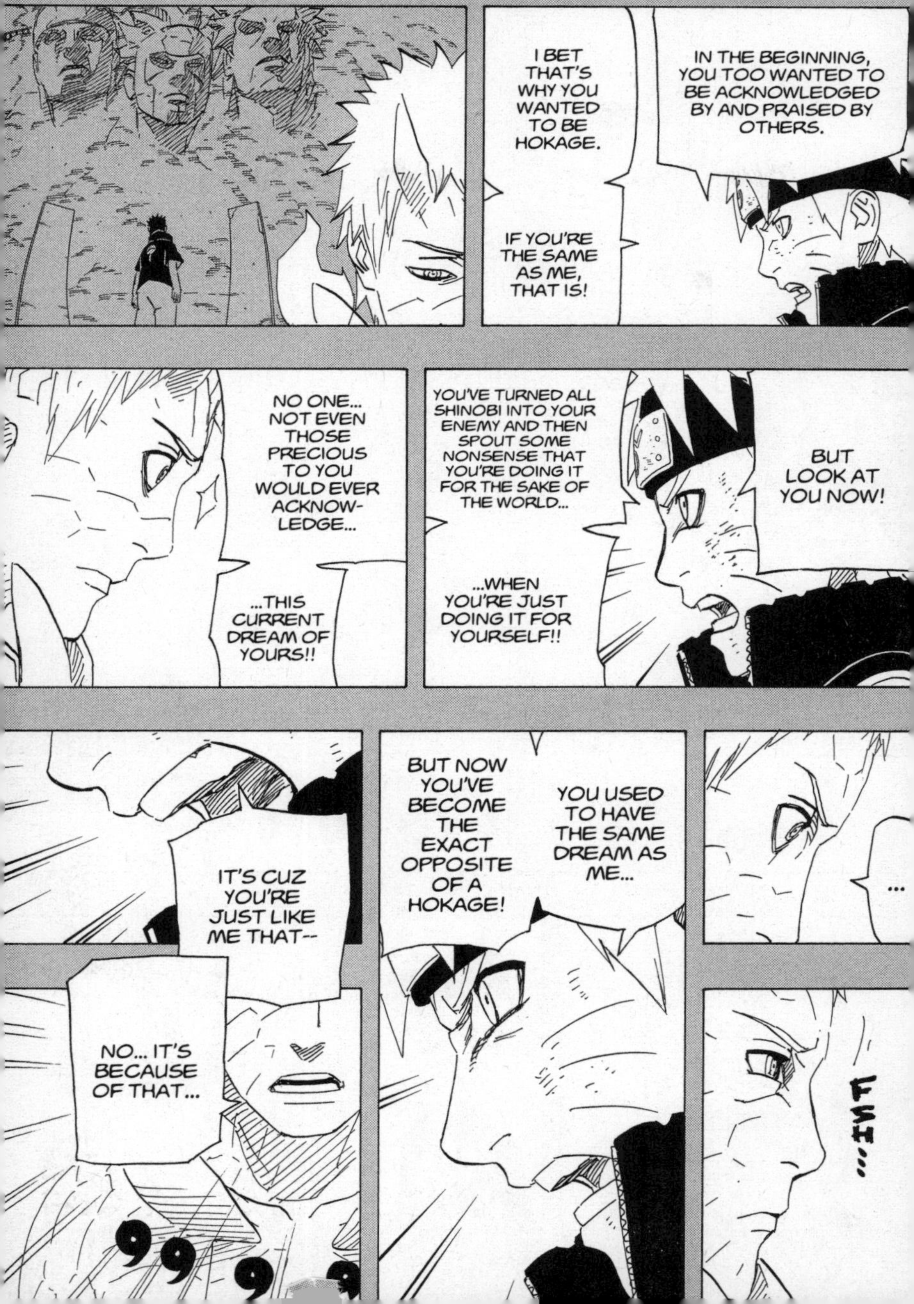
IN THE BEGINNING, YOU TOO WANTED TO BE ACKNOWLEDGED BY AND PRAISED BY OTHERS.
I BET THAT'S WHY YOU WANTED TO BE HOKAGE.
IF YOU'RE THE SAME AS ME, THAT IS!
BUT LOOK AT YOU NOW!
YOU'VE TURNED ALL SHINOBI INTO YOUR ENEMY AND THEN SPOUT SOME NONSENSE THAT YOU'RE DOING IT FOR THE SAKE OF THE WORLD...
...WHEN YOU'RE JUST DOING IT FOR YOURSELF!!
NO ONE... NOT EVEN THOSE PRECIOUS TO YOU WOULD EVER ACKNOW-LEDGE...
...THIS CURRENT DREAM OF YOURS!!
...
FSH...
YOU USED TO HAVE THE SAME DREAM AS ME...
BUT NOW YOU'VE BECOME THE EXACT OPPOSITE OF A HOKAGE!
IT'S CUZ YOU'RE JUST LIKE ME THAT--
NO... IT'S BECAUSE OF THAT...

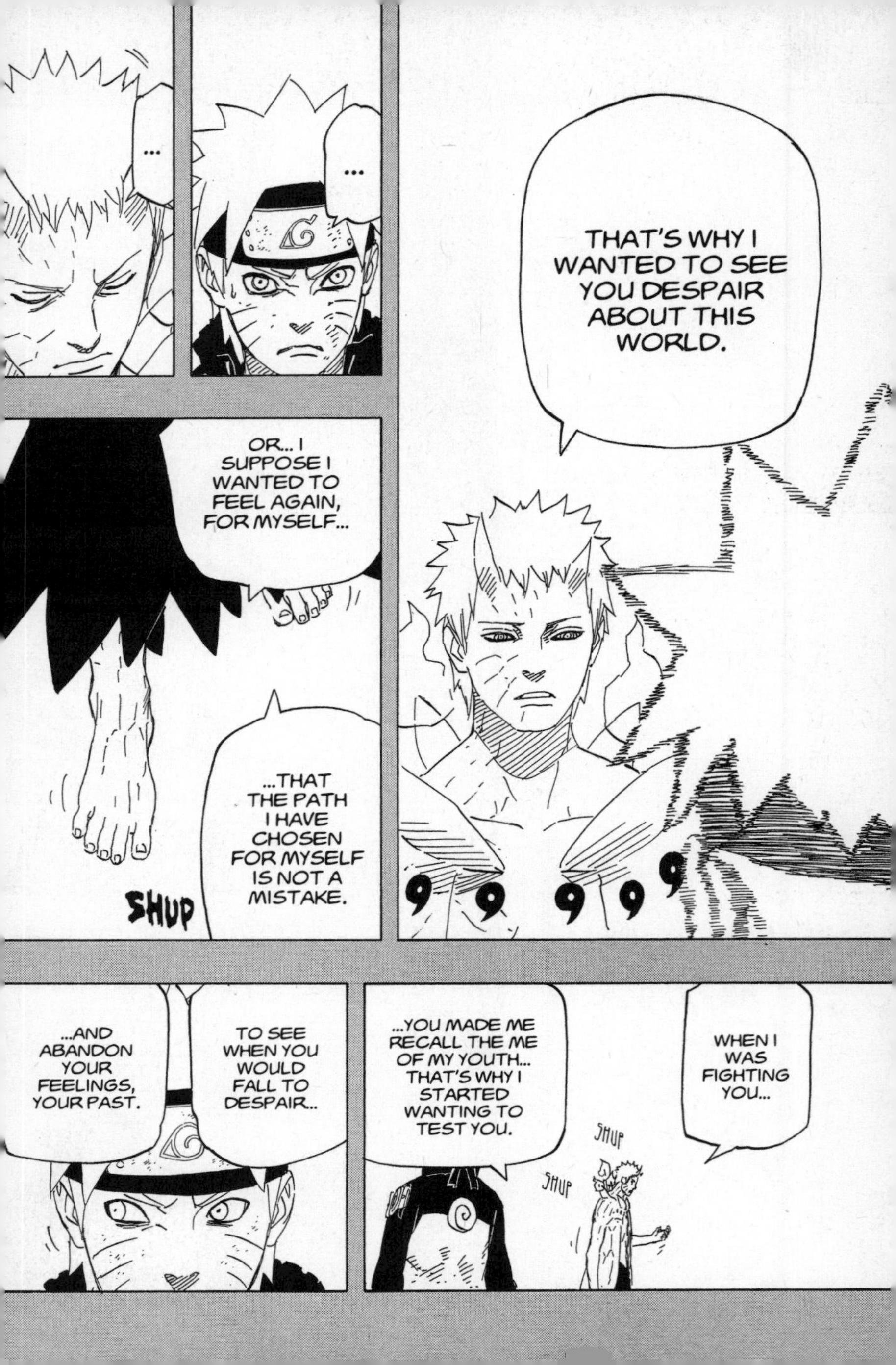
THAT'S WHY I WANTED TO SEE YOU DESPAIR ABOUT THIS WORLD.
...
...
OR... I SUPPOSE I WANTED TO FEEL AGAIN, FOR MYSELF...
...THAT THE PATH I HAVE CHOSEN FOR MYSELF IS NOT A MISTAKE.
SHUP
WHEN I WAS FIGHTING YOU...
...YOU MADE ME RECALL THE ME OF MY YOUTH... THAT'S WHY I STARTED WANTING TO TEST YOU.
SHUP
SHUP
TO SEE WHEN YOU WOULD FALL TO DESPAIR...
...AND ABANDON YOUR FEELINGS, YOUR PAST.

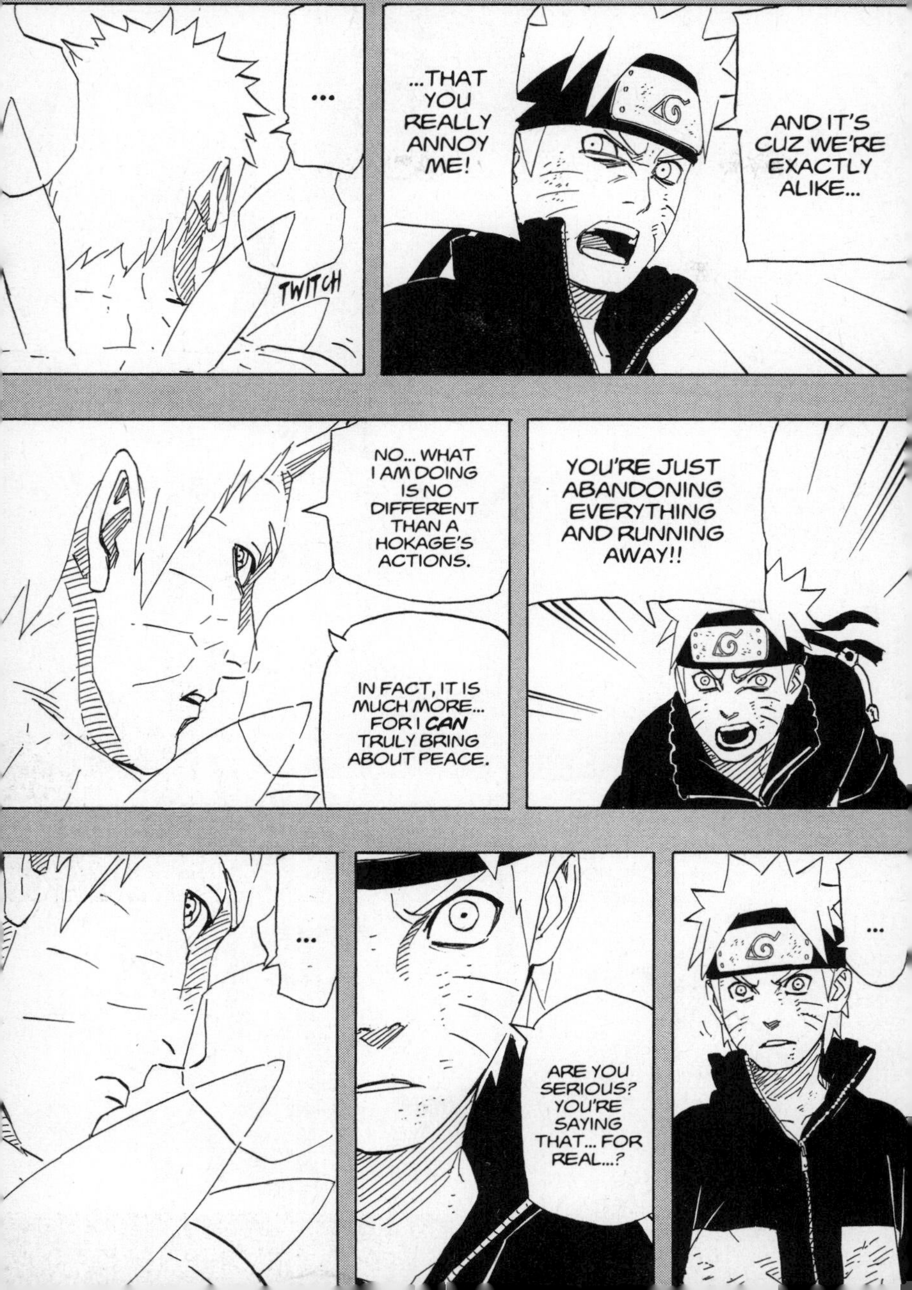
AND IT'S CUZ WE'RE EXACTLY ALIKE...
...THAT YOU REALLY ANNOY ME!
...
TWITCH
YOU'RE JUST ABANDONING EVERYTHING AND RUNNING AWAY!!
NO... WHAT I AM DOING IS NO DIFFERENT THAN A HOKAGE'S ACTIONS.
IN FACT, IT IS MUCH MORE... FOR I CAN TRULY BRING ABOUT PEACE.
...
ARE YOU SERIOUS? YOU'RE SAYING THAT... FOR REAL...?
...

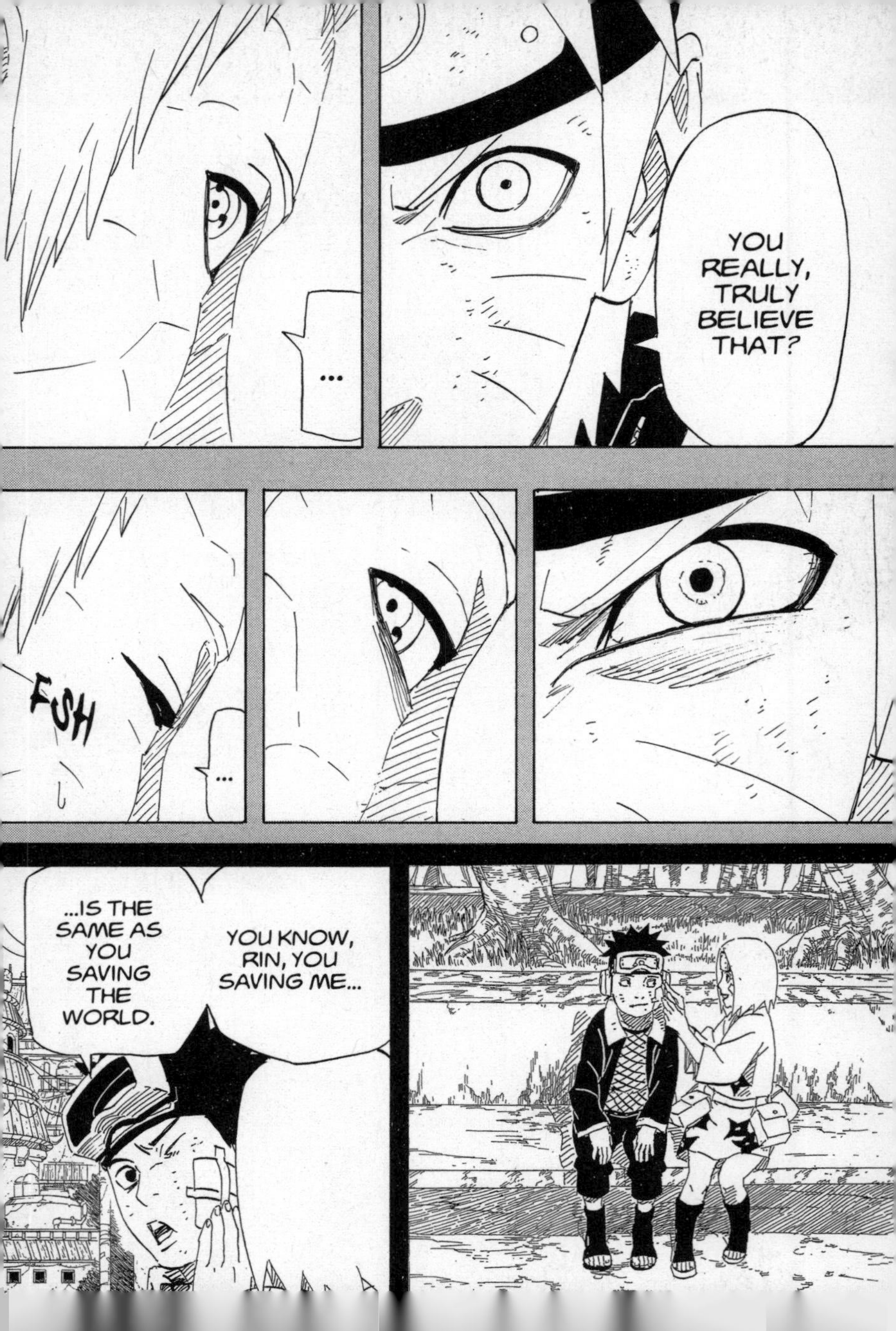
YOU REALLY, TRULY BELIEVE THAT?
...
FSH
...
YOU KNOW, RIN, YOU SAVING ME...
...IS THE SAME AS YOU SAVING THE WORLD.

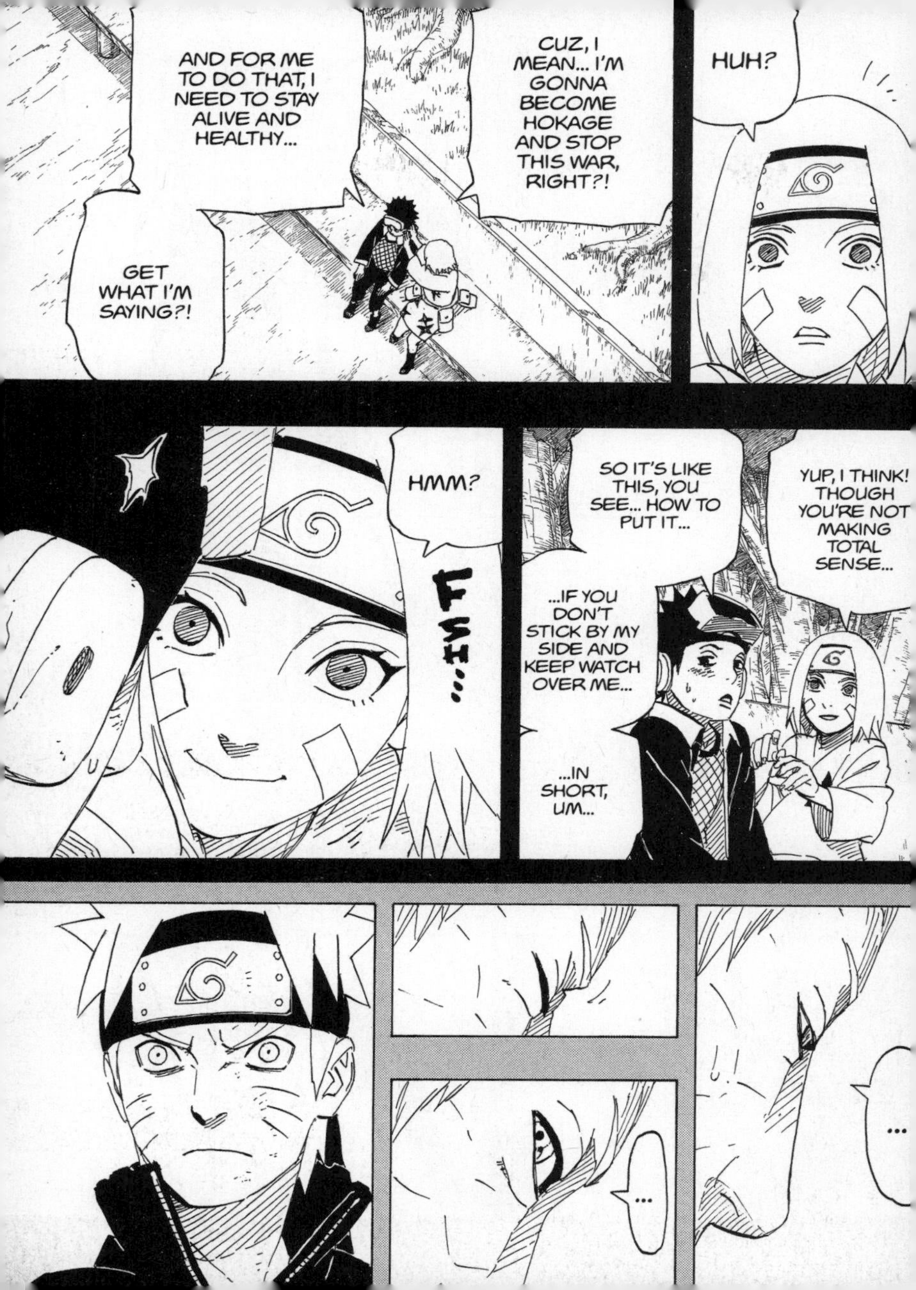

HUH?
CUZ, I MEAN... I'M GONNA BECOME HOKAGE AND STOP THIS WAR, RIGHT?!
AND FOR ME TO DO THAT, I NEED TO STAY ALIVE AND HEALTHY...
GET WHAT I'M SAYING?!
YUP, I THINK! THOUGH YOU'RE NOT MAKING TOTAL SENSE...
SO IT'S LIKE THIS, YOU SEE... HOW TO PUT IT...
...IF YOU DON'T STICK BY MY SIDE AND KEEP WATCH OVER ME...
...IN SHORT, UM...
HMM?
FSH...
...
...

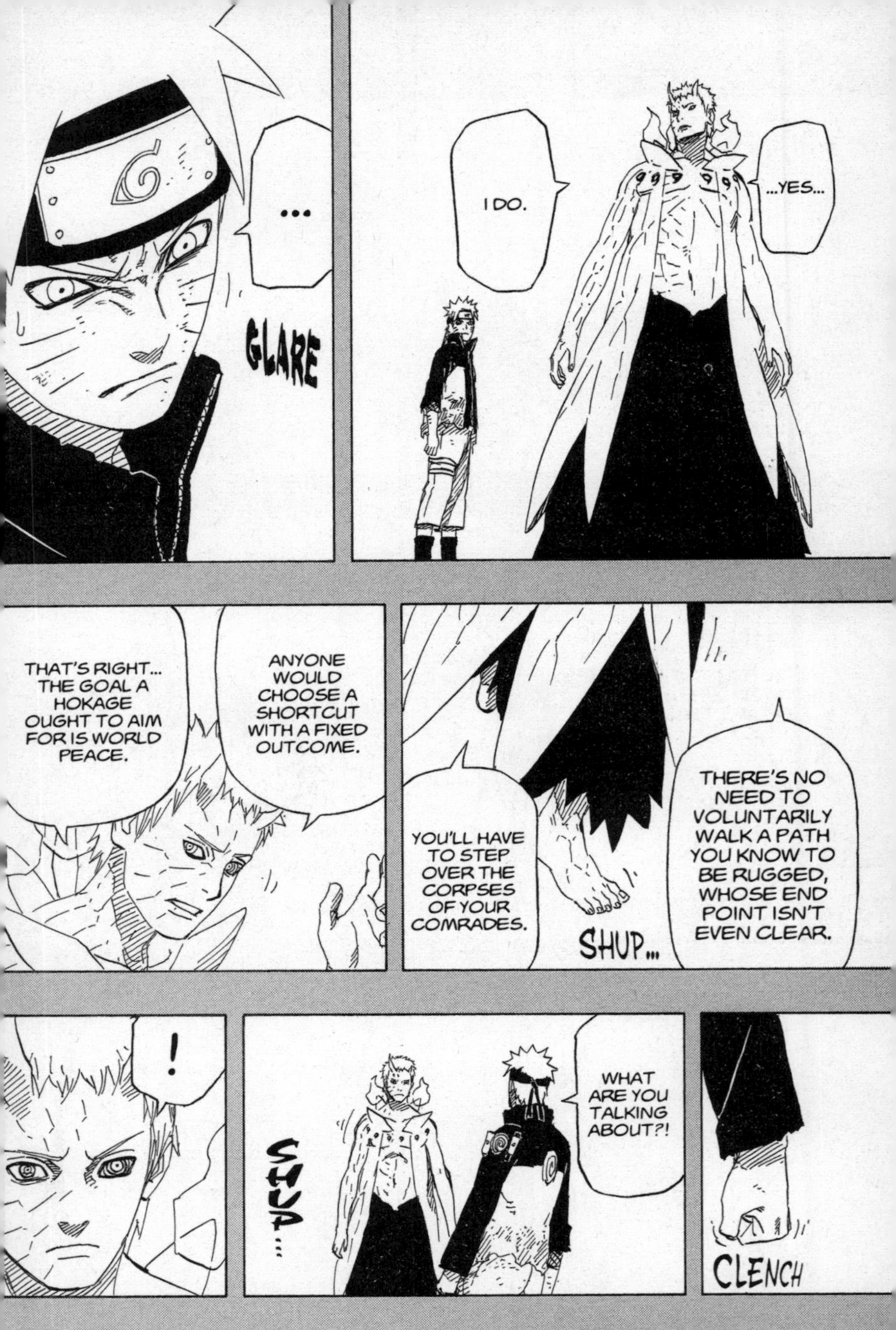
...YES...
I DO.
...
GLARE
THERE'S NO NEED TO VOLUNTARILY WALK A PATH YOU KNOW TO BE RUGGED, WHOSE END POINT ISN'T EVEN CLEAR.
YOU'LL HAVE TO STEP OVER THE CORPSES OF YOUR COMRADES.
SHUP...
ANYONE WOULD CHOOSE A SHORTCUT WITH A FIXED OUTCOME.
THAT'S RIGHT... THE GOAL A HOKAGE OUGHT TO AIM FOR IS WORLD PEACE.
CLENCH
WHAT ARE YOU TALKING ABOUT?!
SHUP...
!

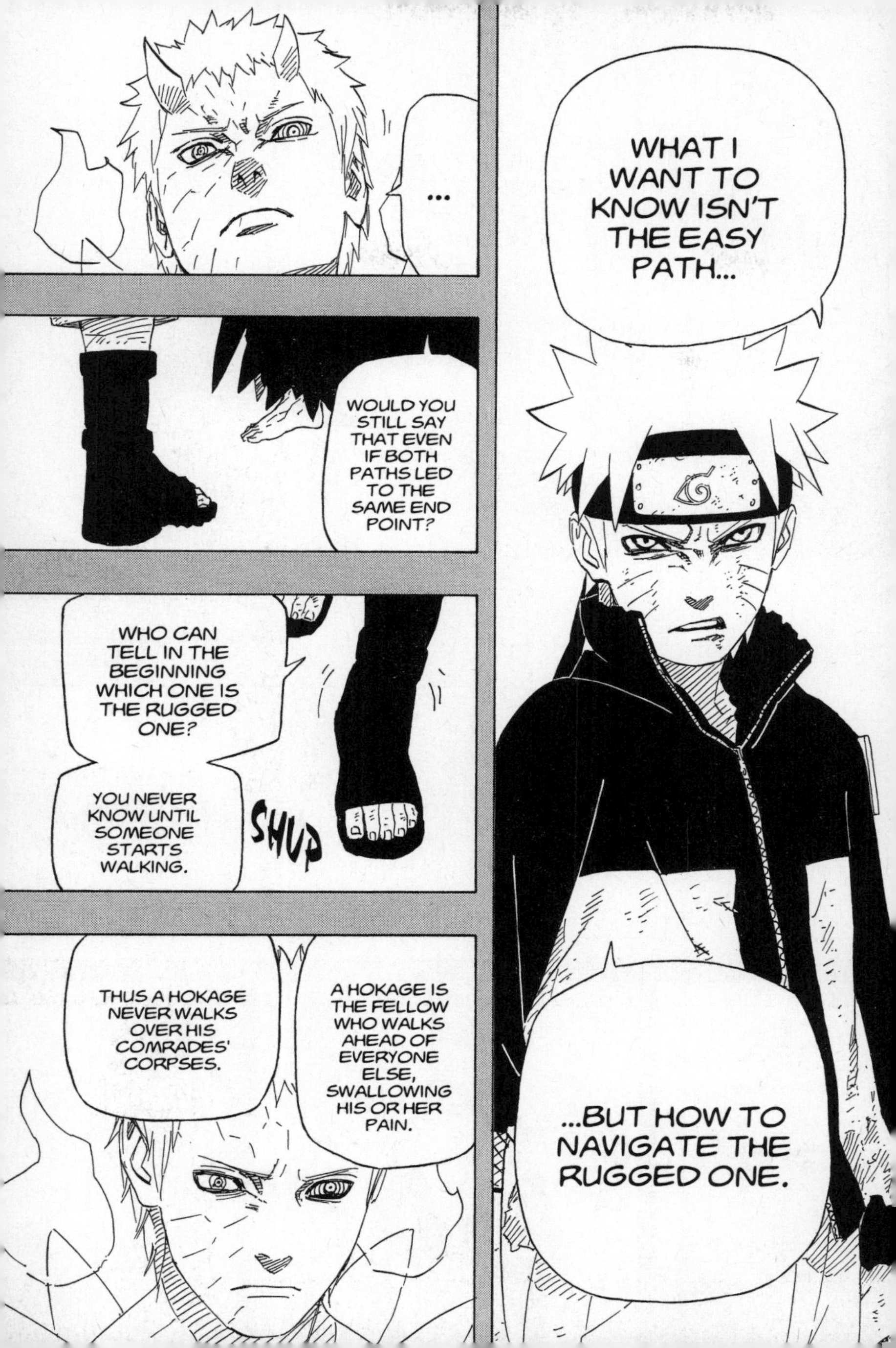

WHAT I WANT TO KNOW ISN'T THE EASY PATH...
...BUT HOW TO NAVIGATE THE RUGGED ONE.
...
WOULD YOU STILL SAY THAT EVEN IF BOTH PATHS LED TO THE SAME END POINT?
WHO CAN TELL IN THE BEGINNING WHICH ONE IS THE RUGGED ONE?
YOU NEVER KNOW UNTIL SOMEONE STARTS WALKING.
SHUP
A HOKAGE IS THE FELLOW WHO WALKS AHEAD OF EVERYONE ELSE, SWALLOWING HIS OR HER PAIN.
THUS A HOKAGE NEVER WALKS OVER HIS COMRADES' CORPSES.

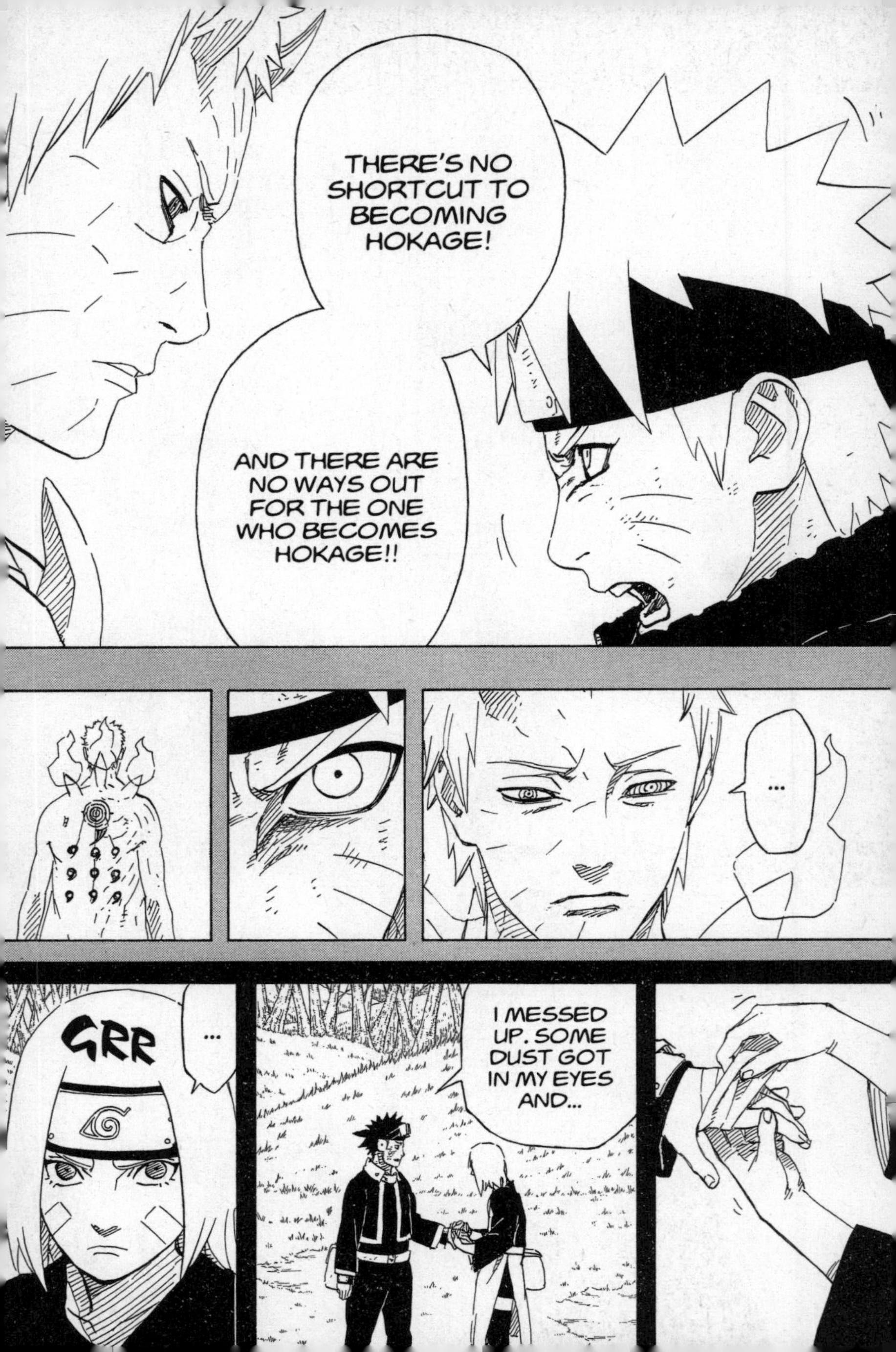

THERE'S NO SHORTCUT TO BECOMING HOKAGE!
AND THERE ARE NO WAYS OUT FOR THE ONE WHO BECOMES HOKAGE!!
...
I MESSED UP. SOME DUST GOT IN MY EYES AND...
GRR
...

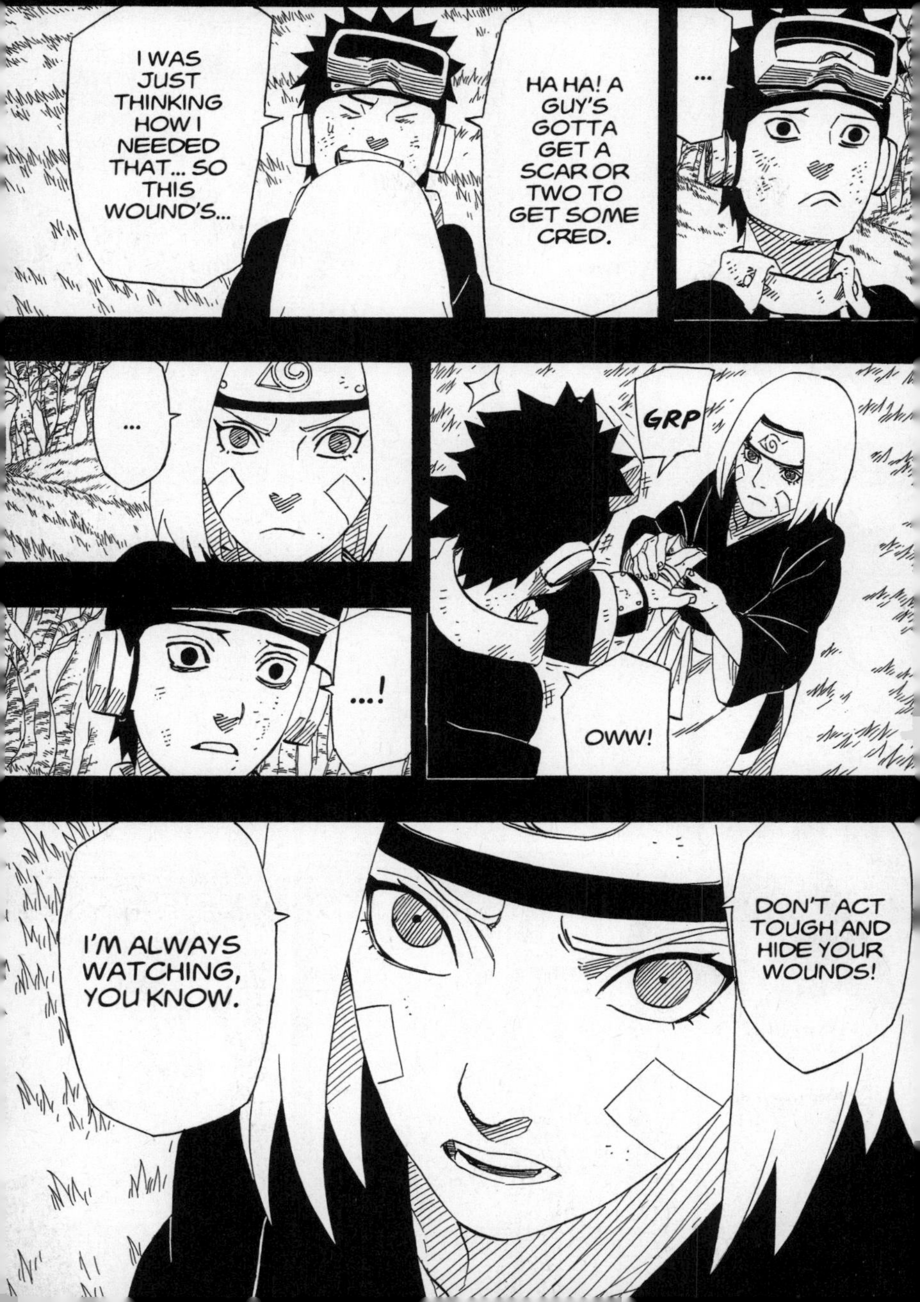
...
HA HA! A GUY'S GOTTA GET A SCAR OR TWO TO GET SOME CRED.
I WAS JUST THINKING HOW I NEEDED THAT... SO THIS WOUND'S...
GRP
OWW!
...
...!
DON'T ACT TOUGH AND HIDE YOUR WOUNDS!
I'M ALWAYS WATCHING, YOU KNOW.

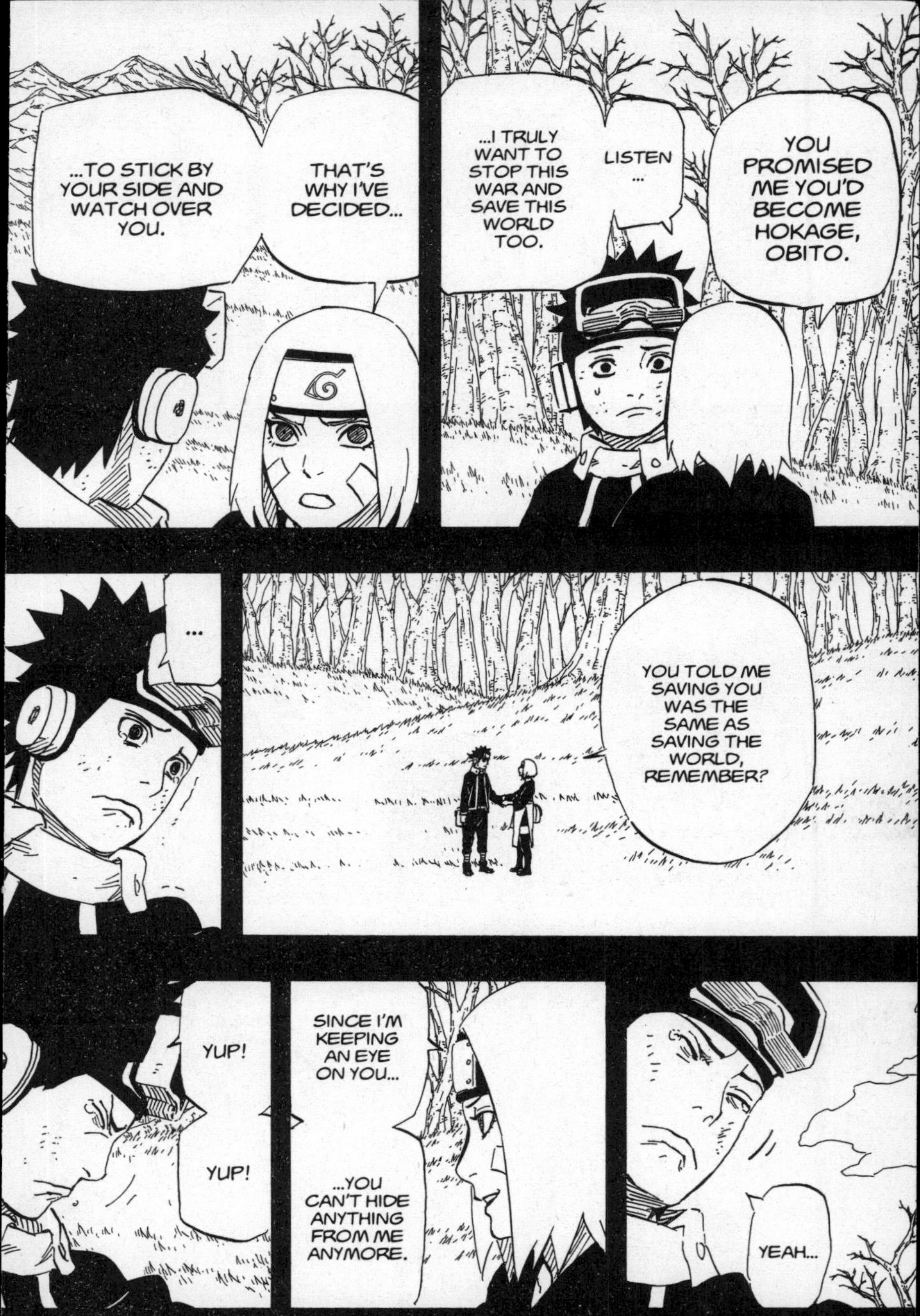
YOU PROMISED ME YOU'D BECOME HOKAGE, OBITO.
LISTEN...
...I TRULY WANT TO STOP THIS WAR AND SAVE THIS WORLD TOO.
THAT'S WHY I'VE DECIDED...
...TO STICK BY YOUR SIDE AND WATCH OVER YOU.
YOU TOLD ME SAVING YOU WAS THE SAME AS SAVING THE WORLD, REMEMBER?
...
YEAH...
SINCE I'M KEEPING AN EYE ON YOU...
...YOU CAN'T HIDE ANYTHING FROM ME ANYMORE.
YUP!
YUP!

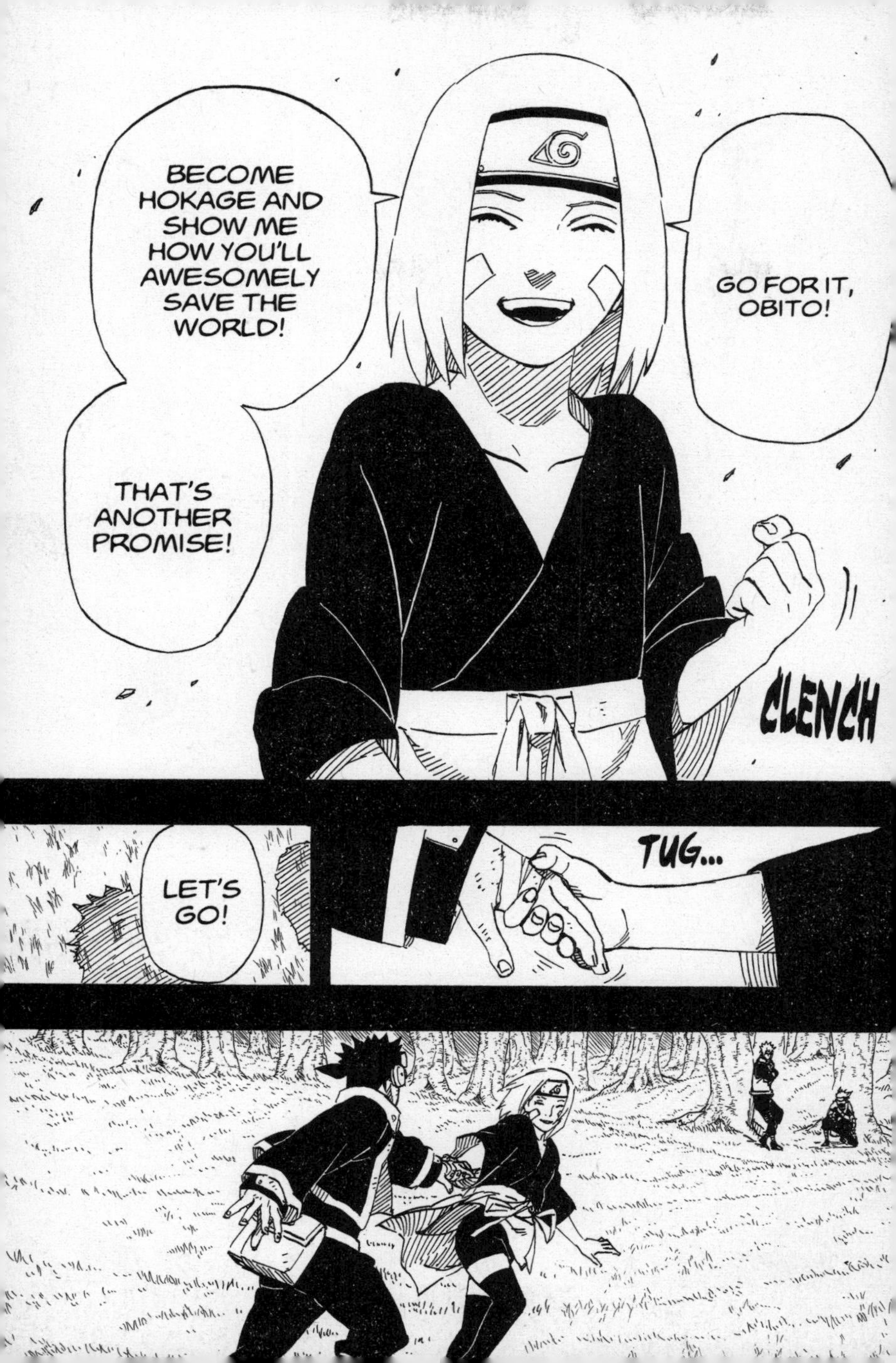
GO FOR IT, OBITO!
BECOME HOKAGE AND SHOW ME HOW YOU'LL AWESOMELY SAVE THE WORLD!
THAT'S ANOTHER PROMISE!
CLENCH
TUG...
LET'S GO!

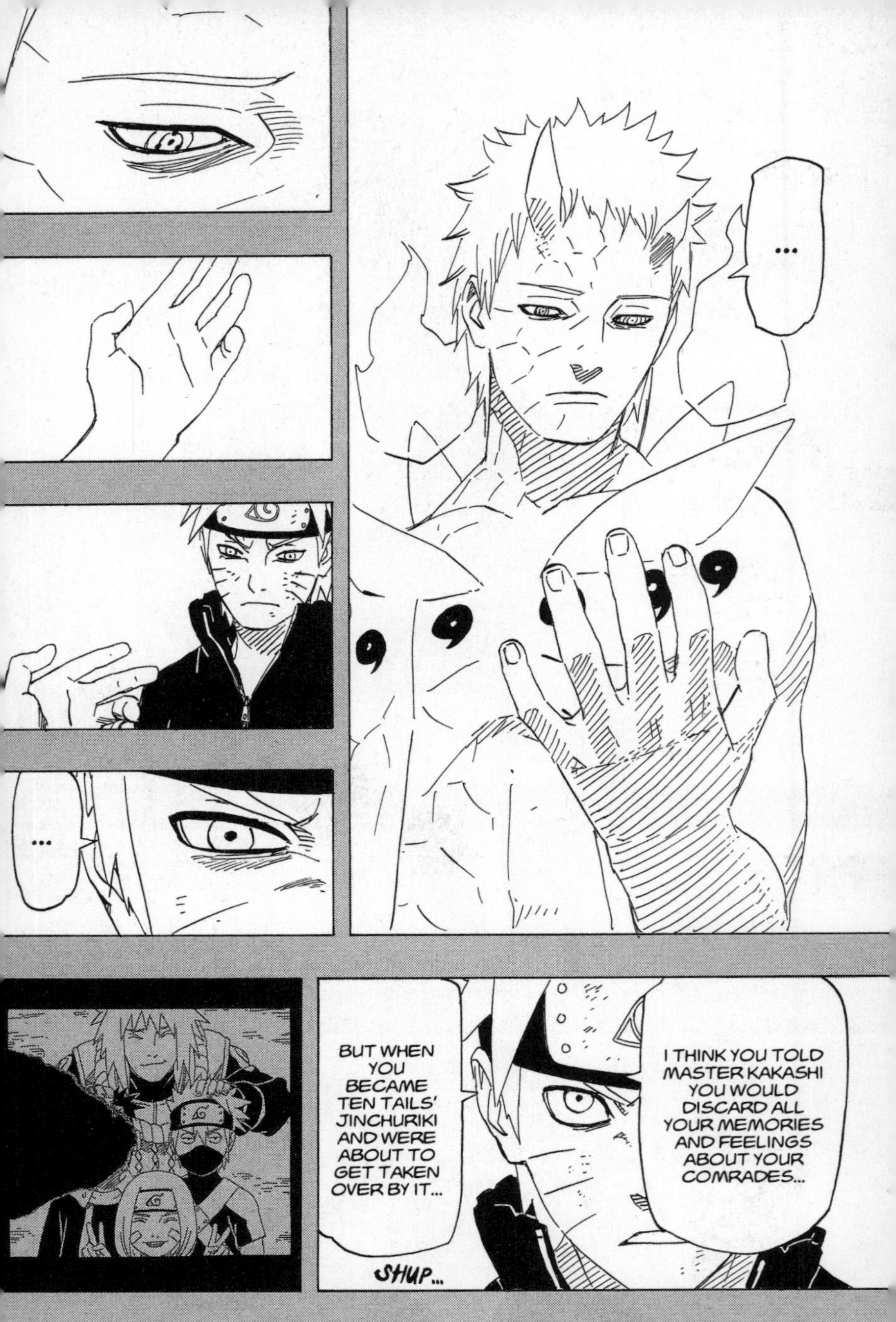
...
...
I THINK YOU TOLD MASTER KAKASHI YOU WOULD DISCARD ALL YOUR MEMORIES AND FEELINGS ABOUT YOUR COMRADES...
BUT WHEN YOU BECAME TEN TAILS' JINCHURIKI AND WERE ABOUT TO GET TAKEN OVER BY IT...
SHUP...

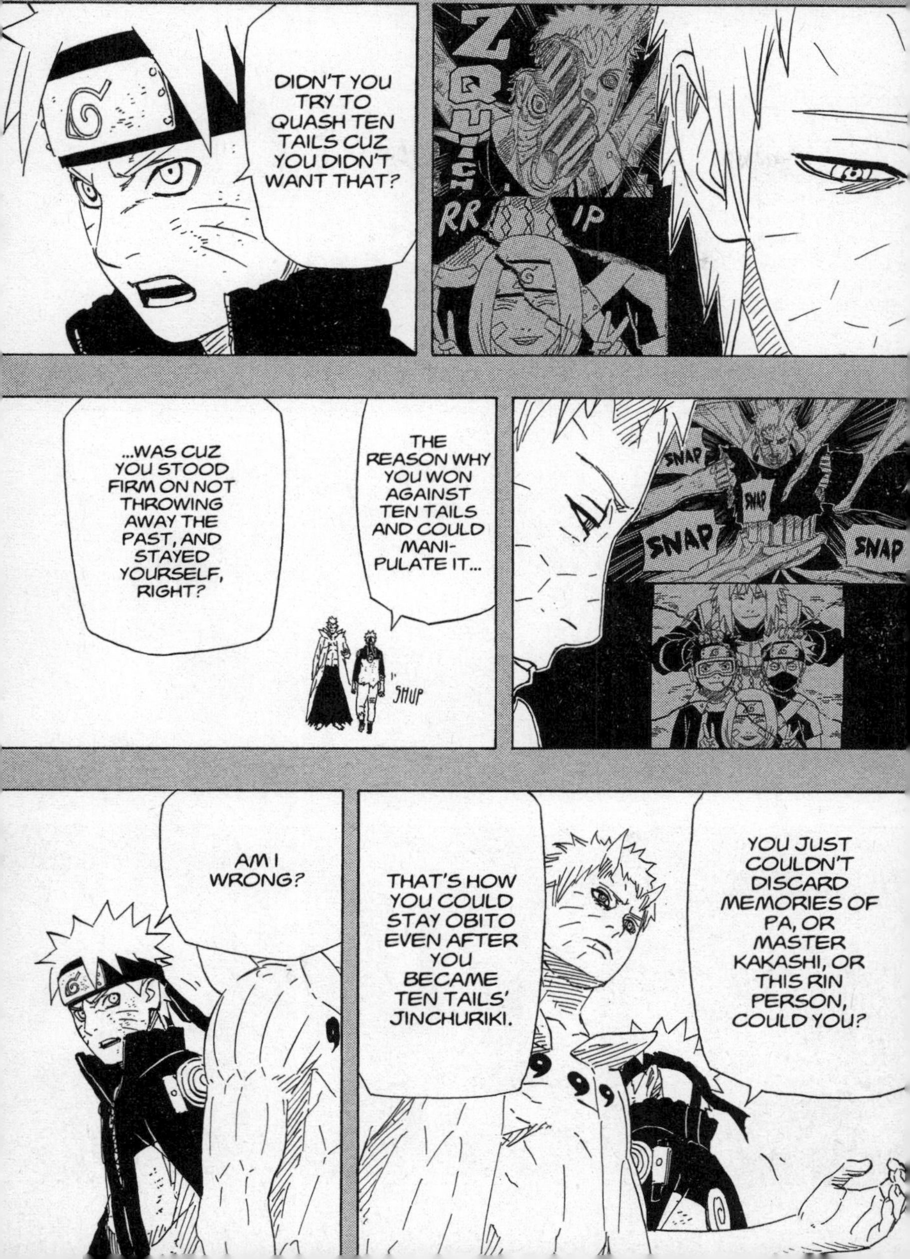
ZQUISH
RRIP
DIDN'T YOU TRY TO QUASH TEN TAILS CUZ YOU DIDN'T WANT THAT?
SNAP
SNAP
SNAP
SNAP
THE REASON WHY YOU WON AGAINST TEN TAILS AND COULD MANI-PULATE IT...
...WAS CUZ YOU STOOD FIRM ON NOT THROWING AWAY THE PAST, AND STAYED YOURSELF, RIGHT?
SHUP
YOU JUST COULDN'T DISCARD MEMORIES OF PA, OR MASTER KAKASHI, OR THIS RIN PERSON, COULD YOU?
THAT'S HOW YOU COULD STAY OBITO EVEN AFTER YOU BECAME TEN TAILS' JINCHURIKI.
AM I WRONG?

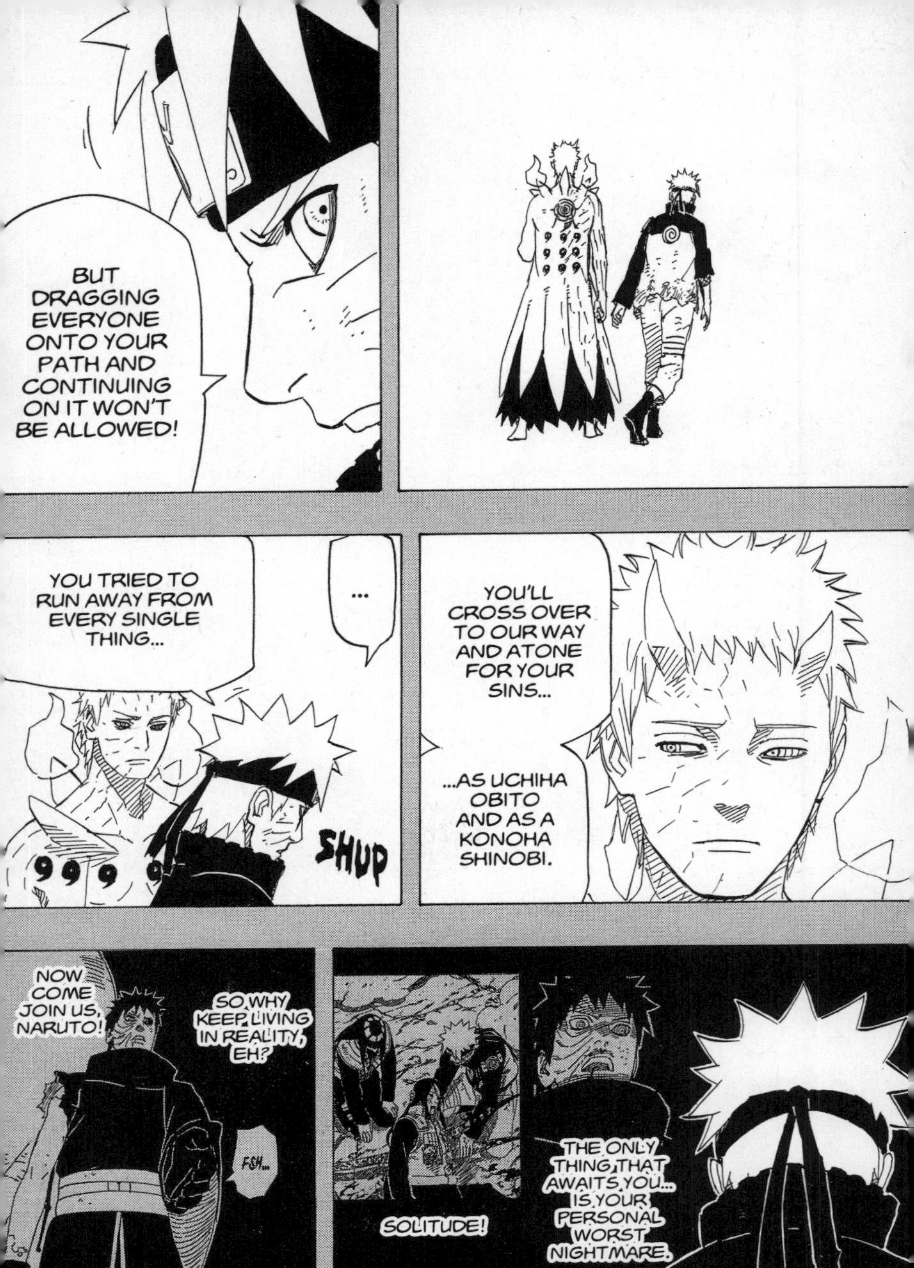
BUT DRAGGING EVERYONE ONTO YOUR PATH AND CONTINUING ON IT WON'T BE ALLOWED!
YOU'LL CROSS OVER TO OUR WAY AND ATONE FOR YOUR SINS...
...AS UCHIHA OBITO AND AS A KONOHA SHINOBI.
...
YOU TRIED TO RUN AWAY FROM EVERY SINGLE THING...
SHUP
THE ONLY THING THAT AWAITS YOU... IS YOUR PERSONAL WORST NIGHTMARE.
SOLITUDE!
SO WHY KEEP LIVING IN REALITY, EH?
NOW COME JOIN US, NARUTO!
FSH...

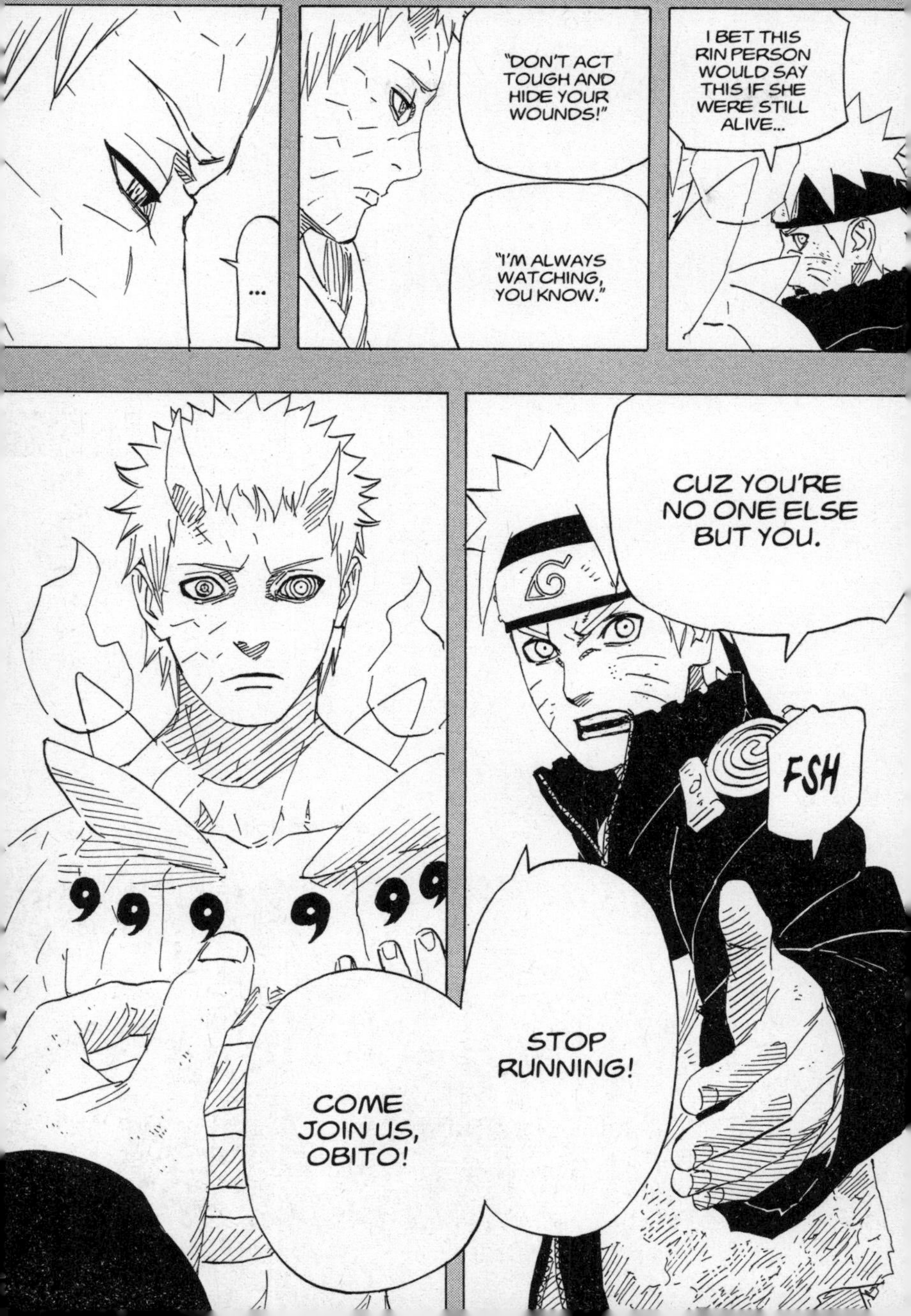
I BET THIS RIN PERSON WOULD SAY THIS IF SHE WERE STILL ALIVE...
"DON'T ACT TOUGH AND HIDE YOUR WOUNDS!"
"I'M ALWAYS WATCHING, YOU KNOW."
...
CUZ YOU'RE NO ONE ELSE BUT YOU.
FSH
STOP RUNNING!
COME JOIN US, OBITO!

Number 654: I'm Uchiha Obito

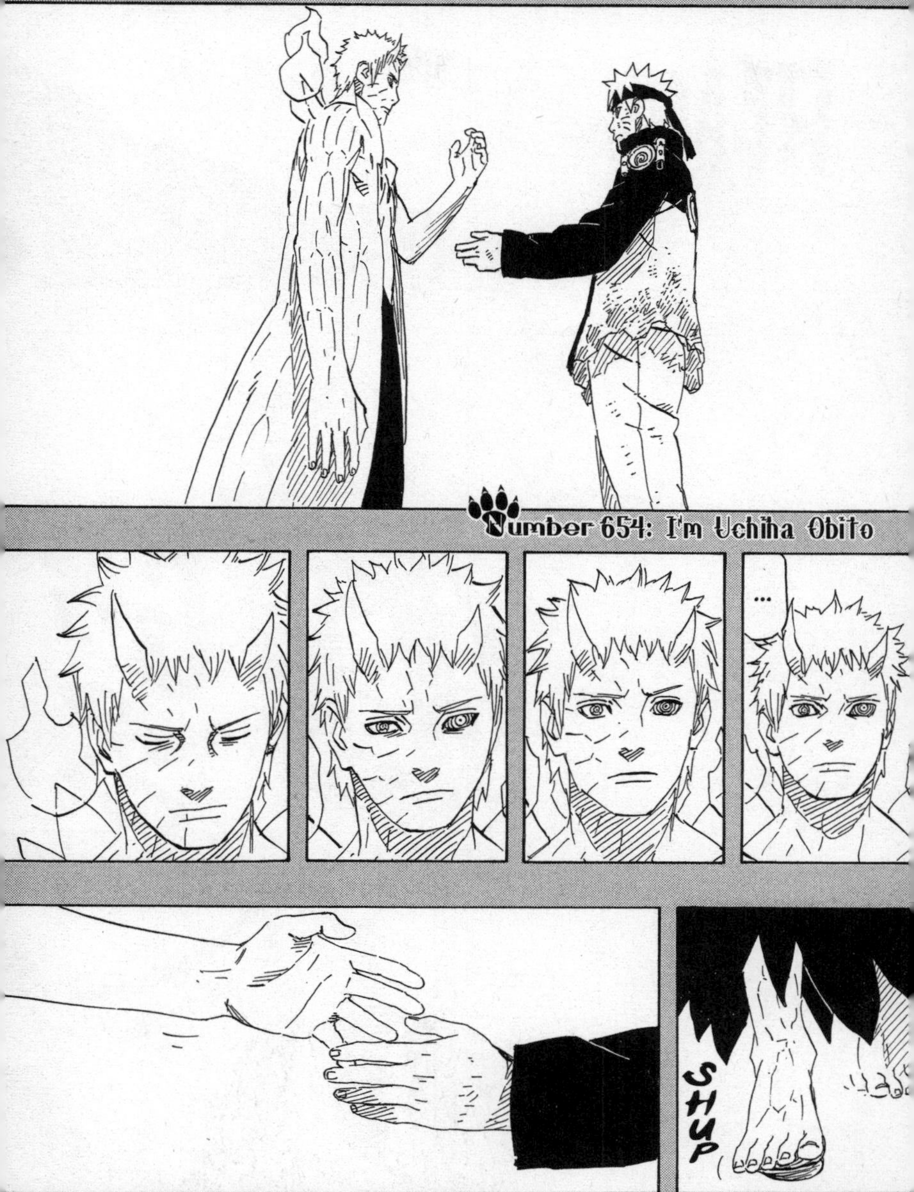
...
SHUP

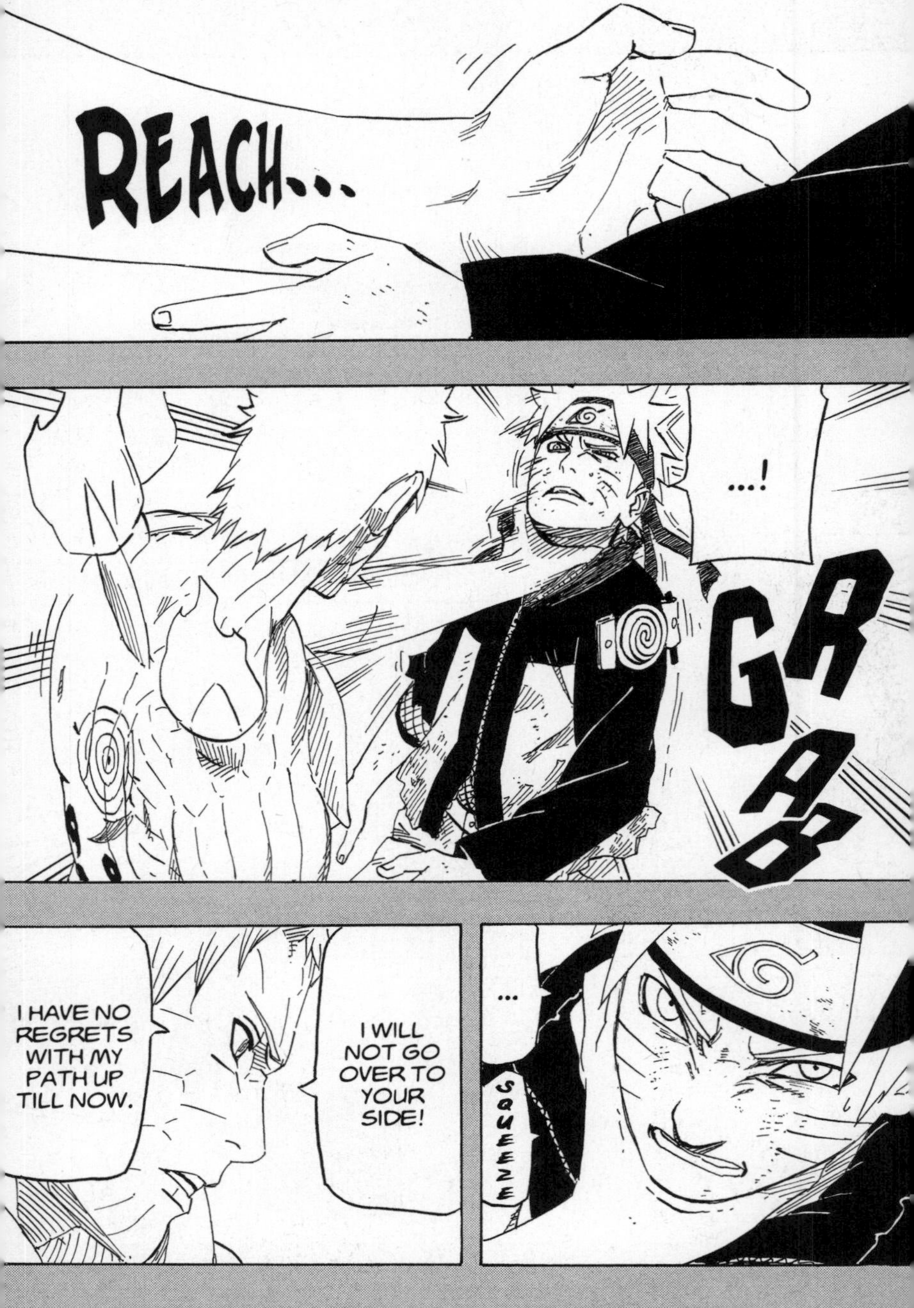
REACH...
...!
GRAB
...
SQUEEZE
I WILL NOT GO OVER TO YOUR SIDE!
I HAVE NO REGRETS WITH MY PATH UP TILL NOW.

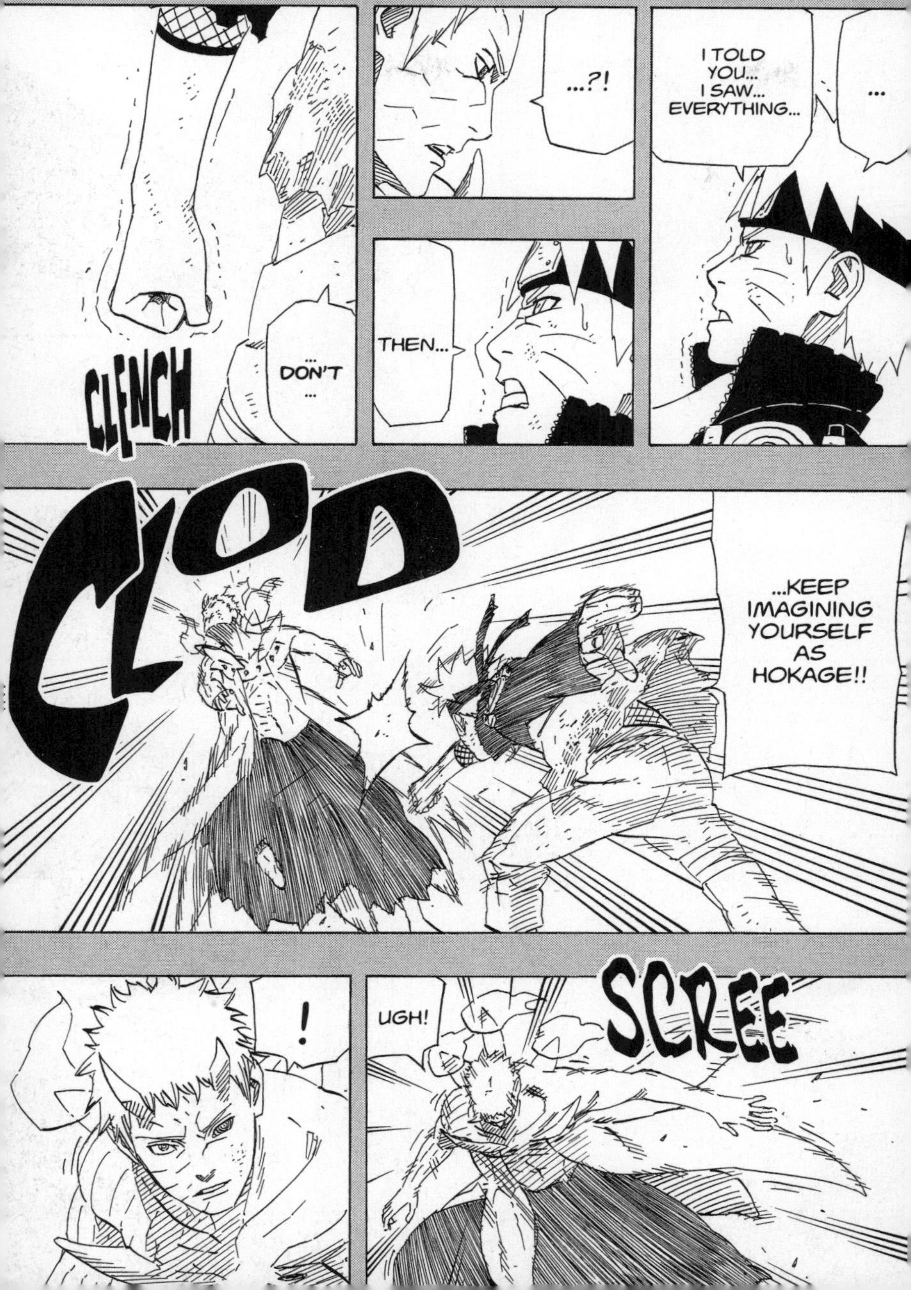
...
I TOLD YOU... I SAW... EVERYTHING...
...?!
THEN...
... DON'T ...
CLENCH
...KEEP IMAGINING YOURSELF AS HOKAGE!!
CLOD
SCREE
UGH!
!

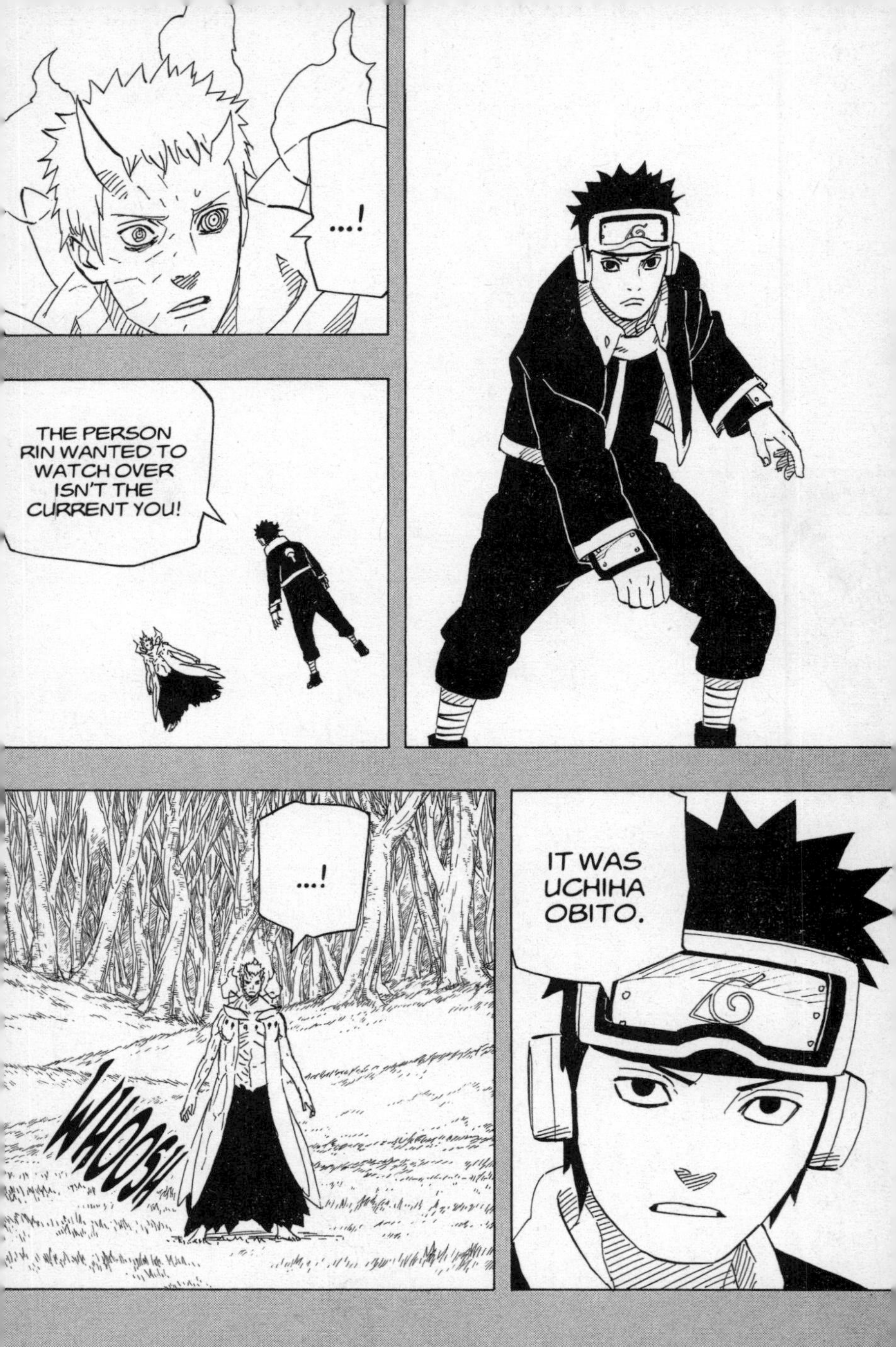
...!
THE PERSON RIN WANTED TO WATCH OVER ISN'T THE CURRENT YOU!
IT WAS UCHIHA OBITO.
...!
WHOOSH

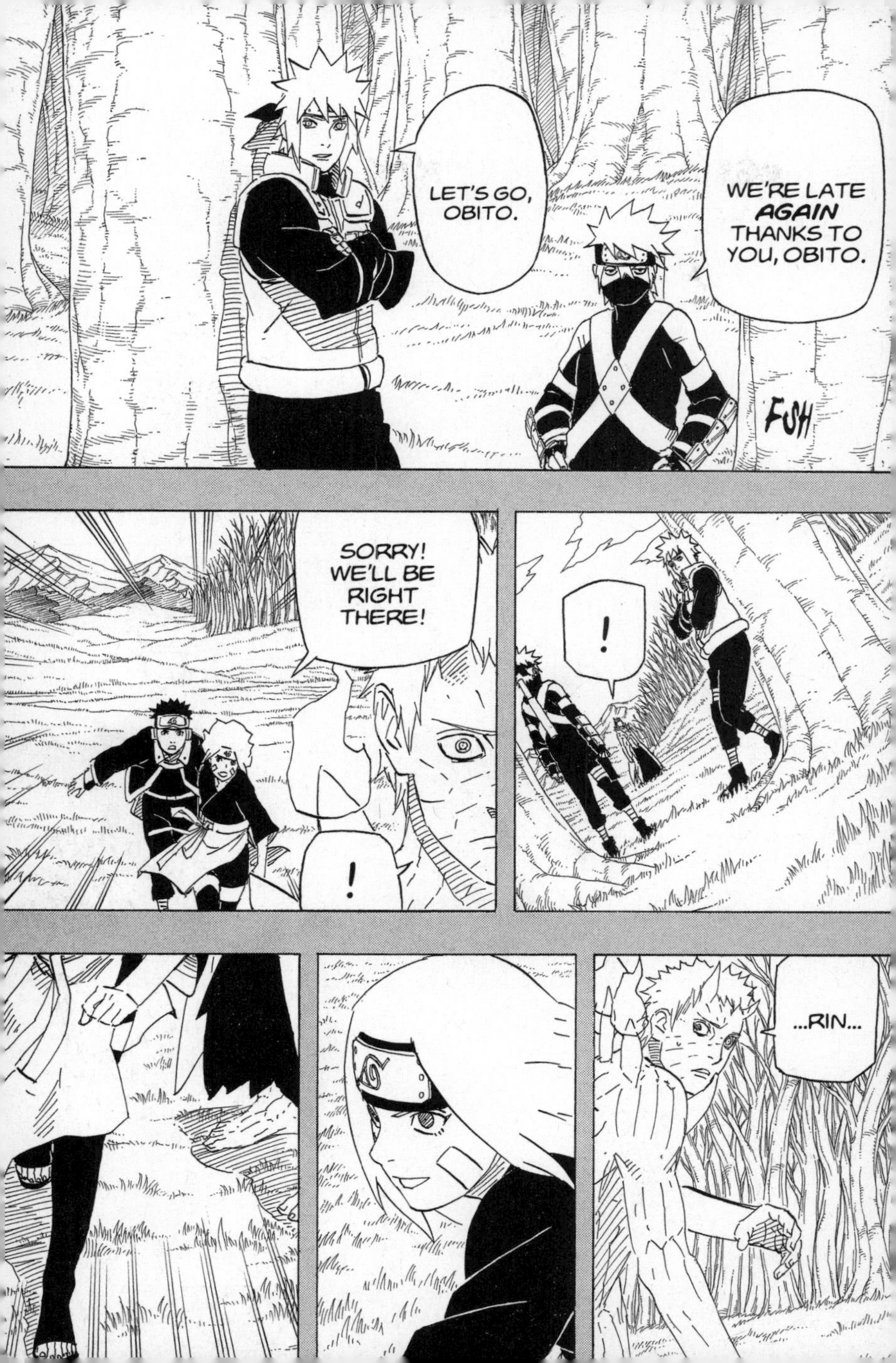
WE'RE LATE AGAIN THANKS TO YOU, OBITO.
LET'S GO, OBITO.
FSH
!
SORRY! WE'LL BE RIGHT THERE!
!
...RIN...

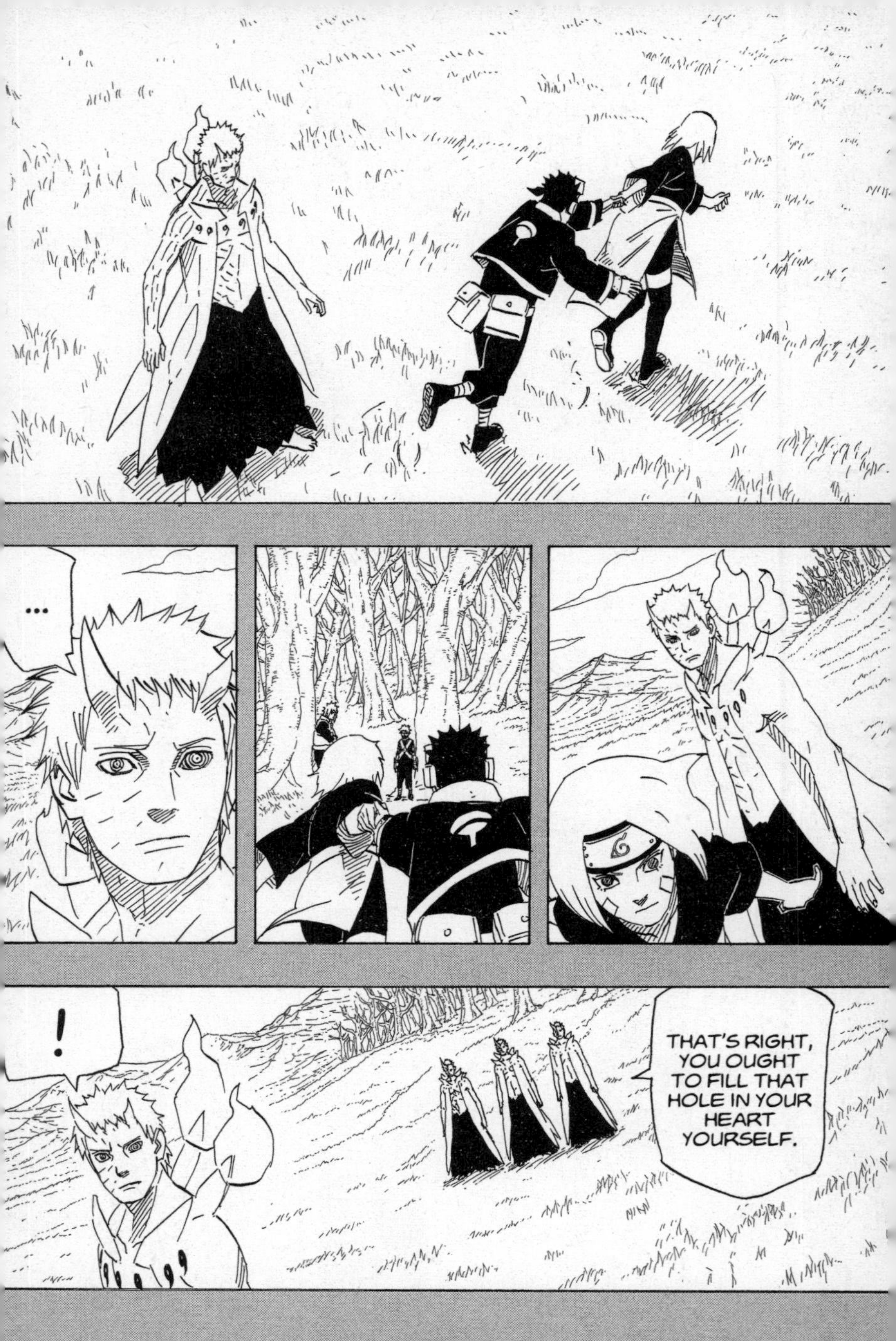
...
THAT'S RIGHT, YOU OUGHT TO FILL THAT HOLE IN YOUR HEART YOURSELF.
!

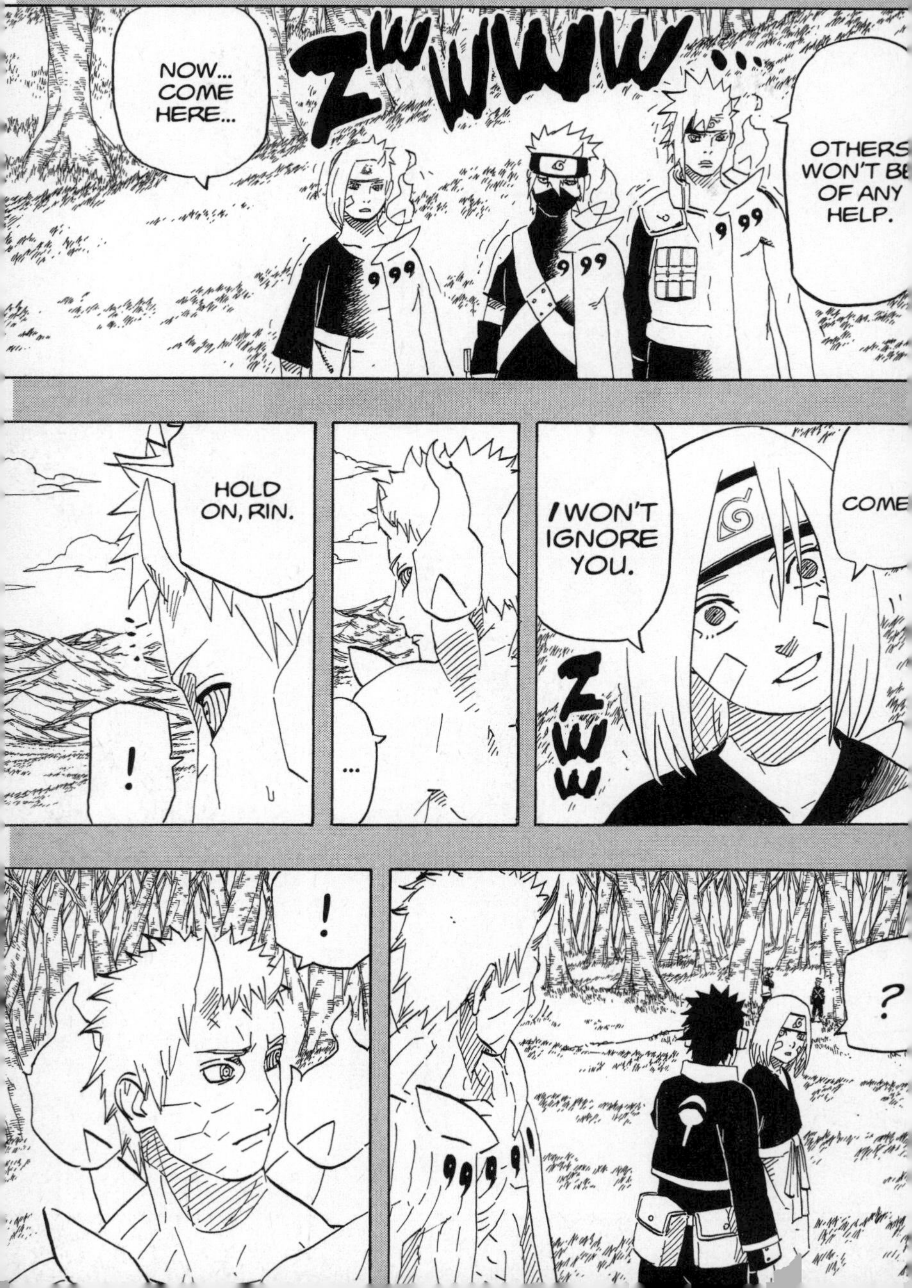
OTHERS WON'T BE OF ANY HELP.
ZWWWW...
NOW... COME HERE...
COME
I WON'T IGNORE YOU.
ZWW
...
HOLD ON, RIN.
!
?
!

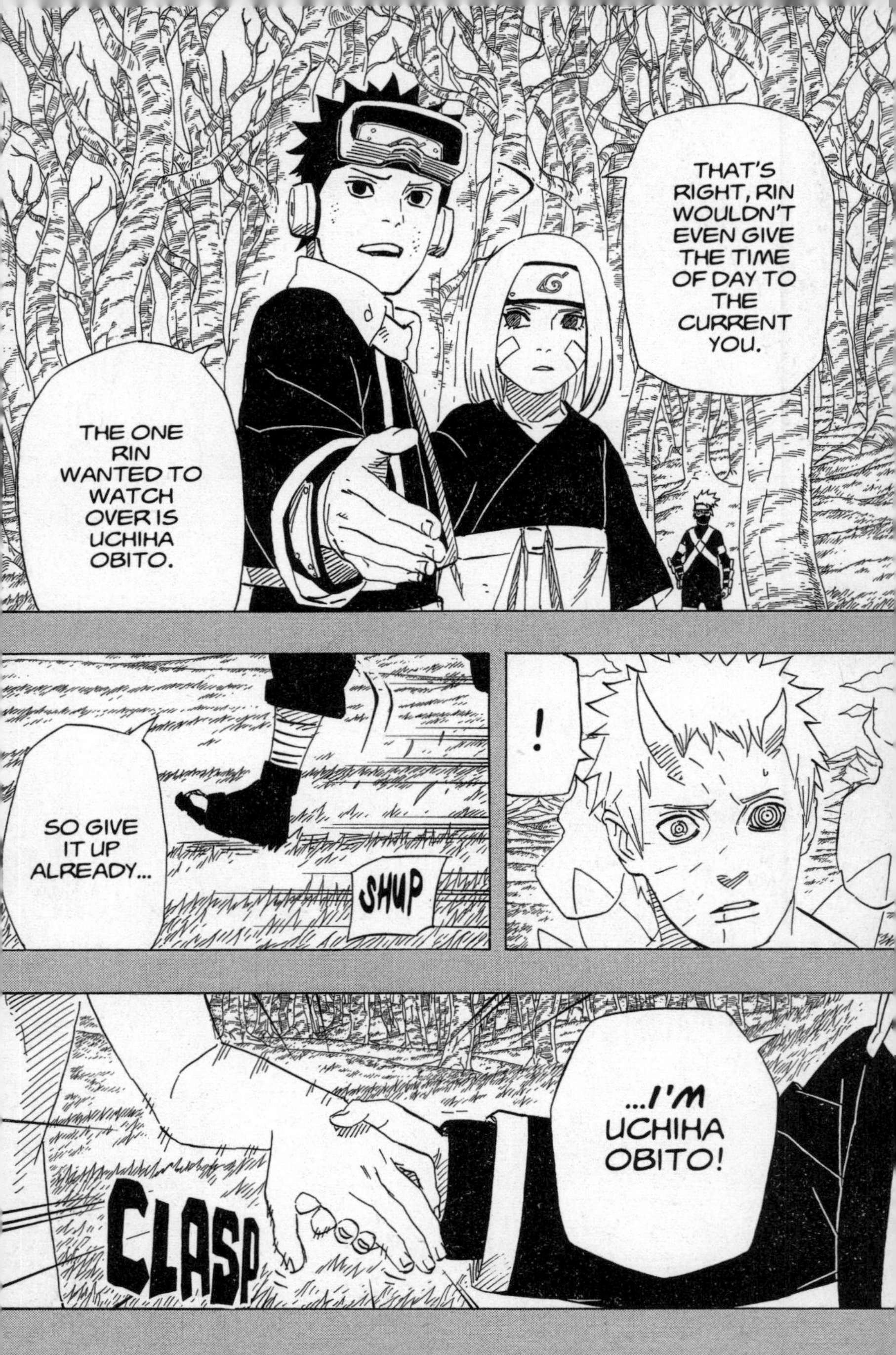
THAT'S RIGHT, RIN WOULDN'T EVEN GIVE THE TIME OF DAY TO THE CURRENT YOU.
THE ONE RIN WANTED TO WATCH OVER IS UCHIHA OBITO.
!
SO GIVE IT UP ALREADY...
SHUP
...I'M UCHIHA OBITO!
CLASP

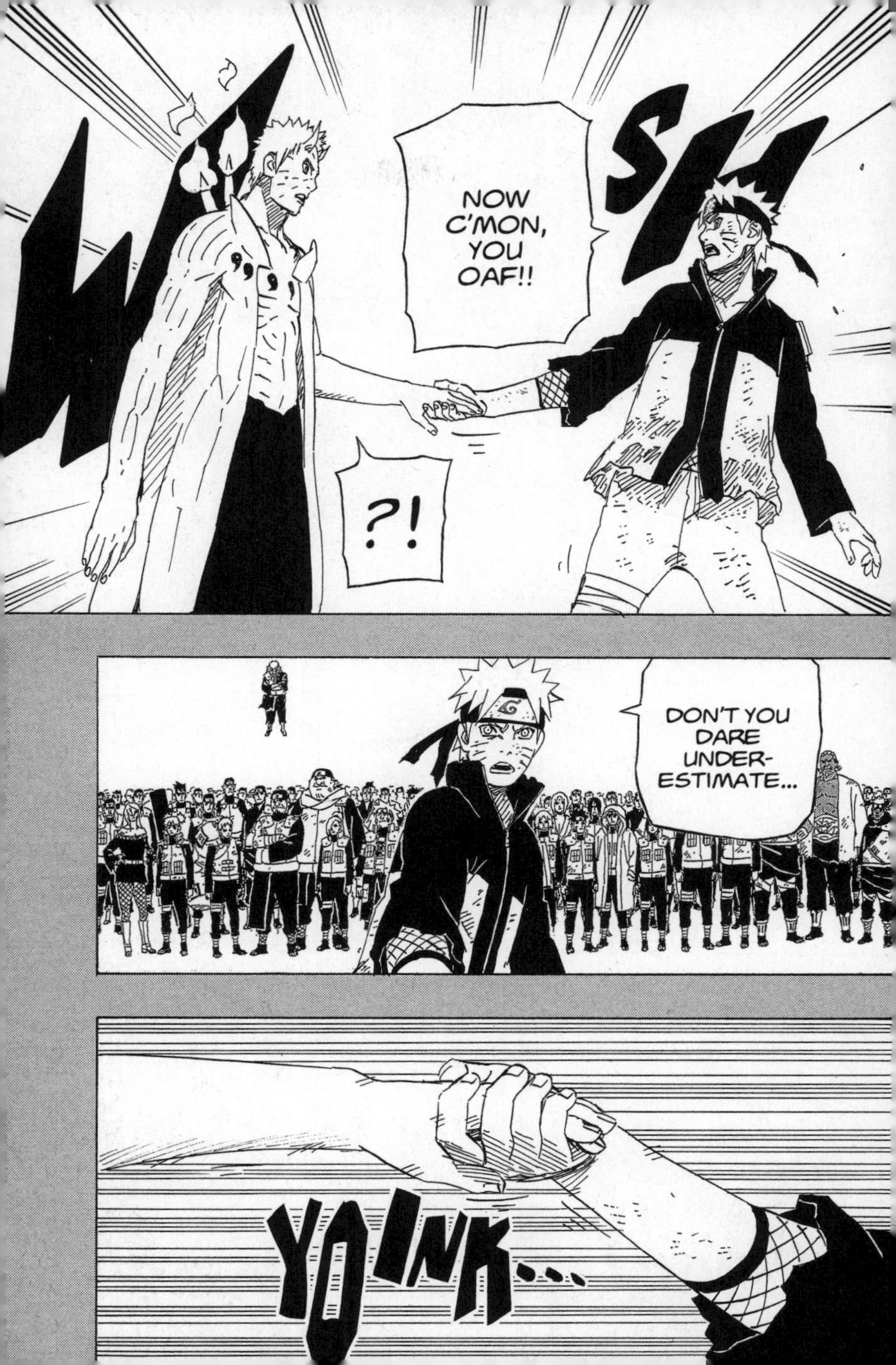
WSH
NOW C'MON, YOU OAF!!
?!
DON'T YOU DARE UNDER-ESTIMATE...
YOINK...

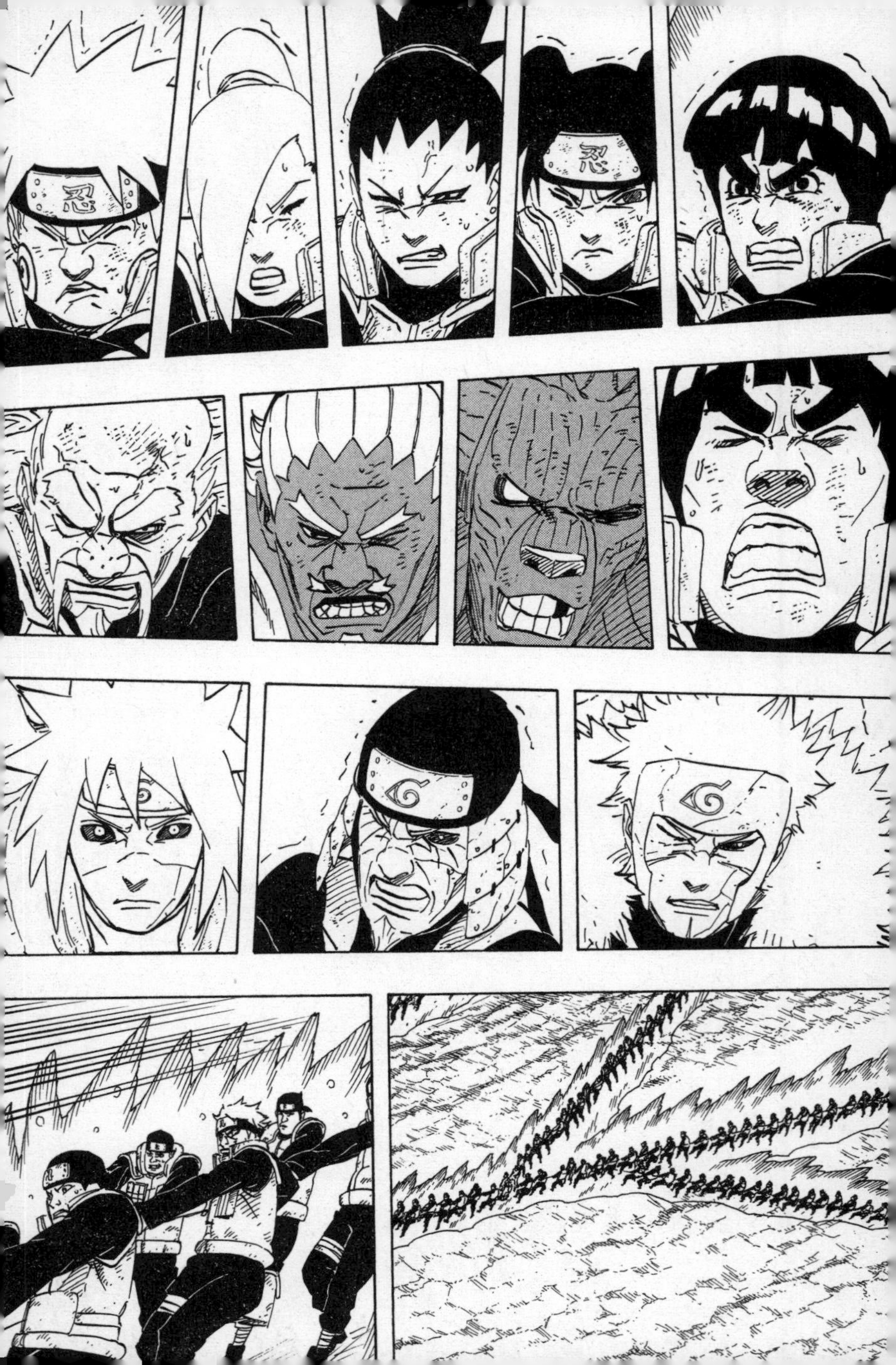

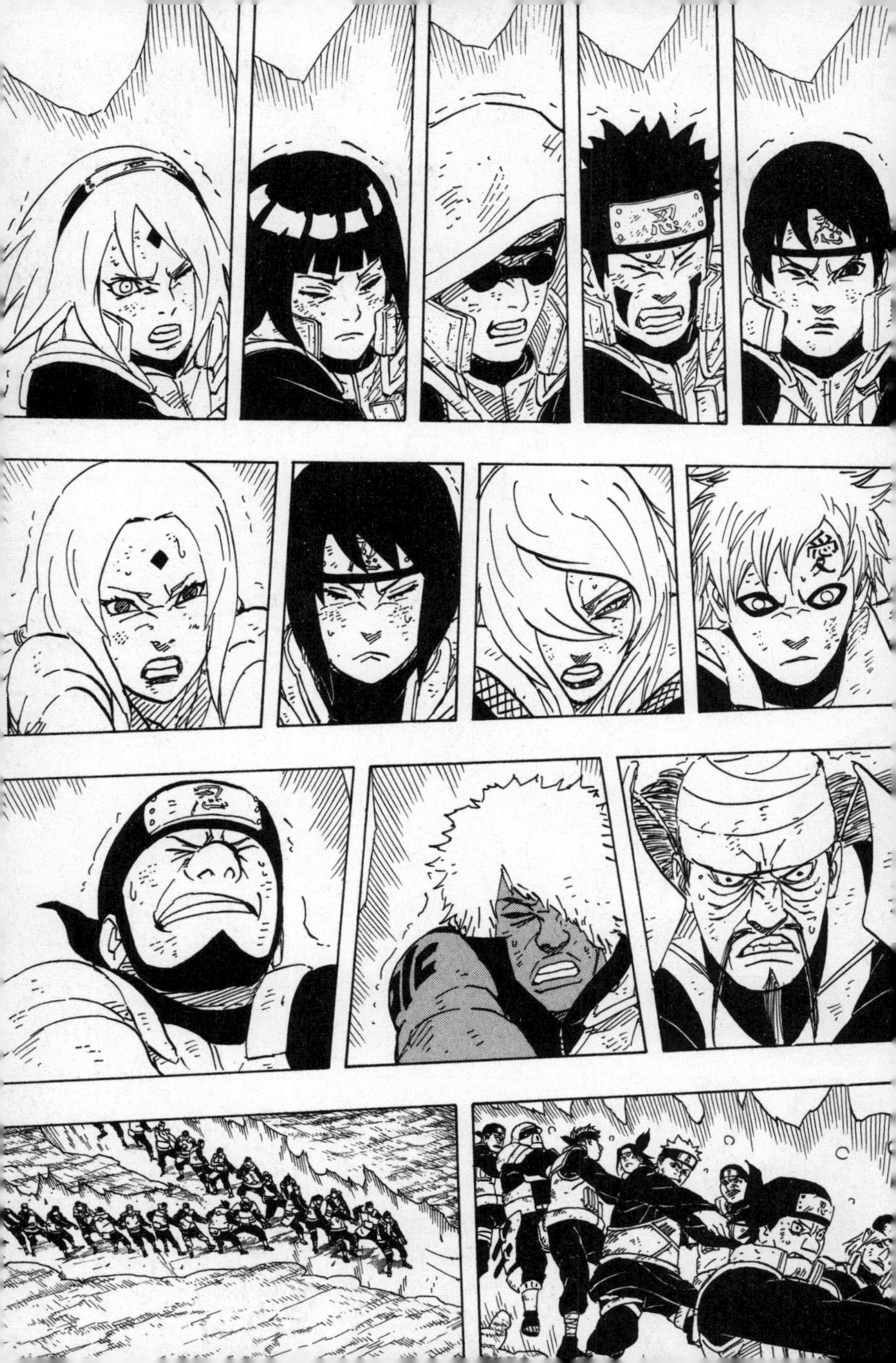

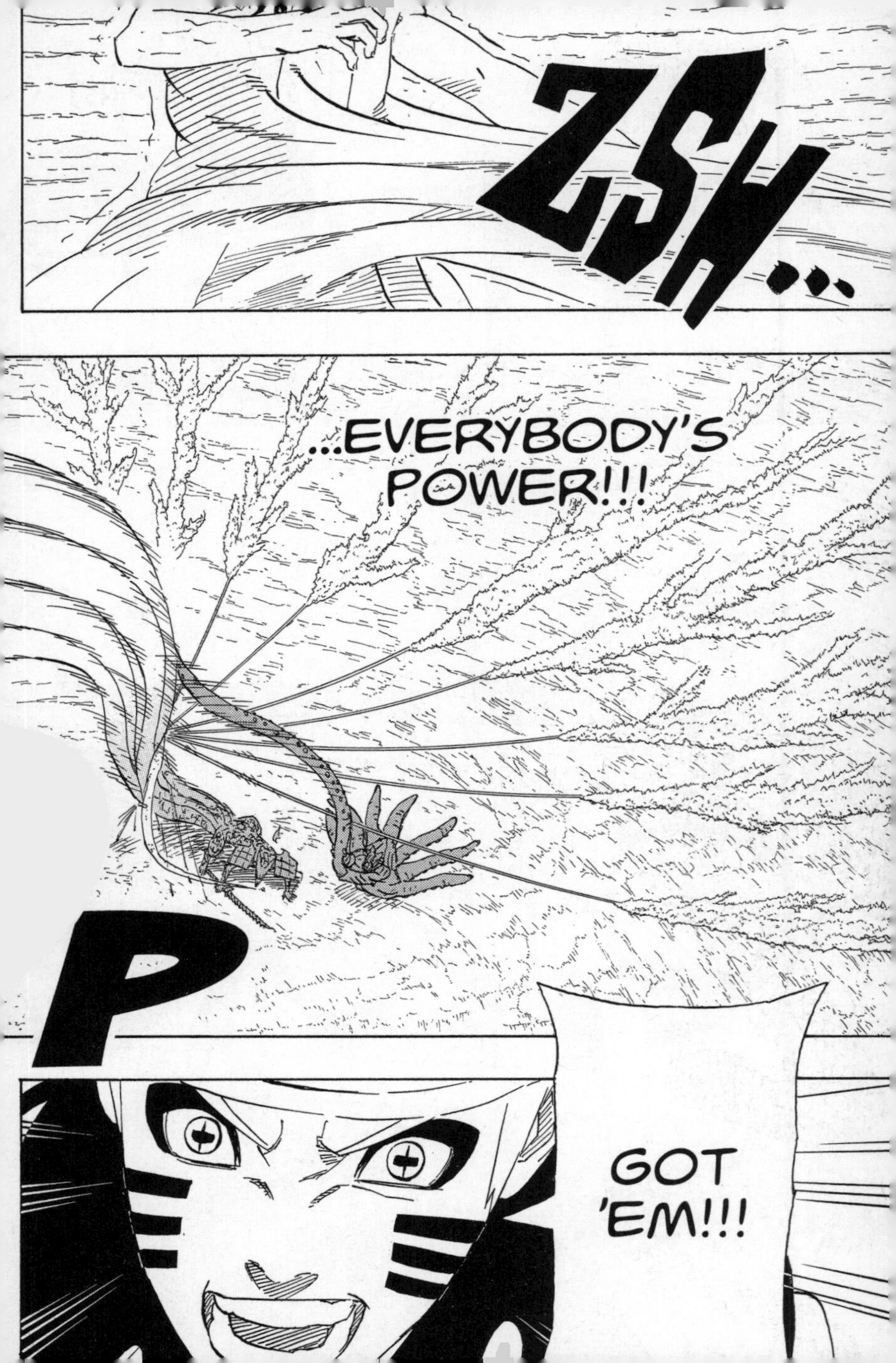
ZSH...
...EVERYBODY'S POWER!!!
P
GOT 'EM!!!

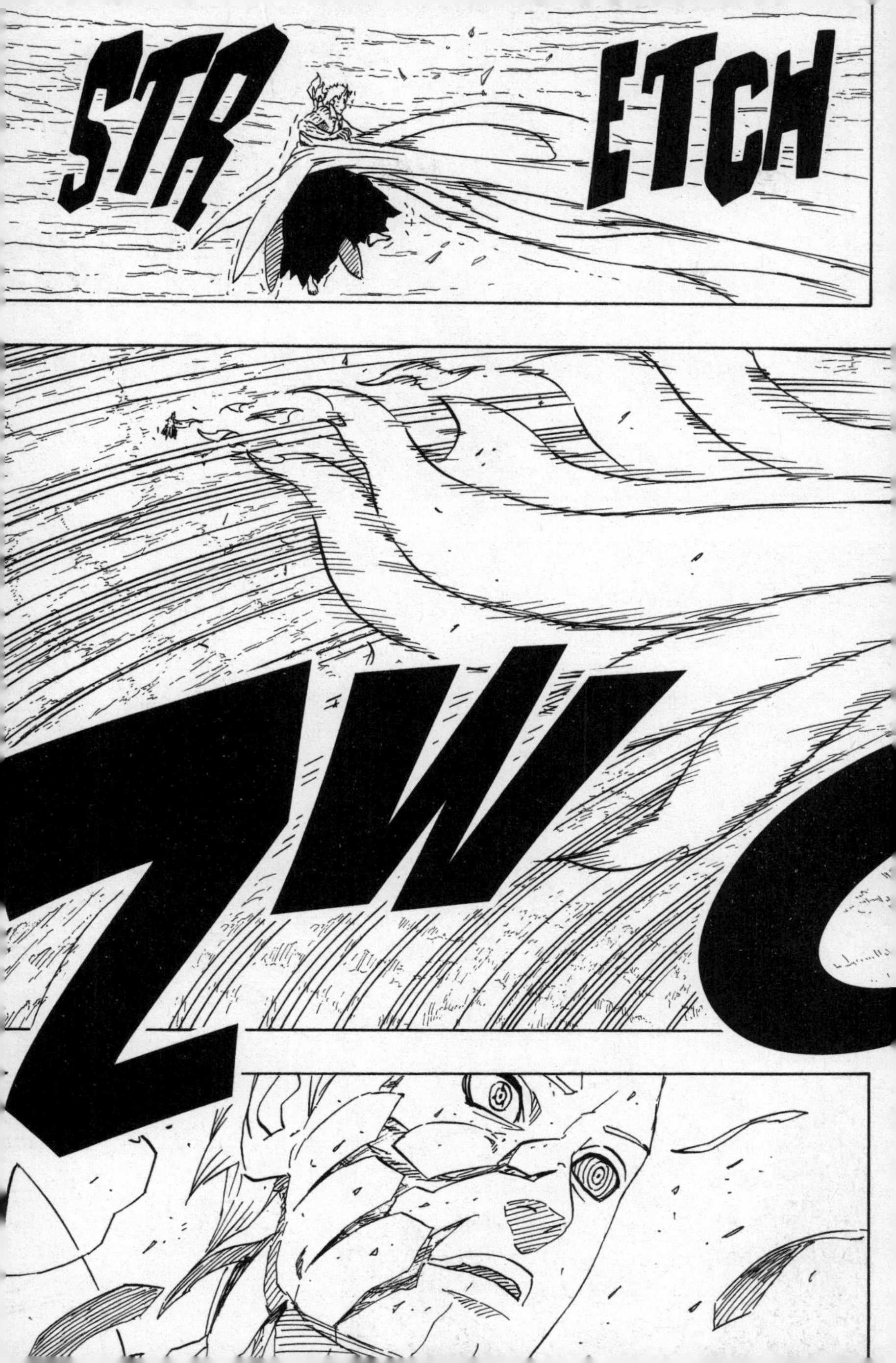
STRETCH
ZW

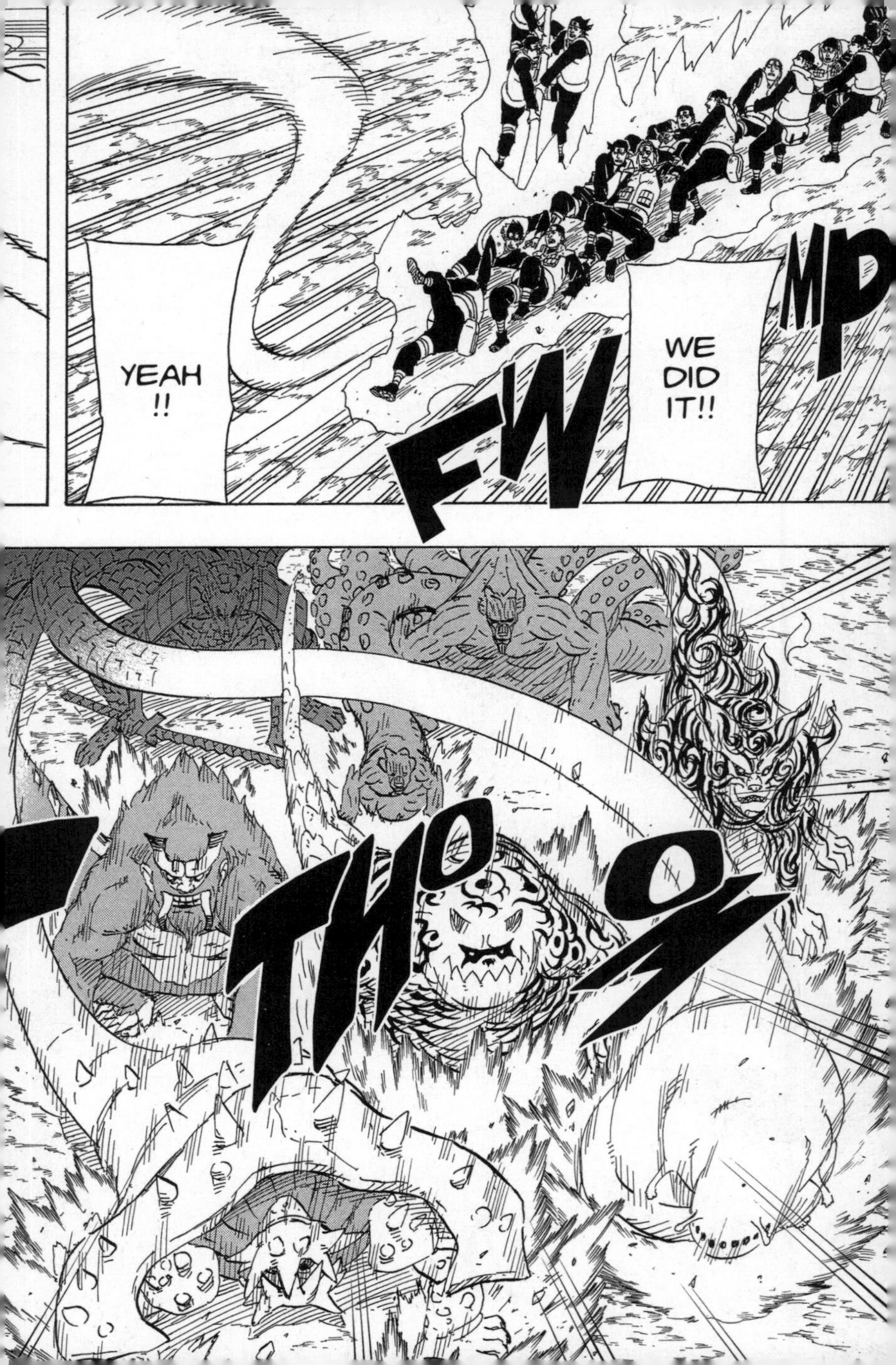
MP
WE DID IT!!
FW
YEAH !!
THOOM

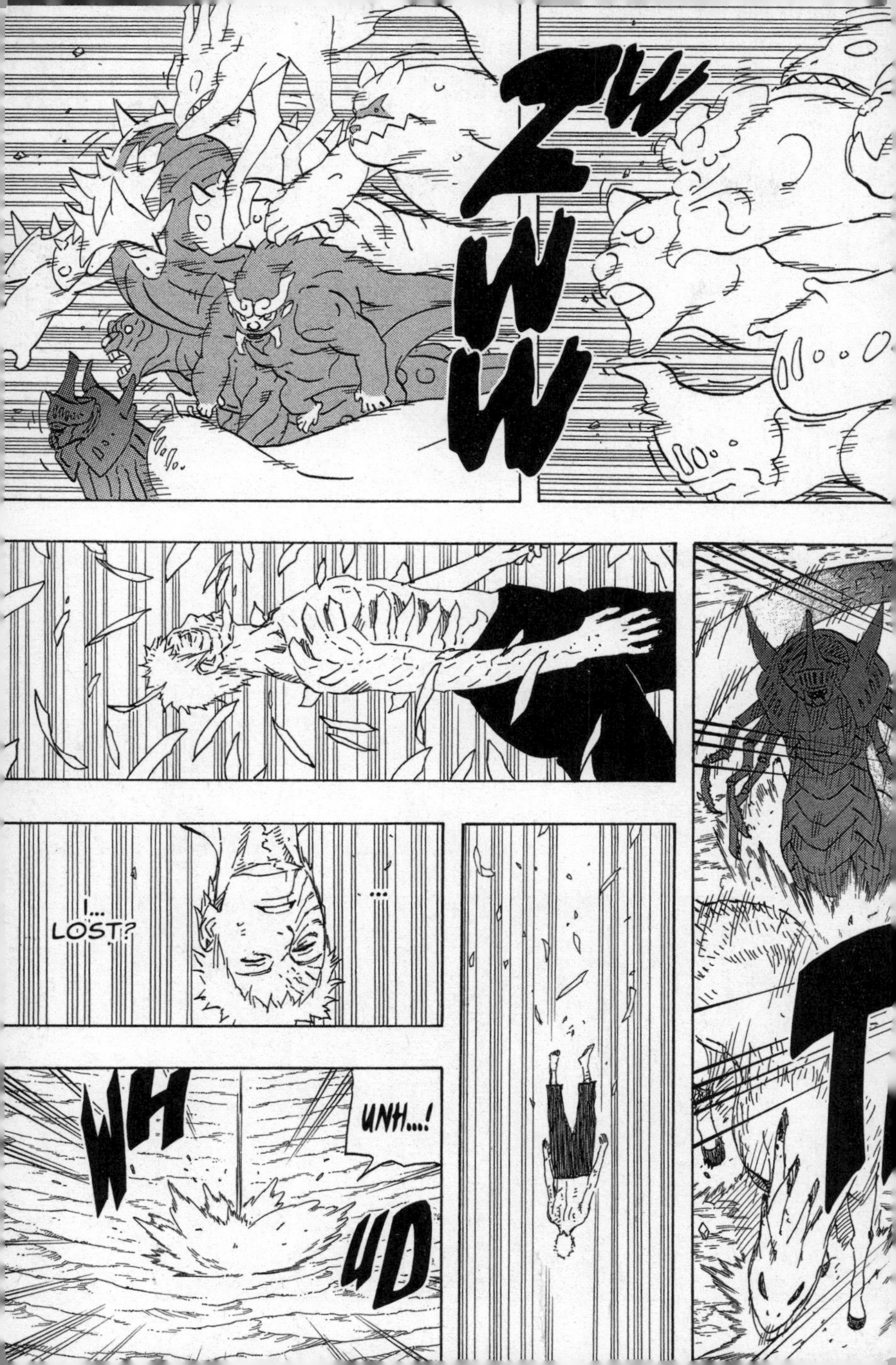
ZWWW
...
I... LOST?
UNH...!
WHUD

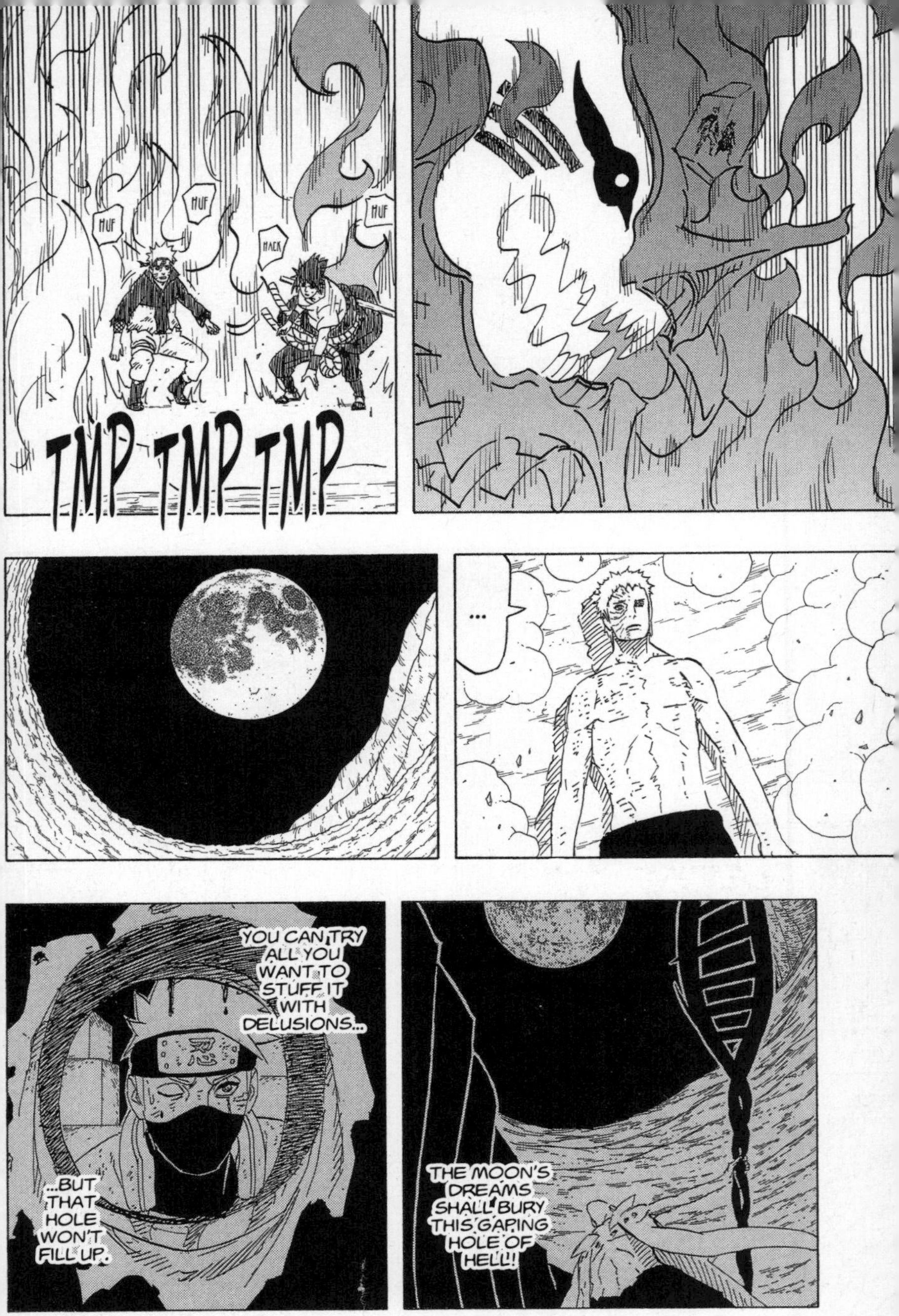
HUF
HACK
HUF
HUF
TMP TMP TMP
...
THE MOON'S DREAMS SHALL BURY THIS GAPING HOLE OF HELL!!
YOU CAN TRY ALL YOU WANT TO STUFF IT WITH DELUSIONS...
...BUT THAT HOLE WON'T FILL UP.

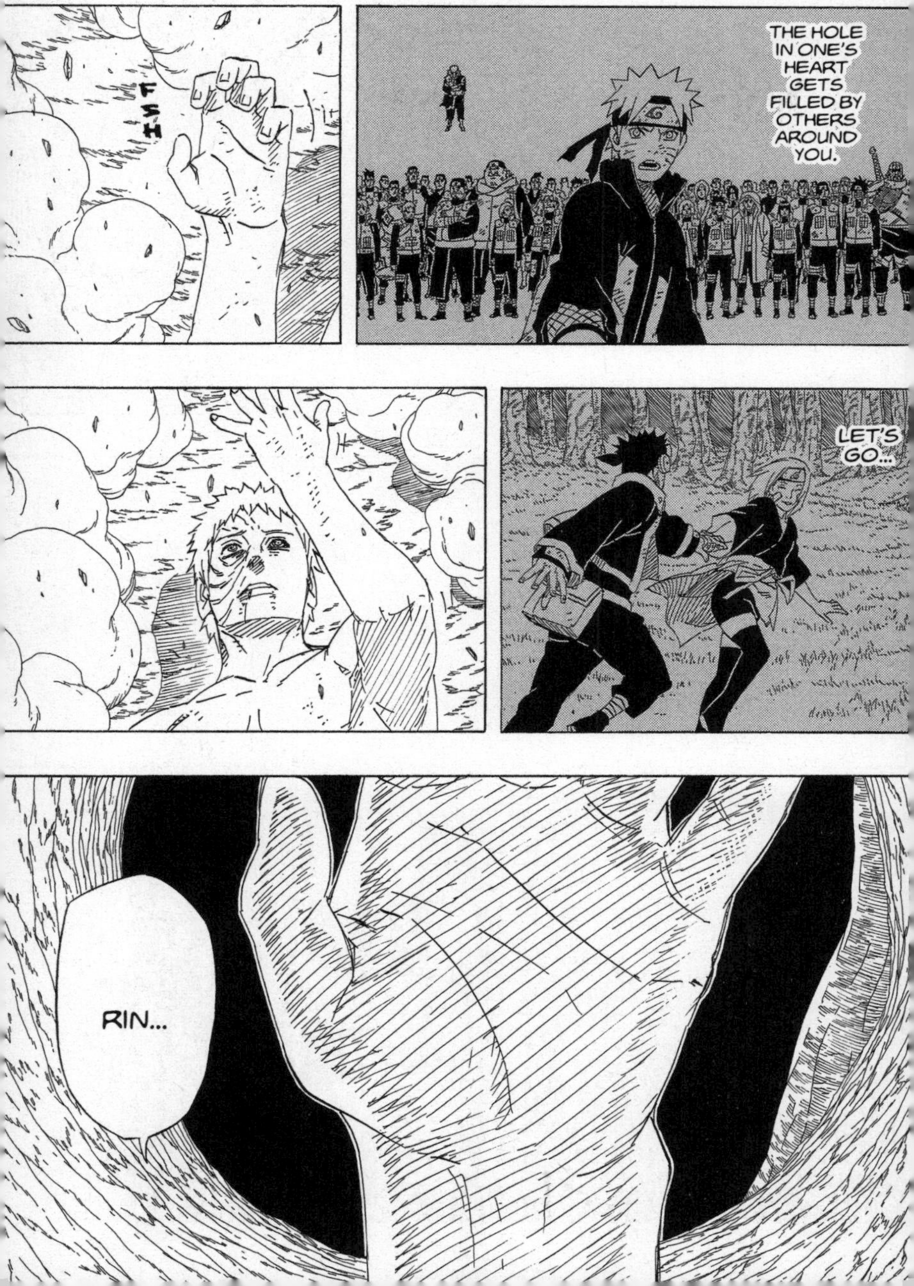
THE HOLE IN ONE'S HEART GETS FILLED BY OTHERS AROUND YOU.
FSH
LET'S GO...
RIN...

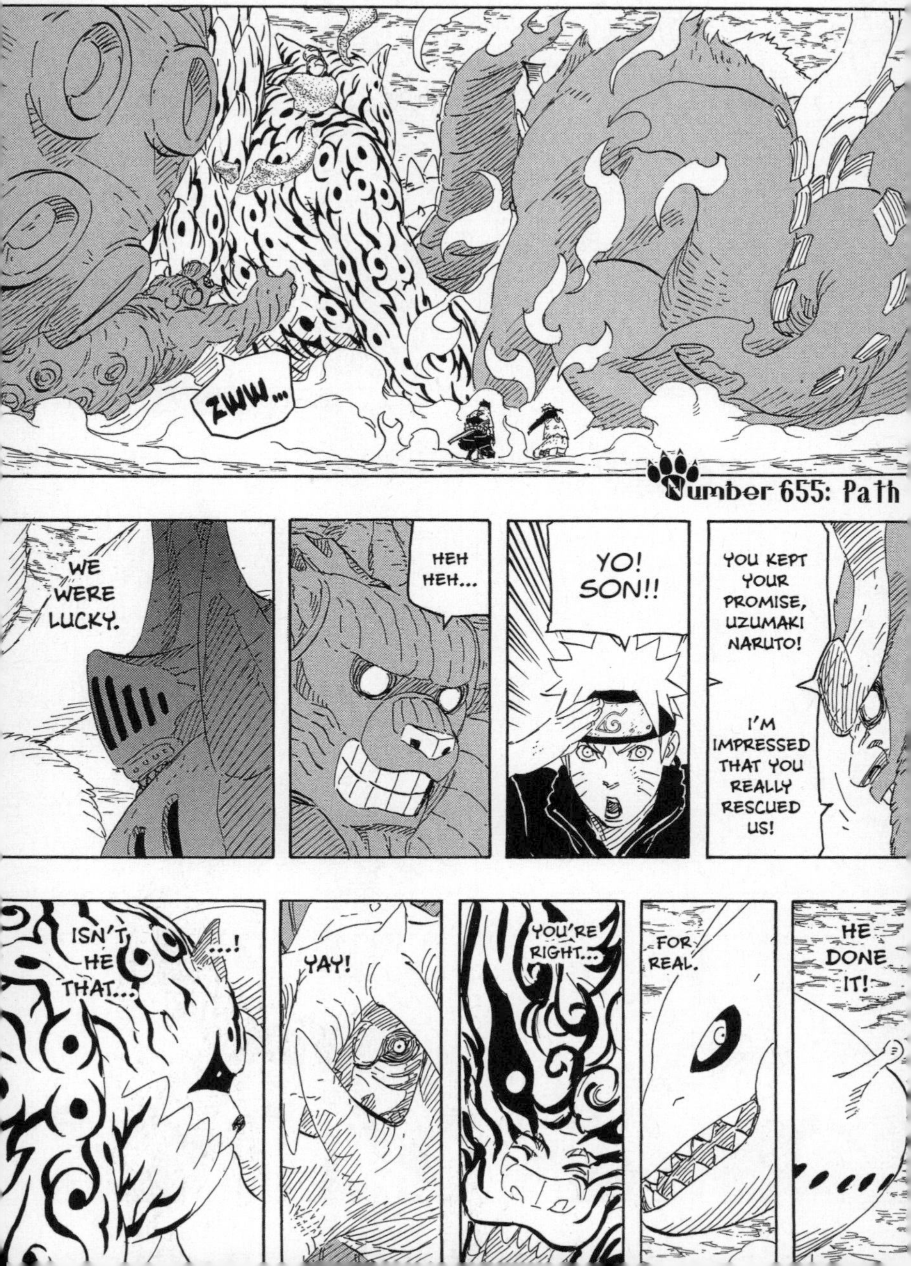
ZWW...
Number 655: Path
YOU KEPT YOUR PROMISE, UZUMAKI NARUTO!
I'M IMPRESSED THAT YOU REALLY RESCUED US!
YO! SON!!
HEH HEH...
WE WERE LUCKY.
HE DONE IT!
......
FOR REAL.
YOU'RE RIGHT...
YAY!
...!
ISN'T HE THAT...

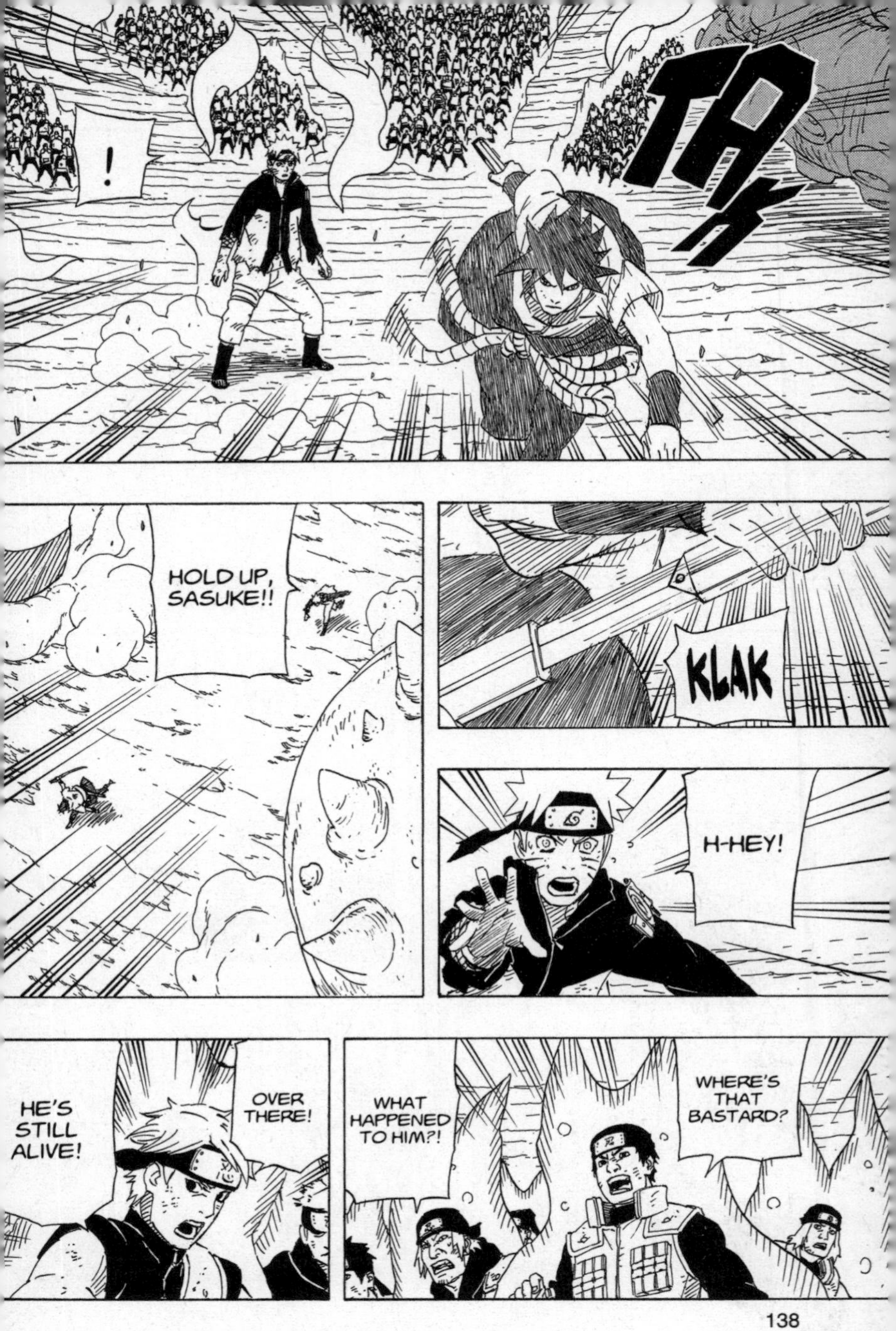
TAK
!
KLAK
H-HEY!
HOLD UP, SASUKE!!
WHERE'S THAT BASTARD?
WHAT HAPPENED TO HIM?!
OVER THERE!
HE'S STILL ALIVE!

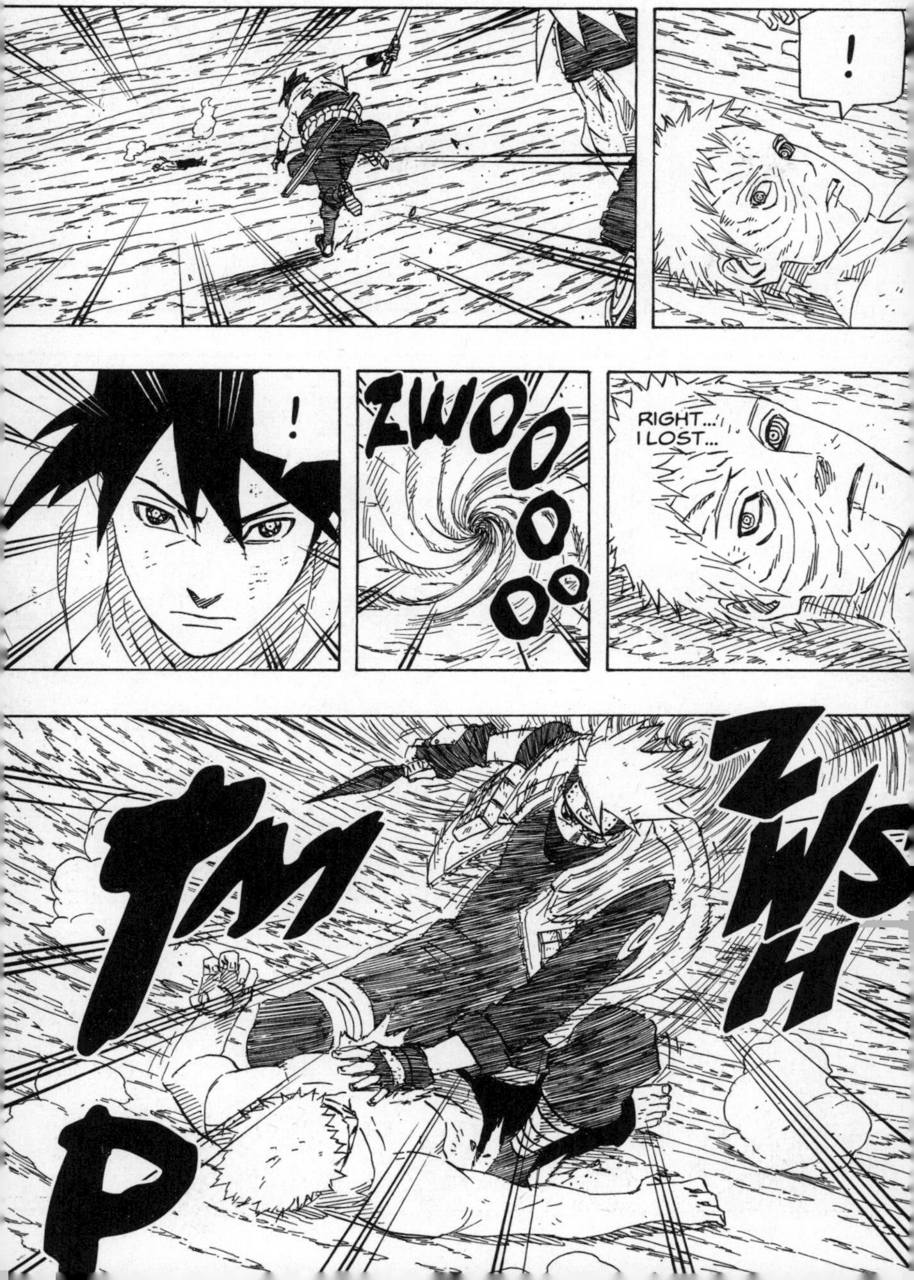
!
RIGHT... I LOST...
ZWOOOOOO
!
ZWSH
TMP

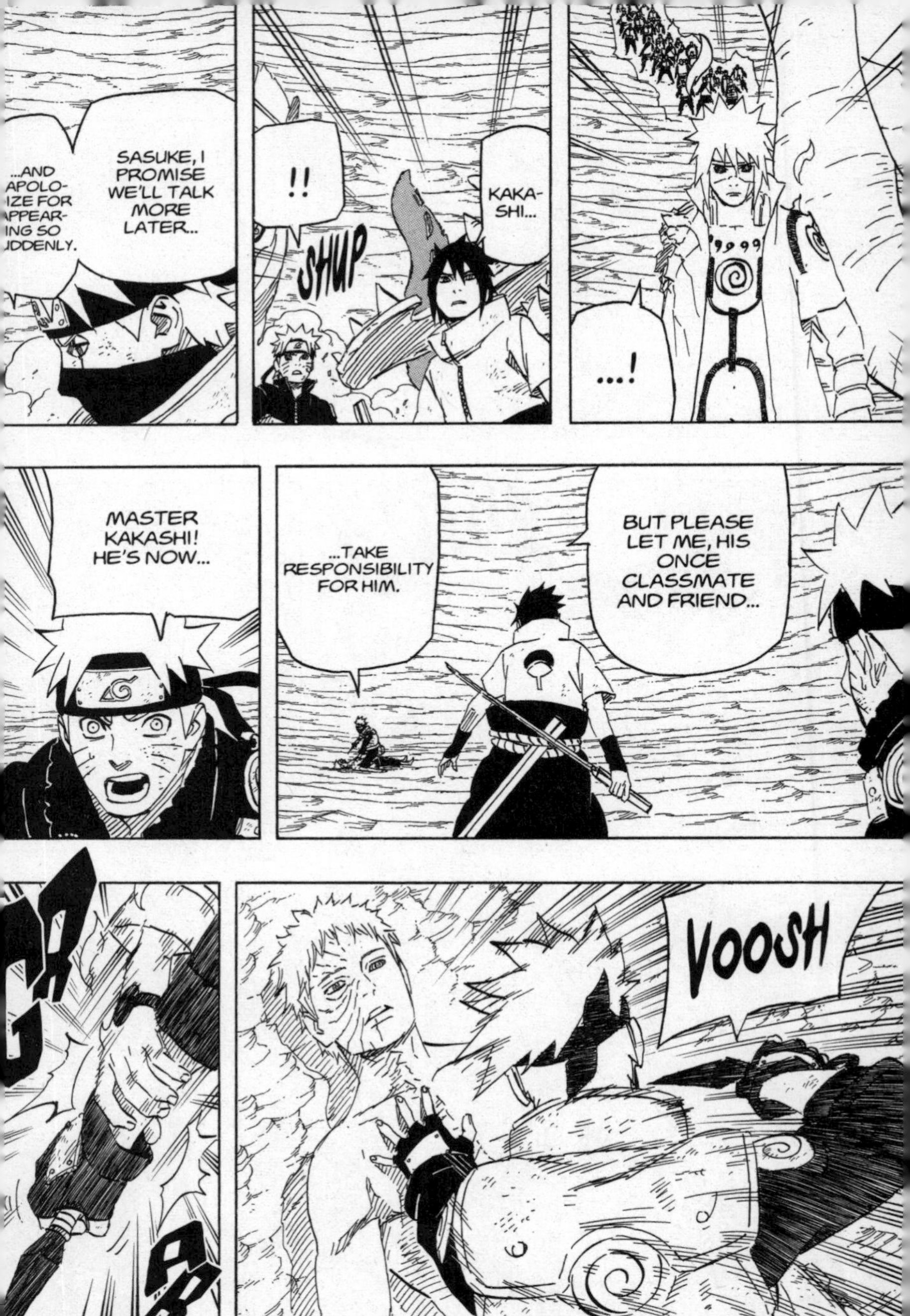
...!
KAKA-SHI...
!!
SHUP
SASUKE, I PROMISE WE'LL TALK MORE LATER...
...AND APOLO- IZE FOR PPEAR- NG SO UDDENLY.
BUT PLEASE LET ME, HIS ONCE CLASSMATE AND FRIEND...
...TAKE RESPONSIBILITY FOR HIM.
MASTER KAKASHI! HE'S NOW...
VOOSH

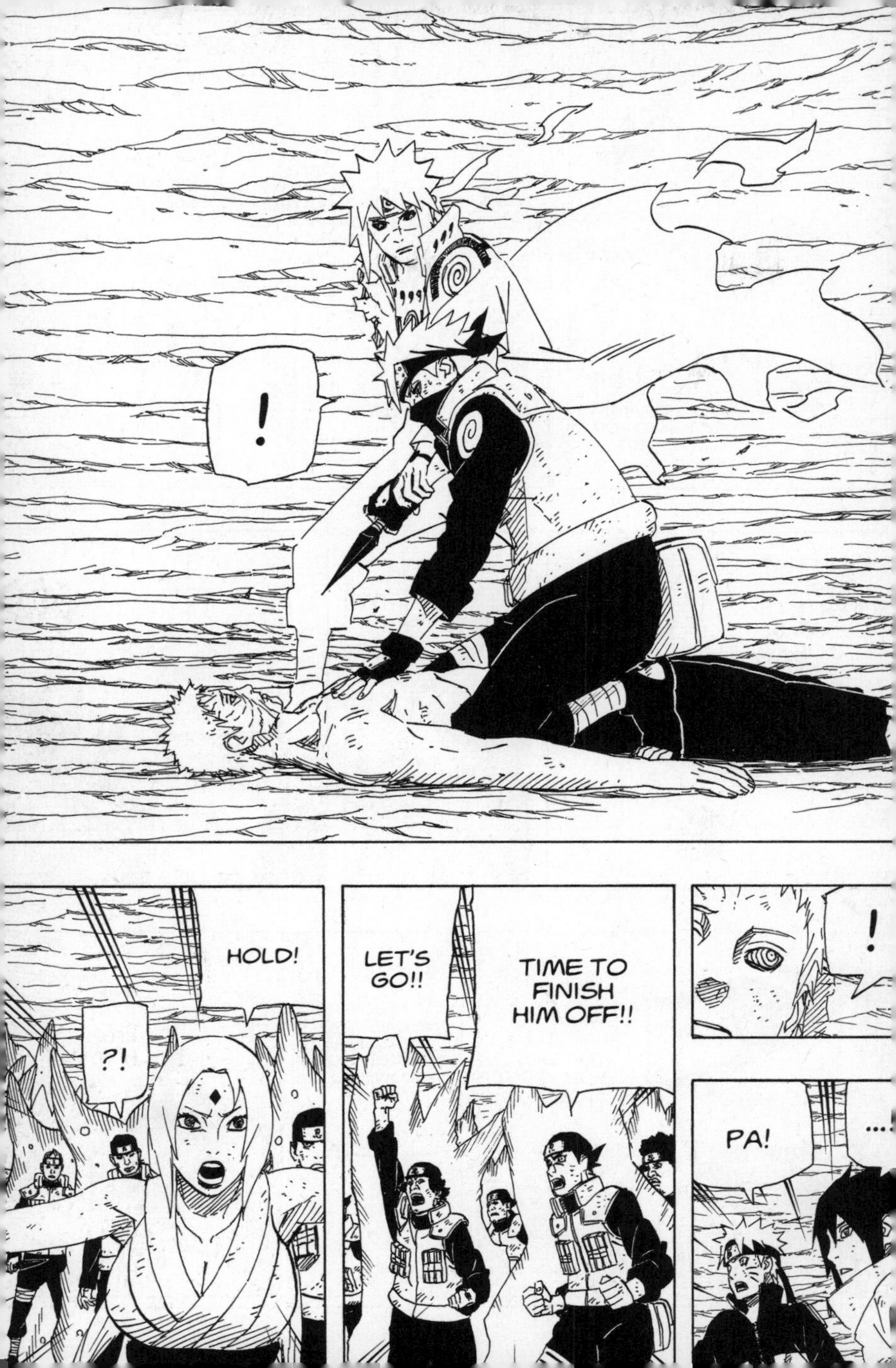
!
!
...
PA!
TIME TO FINISH HIM OFF!!
LET'S GO!!
HOLD!
?!

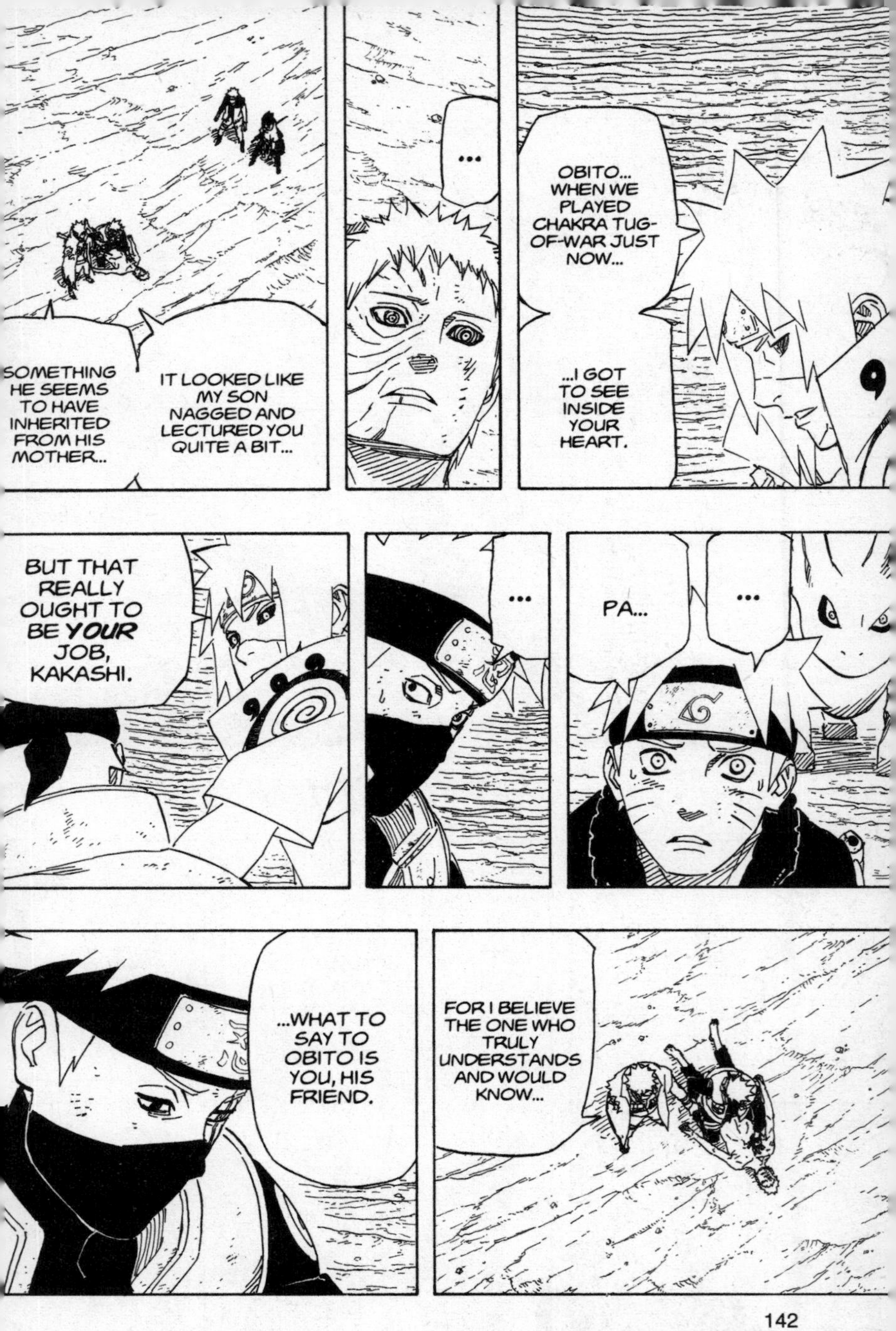
OBITO... WHEN WE PLAYED CHAKRA TUG-OF-WAR JUST NOW...
...I GOT TO SEE INSIDE YOUR HEART.
...
IT LOOKED LIKE MY SON NAGGED AND LECTURED YOU QUITE A BIT...
SOMETHING HE SEEMS TO HAVE INHERITED FROM HIS MOTHER...
...
PA...
...
BUT THAT REALLY OUGHT TO BE **YOUR** JOB, KAKASHI.
FOR I BELIEVE THE ONE WHO TRULY UNDERSTANDS AND WOULD KNOW...
...WHAT TO SAY TO OBITO IS YOU, HIS FRIEND.

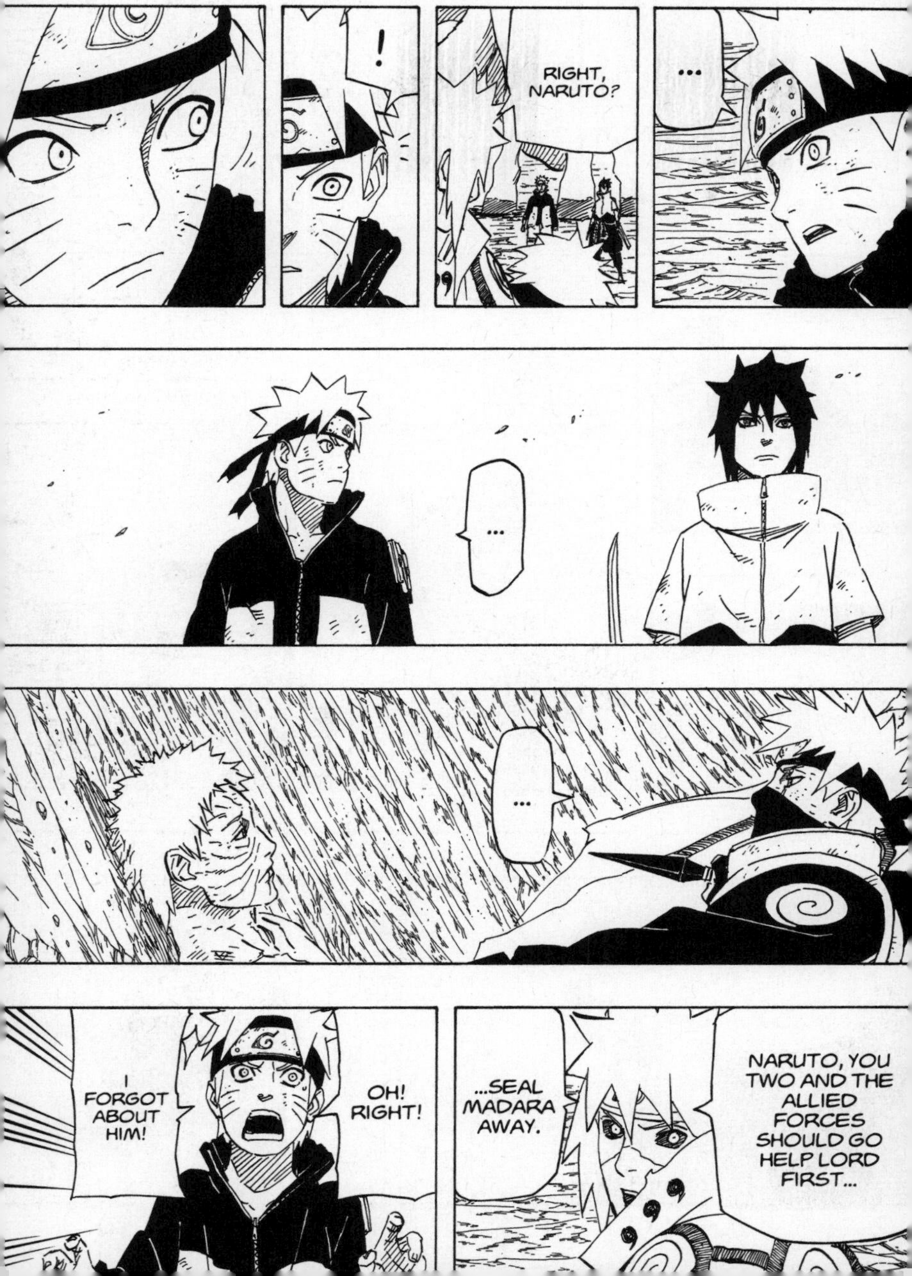
...
RIGHT, NARUTO?
!
...
...
NARUTO, YOU TWO AND THE ALLIED FORCES SHOULD GO HELP LORD FIRST...
...SEAL MADARA AWAY.
OH! RIGHT!
I FORGOT ABOUT HIM!

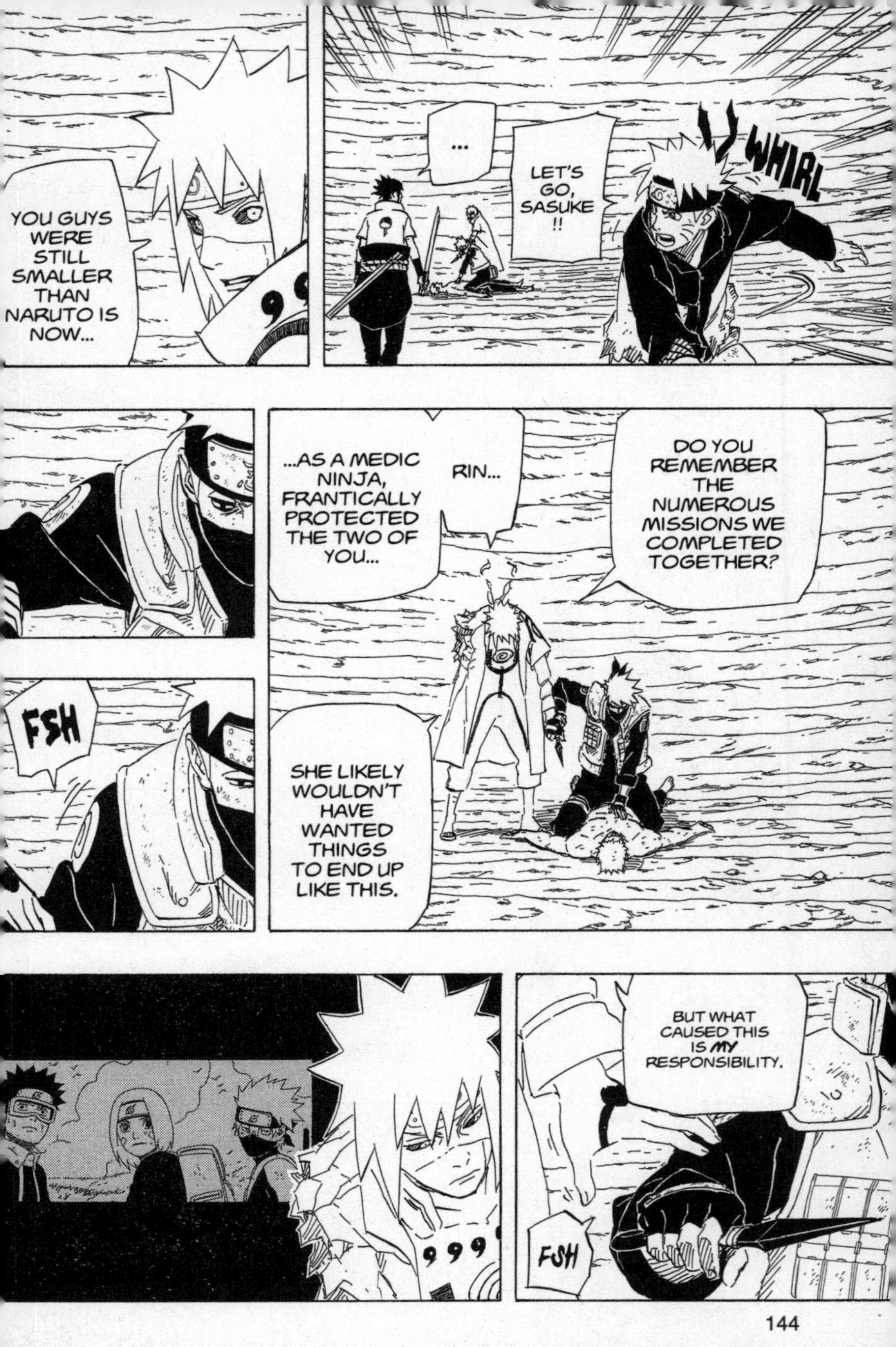
WHIRL
LET'S GO, SASUKE!!
...
YOU GUYS WERE STILL SMALLER THAN NARUTO IS NOW...
DO YOU REMEMBER THE NUMEROUS MISSIONS WE COMPLETED TOGETHER?
RIN...
...AS A MEDIC NINJA, FRANTICALLY PROTECTED THE TWO OF YOU...
SHE LIKELY WOULDN'T HAVE WANTED THINGS TO END UP LIKE THIS.
FSH
BUT WHAT CAUSED THIS IS *MY* RESPONSIBILITY.
FSH

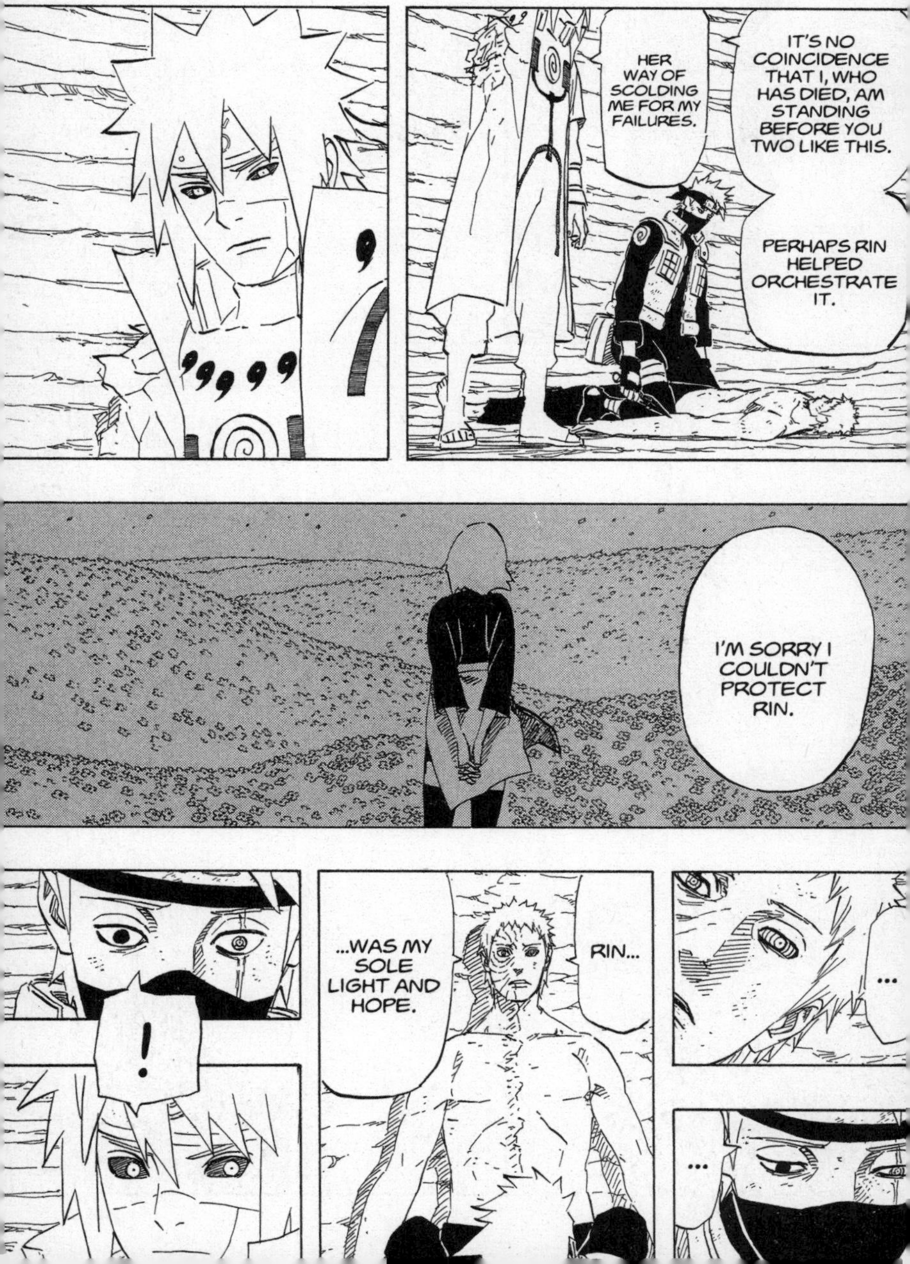
IT'S NO COINCIDENCE THAT I, WHO HAS DIED, AM STANDING BEFORE YOU TWO LIKE THIS.
PERHAPS RIN HELPED ORCHESTRATE IT.
HER WAY OF SCOLDING ME FOR MY FAILURES.
I'M SORRY I COULDN'T PROTECT RIN.
...
...
RIN...
...WAS MY SOLE LIGHT AND HOPE.
!

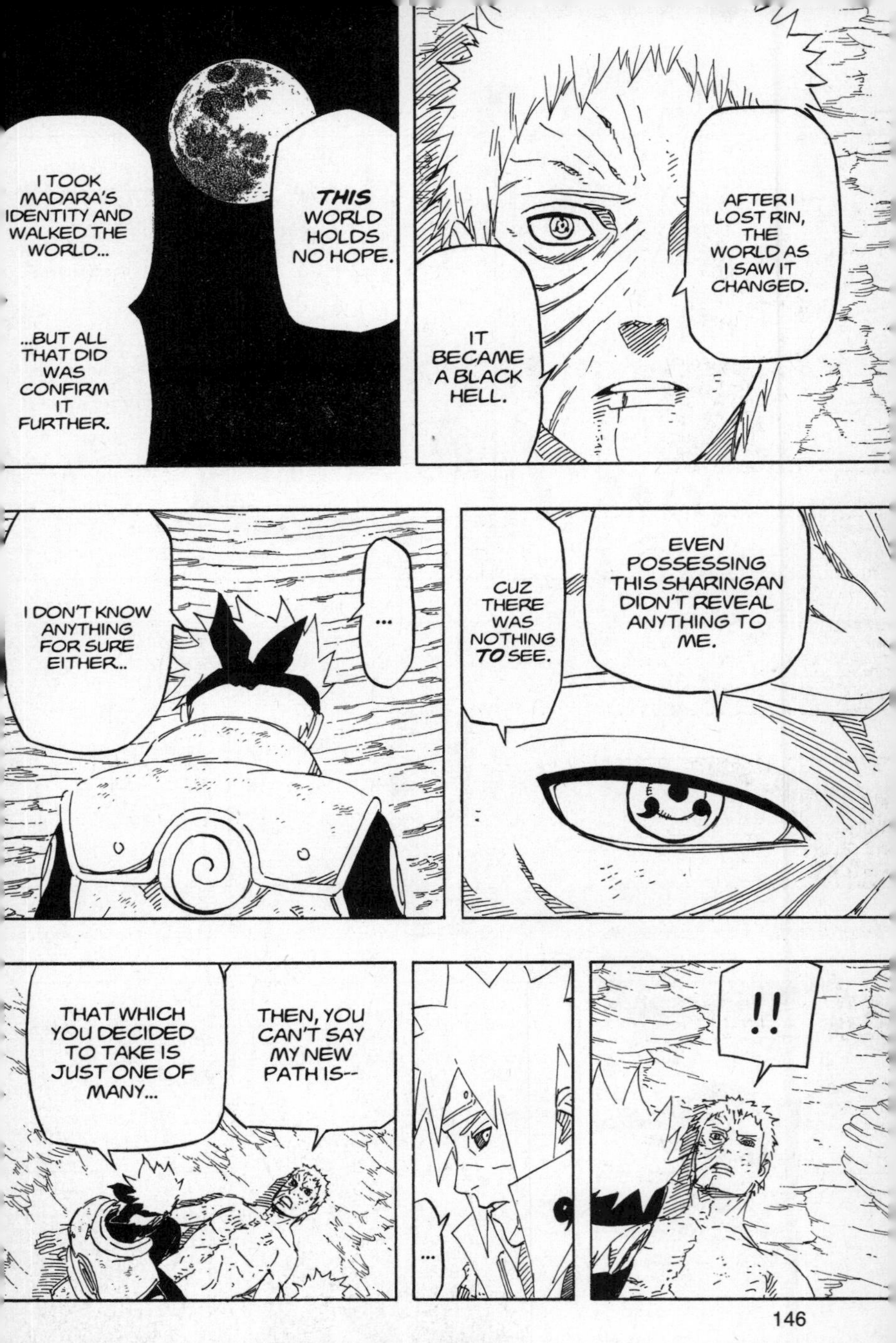
AFTER I LOST RIN, THE WORLD AS I SAW IT CHANGED.
IT BECAME A BLACK HELL.
THIS WORLD HOLDS NO HOPE.
I TOOK MADARA'S IDENTITY AND WALKED THE WORLD...
...BUT ALL THAT DID WAS CONFIRM IT FURTHER.
EVEN POSSESSING THIS SHARINGAN DIDN'T REVEAL ANYTHING TO ME.
CUZ THERE WAS NOTHING ***TO*** SEE.
...
I DON'T KNOW ANYTHING FOR SURE EITHER...
!!
...
THEN, YOU CAN'T SAY MY NEW PATH IS--
THAT WHICH YOU DECIDED TO TAKE IS JUST ONE OF MANY...

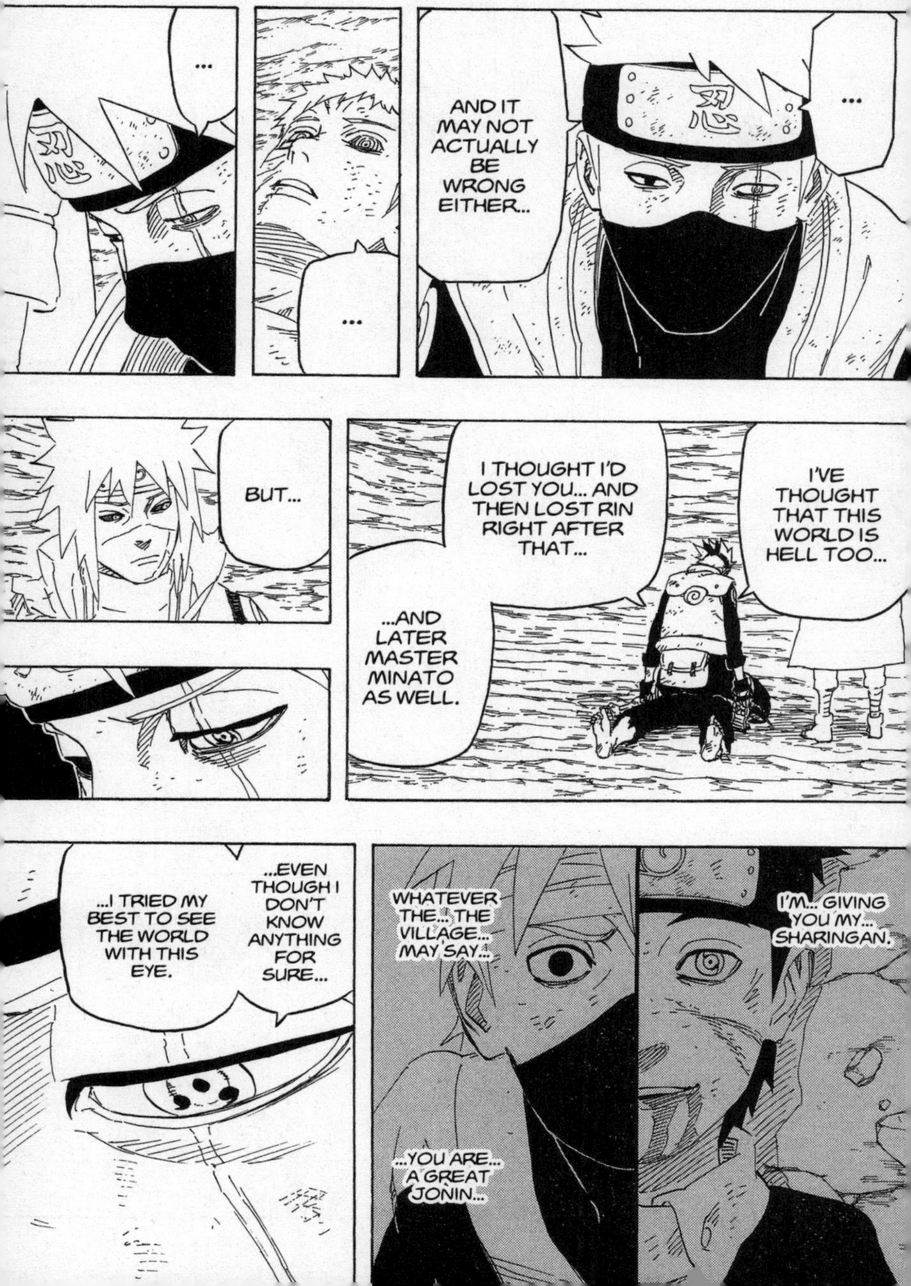
...
AND IT MAY NOT ACTUALLY BE WRONG EITHER...
...
...
I'VE THOUGHT THAT THIS WORLD IS HELL TOO...
I THOUGHT I'D LOST YOU... AND THEN LOST RIN RIGHT AFTER THAT...
...AND LATER MASTER MINATO AS WELL.
BUT...
I'M... GIVING YOU MY... SHARINGAN.
WHATEVER THE... THE VILLAGE... MAY SAY...
...YOU ARE... A GREAT JONIN...
...EVEN THOUGH I DON'T KNOW ANYTHING FOR SURE...
...I TRIED MY BEST TO SEE THE WORLD WITH THIS EYE.

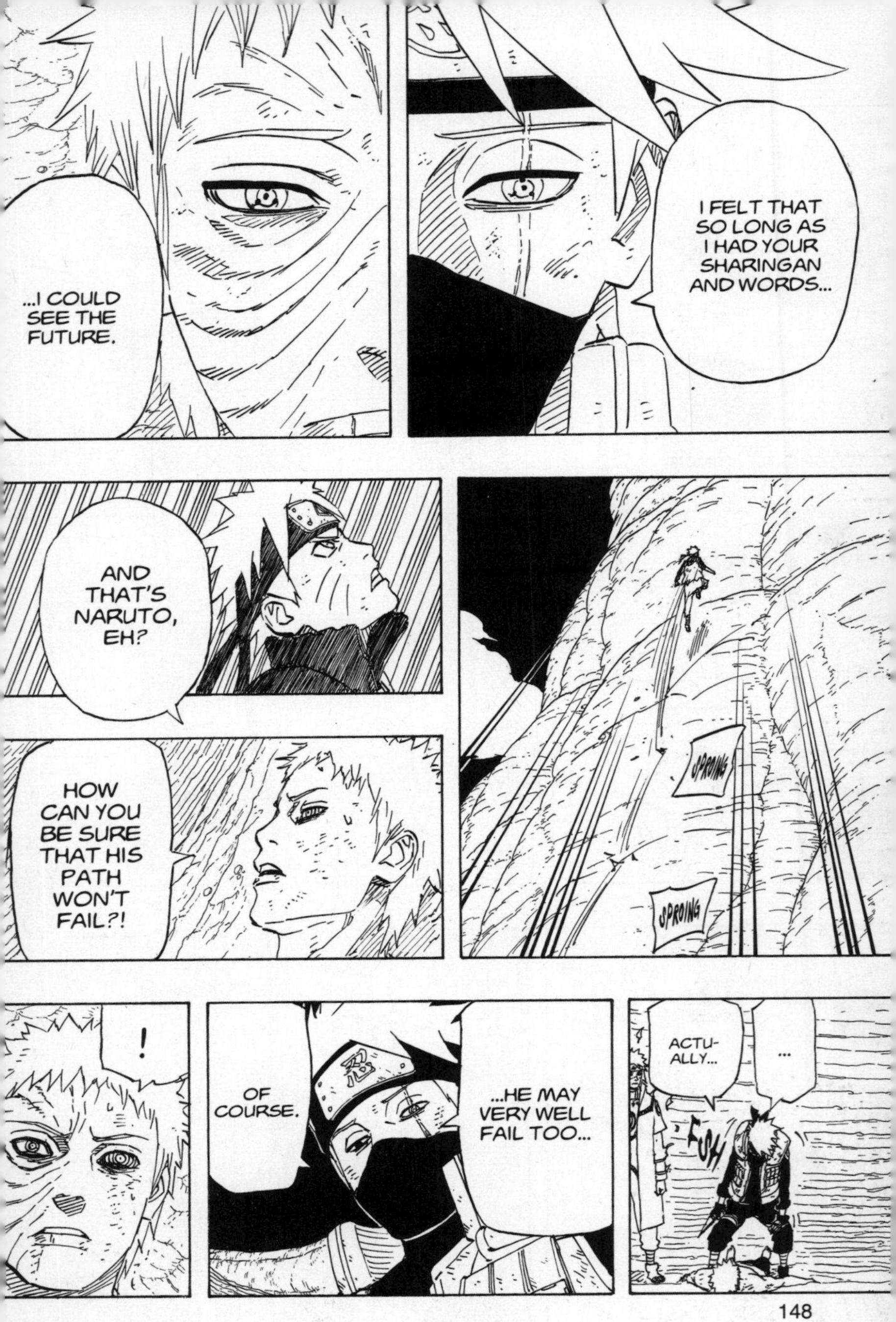
I FELT THAT SO LONG AS I HAD YOUR SHARINGAN AND WORDS...
...I COULD SEE THE FUTURE.
SPROING
SPROING
AND THAT'S NARUTO, EH?
HOW CAN YOU BE SURE THAT HIS PATH WON'T FAIL?!
...
ACTU-ALLY...
FSH
...HE MAY VERY WELL FAIL TOO...
OF COURSE.
!

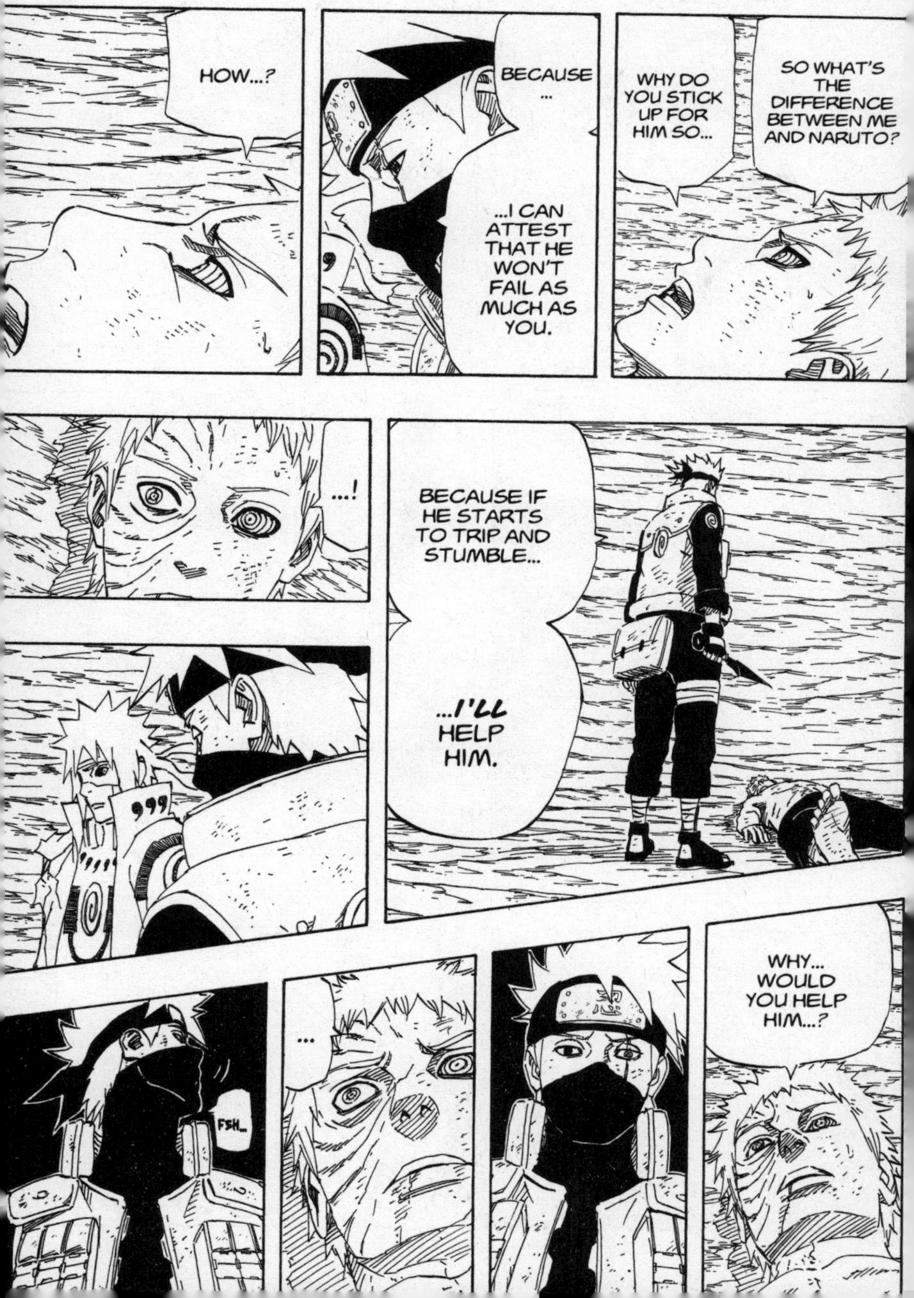
SO WHAT'S THE DIFFERENCE BETWEEN ME AND NARUTO?
WHY DO YOU STICK UP FOR HIM SO...
BECAUSE ...
...I CAN ATTEST THAT HE WON'T FAIL AS MUCH AS YOU.
HOW...?
BECAUSE IF HE STARTS TO TRIP AND STUMBLE...
...I'LL HELP HIM.
...!
WHY... WOULD YOU HELP HIM...?
...
FSH...

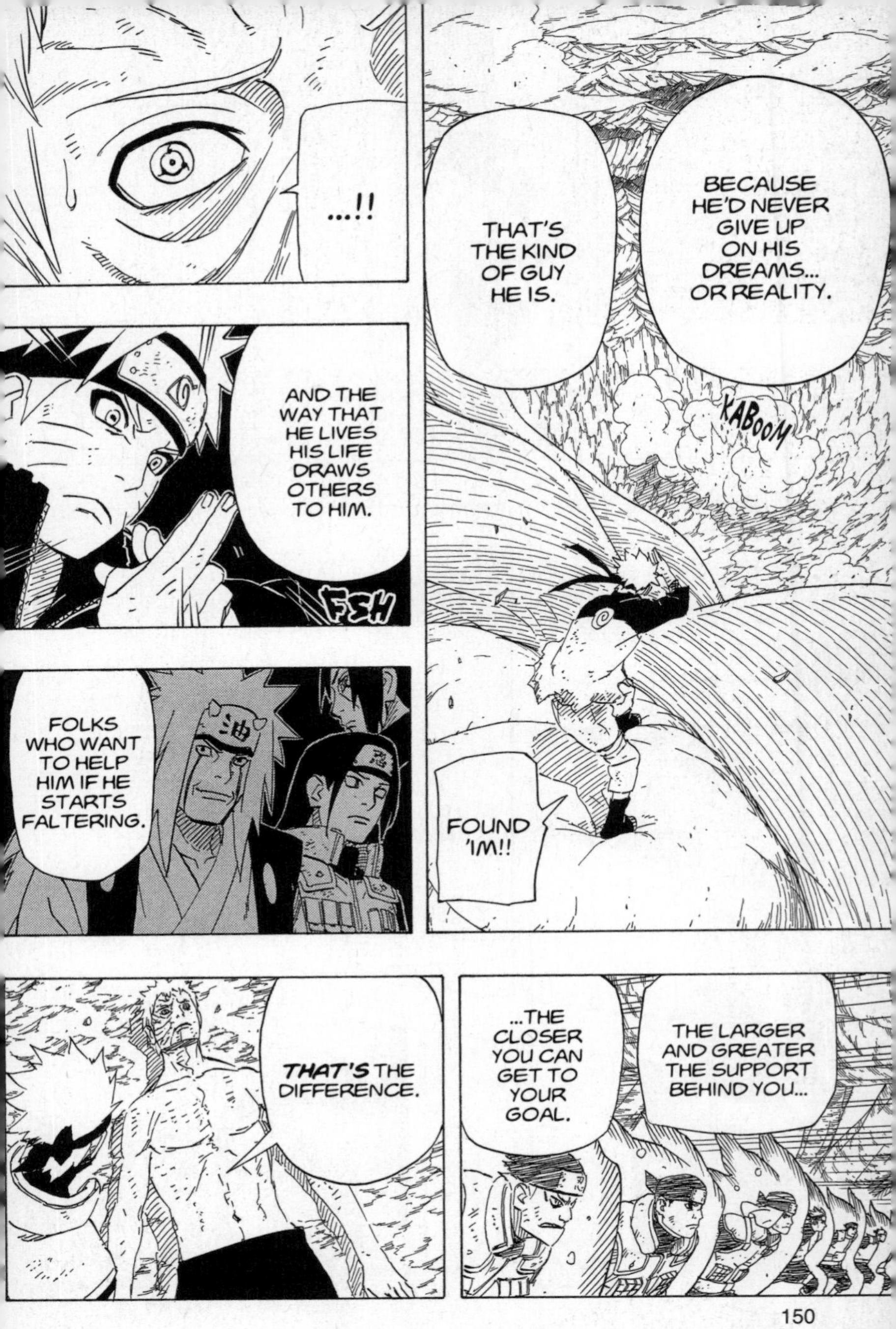
BECAUSE HE'D NEVER GIVE UP ON HIS DREAMS... OR REALITY.
THAT'S THE KIND OF GUY HE IS.
KABOOM
FOUND 'IM!!
...!!
AND THE WAY THAT HE LIVES HIS LIFE DRAWS OTHERS TO HIM.
FSH
FOLKS WHO WANT TO HELP HIM IF HE STARTS FALTERING.
THE LARGER AND GREATER THE SUPPORT BEHIND YOU...
...THE CLOSER YOU CAN GET TO YOUR GOAL.
THAT'S THE DIFFERENCE.

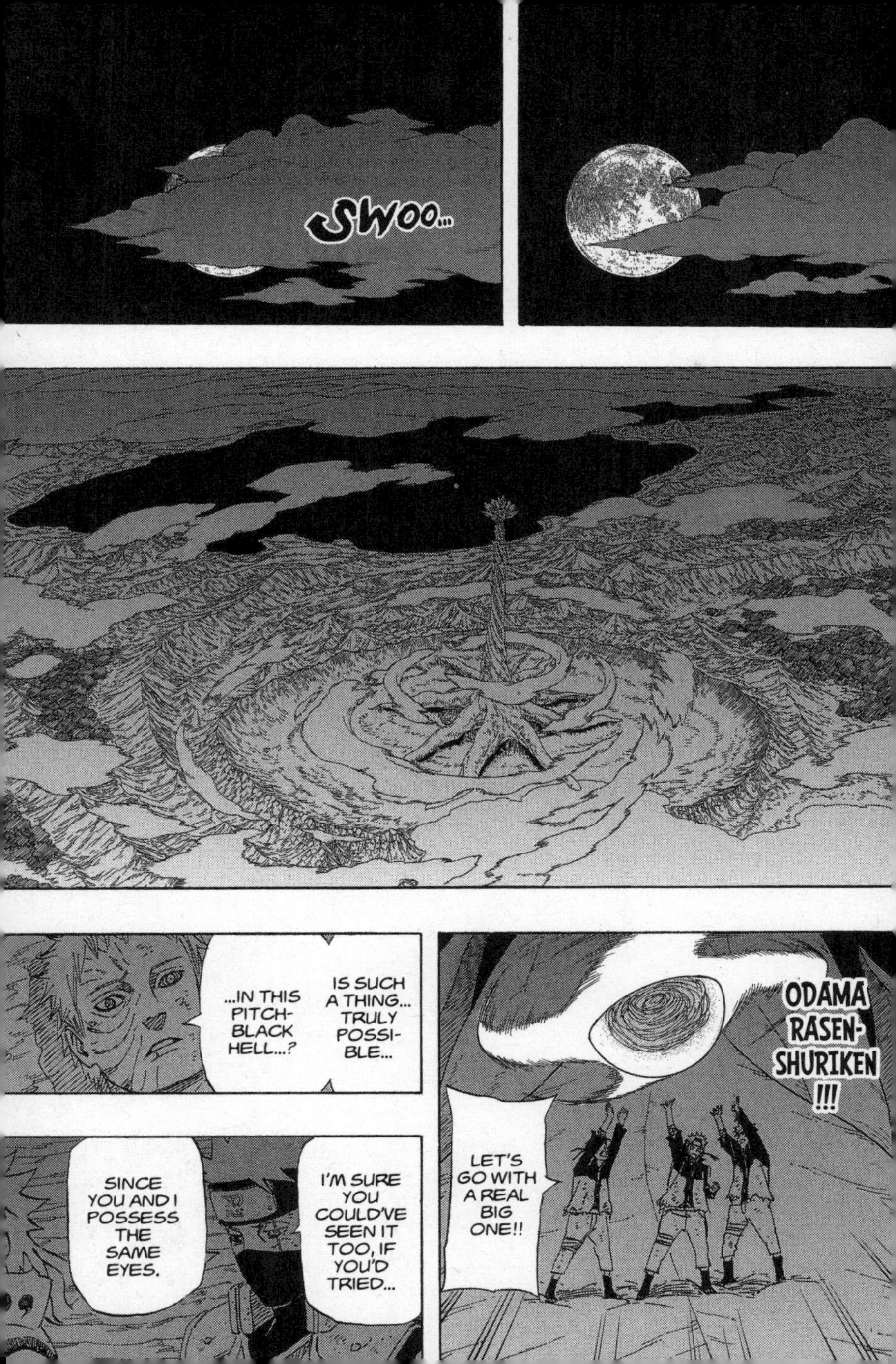
SWOO...
ODAMA RASEN-SHURIKEN!!!
LET'S GO WITH A REAL BIG ONE!!
IS SUCH A THING... TRULY POSSIBLE...
...IN THIS PITCH-BLACK HELL...?
I'M SURE YOU COULD'VE SEEN IT TOO, IF YOU'D TRIED...
SINCE YOU AND I POSSESS THE SAME EYES.

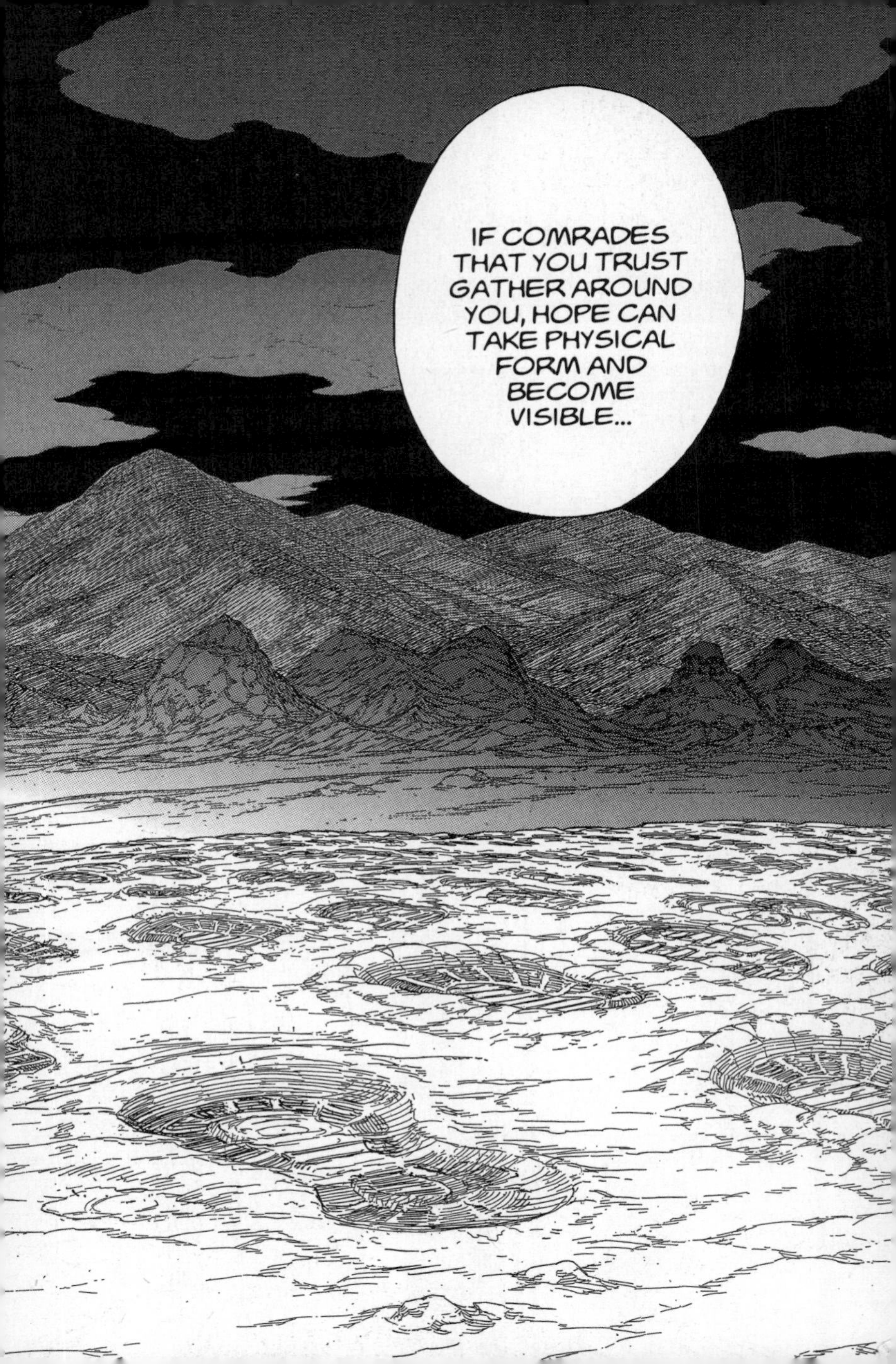
IF COMRADES THAT YOU TRUST GATHER AROUND YOU, HOPE CAN TAKE PHYSICAL FORM AND BECOME VISIBLE...

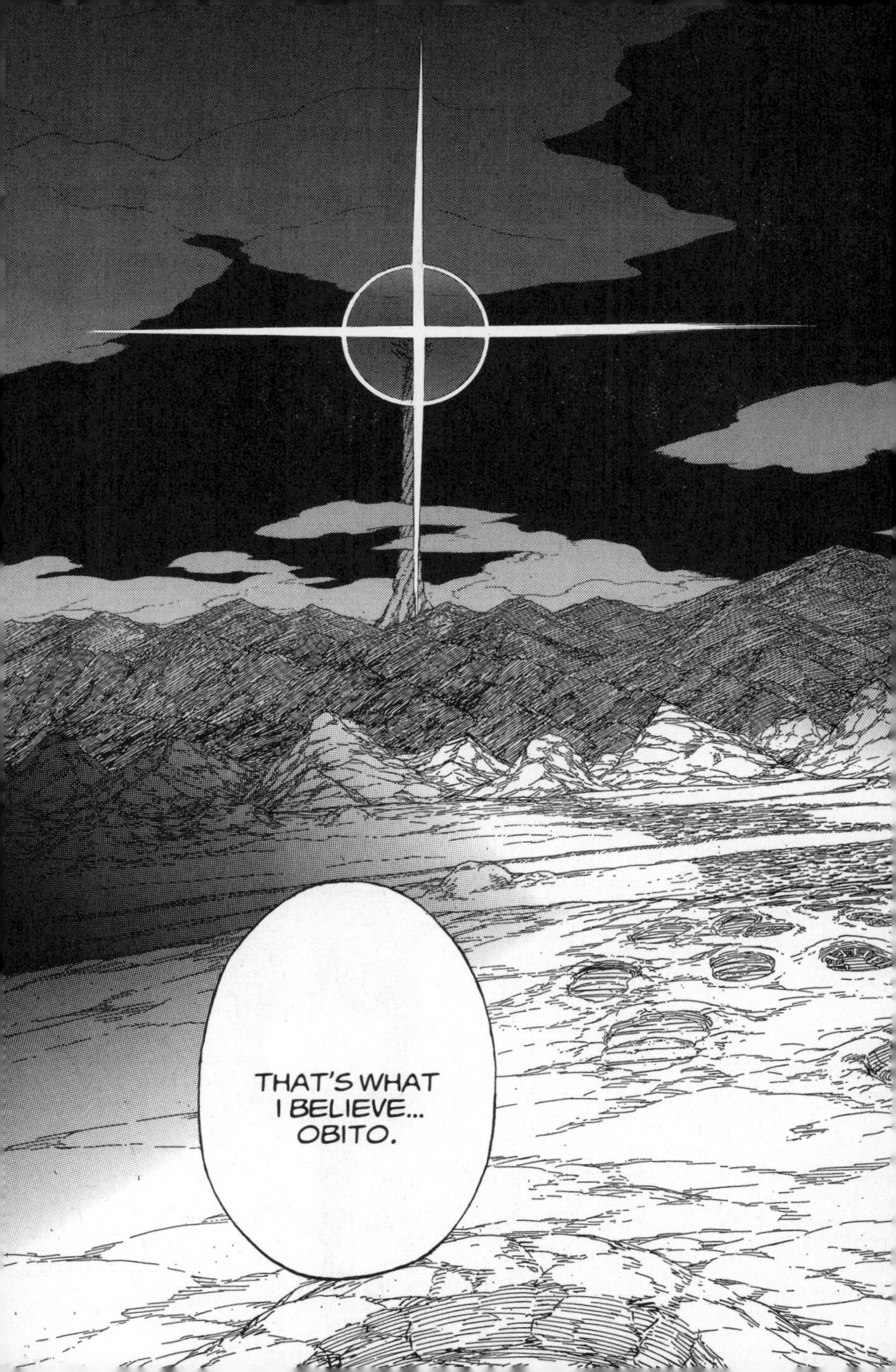
THAT'S WHAT I BELIEVE... OBITO.

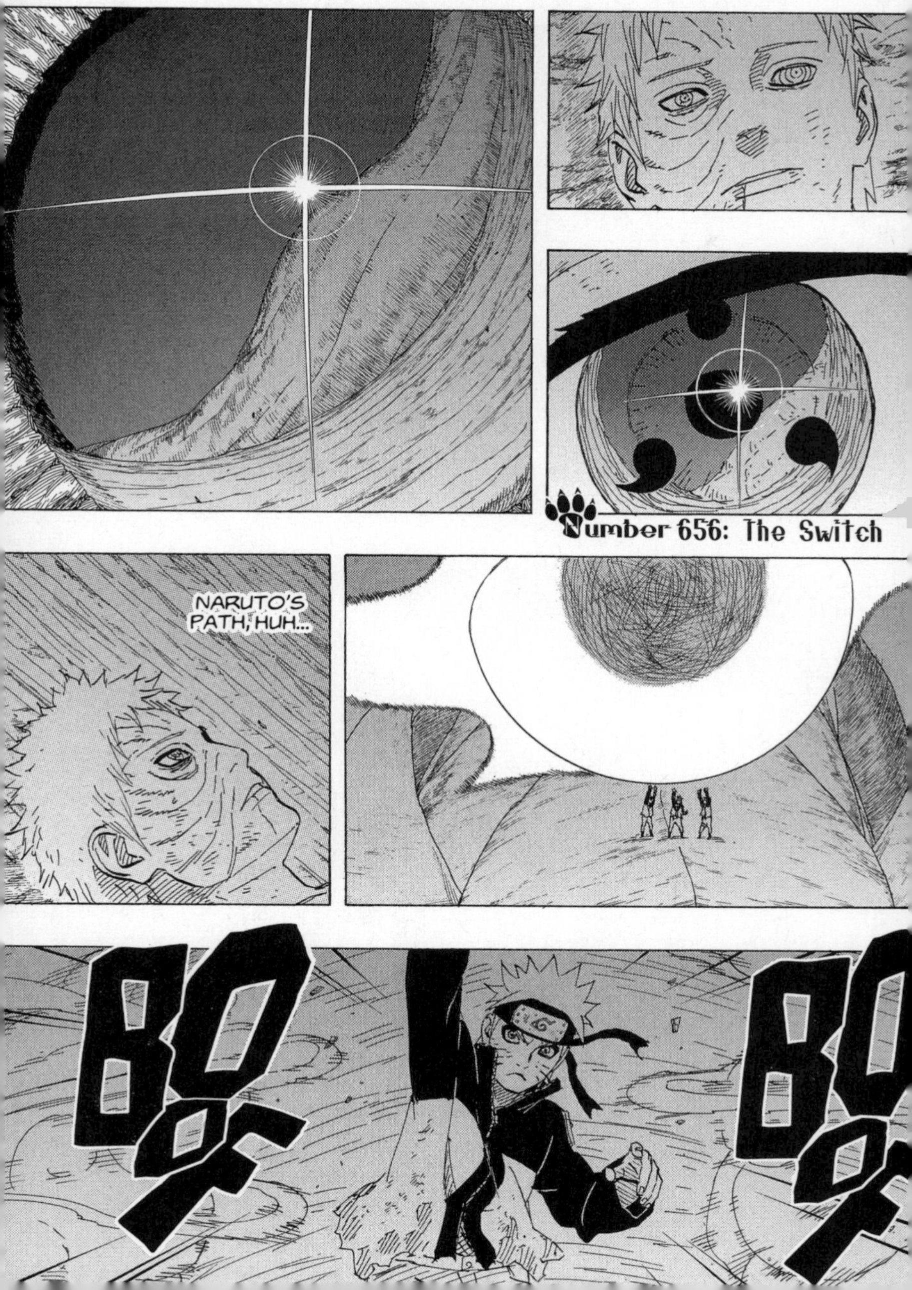
Number 656: The Switch
NARUTO'S PATH, HUH...
BOOF
BOOF

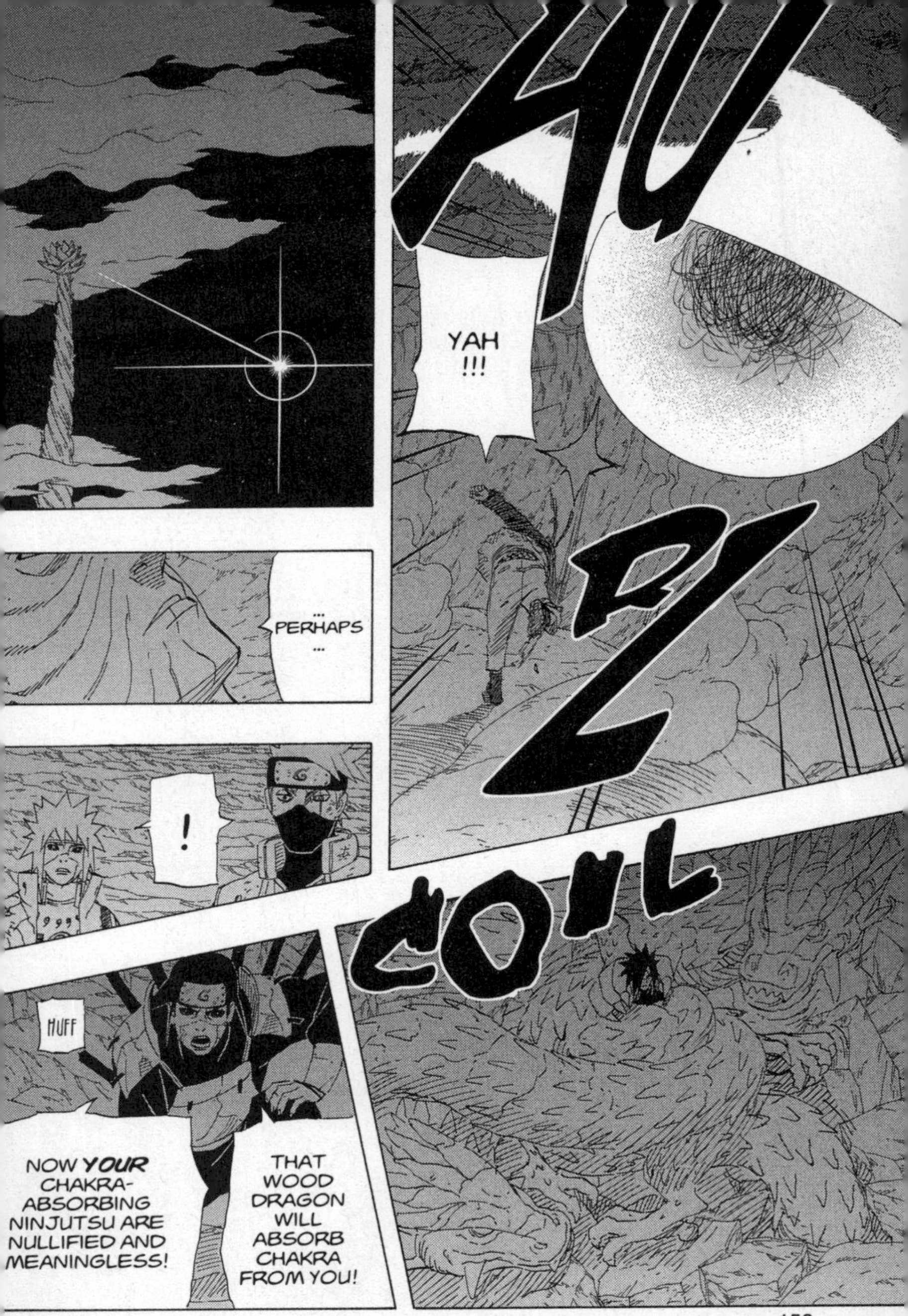
YAH !!!
... PERHAPS ...
!
COIL
HUFF
THAT WOOD DRAGON WILL ABSORB CHAKRA FROM YOU!
NOW YOUR CHAKRA-ABSORBING NINJUTSU ARE NULLIFIED AND MEANINGLESS!

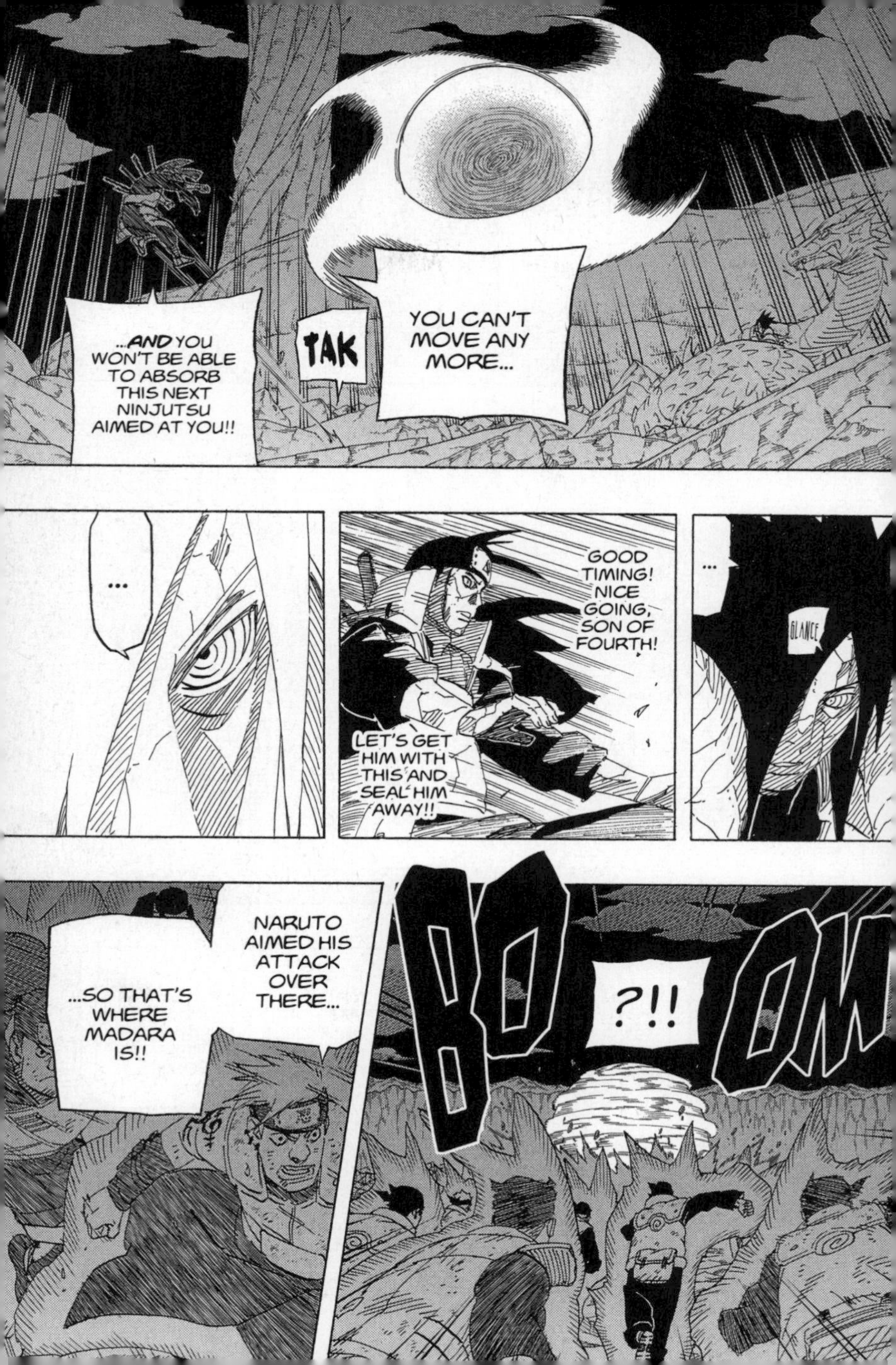

YOU CAN'T MOVE ANY MORE...
TAK
...AND YOU WON'T BE ABLE TO ABSORB THIS NEXT NINJUTSU AIMED AT YOU!!
...
GLANCE
GOOD TIMING! NICE GOING, SON OF FOURTH!
LET'S GET HIM WITH THIS AND SEAL HIM AWAY!!
...
BOOM
?!!
NARUTO AIMED HIS ATTACK OVER THERE...
...SO THAT'S WHERE MADARA IS!!

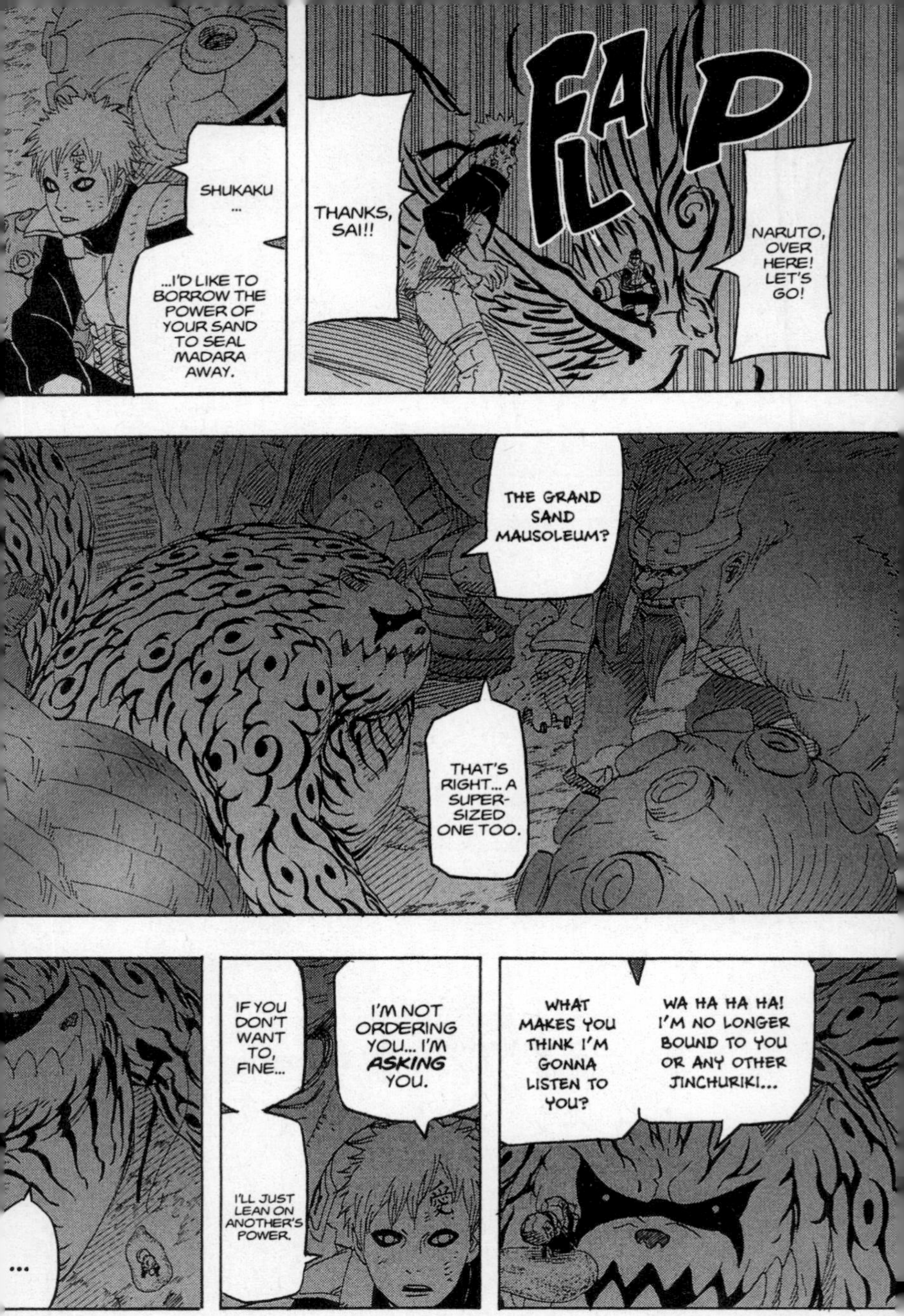
FLAP
NARUTO, OVER HERE! LET'S GO!
THANKS, SAI!!
SHUKAKU ...
...I'D LIKE TO BORROW THE POWER OF YOUR SAND TO SEAL MADARA AWAY.
THE GRAND SAND MAUSOLEUM?
THAT'S RIGHT... A SUPER-SIZED ONE TOO.
WA HA HA HA! I'M NO LONGER BOUND TO YOU OR ANY OTHER JINCHURIKI...
WHAT MAKES YOU THINK I'M GONNA LISTEN TO YOU?
I'M NOT ORDERING YOU... I'M **ASKING** YOU.
IF YOU DON'T WANT TO, FINE...
I'LL JUST LEAN ON ANOTHER'S POWER.
...

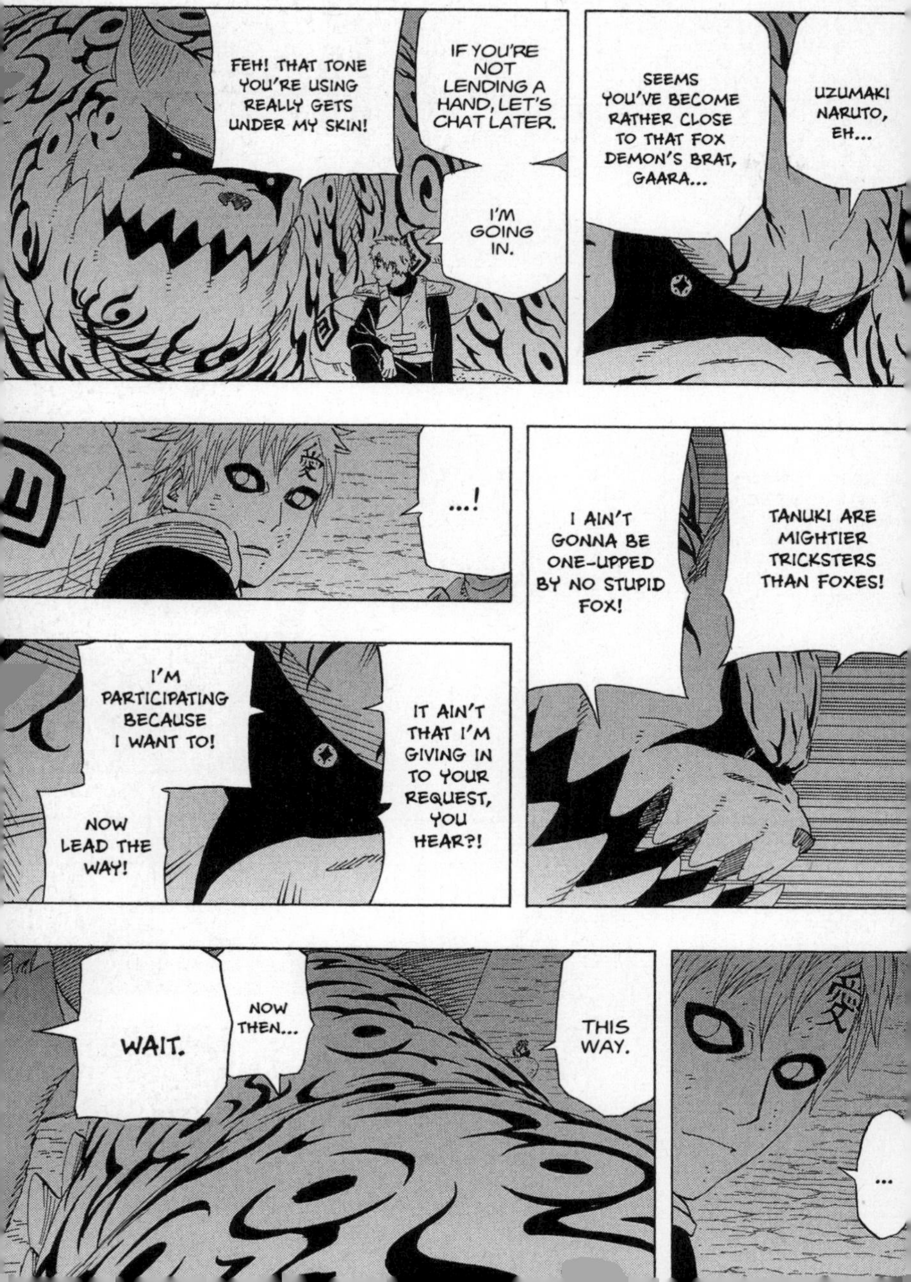
UZUMAKI NARUTO, EH...
SEEMS YOU'VE BECOME RATHER CLOSE TO THAT FOX DEMON'S BRAT, GAARA...
IF YOU'RE NOT LENDING A HAND, LET'S CHAT LATER.
I'M GOING IN.
FEH! THAT TONE YOU'RE USING REALLY GETS UNDER MY SKIN!
TANUKI ARE MIGHTIER TRICKSTERS THAN FOXES!
I AIN'T GONNA BE ONE-UPPED BY NO STUPID FOX!
...!
IT AIN'T THAT I'M GIVING IN TO YOUR REQUEST, YOU HEAR?!
I'M PARTICIPATING BECAUSE I WANT TO!
NOW LEAD THE WAY!
...
THIS WAY.
NOW THEN...
WAIT.

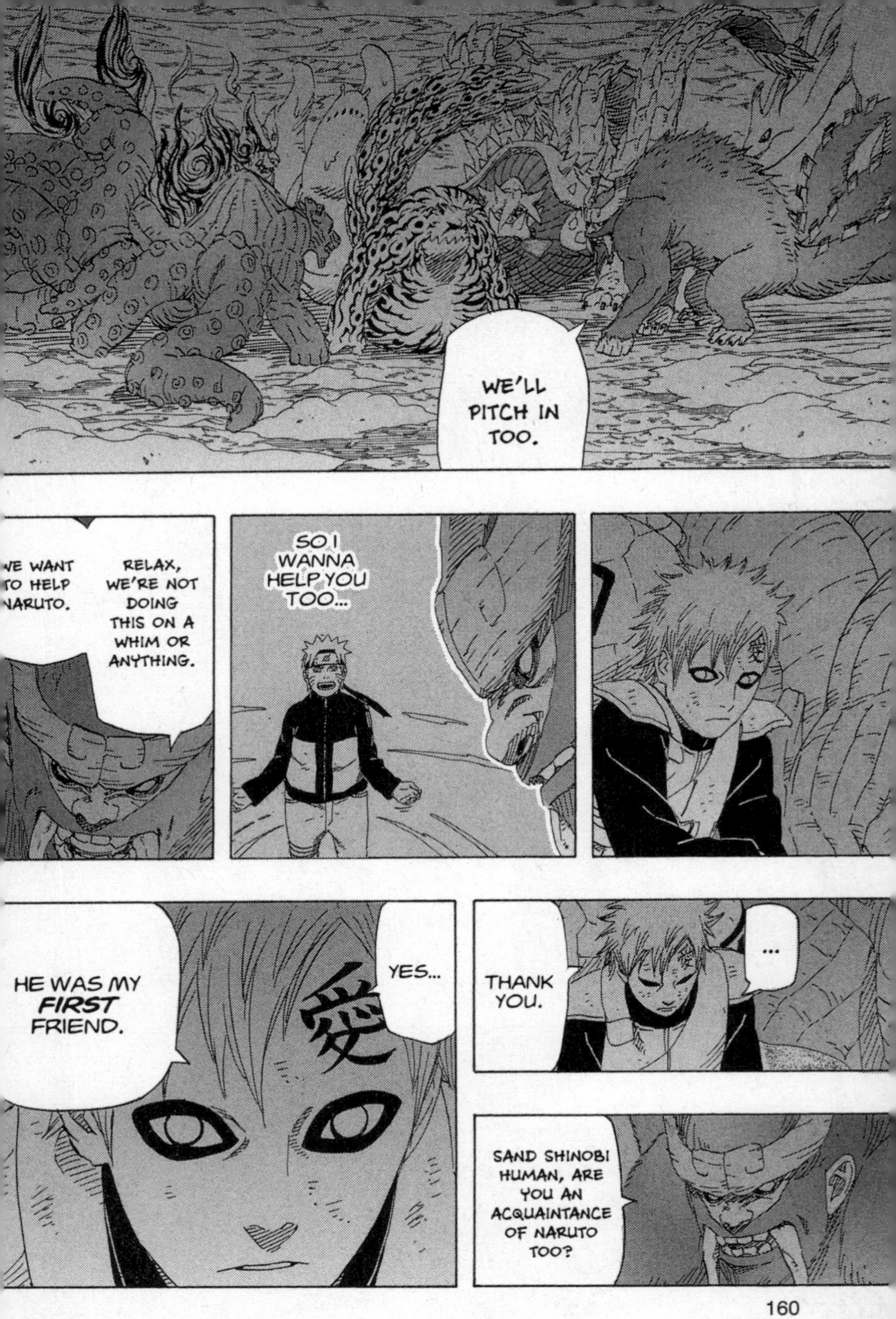
WE'LL PITCH IN TOO.
SO I WANNA HELP YOU TOO...
RELAX, WE'RE NOT DOING THIS ON A WHIM OR ANYTHING.
WE WANT TO HELP NARUTO.
...
THANK YOU.
SAND SHINOBI HUMAN, ARE YOU AN ACQUAINTANCE OF NARUTO TOO?
YES...
HE WAS MY *FIRST* FRIEND.

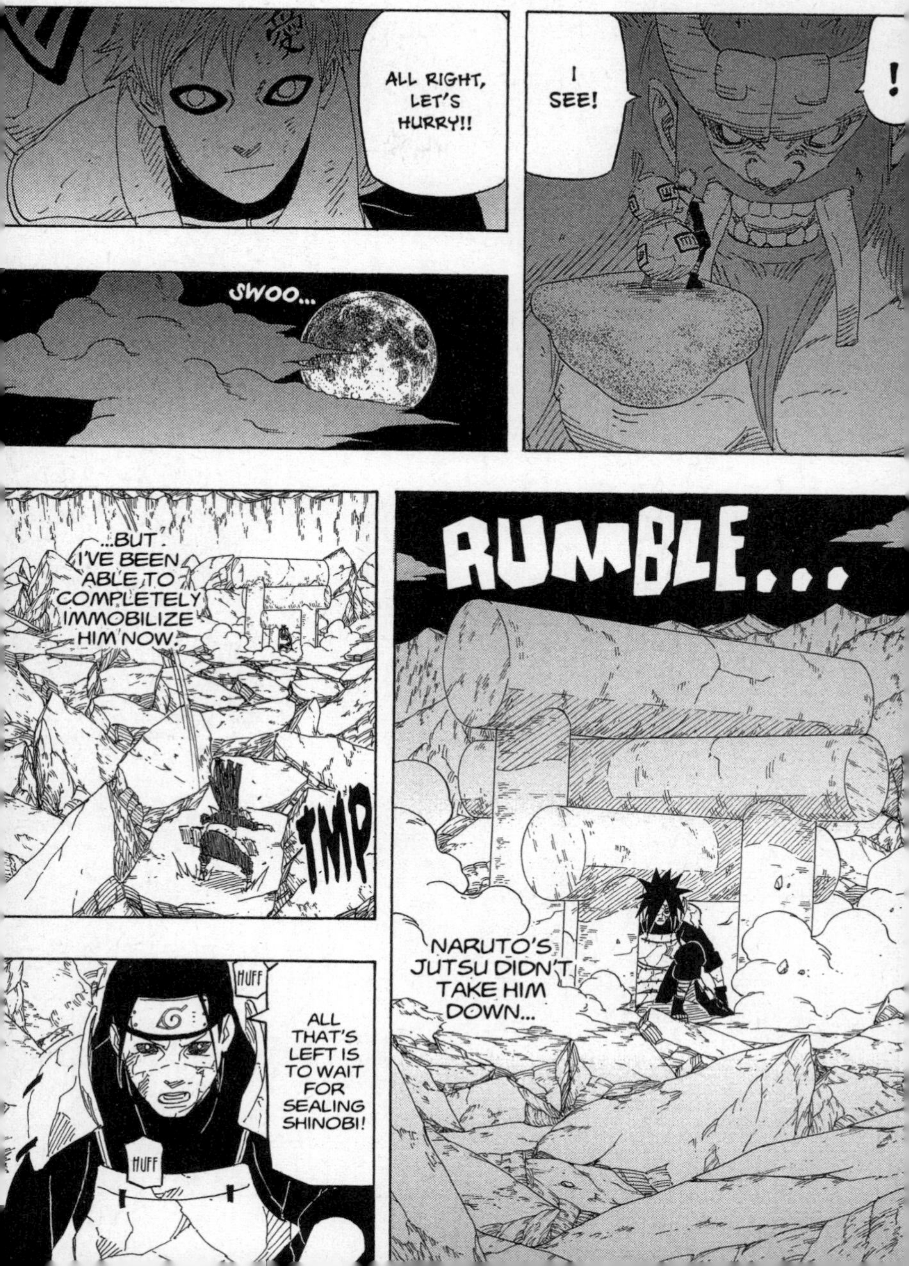
!
I SEE!
ALL RIGHT, LET'S HURRY!!
SWOO...
RUMBLE...
NARUTO'S JUTSU DIDN'T TAKE HIM DOWN...
...BUT I'VE BEEN ABLE TO COMPLETELY IMMOBILIZE HIM NOW.
TMP
HUFF
ALL THAT'S LEFT IS TO WAIT FOR SEALING SHINOBI!
HUFF

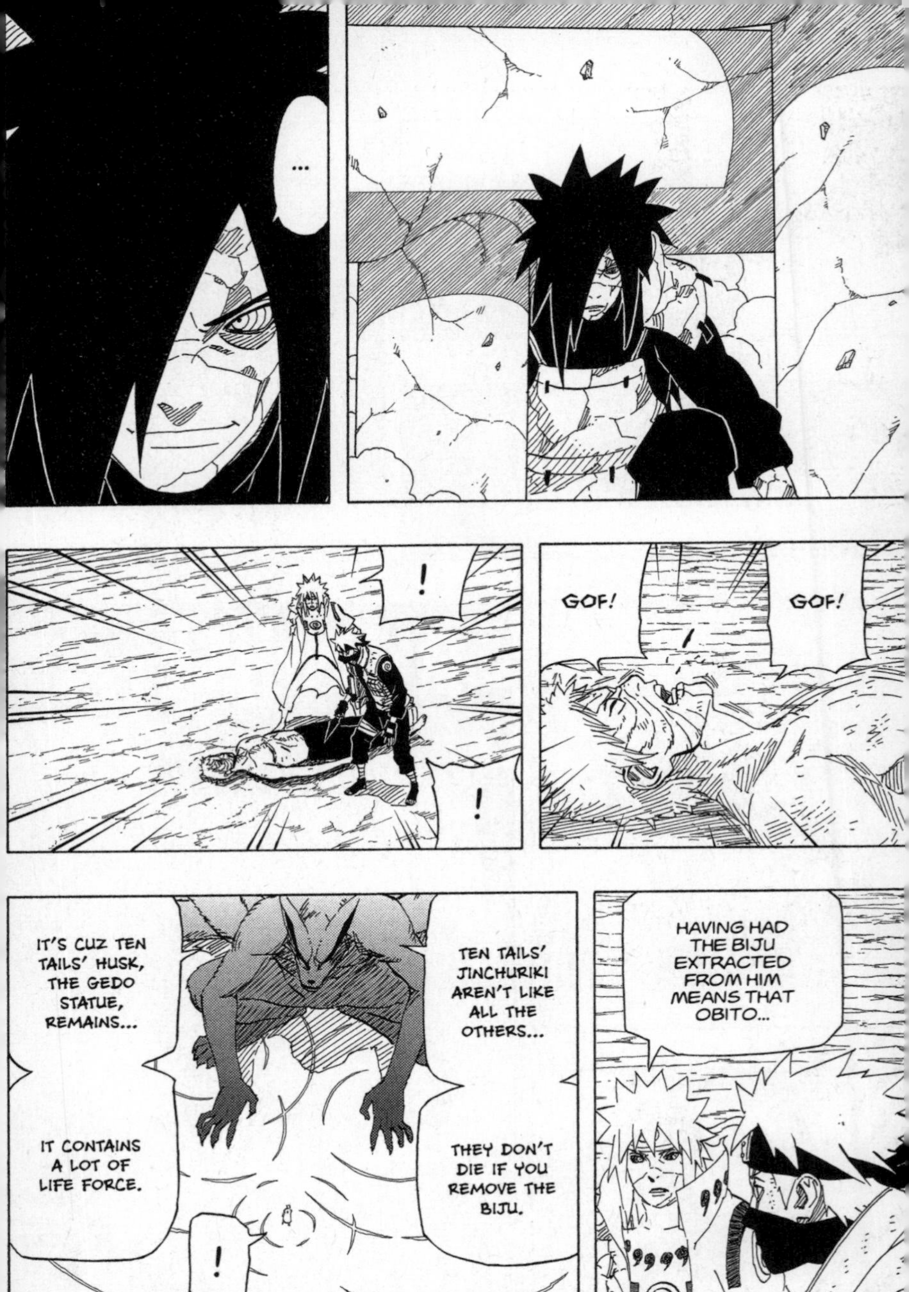
...
GOF!
GOF!
!
!
HAVING HAD THE BIJU EXTRACTED FROM HIM MEANS THAT OBITO...
TEN TAILS' JINCHURIKI AREN'T LIKE ALL THE OTHERS...
IT'S CUZ TEN TAILS' HUSK, THE GEDO STATUE, REMAINS...
THEY DON'T DIE IF YOU REMOVE THE BIJU.
IT CONTAINS A LOT OF LIFE FORCE.
!

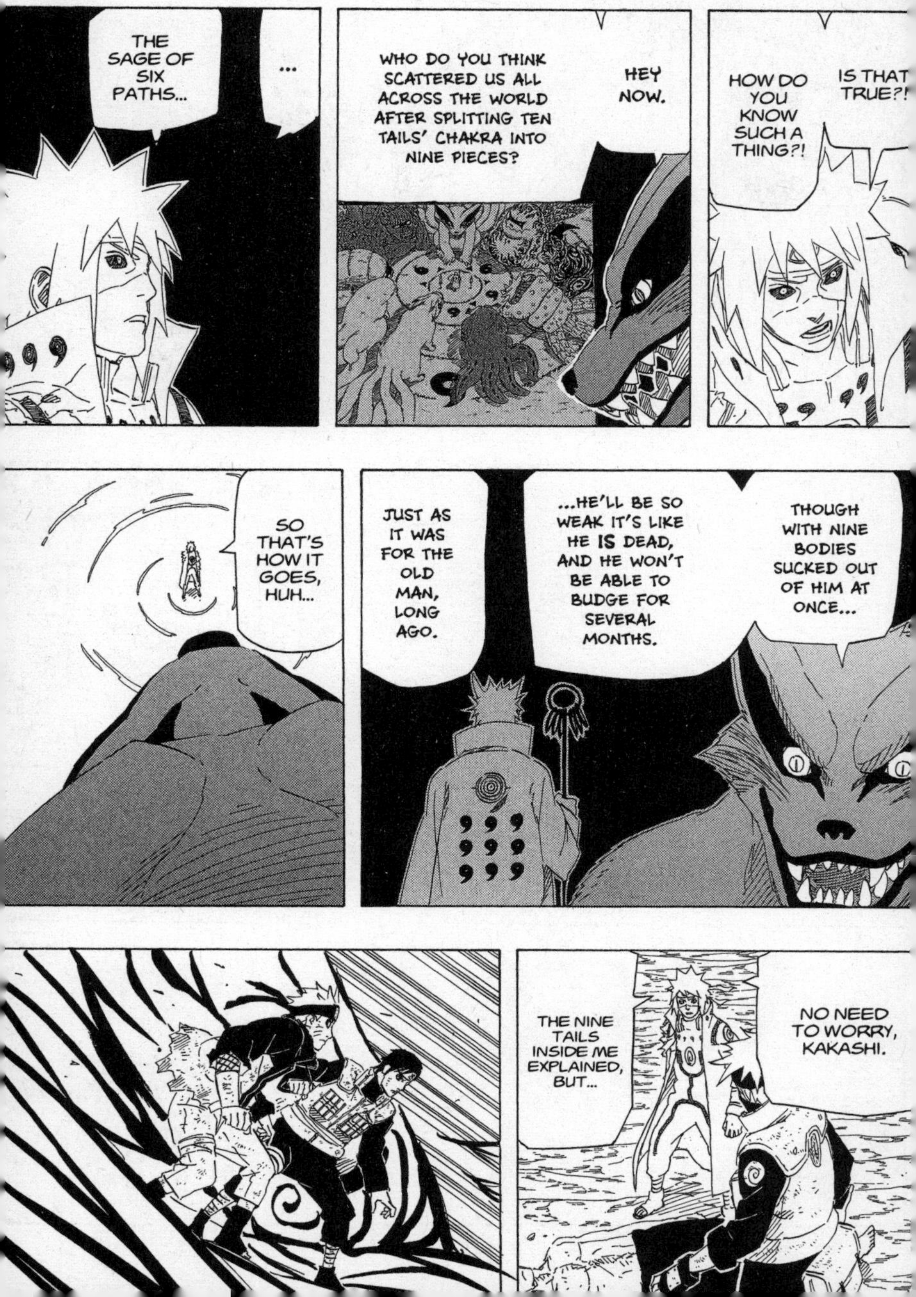
IS THAT TRUE?!
HOW DO YOU KNOW SUCH A THING?!
HEY NOW.
WHO DO YOU THINK SCATTERED US ALL ACROSS THE WORLD AFTER SPLITTING TEN TAILS' CHAKRA INTO NINE PIECES?
...
THE SAGE OF SIX PATHS...
THOUGH WITH NINE BODIES SUCKED OUT OF HIM AT ONCE...
...HE'LL BE SO WEAK IT'S LIKE HE **IS** DEAD, AND HE WON'T BE ABLE TO BUDGE FOR SEVERAL MONTHS.
JUST AS IT WAS FOR THE OLD MAN, LONG AGO.
SO THAT'S HOW IT GOES, HUH...
NO NEED TO WORRY, KAKASHI.
THE NINE TAILS INSIDE ME EXPLAINED, BUT...

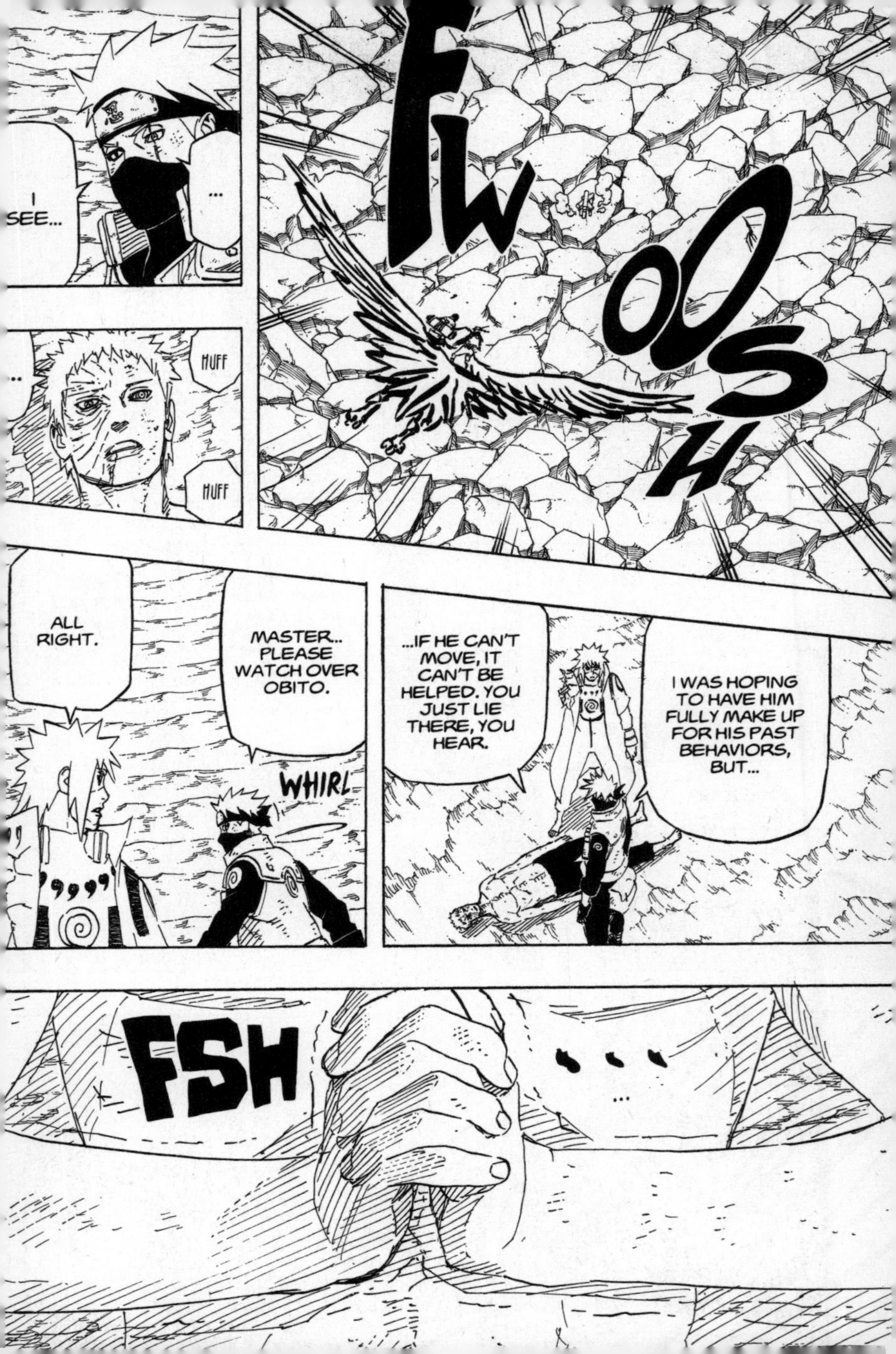
FWOOSH
...
I SEE...
HUFF
...
HUFF
I WAS HOPING TO HAVE HIM FULLY MAKE UP FOR HIS PAST BEHAVIORS, BUT...
...IF HE CAN'T MOVE, IT CAN'T BE HELPED. YOU JUST LIE THERE, YOU HEAR.
MASTER... PLEASE WATCH OVER OBITO.
WHIRL
ALL RIGHT.
...
...
FSH

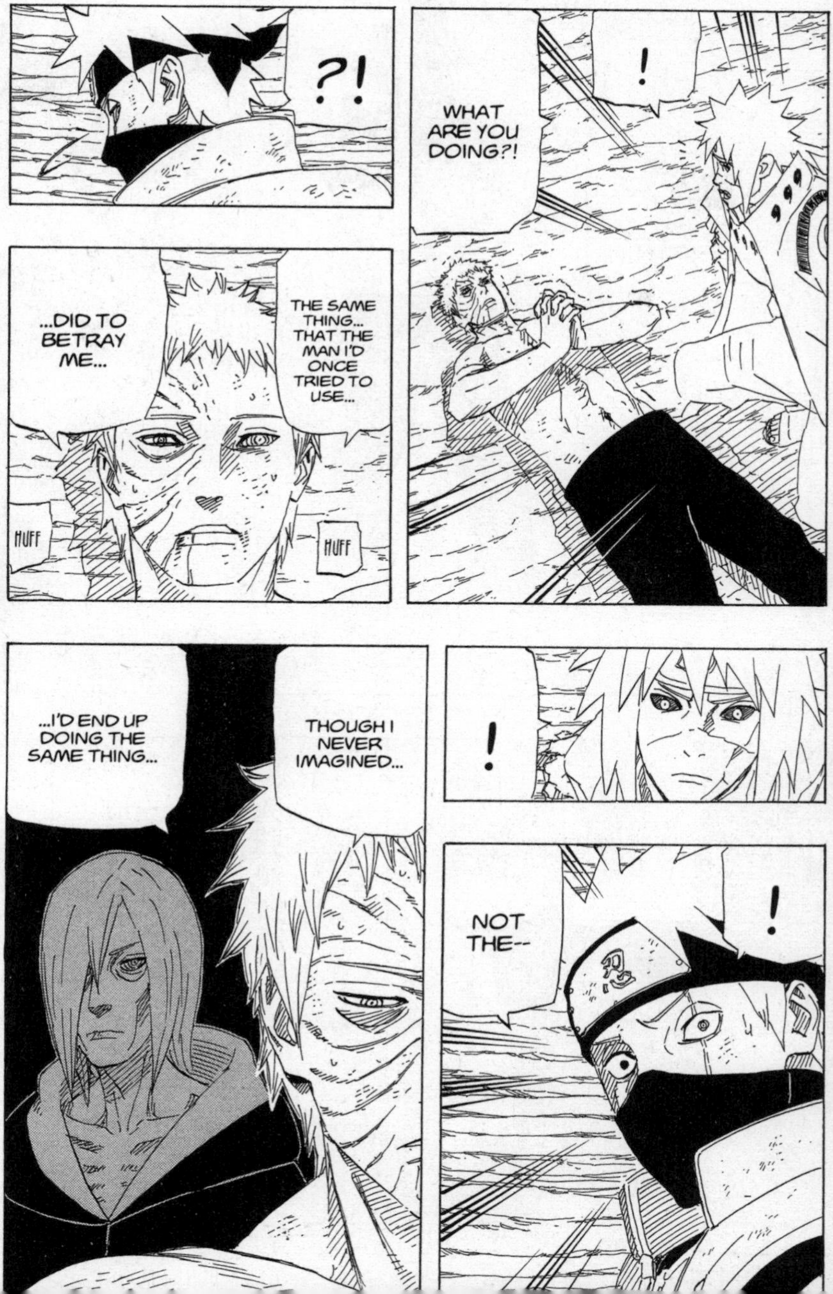
!
WHAT ARE YOU DOING?!
?!
THE SAME THING... THAT THE MAN I'D ONCE TRIED TO USE...
...DID TO BETRAY ME...
HUFF
HUFF
!
!
NOT THE--
THOUGH I NEVER IMAGINED...
...I'D END UP DOING THE SAME THING...

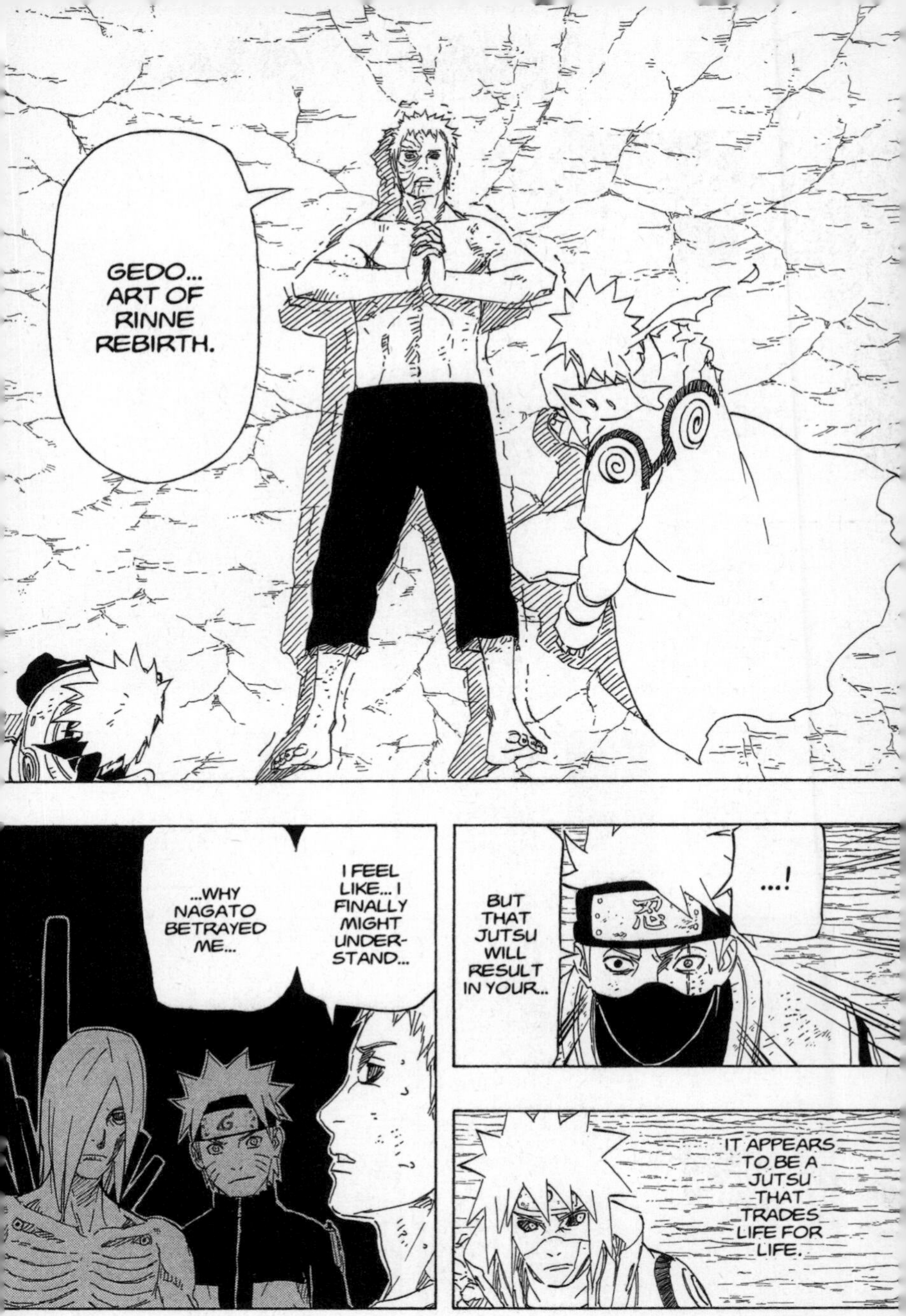
GEDO... ART OF RINNE REBIRTH.
...!
BUT THAT JUTSU WILL RESULT IN YOUR..
IT APPEARS TO BE A JUTSU THAT TRADES LIFE FOR LIFE.
I FEEL LIKE... I FINALLY MIGHT UNDER-STAND...
...WHY NAGATO BETRAYED ME...

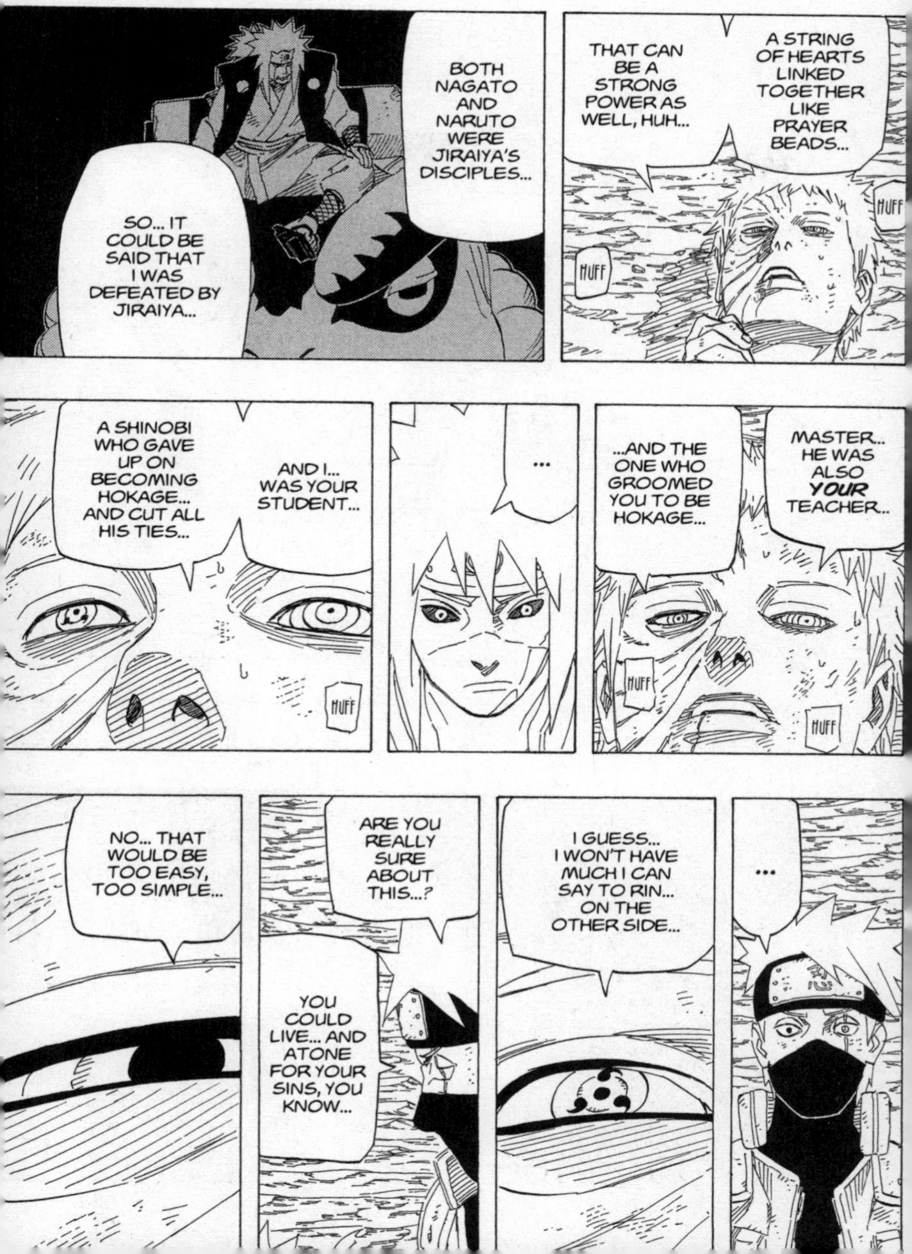
A STRING OF HEARTS LINKED TOGETHER LIKE PRAYER BEADS...
THAT CAN BE A STRONG POWER AS WELL, HUH...
HUFF
HUFF
BOTH NAGATO AND NARUTO WERE JIRAIYA'S DISCIPLES...
SO... IT COULD BE SAID THAT I WAS DEFEATED BY JIRAIYA...
MASTER... HE WAS ALSO *YOUR* TEACHER...
...AND THE ONE WHO GROOMED YOU TO BE HOKAGE...
HUFF
HUFF
...
AND I... WAS YOUR STUDENT...
A SHINOBI WHO GAVE UP ON BECOMING HOKAGE... AND CUT ALL HIS TIES...
HUFF
...
I GUESS... I WON'T HAVE MUCH I CAN SAY TO RIN... ON THE OTHER SIDE...
ARE YOU REALLY SURE ABOUT THIS...?
YOU COULD LIVE... AND ATONE FOR YOUR SINS, YOU KNOW...
NO... THAT WOULD BE TOO EASY, TOO SIMPLE...

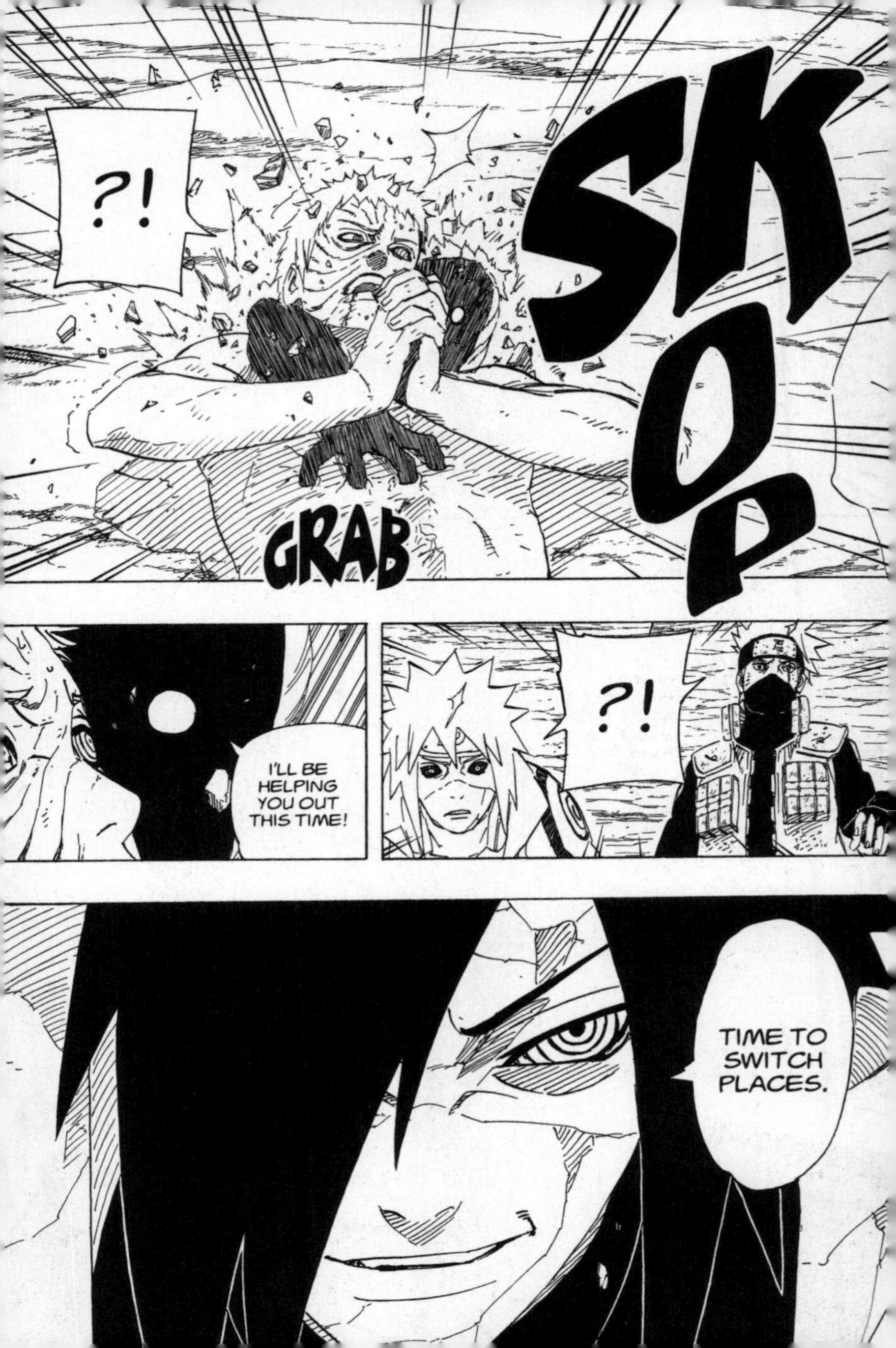
SKOOP
?!
GRAB
?!
I'LL BE HELPING YOU OUT THIS TIME!
TIME TO SWITCH PLACES.

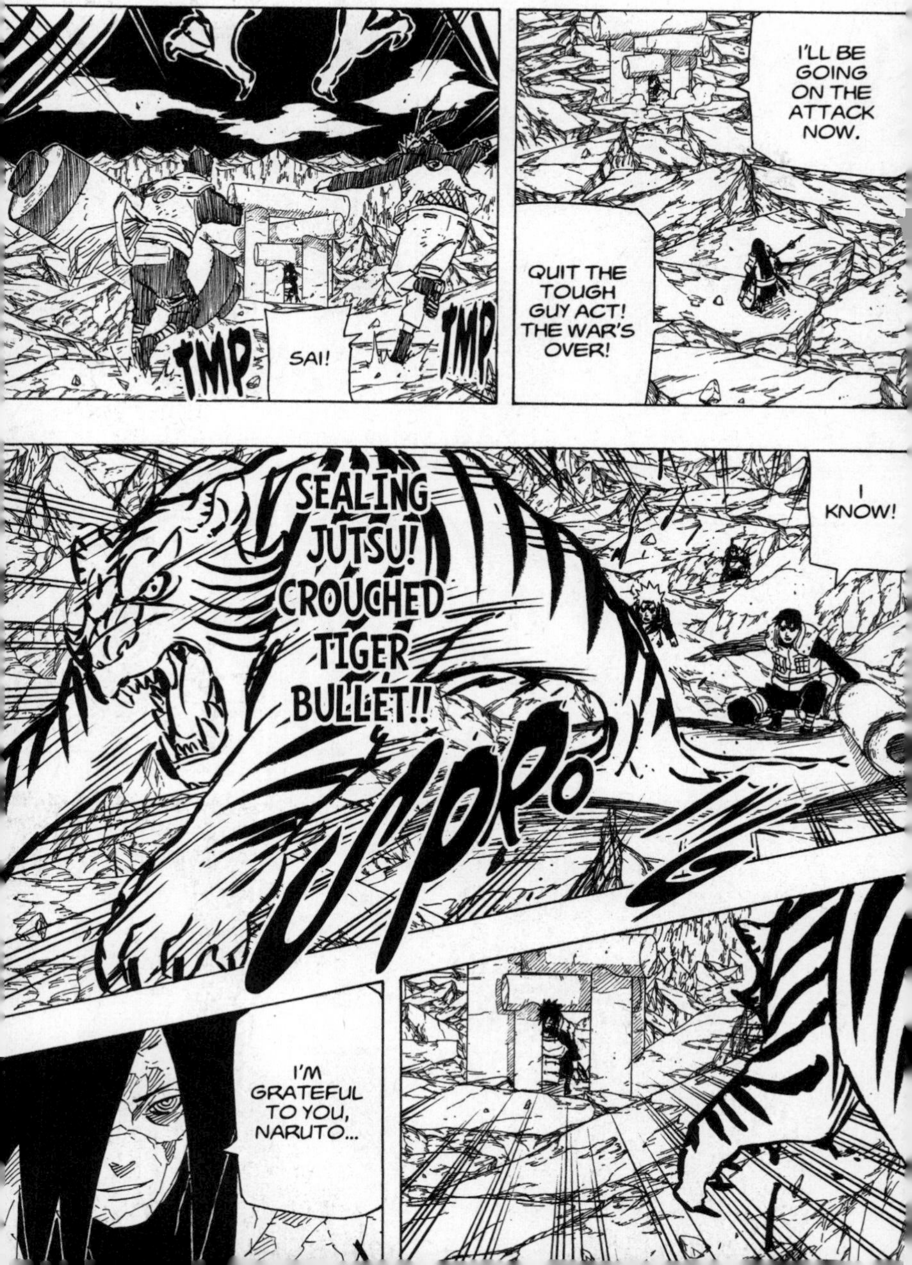
I'LL BE GOING ON THE ATTACK NOW.
QUIT THE TOUGH GUY ACT! THE WAR'S OVER!
TMP
SAI!
TMP
I KNOW!
SEALING JUTSU! CROUCHED TIGER BULLET!!
I'M GRATEFUL TO YOU, NARUTO...

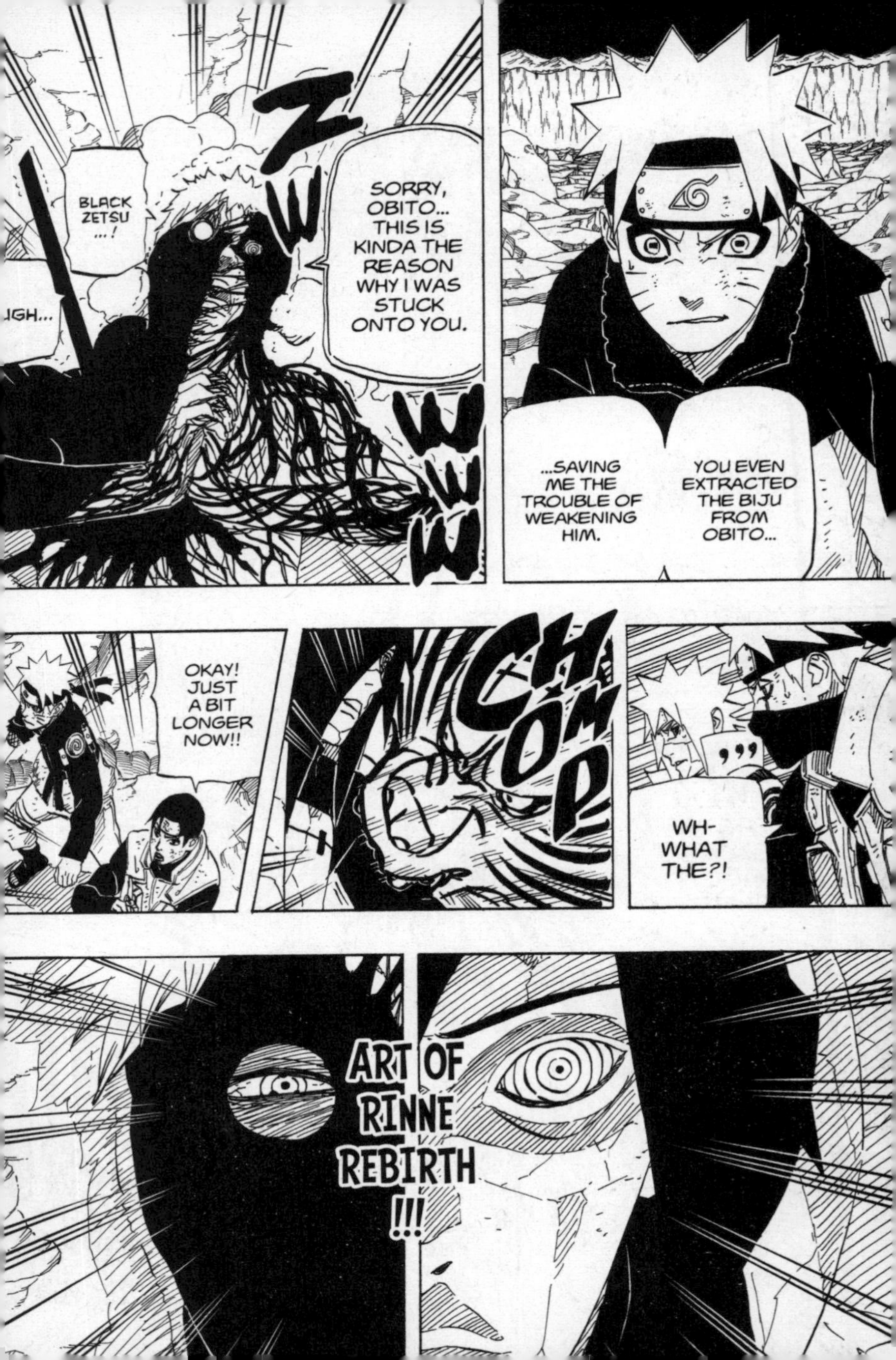
YOU EVEN EXTRACTED THE BIJU FROM OBITO...
...SAVING ME THE TROUBLE OF WEAKENING HIM.
SORRY, OBITO... THIS IS KINDA THE REASON WHY I WAS STUCK ONTO YOU.
ZWWWWW
BLACK ZETSU ...!
WH- WHAT THE?!
...
CHOMP
OKAY! JUST A BIT LONGER NOW!!
ART OF RINNE REBIRTH !!!

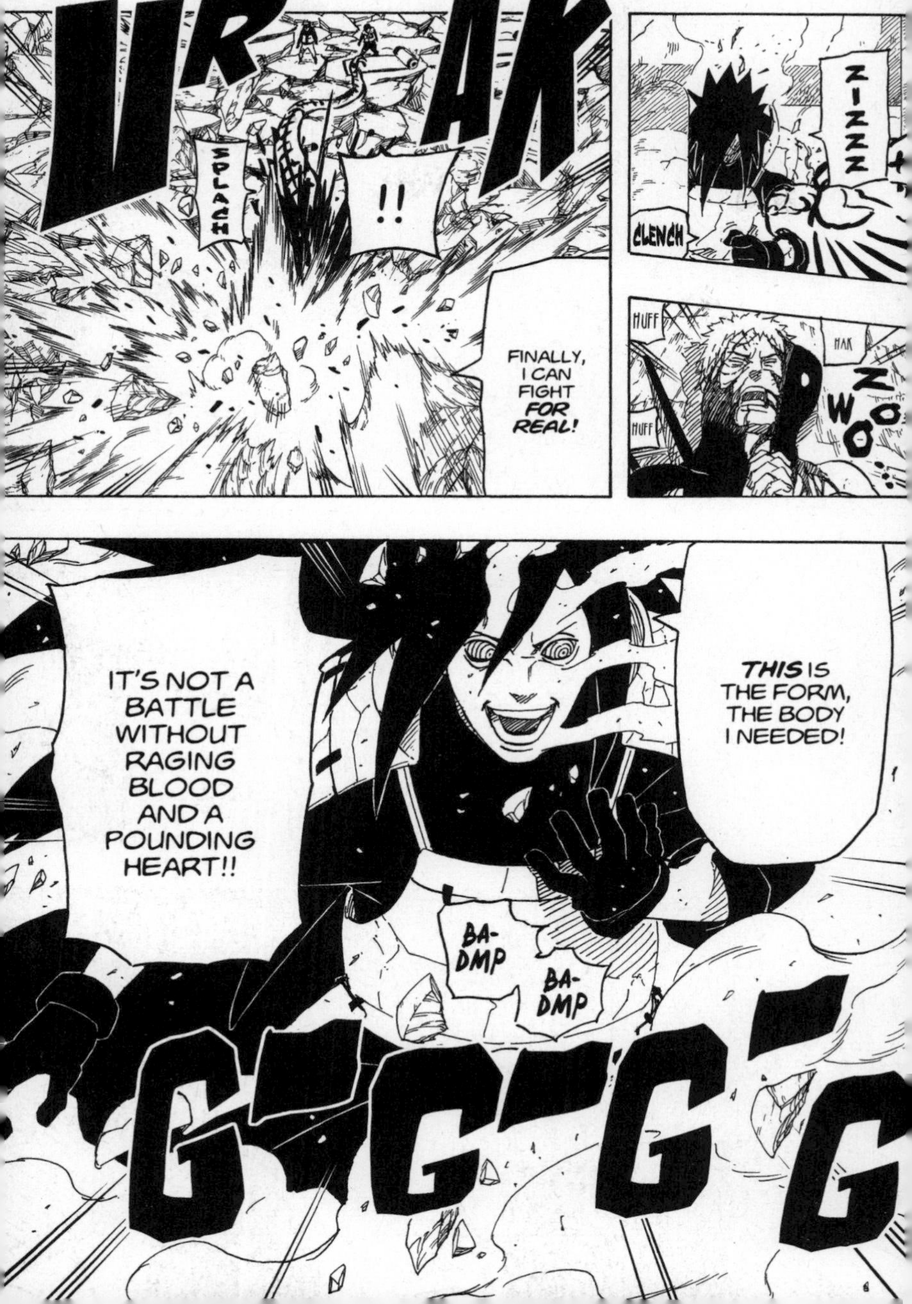

ZIZZZ
CLENCH
HUFF
HAK
HUFF
ZWOO
VRAK
SPLACH
!!
FINALLY, I CAN FIGHT FOR REAL!
THIS IS THE FORM, THE BODY I NEEDED!
IT'S NOT A BATTLE WITHOUT RAGING BLOOD AND A POUNDING HEART!!
BA-DMP
BA-DMP
GGGG

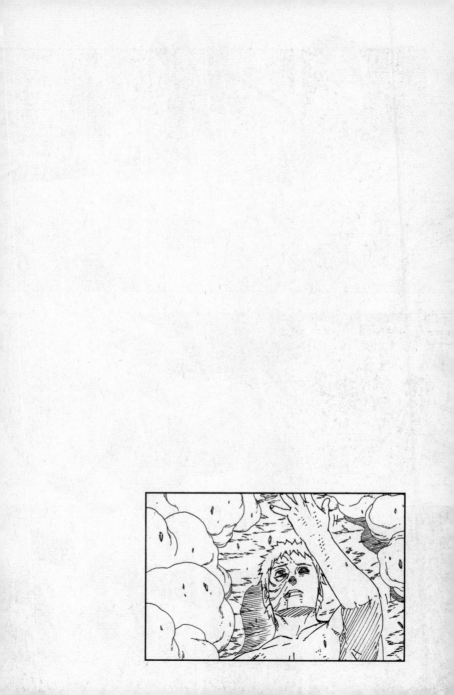

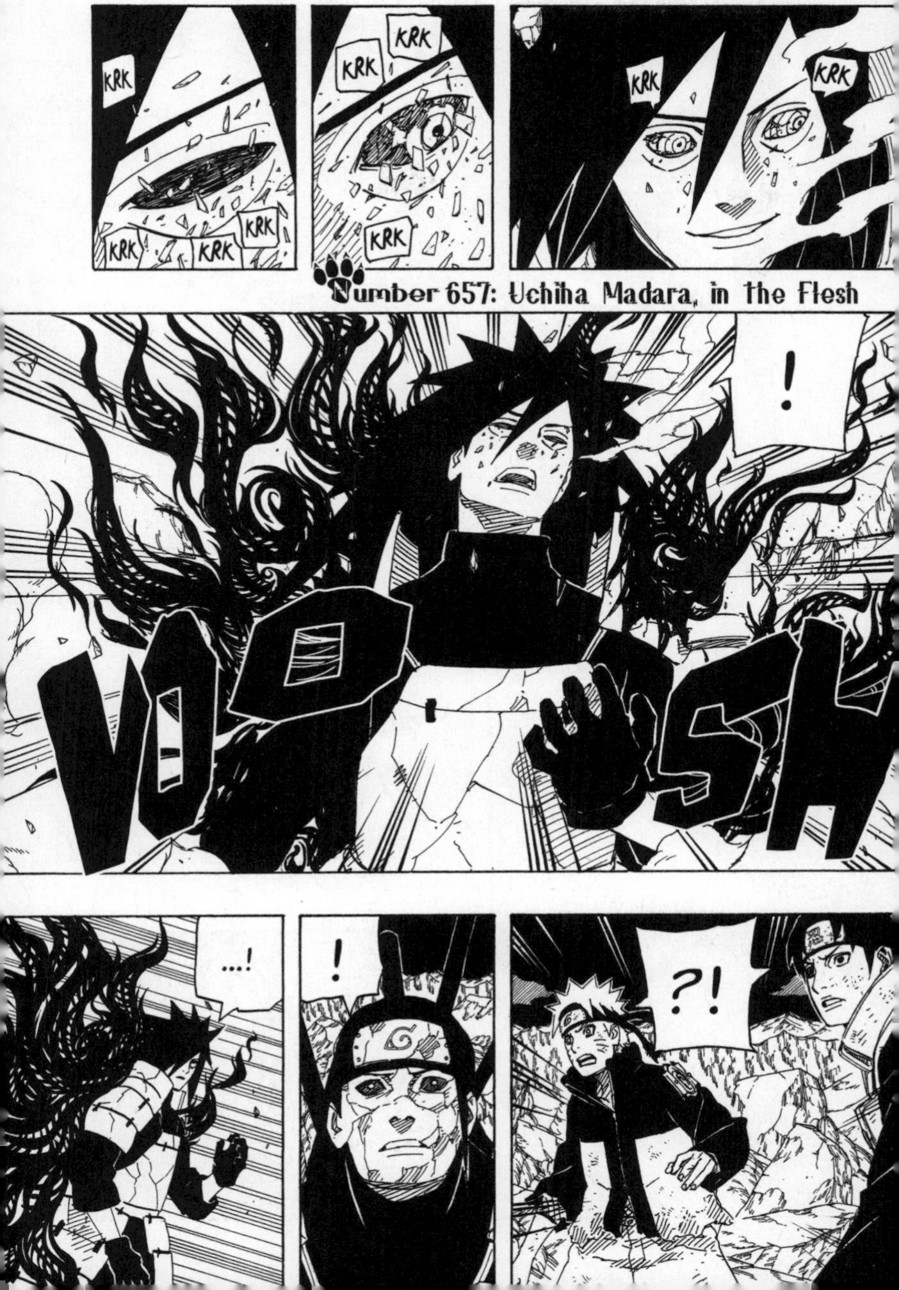
KRK
KRK
KRK
KRK
KRK
KRK
KRK
KRK
KRK
Number 657: Uchiha Madara, in the Flesh
!
VOOSH
?!
!
...!

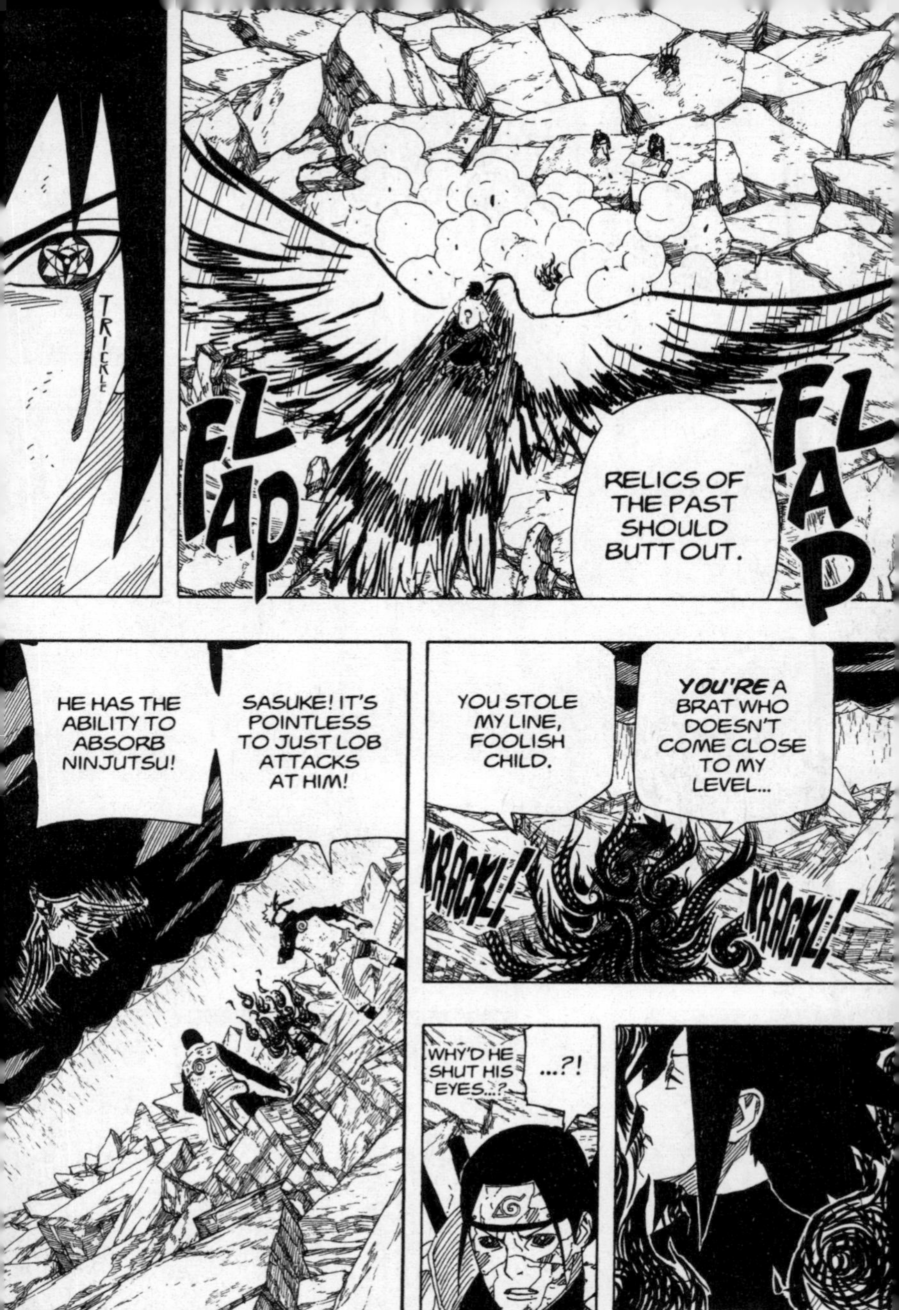
FLAP
RELICS OF THE PAST SHOULD BUTT OUT.
FLAP
TRICKLE
YOU'RE A BRAT WHO DOESN'T COME CLOSE TO MY LEVEL...
YOU STOLE MY LINE, FOOLISH CHILD.
KRACKL!
KRACKL!
...?!
WHY'D HE SHUT HIS EYES...?
SASUKE! IT'S POINTLESS TO JUST LOB ATTACKS AT HIM!
HE HAS THE ABILITY TO ABSORB NINJUTSU!

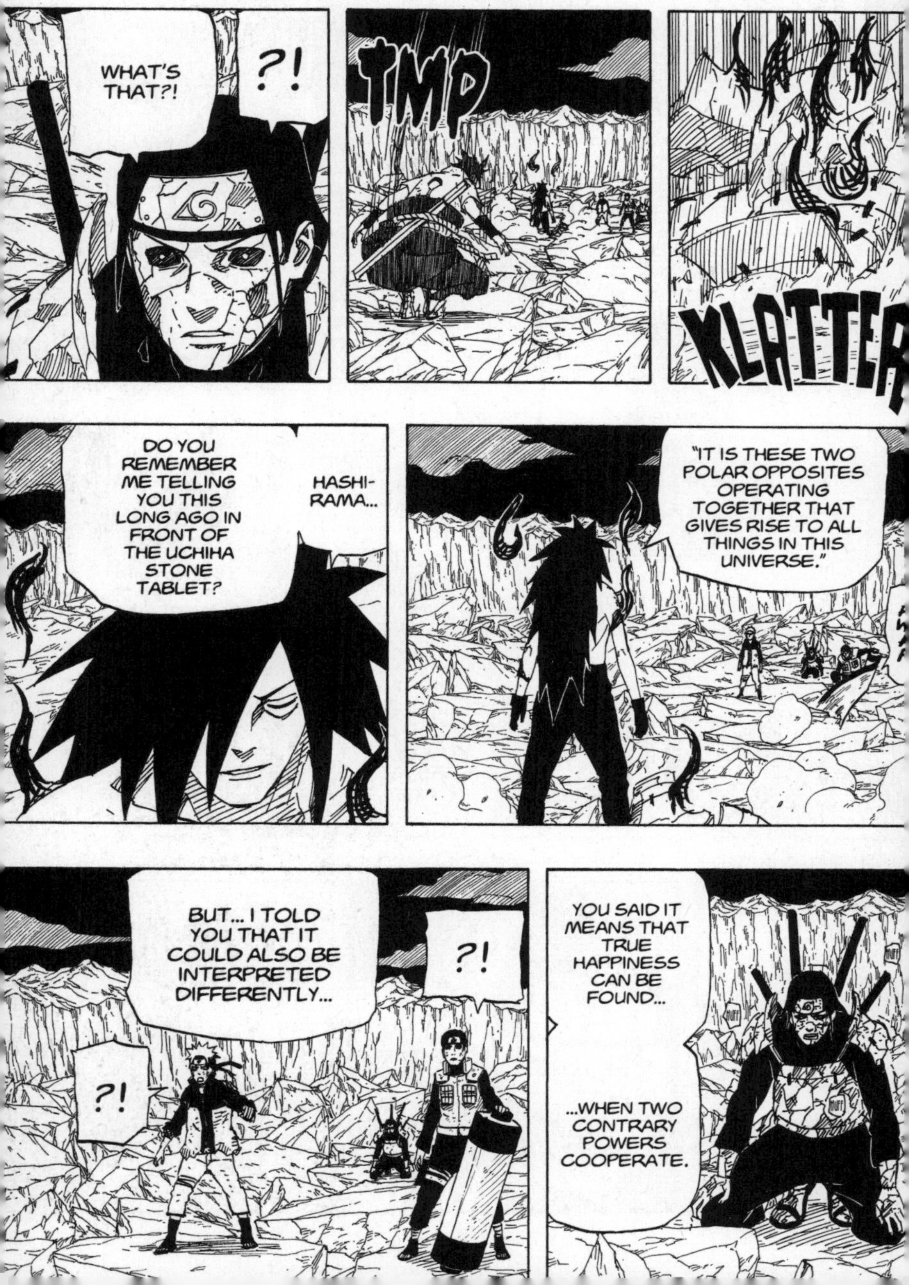
KLATTER
TMP
?!
WHAT'S THAT?!
"IT IS THESE TWO POLAR OPPOSITES OPERATING TOGETHER THAT GIVES RISE TO ALL THINGS IN THIS UNIVERSE."
HASHI-RAMA...
DO YOU REMEMBER ME TELLING YOU THIS LONG AGO IN FRONT OF THE UCHIHA STONE TABLET?
YOU SAID IT MEANS THAT TRUE HAPPINESS CAN BE FOUND...
...WHEN TWO CONTRARY POWERS COOPERATE.
?!
BUT... I TOLD YOU THAT IT COULD ALSO BE INTERPRETED DIFFERENTLY...
?!

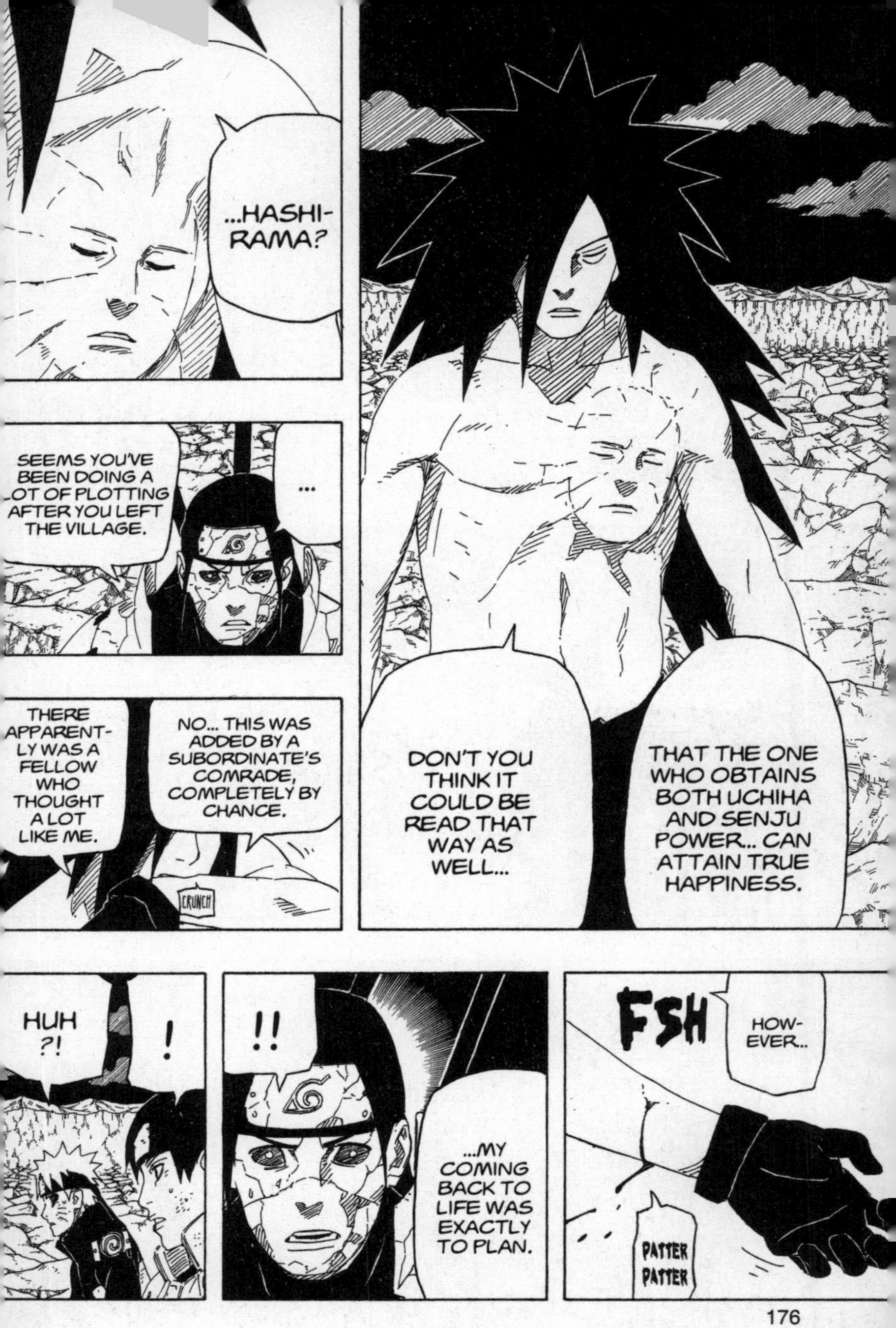
THAT THE ONE WHO OBTAINS BOTH UCHIHA AND SENJU POWER... CAN ATTAIN TRUE HAPPINESS.
DON'T YOU THINK IT COULD BE READ THAT WAY AS WELL...
...HASHI-RAMA?
...
SEEMS YOU'VE BEEN DOING A LOT OF PLOTTING AFTER YOU LEFT THE VILLAGE.
NO... THIS WAS ADDED BY A SUBORDINATE'S COMRADE, COMPLETELY BY CHANCE.
THERE APPARENT-LY WAS A FELLOW WHO THOUGHT A LOT LIKE ME.
CRUNCH
HOW-EVER...
FSH
PATTER PATTER
!!
...MY COMING BACK TO LIFE WAS EXACTLY TO PLAN.
!
HUH ?!

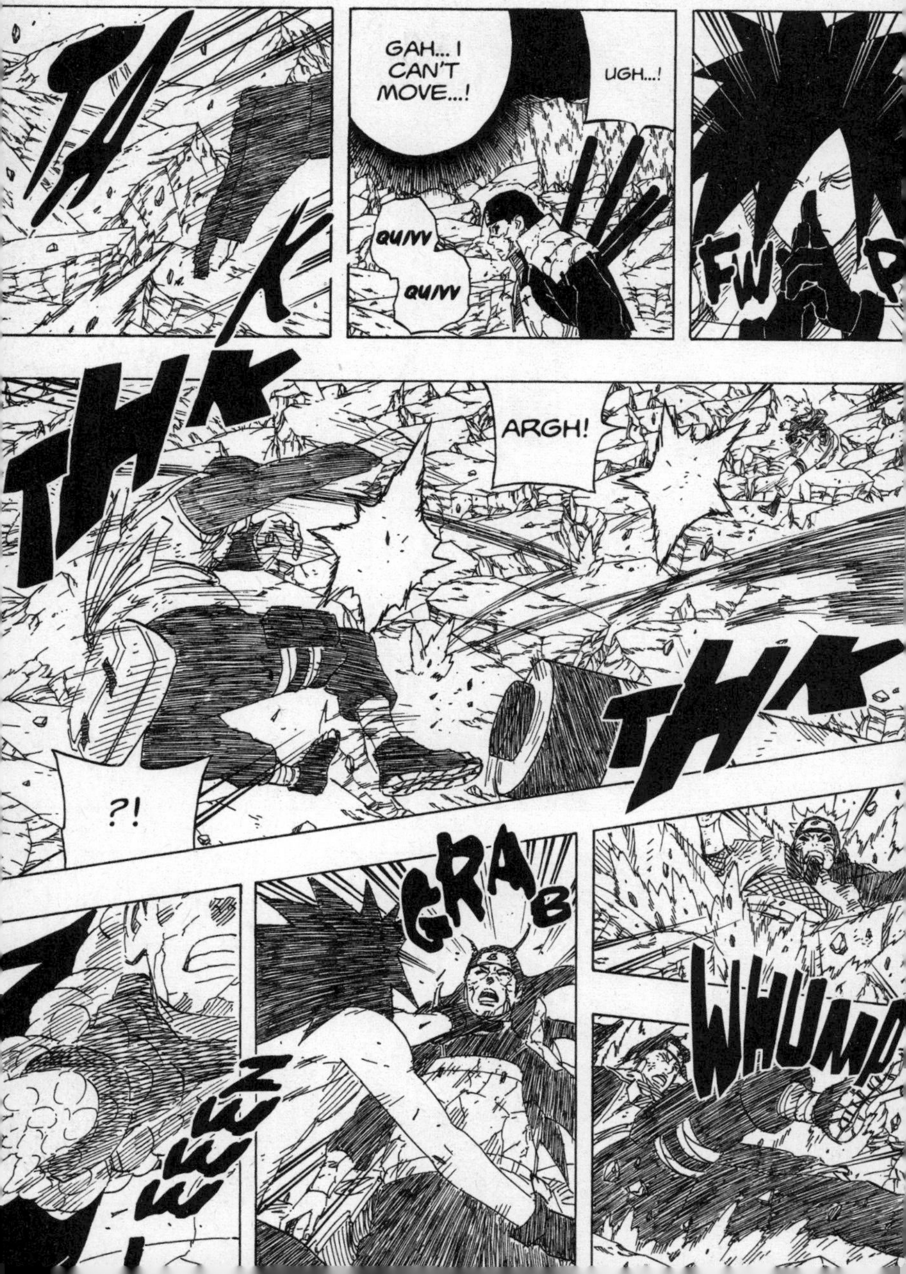
FWAP
GAH... I CAN'T MOVE...!
UGH...!
QUIVV
QUIVV
THWK
THWK
ARGH!
THWK
?!
WHUMP
GRAB

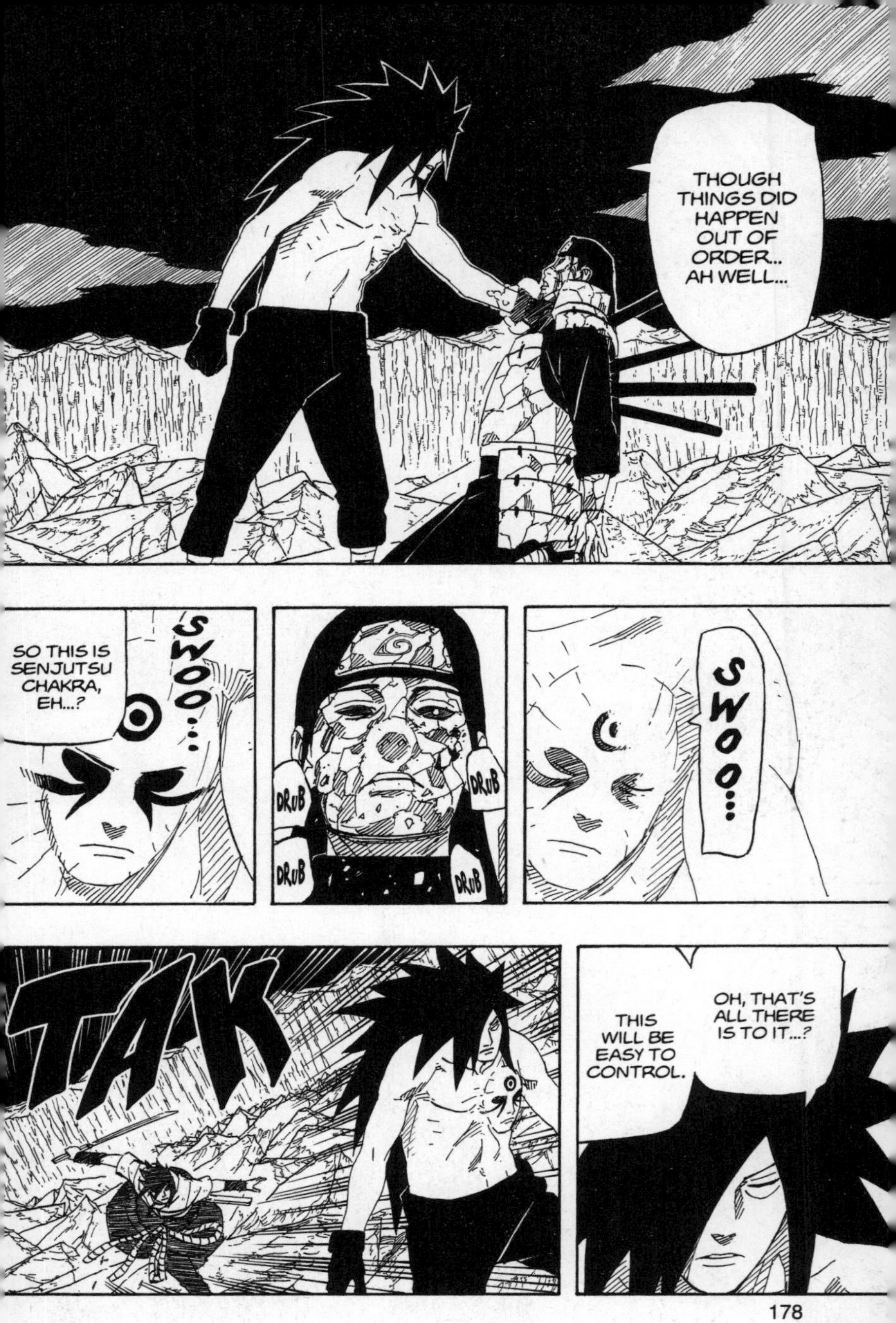
THOUGH THINGS DID HAPPEN OUT OF ORDER... AH WELL...
SWOO...
DRUB
DRUB
DRUB
DRUB
SO THIS IS SENJUTSU CHAKRA, EH...?
SWOO...
OH, THAT'S ALL THERE IS TO IT...?
THIS WILL BE EASY TO CONTROL.
TAK

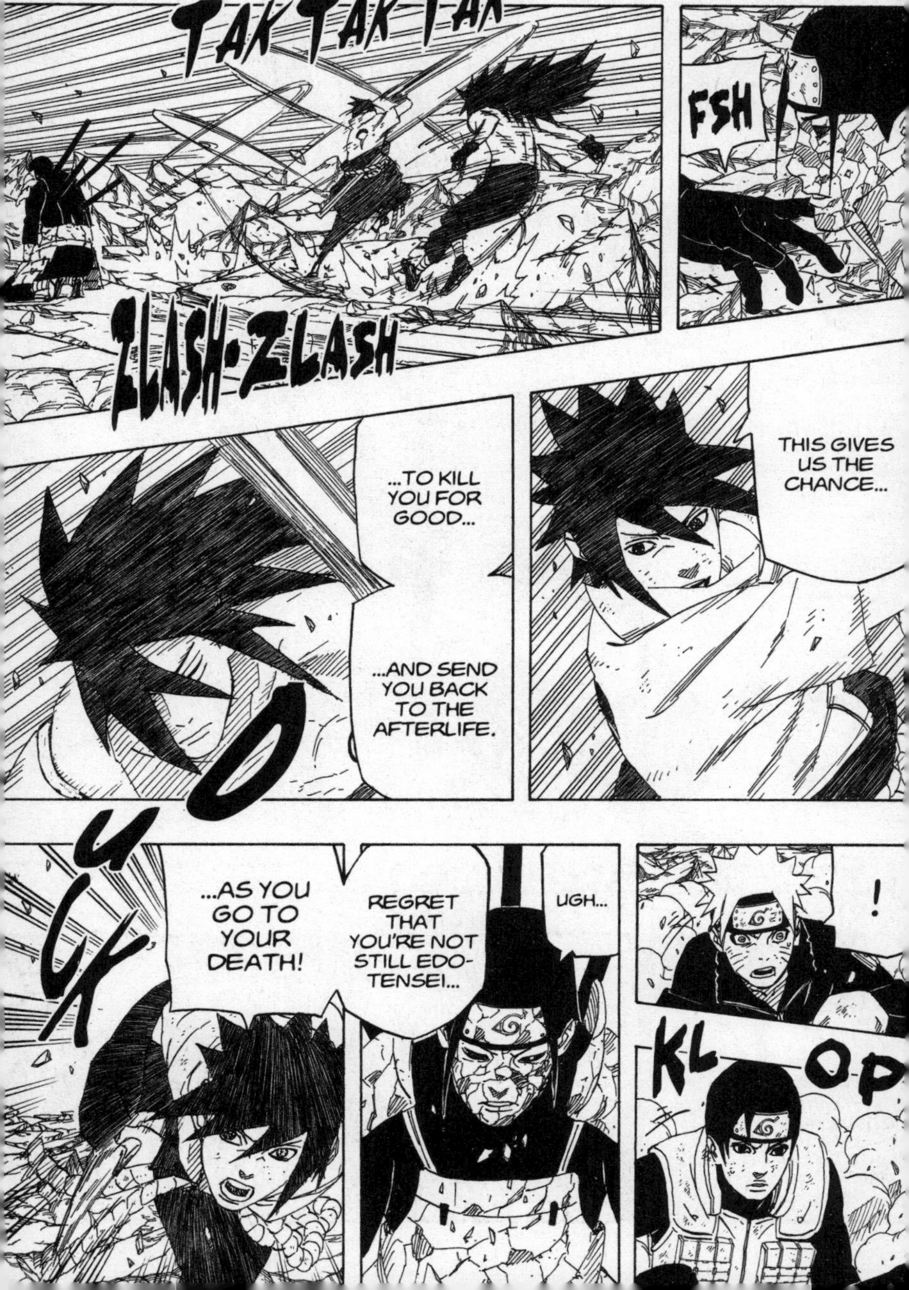
FSH
TAK TAK TAK
ZLASH-ZLASH
THIS GIVES US THE CHANCE...
...TO KILL YOU FOR GOOD...
...AND SEND YOU BACK TO THE AFTERLIFE.
!
KL-OP
UGH...
REGRET THAT YOU'RE NOT STILL EDO-TENSEI...
...AS YOU GO TO YOUR DEATH!

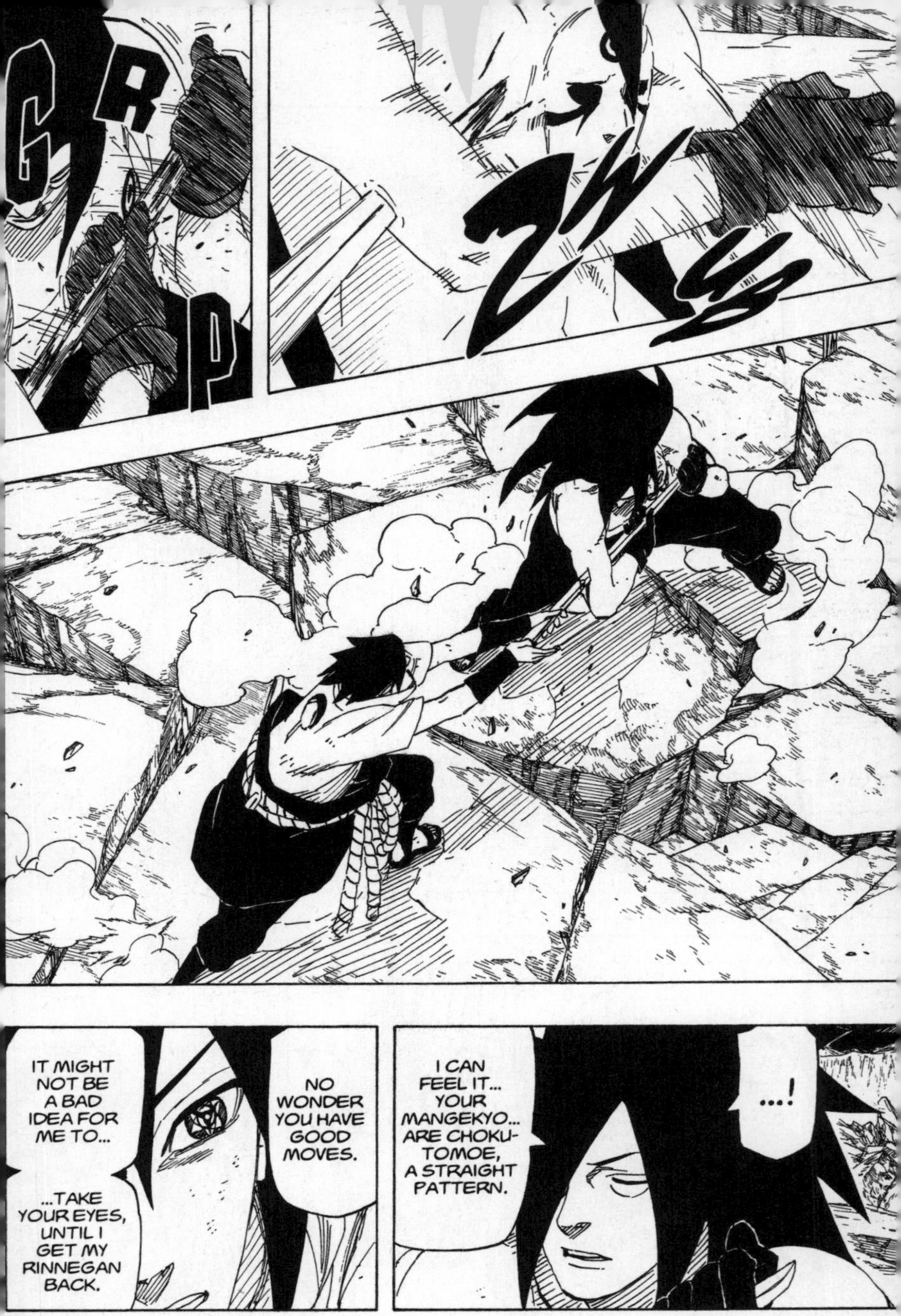
ZWUP
GRIP
...!
I CAN FEEL IT... YOUR MANGEKYO... ARE CHOKU-TOMOE, A STRAIGHT PATTERN.
NO WONDER YOU HAVE GOOD MOVES.
IT MIGHT NOT BE A BAD IDEA FOR ME TO...
...TAKE YOUR EYES, UNTIL I GET MY RINNEGAN BACK.

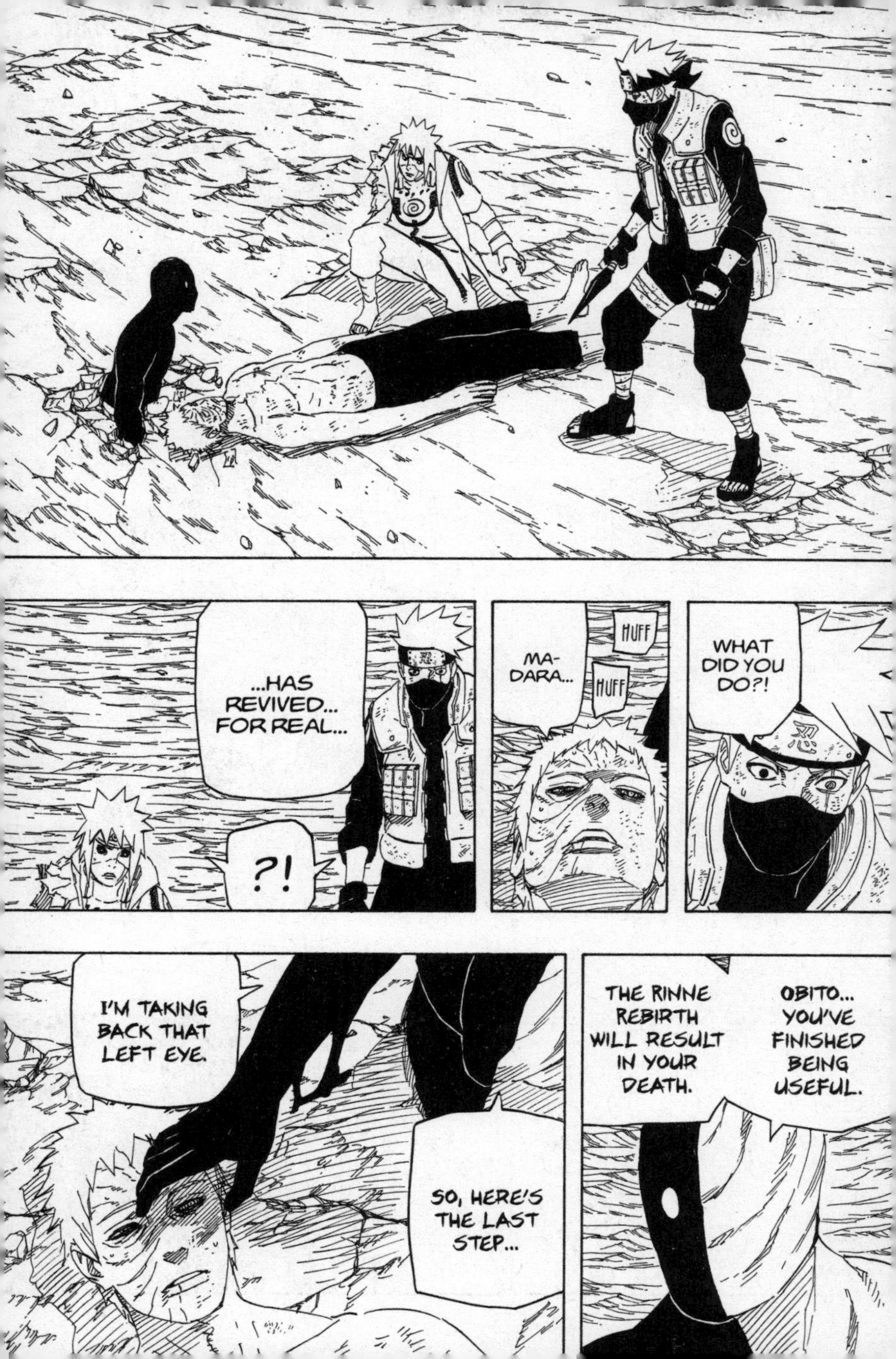
WHAT DID YOU DO?!
HUFF
MA-DARA...
HUFF
...HAS REVIVED... FOR REAL...
?!
OBITO... YOU'VE FINISHED BEING USEFUL.
THE RINNE REBIRTH WILL RESULT IN YOUR DEATH.
SO, HERE'S THE LAST STEP...
I'M TAKING BACK THAT LEFT EYE.

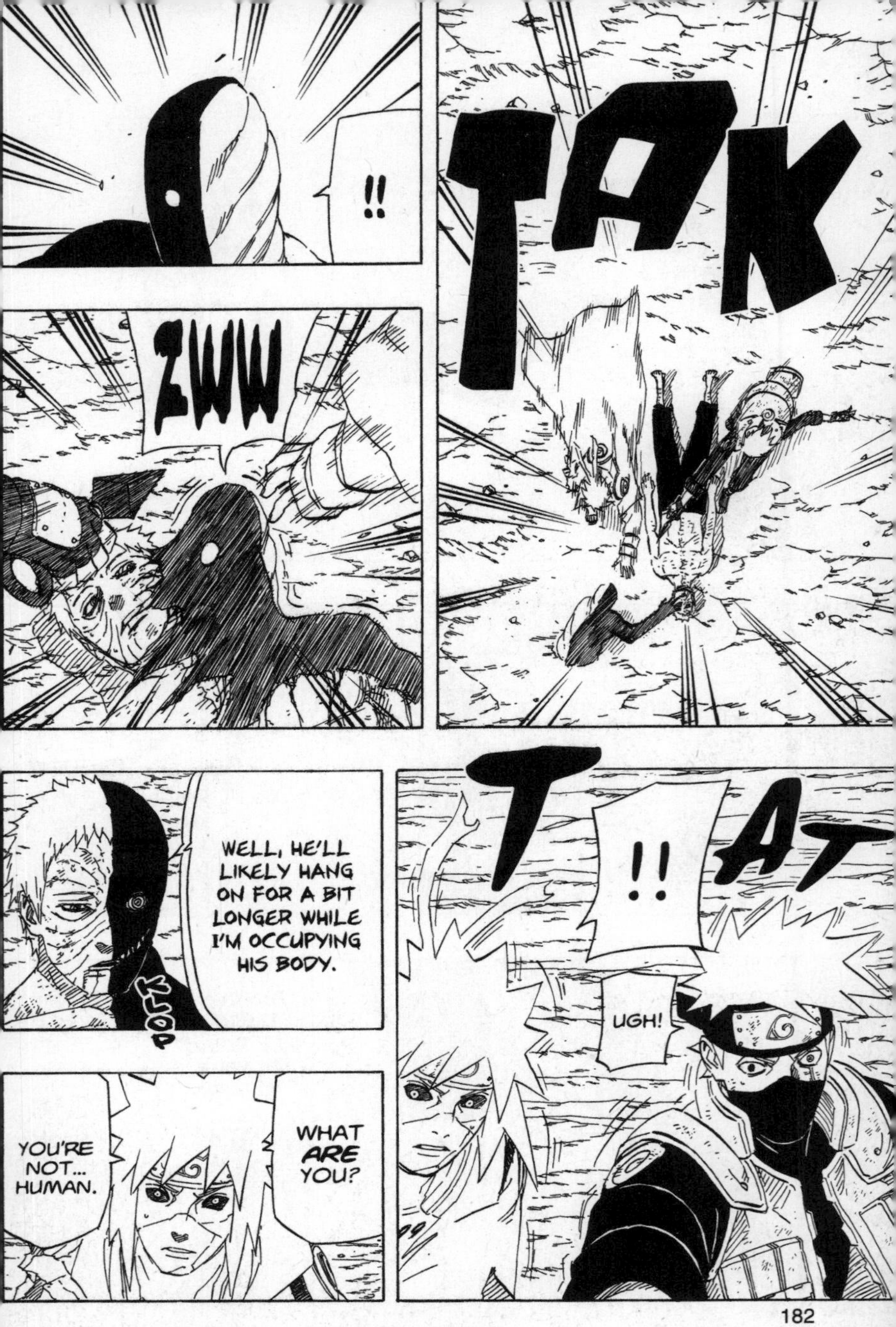
TAK
!!
ZWW
TAT
!!
UGH!
WELL, HE'LL LIKELY HANG ON FOR A BIT LONGER WHILE I'M OCCUPYING HIS BODY.
KLOP
WHAT ARE YOU?
YOU'RE NOT... HUMAN.

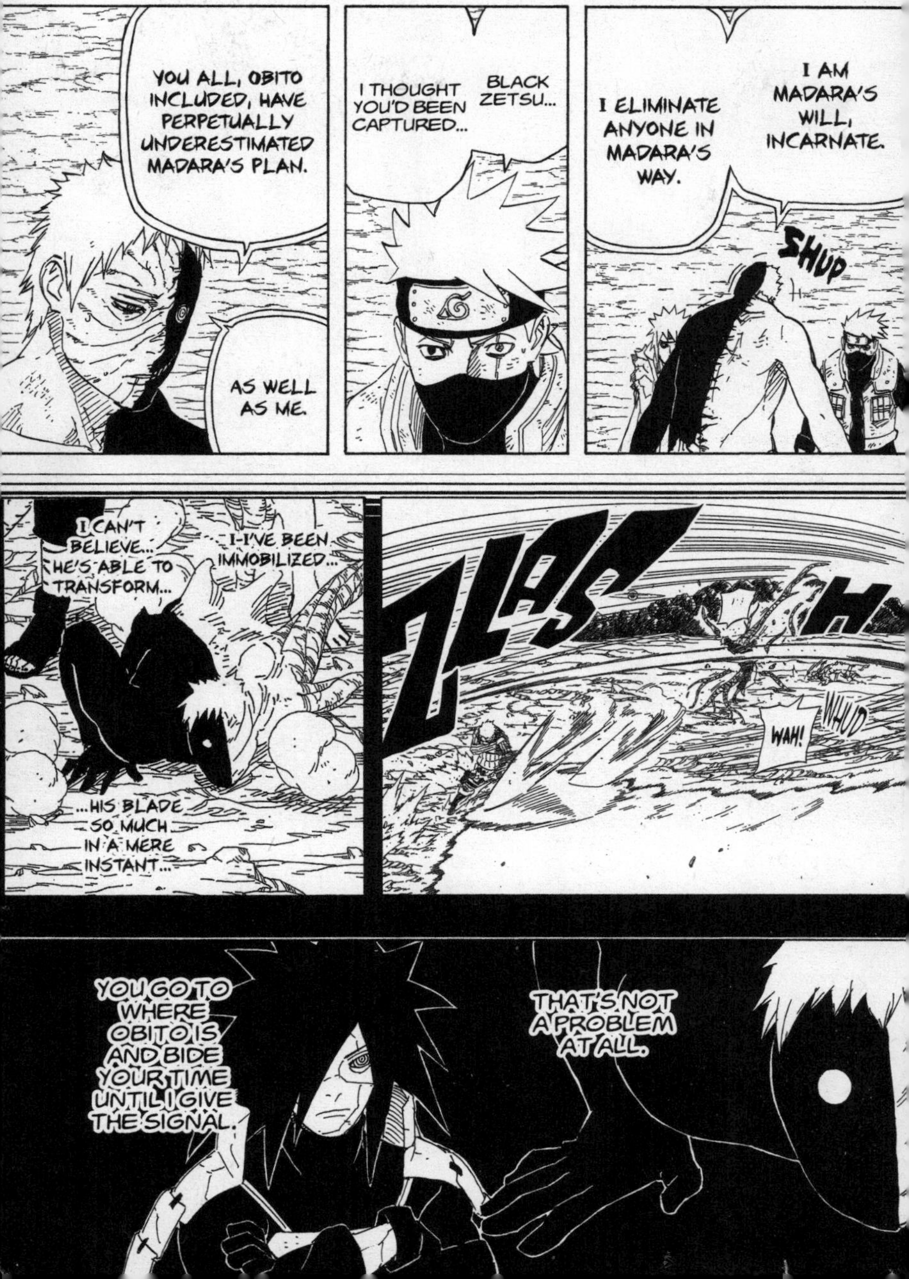
I AM MADARA'S WILL, INCARNATE.
I ELIMINATE ANYONE IN MADARA'S WAY.
SHUP
BLACK ZETSU...
I THOUGHT YOU'D BEEN CAPTURED...
YOU ALL, OBITO INCLUDED, HAVE PERPETUALLY UNDERESTIMATED MADARA'S PLAN.
AS WELL AS ME.
ZLASH
WHUD
WAH!
I-I'VE BEEN IMMOBILIZED...
I CAN'T BELIEVE... HE'S ABLE TO TRANSFORM...
...HIS BLADE SO MUCH IN A MERE INSTANT...
YOU GO TO WHERE OBITO IS AND BIDE YOUR TIME UNTIL I GIVE THE SIGNAL.
THAT'S NOT A PROBLEM AT ALL.

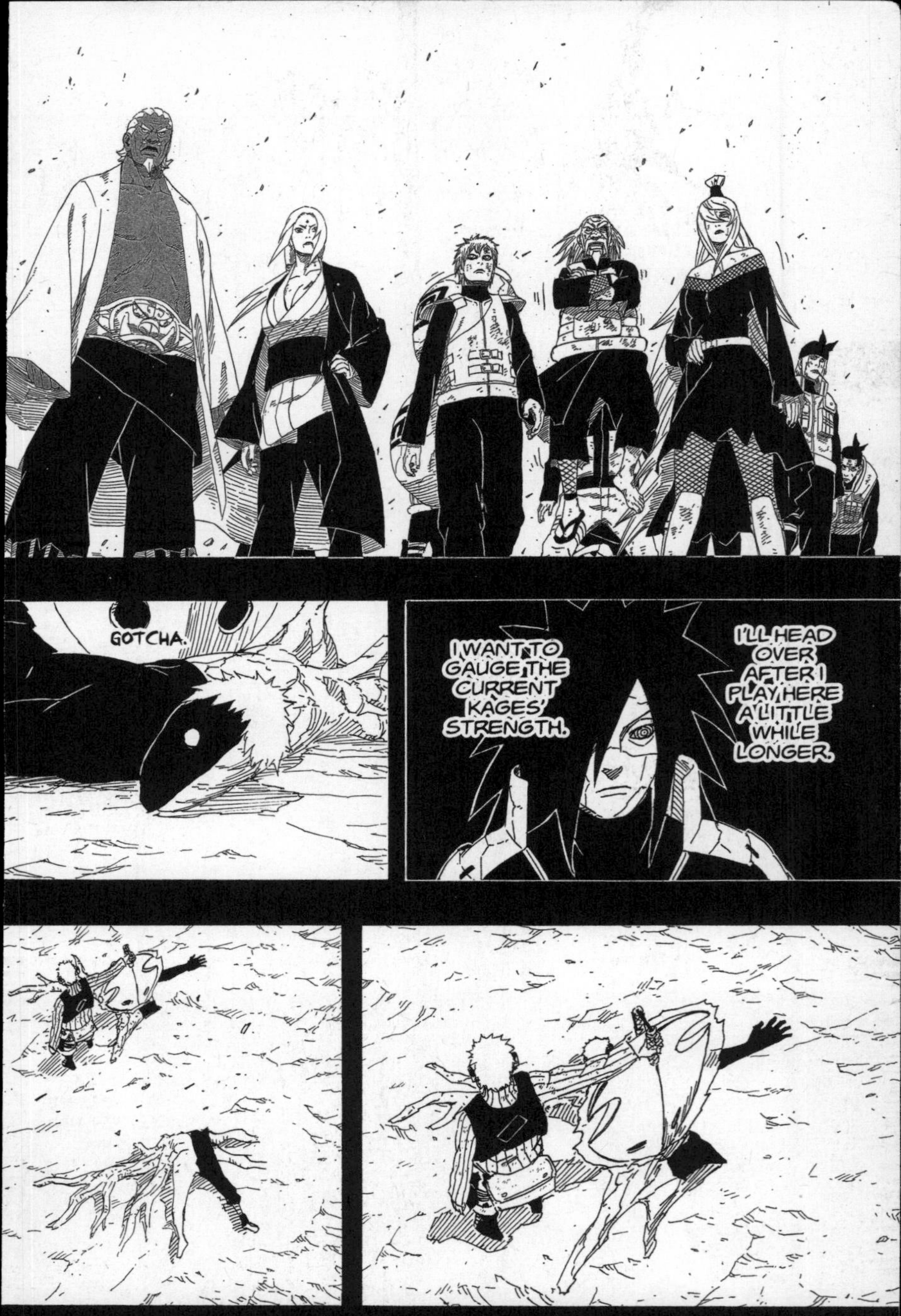
I'LL HEAD OVER AFTER I PLAY HERE A LITTLE WHILE LONGER.
I WANT TO GAUGE THE CURRENT KAGES' STRENGTH.
GOTCHA.

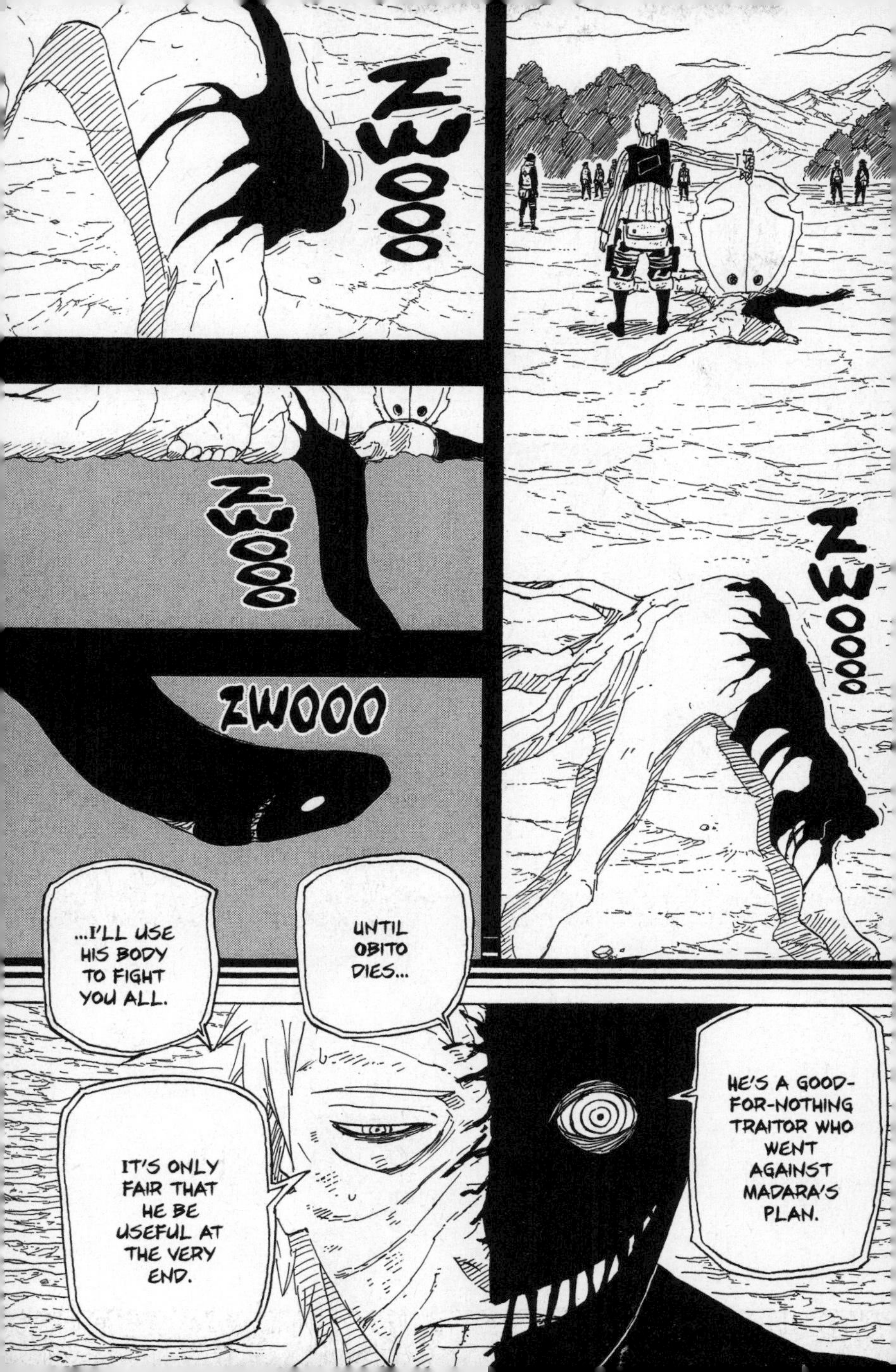
ZWOOOO
ZWOOO
ZWOOO
ZWOOO
HE'S A GOOD-FOR-NOTHING TRAITOR WHO WENT AGAINST MADARA'S PLAN.
UNTIL OBITO DIES...
...I'LL USE HIS BODY TO FIGHT YOU ALL.
IT'S ONLY FAIR THAT HE BE USEFUL AT THE VERY END.

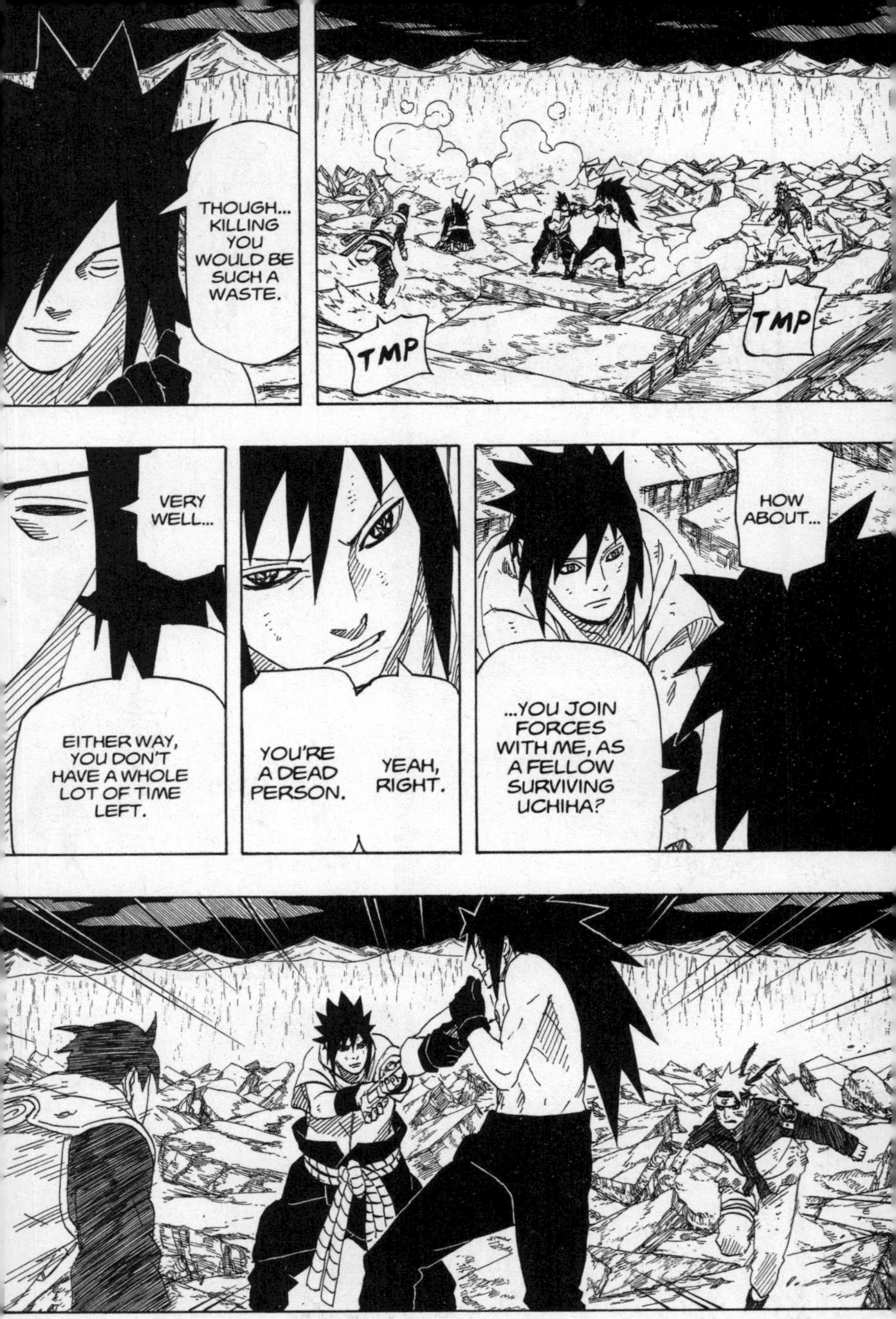
TMP
TMP
THOUGH... KILLING YOU WOULD BE SUCH A WASTE.
HOW ABOUT...
...YOU JOIN FORCES WITH ME, AS A FELLOW SURVIVING UCHIHA?
YEAH, RIGHT.
YOU'RE A DEAD PERSON.
VERY WELL...
EITHER WAY, YOU DON'T HAVE A WHOLE LOT OF TIME LEFT.

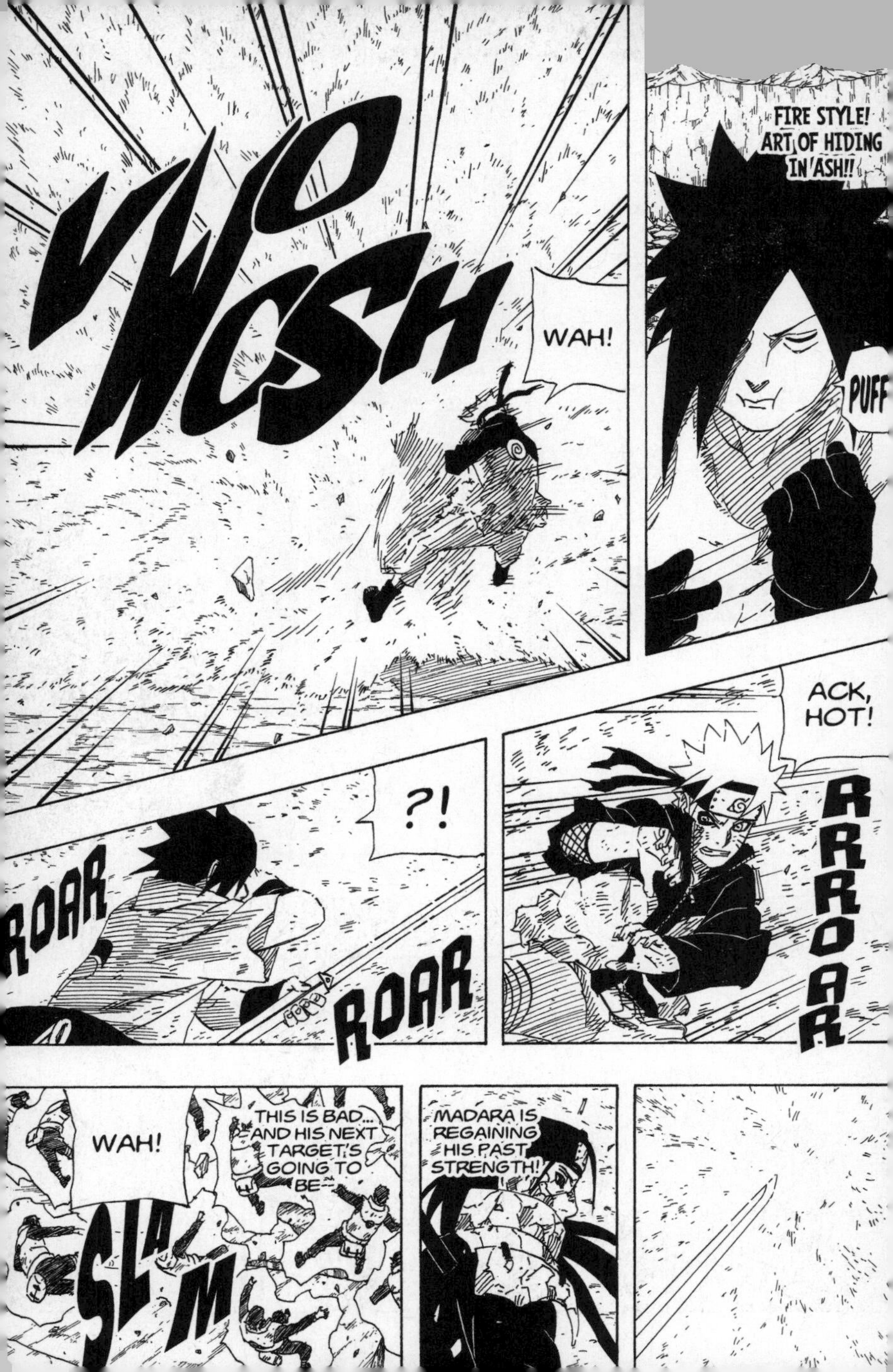
FIRE STYLE! ART OF HIDING IN ASH!!
PUFF
WHOOSH
WAH!
ACK, HOT!
RRRROAR
?!
ROAR
ROAR
MADARA IS REGAINING HIS PAST STRENGTH!
THIS IS BAD... AND HIS NEXT TARGET'S GOING TO BE--
WAH!
SLAM

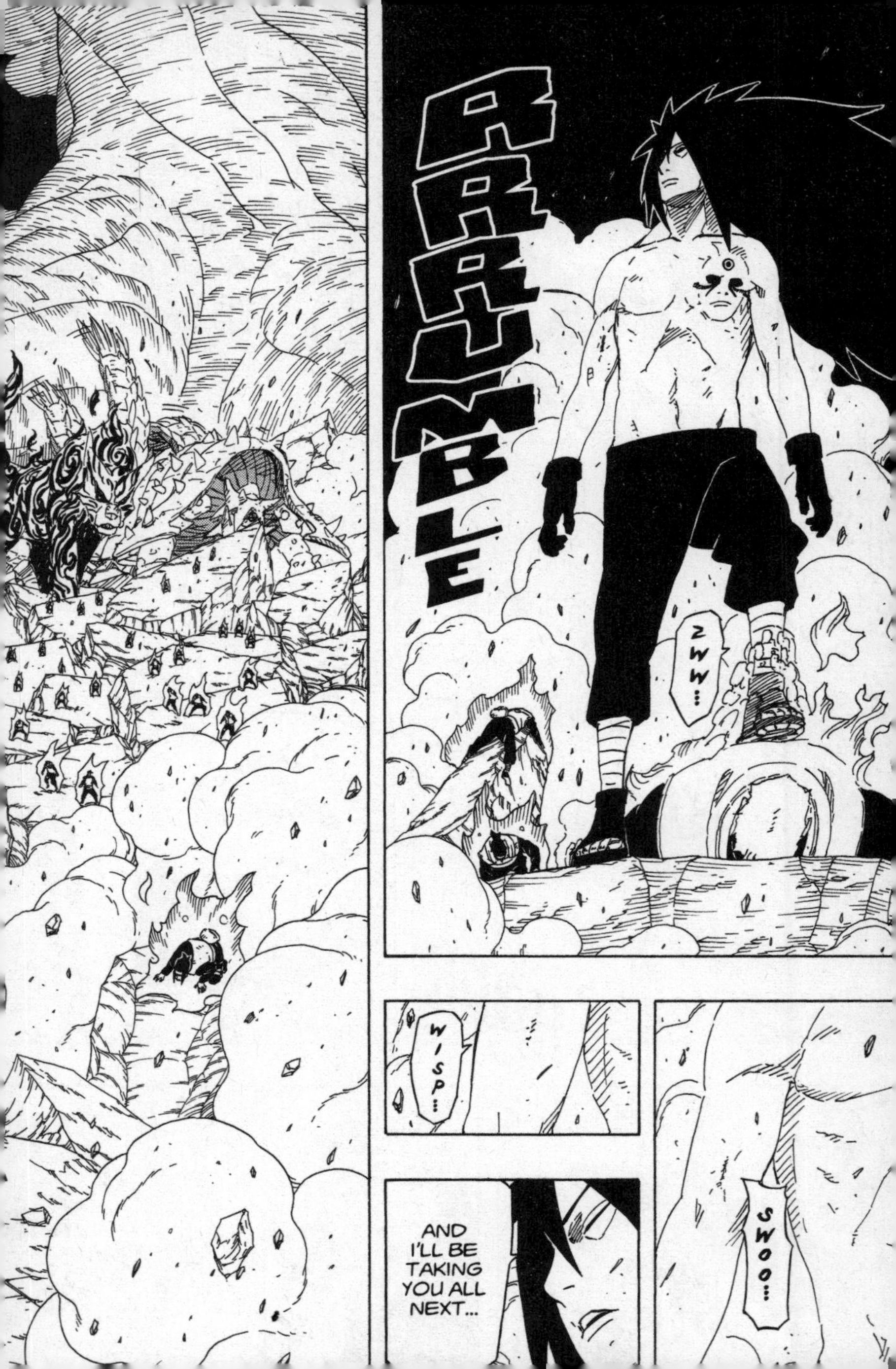
RRRUMBLE
ZWW...
SWOO...
WISP...
AND I'LL BE TAKING YOU ALL NEXT...

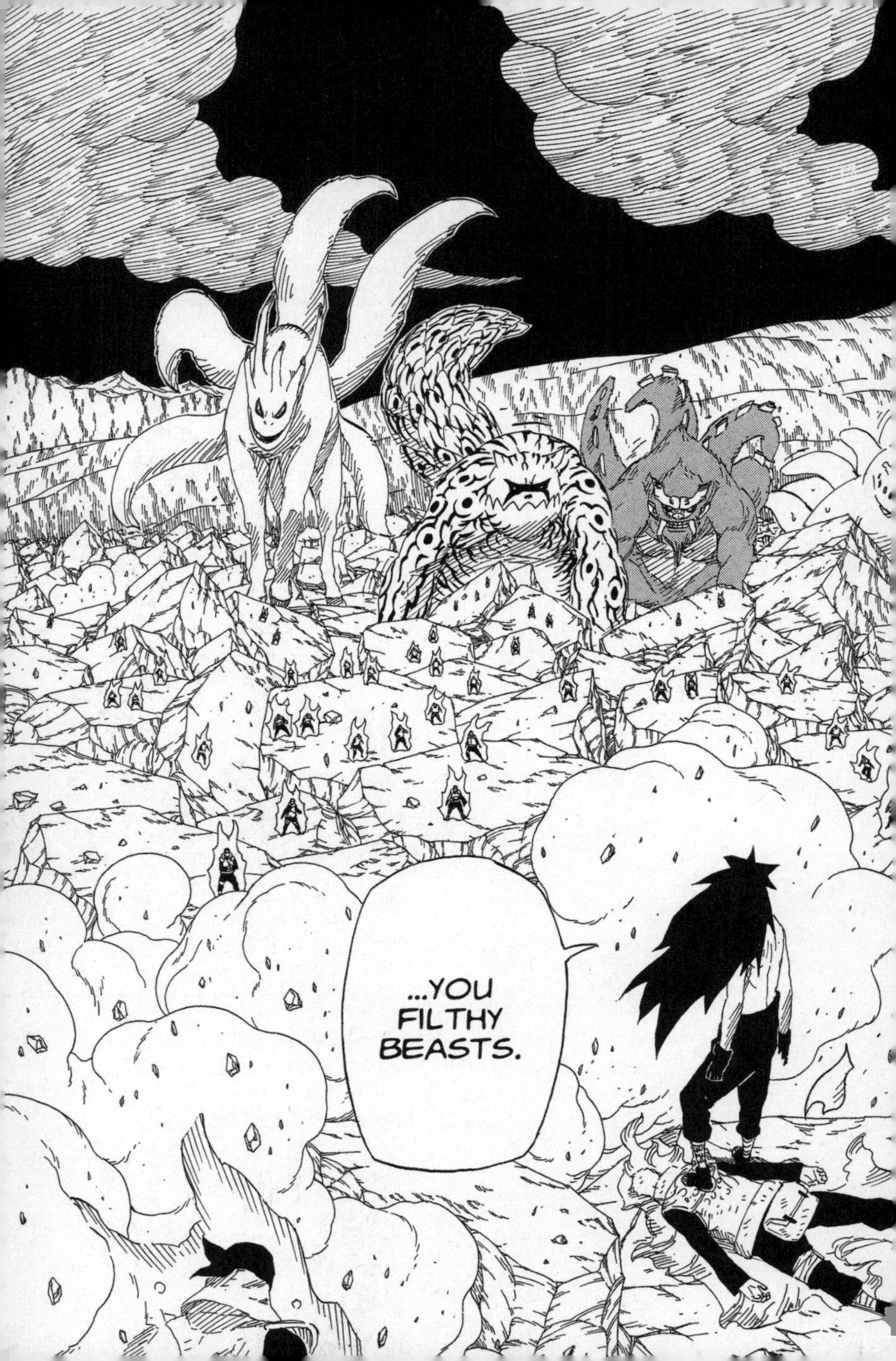
...YOU FILTHY BEASTS.

IN THE NEXT VOLUME...

THE START OF A CRIMSON SPRING

The victory against Obito is short-lived as Madara is finally fully revived. The legendary ninja appears unstoppable as he regains his former powers and sets his sights on the biju. The devastating moment when Naruto loses the Nine Tails may be at hand!

AVAILABLE MARCH 2015!